This book belongs to Cos E

Kindly donated to F+G — pl

C000233463

!

The NEC 3 Engineering and Construction Contract

The NEC 3 Engineering and Construction Contract

A Commentary

Second Edition

Brian Eggleston
CEng, FICE, FIStructE, FCIArb

Blackwell
Science

Blackwell Science, a Blackwell Publishing company
Blackwell Science Ltd, 9600 Garsington Road, Oxford OX4 2DQ, UK
  Tel: +44 (0) 1865 776868
Blackwell Publishing Inc., 350 Main Street, Malden, MA 02148-5020, USA
  Tel: +1 781 388 8250
Blackwell Science Asia Pty Ltd, 550 Swanston Street, Carlton, Victoria 3053, Australia
  Tel: +61 (0)3 8359 1011

First published 1996 by Blackwell Science as The New Engineering Contract: A Commentary
Reissued in paperback 2000
Second retitled edition published 2006 by Blackwell Science

3   2008

ISBN 978-0-632-05386-5

Library of Congress Cataloging-in-Publication Data
Eggleston, Brian, CEng.
The NEC 3 engineering and construction contract : a commentary/Brian Eggleston. – 2nd ed.
   p. cm.
Rev. ed. of: The new engineering contract. 1996
Includes bibliographical references and index.
ISBN 978-0-632-05386-5 (hardback : alk. paper)
ISBN 0-632-05386-0 (hardback : alk. paper)
1. Engineering contracts–Great Britain.   I. Eggleston, Brian, CEng.
New engineering contract.   II. Title.
KD1641.E354 2006
343.41′07862–dc22
2006014908

A catalogue record for this title is available from the British Library

Set in 10/12 pt Palatino
by SNP Best-set Typesetter Ltd, Hong Kong
Printed and bound in Great Britain
by TJ International Ltd, Padstow, Cornwall

The publisher's policy is to use permanent paper from mills that operate a sustainable forestry policy, and which has been manufactured from pulp processed using acid-free and elementary chlorine-free practices. Furthermore, the publisher ensures that the text paper and cover board used have met acceptable environmental accreditation standards.

For further information on Blackwell Publishing, visit our website:
www.blackwellpublishing.com/construction

Contents

Contents

Preface

In the preface to my 1996 book on the second edition of the New Engineering Contract (ECC 2) I questioned whether it was necessary to scrutinise the detail of the contract when faith in its principles might be more important to users than the detail of its provisions. However, I went on to suggest that if the contract succeeded and gained widespread use then commercial pressures would prevail and the contract would need to be robust enough to withstand detailed analysis and criticism.

It was soon evident that ECC 2 was becoming a popular contract of choice for civil engineering works and for building works – and its usage remains on an upward curve. It has certainly succeeded. But it was also soon evident that there were problems with the contract, particularly with its compensation event procedures. The need for a third edition was obvious and urgent.

NEC 3 took a few years longer than expected to produce. Perhaps this reflected the difficulties of amending clauses written in a unique style with minimalistic drafting. Perhaps remaining true to the original concepts of the contract inhibited change. When NEC 3 did eventually emerge in 2005 it was not the comprehensive revision which might have been expected. Some useful changes to compensation event procedures had been made, a few gaps had been plugged here and there, and a few new clauses added. At first sight it seemed that not much had changed. But getting into the detail revealed a different picture. There has been significant change – probably far more than the draftsmen intended – and not all of it for the better.

My endeavour in writing this book has been to try to explain in ordinary language what the clauses of NEC 3 say and what I think they mean. Not everyone will share my views but if they do no more than provide food for thought I hope they will make some contribution to the use and development of the contract.

Brian Eggleston
May 2006

Author's note

Phraseology

The New Engineering Contract is a family of contract documents and the proper use of the acronym NEC is as a prefix rather than as the name of any single contract. This book is principally a commentary on the third edition of the NEC Engineering and Construction Contract – the main contract in the family. For convenience that contract is referred to throughout this book simply as NEC 3. Its predecessor is referred to as ECC 2.

Capitals

NEC 3 relies heavily on defined terms which have capital initials and identified terms which are in italics. However, for reasons of style which I hope make for easier reading, capitals and italics have been used sparingly in this book, and therefore both defined terms and identified terms appear usually in ordinary case.

Text of NEC 3

Very little of the text of NEC 3 is quoted in this book. I have assumed that readers will have to hand a copy of NEC 3 and the other forms in the family as appropriate.

Commentary on the text is against the June 2005 publication of NEC 3.

Content of book

I have endeavoured to cover in this book all the clauses of NEC 3 and all the changes from ECC 2. I have retained the general layout and some of the content of my book on ECC 2 whilst extending commentary on compensation events from one to five chapters.

Table of clause numbers

The published version of the NEC 3 contract contains a comprehensive index of subjects referenced to clause numbers. In this book a full table of clause numbers with descriptions is referenced to chapter sections. The table is set out on pages 359–78.

Readers of this book who wish to have the benefit of a subject index will find it a straightforward matter to move from the subjects in the NEC 3 contract to the chapter sections in this book.

Chapter 1
Introduction

1.1 Development of NEC contracts

NEC 3 is a generic name for a family of contracts published for the Institution of Civil Engineers by Thomas Telford Services Ltd. NEC stands for New Engineering Contract and it is by this name that the contracts are generally known. The main contract and the subcontract were first published as consultative editions in January 1991. First formal editions followed in March 1993; second editions in November 1995; and third editions in June 2005.

It was always intended that there would be a family of New Engineering Contracts and in the short space of time between 1991 and 2005 other contracts were produced such that by 2005 the NEC 3 family comprised:

- the NEC 3 Engineering and Construction Contract
- the NEC 3 Engineering and Construction Subcontract
- the NEC 3 Professional Services Contract
- the NEC 3 Short Contract
- the NEC 3 Short Subcontract
- the NEC 3 Adjudicator's Contract
- the NEC 3 Term Services Contract
- the NEC 3 Framework Contract

The contracts are supported by officially published guidance notes, flow charts and an advisory document entitled *NEC 3 Procurement and Contract Strategies*. The Engineering and Construction Contract has six main procurement options and although one document (the *Black Book*) covers all six, each option is separately published. In all, as at June 2005, the complete set of NEC 3 documents comprised twenty-three volumes.

Background to NEC contracts

The background to the development of the New Engineering Contract does much to explain its style and content. In the 1980s there was on-going debate within the Institution of Civil Engineers, the lead body for the production of the ICE Conditions of Contract – at that time the standard form used for most civil engineering works in the UK – as to the direction of future contract strategies. At issue were questions as to whether the then existing standard forms adequately served the best interests of the parties by focusing on the obligations and responsibilities of the parties rather than on good management, and whether an entirely new approach was needed to promote co-operation and to reduce confrontation. The prevailing view was that something new was needed, particularly for sizeable contracts where attention to good project management was the key to successful completion. So although confidence remained high that the standard ICE forms would remain the popular choice for routine civil engineering works, the Institution embarked upon the drafting and production of what is now the New Engineering Contract.

The drafting team was charged with three specific objectives for the contract:

- that it should be more flexible in its scope than existing standard forms
- that it should provide greater stimulus to good project management than existing forms
- that it should be expressed more simply and clearly than existing forms

It was, therefore, a matter of policy that the New Engineering Contract should be different from other standard forms in style and content.

For users of the contract the difference is of very significant practical effect. It used to be said that a good contract was never taken out of the drawer until it was needed. For the New Engineering Contract that rule does not apply. It is as much a manual of project management as a set of contractual conditions – and it should never be taken off the desk and put in the drawer.

Prospects for the future

The rapid expansion of use of the New Engineering Contract has been a remarkable success story. Contrary to intentions and to expectations the contract has within just a few years replaced ICE Conditions of Contract as the contract of popular choice for civil engineering works and it is already in widespread use for building, process and plant works. Although much used for major projects it is also used at more mundane levels. With the support base it has now built amongst clients and professionals, and with the range of contracts now available, there are real prospects that the New Engineering Contract in its various forms will become the dominant contract of the future.

1.2 Characteristics of NEC contracts

As noted above the New Engineering Contract was drafted with the objectives of achieving flexibility, stimulus to good project management, clarity and simplicity.

Flexibility

Flexibility is perhaps the most ambitious of these objectives. Thus the NEC 3 Engineering and Construction Contract aims to be an all purpose contract for all construction and engineering disciplines at home or abroad. It offers this through a combination of uniquely drafted provisions and a complex structure of options. Four distinct features are presented:

- discipline specific terminology and references to the practices of particular industries are avoided. Reliance is placed on a framework of general provisions written largely in non-technical language
- responsibility for design is not fixed with either the employer or the contractor but can be set at any amount from nil to total with either party
- primary options give a choice of pricing mechanism from lump sum to cost, *plus*
- secondary options allow the employer to build up the provisions in the contract to suit his individual policies

Stimulus to good management

Again, as noted above, much of the inspiration for the development of NEC contracts came from a belief that existing forms of contract no longer adequately served the best interests of the parties. The argument was put that expanding procurement strategies, changing practices in contracting, and developments in project management required contracts to focus as much on management as on the obligations and liabilities of the parties. So NEC contracts lay great emphasis on communications, co-operation, programming, and the need for clear definition at the outset of various types of information. Reports from users of NEC contracts suggest that improvements in project management are being achieved and that job satisfaction for those involved is better than with traditional contracts.

Clarity and simplicity

The approach adopted by the drafting team towards the objective that NEC contracts should be expressed more simply and clearly than existing forms of contract was to start from scratch rather than to build on old foundations. So NEC contracts are intentionally and conspicuously different from other standard forms in style and structure. They are written in non-legalistic language using short sentences and avoiding cross-references. Familiar phrases such as 'extension of time' and 'variations' are absent as is the regular use of the word 'shall' to signify obligations.

However, there is a price to pay for this brevity. Taken by themselves, the contracts are, at least for first time readers, more of a mystery than a model of clarity and simplicity. Fortunately, there are guidance notes and flow charts to assist in general understanding and the application of the contracts.

Legal interpretation of the contracts is not so easily solved. Neither the guidance notes nor the flow charts are intended to be used for legal interpretation and the application of legal precedents from traditional forms of contract written in conventional drafting style can only be surmised. Which raises the question, have NEC contracts sacrificed legal certainty in pursuit of a new order? There are certainly some who feel that discarding conventional drafting amounts to discarding the accumulated contractual wisdom of generations. Throwing the baby out with the bath water is how one eminent construction lawyer put it. But others are far more optimistic and they suggest that to focus on the words of NEC contracts is to miss the point of the message; and that the courts, if called upon to do so, will have no difficulty in discovering the true intentions of the parties.

1.3 *Structure of the NEC 3 Engineering and Construction Contract*

In this chapter and thereafter in this book, NEC 3 means the NEC 3 Engineering and Construction Contract. ECC 2 means the second edition of the Engineering and Construction Contract.

Each NEC 3 contract is uniquely put together to meet the employer's needs by assembling clauses from the option structure and by particularisation in accompanying documents.

Option structure

In order to create a set of NEC 3 conditions for a particular contract, the employer:

- makes a selection from the six main options as to which type of pricing mechanism is to apply
- includes in the contract the nine sections of core clauses
- specifies which dispute resolution option applies
- includes such selection (if any) from the seventeen detailed secondary option clauses as he thinks fit
- includes in the contract under secondary option Z any additional clauses required by him or as agreed with the contractor

Main options

The main options comprise six types of payment mechanism:

- Option A – priced contract with activity schedule
- Option B – priced contract with bill of quantities

- Option C – target contract with activity schedule
- Option D – target contract with bill of quantities
- Option E – cost reimbursable contract
- Option F – management contract

Each of the main options is published in a separate volume which includes the relevant core clauses for the particular option. Additionally there is a single volume (the *Black Book*) covering all six options.

Core clauses

The core clauses are grouped into nine sections, numbered as follows:

(1) general
(2) contractor's main responsibilities
(3) time
(4) testing and defects
(5) payment
(6) compensation events
(7) title
(8) risks and insurance
(9) termination

For each section there is a common set of core clauses and for some of the main options there are additional core clauses. There are two sets of dispute resolution clauses, labelled Options W1 and W2, from which a choice must be made.

Secondary options

The secondary option clauses are labelled under X, Y(UK)2, and Z prefixes. Not all would normally be regarded as secondary. Included within them are some matters such as retention and liquidated damages for late completion which most traditional contracts treat as essential. Other matters such as performance bonds and performance related damages are more obviously contract specific. The full list of secondary option clauses is considered in Chapter 3.

1.4 Feedback from ECC 2

It was evident from the usage growth of ECC 2 that the contract had many admirers and satisfied users. Anecdotal evidence suggested that when ECC 2 contracts were properly prepared, adequately staffed, and administered by a project manager who understood the philosophy of the contract and recognised the duties involved, they generally operated well. However, there were reports of contractors losing large sums of money on some ECC 2 contracts and it is no secret that many disputes were referred to adjudication on both small and large ECC 2 contracts.

Feedback indicated various types of problems, in particular:

- preparation problems – these mainly related to incomplete works information and to a lesser extent incomplete contract data
- staffing problems – there is little doubt that it took some time for employers, contractors, and project managers to recognise the staffing needs of ECC 2 contracts – with the result that some contracts were understaffed and never properly operated, whilst others were staffed to the required strength but non-recoverable costs were sustained
- people problems – the requirement in ECC 2 for the parties and the project manager to act in a spirit of mutual trust and co-operation was frequently not understood or followed – one particular problem being the involvement of persons with management styles inherited from old style adversarial contracts
- compensation event problems – these were many and various with perhaps the most common being complaints of procedural overload, difficulties and costs of assessments, failures to use the quotation system, and confusion over time-bars

Preparation, staffing and people problems can hopefully be resolved by training and experience. Some of the compensation event problems of ECC 2 have been addressed in NEC 3.

1.5 *Changes from ECC 2*

The amount of change from ECC 2 to NEC 3 is quite small in volume terms – perhaps no more than 5% or so of the text. However, that belies the importance of the changes. There are new provisions of considerable potential impact and changes which significantly affect the operation of the contract. And as with changes generally to contracts and other formal documents, a change in one clause, however small, can have effects not immediately apparent on other clauses. For these reasons and because there has been quite an amount of re-arrangement and re-numbering, NEC 3 is best treated as a new contract rather than an update of ECC 2.

Significant new features

- key dates — these are dates set by the employer by which the contractor has to bring a stated part of the works to a specified condition
- risk register — a register maintained by the project manager and intended to include all risks stated in the contract data or subsequently identified by the project manager and the contractor

- key performance indicators — aspects of performance for which targets are set in an incentive schedule
- prevention provisions — new clauses by which the employer carries the time and cost risks of events similar to, but potentially wider than, *force majeure*
- entire agreement clause — statement that the contract is the entire agreement between the parties
- quotations treated as having been accepted — new provisions indicating the contractor's right to submit quotations for compensation events
- limitation of liability — new option clause limiting the contractor's liability to the employer for indirect or consequential loss
- delay damages — proportioning down clause included for parts of the works taken over before completion

Significant changes

- cost schedules — increased use of shorter schedule of cost components to simplify assessment of compensation events
- rates and lump sums — by agreement rates and lump sums can be used to assess compensation events
- fee percentages — separate fee percentages for subcontracted work and direct work
- conditions precedent — revised and clarified provisions on notices and timing restrictions for the submission of compensation events
- interest — revised and clarified provisions on entitlements to interest
- dispute resolution — choice to be made between alternative sets of provisions

1.6 Points of interest in NEC 3

Entire agreement

New NEC 3 clause 12.4 states that the contract is the entire agreement between the parties. Precisely what this means is open to debate but there are various possibilities – all of which give rise to potentially important consequences. Lawyers will probably seek to clarify this clause for particular contracts.

Exclusion of common law rights

The question of whether the compensation event system acts to exclude the contractor's common law rights to damages for breach is not entirely settled in NEC 3. New clause 12.4 may have a bearing on the matter as may the new clause 63.4 which refers to rights of the parties. However, there remain aspects of the compensation event system which are difficult to reconcile with the concept of loss of common law rights.

Conditions precedent to entitlement

ECC 2 was far from clear as to what was legally intended by its requirement for compensation events to be notified within two weeks. New provisions in NEC 3 aim to rectify the situation by limiting entitlement to cost and time changes to notifications given within eight weeks of an event. However, this does not apply to compensation events which the project manager should have notified. There are various other aspects of the clause itself which add doubts as to the likely efficacy of its application. Perhaps a bigger problem is that there does not appear to be anything in NEC 3 empowering the project manager to concern himself with conditions precedent and time-bars.

Powers of the project manager

The intention of ECC 2 was probably that the project manager would act more as the employer's agent than as an independent contract administrator and supervisor. This view of his role took something of a knock in the 2005 case of *Corber* v. *Bechtel*. But by entirely separate development NEC 3 seems to have moved towards a more restricted role for the project manager. New clause 12.3 requires changes to the contract to be agreed and signed by the parties – a provision which would fit naturally into most contracts but less so in NEC 3 where many contractual restrictions and obligations are found in the works information.

Changes to works information

The extent of the project manager's power to change the works information under ECC 2 was not expressly restricted in the conventional manner to changes necessary or desirable for the completion and functioning of the works. However, common sense dictated that there should be some restriction. Under NEC 3 the proper approach to considering what changes to the works information are permissible may be to examine where the project manager derives his power from and how the contractor's obligations are defined rather than examining possible restrictions.

Prevention

The inclusion in NEC 3 of provisions putting the risk of what are called 'prevention' matters on the employer will concern many employers and their lawyers. The matters covered by the provisions include what might normally be called *'force majeure'* or 'beyond control of the parties' matters, and the usual rule would be that loss lies where it falls. For that reason alone some employers will wish to see the provisions deleted. Another likely reason is that the provisions as drafted are capable of very wide interpretation and their scope could be argued to extend to all manner of problems encountered by the contractor.

Quotations for compensation events

Strengthening of the quotation system for compensation events by the inclusion in NEC 3 of provisions whereby default by the project manager in operating the contractual rules leads to quotations being treated as accepted will be welcomed by contractors. However, it is something of a surprise that such quotations can be disputed by the employer and altered by an adjudicator. In this respect they are either not being treated as accepted or it is the case, which seems unlikely, that all quotations accepted by the project manager can be challenged by the employer and reviewed by an adjudicator.

Assessment of compensation events

The changes for simplification of assessments of compensation events by greater use of the shorter schedule of cost components and possible use of rates and lump sums will be generally welcomed. There will, however, be disappointment that the changes do not address the fundamental problem that the assessment rules are not suited to low value events or for contracts with frequent and multiple events. There may also be concern as to how the new provision in NEC 3 that assessments should divide actual and forecast costs according to when instructions for quotations were given or should have been given is intended to operate. Retrospective forecasting may be envisaged but it is difficult to see it applying in adjudication.

Dispute resolution

The inclusion in NEC 3 of alternative dispute resolution procedures for contracts which are subject to the Housing Grants, Construction and Regeneration Act 1996, and contracts which are not, will not necessarily lead to the choice which might be expected. The statutory right to adjudication under the Act still applies to qualifying contracts even if the non-compliant alternative is chosen. The big difference between the two alternatives can be simply expressed – one imposes time limits and restrictions on the disputes which can be referred to adjudication, the other allows any dispute to be referred at any time. Subject to retention of any statutory rights it is a matter for the parties as to which of these they prefer.

One surprising and disappointing aspect of the dispute resolution procedures of NEC 3 is that they fail to include the range of procedures now becoming commonplace in construction contracts. Most notably, they fail to include conciliation or mediation which, given the complexities of the contract and its requirement for the parties to act in a spirit of mutual trust and co-operation, might well be the best choice the parties could make for resolving their disputes.

Chapter 2
Main options

2.1 Introduction

NEC 3 retains the six main options, A to F, included in ECC 2 with one major change. Whereas ECC 2 grouped dispute resolution clauses with termination clauses in section 9 of Options A to F, NEC 3 separates the clauses leaving section 9 solely for termination and putting dispute resolution into two new alternative main options W1 and W2. Option W1 matches the procedures in the main body of ECC 2, Option W2 matches the procedures in ECC 2's secondary option Y(UK)2. Broadly, the intention in NEC 3 is that Option W2 will be used for contracts subject to the Housing Grants, Construction and Regeneration Act 1996 and Option W1 will be used for all other contracts. However, as discussed later in this chapter, that will not always be the case.

The main options

The main options of NEC 3 are:

- Option A – priced contract with activity schedule
- Option B – priced contract with bill of quantities
- Option C – target contract with activity schedule
- Option D – target contract with bill of quantities
- Option E – cost reimbursable contract
- Option F – management contract
- dispute resolution Option W1
- dispute resolution Option W2

The main options provide, in descending order, a broad scale of distribution of price risk with Option A providing maximum certainty of price for the employer and Option F providing the least.

The employer is required to state in part one of the contract data which main option is to be used and which dispute resolution option is selected. In most cases the choice will be entirely that of the employer. However, sometimes potential tenderers are invited to propose which main option should apply as part of pre-qualification procedures. When partnering is intended prospective contractors may be allowed to have a say in which main option should be used.

Users of NEC 3 should be alert to the fact that each main option has its own particular clauses which are additional to the core clauses in the main

nine sections of the contract. In particular a point to note is that although the
definitions in the core clauses stop at number 19 in clause 11 of the base
contract, there are other definitions particular to Options A to F which take
the numbering through to 33.

Construction management

There is no named main option in NEC 3 for construction management – the
system in which the contractor provides only management services to the
employer with the works packages let as contracts directly between the works
contractors and the employer. However, this need not be a barrier to the use
of NEC 3 for construction management.

For construction management the employer should appoint a construction
management contractor as project manager under the NEC professional services contract. The duties of the construction manager would be to advise the
employer on the placing of the works contracts under whichever main options
of NEC 3 are most appropriate and then to project manage the works contracts. For an interesting case on the duties of construction managers see *Great
Eastern Hotel Ltd* v. *John Laing Ltd* (2005).

2.2 Contract strategy

Contract strategy is not an exact science. There are some guiding principles
but every employer is unique in his aspirations, his circumstances and his
preferences.

For some employers certainty of price is the dominant aspiration and then,
given few restrictive circumstances and few particular preferences, the
obvious strategic choice will be a lump sum contract with contractor's design.
For other employers certainty of price may be secondary to considerations of
quality, operations/restrictions, or the need for a quick start and a fast finish.
Which method of procurement, which type of contract, and which form of
contract then become more complex questions. Some employers, on the
strength of past experiences or hopes for the future, develop preferences for
certain methods of procurement and certain forms of contract. Rational analysis of selection criteria to determine contract strategy may then become
secondary to selection of the most suitable contractor.

One of the main strengths of NEC 3 is its flexibility. If an employer does
develop a preference for its use he is nothing like as limited in his choice of
procurement route as with other standard forms. He has six main options to
choose from and construction management available as a further option. It
is not appropriate in this book to provide a detailed review of the theories of
contract strategy but for those who do need to study the subject useful starting points are CIRIA Report R85 *Target and Cost-reimbursable Construction
Contracts* or the RIBA publication *Which Contract*. As a checklist for matters
to consider, however, the following may be helpful:

- which party is to be responsible for design
- how important to the employer is certainty of price
- what views prevail on the allocation of risk
- how firmly known are the employer's requirements and what likelihood is there of change
- what operating restrictions apply on the employer's premises or in the construction of the works
- what emphasis is to be placed on early commencement and/or rapid completion
- what flexibility does the employer need in the contractual arrangements – e.g. to terminate at will
- how anxious is the employer to avoid or to minimise formal disputes and legal proceedings
- how important to the employer is the concept of single point responsibility

Responsibility for design

The general principle which should influence which party is responsible for design is that of competence – which party can most competently undertake the design?

If professional design firms are to be employed, whether it be by the employer or by the contractor, the question of competence in this general sense does not arise. But with contractor's design an obvious advantage for the employer is that a choice of designs may be put forward by the tenderers. A further potential advantage is that the contractor's expertise is more likely to be used to the full when the freedom to develop that expertise in the design is permitted.

If the employer already has his own in-house design resources it may be neither efficient nor economic to place design responsibility with the contractor. Or it may be that in-house design teams are more closely in tune with the employer's requirements than any contractor could be. Moreover, in some situations there are matters of confidentiality as to the purpose or operation of the works which are wholly decisive as to whether design briefs can be issued to tenderers and as to which party is responsible for design. In other situations there may be a reliance on specialist know how or patented designs which is itself decisive as to design responsibility.

But as a general rule if the employer is able to specify his requirements in terms of a performance specification or quality standards there is much to be said for contractor's design. Not only may the standard of liability of a contractor for his design (fitness for purpose) be higher than that of a professional designer (skill and care) but the scope for claims for extra payment from the contractor arising out of the designer's defaults and deficiencies is eliminated.

As to how the allocation of responsibility for design influences choice between the main options of NEC 3 the main points to note are:

- Option A – lump sum contract
  Ideally suited to contractor's design but can be used for employer's design
  or divided design responsibility providing the employer's design element
  is complete at the time of tender.
- Option B – remeasurement contract
  Not suited to contractor's design because of the reliance on bills of quanti-
  ties and the difficulties posed by the contractor producing his own bills of
  quantities.
- Option C – target contract (lump sum base)
  As Option A but allows the employer more flexibility in developing his
  own design.
- Option D – target contract (bill of quantities base)
  Suffers from similar problems to Option B.
- Option E – cost reimbursable contract
  Permits maximum flexibility in allocation of design responsibility and
  allows development of the design as the works proceed.
- Option F – management contract
  Not suitable for allocation of the whole of design responsibility to the
  contractor unless placed as a 'design and manage' contract but particularly
  suitable for contracts with a high reliance on specialist subcontractors who
  undertake their own design.

Certainty of price

For many employers certainty of price is the decisive factor in contract strategy. Commercial pressures may dictate that either a project can be completed
within a set budget or it is not worth commencing.

Option A (the lump sum contract) offers the best prospects for certainty
of price – particularly when used with contractor's design.

Option C (the target contract based on lump sum) fixes with some degree
of certainty the maximum price but at tender it is less precise than Option A
in fixing the likely contract price.

Options B and D (both bill of quantities based) put the risk of accuracy of
billed quantities and the consequences of re-measure on the employer and
consequently both suffer from lack of price certainty.

Option E (the cost reimbursable contract) relieves the contractor of any risk
on price (other than in his fee). Consequently not only is the employer at risk
on the price, with the contract itself providing no certainty of price, but the
contractor has little incentive by way of any target to minimise costs. Clearly
Option E is not suitable if the employer is looking for certainty of price.

Option F (the management contract) is a cost reimbursable contract in so
far that the employer and not the contractor takes the risk on the costs of the
works contracts. However, management contracts are frequently arranged on
the basis of lump sum works contracts and this can introduce a good measure
of cost control into the system. If the quotations for the works contracts can
all be obtained before the letting of the management contract there can also
be a good measure of price certainty.

Allocation of risk

The guiding principle on allocation of risk is that risk should be allocated to the party best able to control it. Most contracts, including NEC 3, show some regard for this principle but few, and NEC 3 is no exception, take it to its ultimate conclusion. Two other factors frequently prevail.

One of these is that it is often considered better for the employer to pay for what does happen rather than what might happen – hence, unforeseen ground condition clauses. The other is that in the interests of fairness (and in some cases coincidental commercial interests) it is often accepted that the contractor should not be required to carry risks which are uninsurable or which arise from matters beyond the influence of either party – for example, changes in statute which affect the costs of construction. Taken together, the result of the above is that the employer can end up carrying some risks over which he has no control whatsoever. Thus if the government puts up labour taxes the employer usually pays the additional contract costs although it is only the contractor who has any control over those costs.

When it comes to the selection of a main option of NEC 3 the employer is fully justified in asking how the various options deal with the allocation of risk. The answer, surprisingly perhaps, is that apart from the variables inherent in the pricing mechanisms of the main options and the variables which can be introduced through choice of secondary options, NEC 3 operates a policy of common allocation of risk through all its main options.

NEC 3 does this quite deliberately to provide consistency in the application of its core clauses and its compensation events. But it is certainly questionable whether the employer's interests are always best served by the policy. For example, is it appropriate that target cost prices should be adjustable for the full range of compensation events; and, is there a proper place for unforeseen ground conditions clauses in design and build contracts?

The answers to these questions are not wholly academic even if employers desist, as they are encouraged to do by the promoters of NEC 3, from making changes to the core clauses and to the set list of compensation events to suit their particular projects. What employers need to do is to take note of the common aspects of allocation of risk in the main options and to consider what influence that should have on contract strategy generally.

So, for example, an employer wishing to develop a difficult site with uncertain ground conditions might well decide – returning to the principle that risk should be allocated to the party best able to control it – that retaining responsibility for design would be more appropriate than contractor's design and that Option B might be more favourable than Option A in obtaining competitive tenders.

The employer's requirements

The aspects of the employer's requirements which influence the selection of the main option of NEC 3 are various. They include:

- the degree of finalisation of the requirements
- the likelihood of change in the requirements
- the extent to which the requirements are performance based
- the extent to which the requirements are confidential
- the extent to which the requirements involve active participation of the employer in the construction of the works

As for finalisation of the requirements and the likelihood of change, the simple rule of contract procurement is that you should only buy on a lump sum basis when you know in advance what you want. Changes and variations are likely to be expensive and associated claims for delay and disruption even more so. Not uncommonly the apparent certainty of the lump sum price evaporates as changes, variations and claims are paid on cost plus. It makes good commercial sense, therefore, for employers who know they are likely to end up paying cost plus to embark on a cost plus contract in the first place. They will then have some control over the costs from the outset and they can consider whether a target price contract is appropriate so as to provide the incentive for all costs to be minimised.

Options A and B of NEC 3, being firm price contracts, are clearly least suited to change and/or development of the employer's requirements as the works progress. Options E and F, being cost plus contracts are clearly best suited. They allow the employer maximum flexibility.

The two target contract main options, C and D, provide an intermediate level of choice. They do allow flexibility but they require a reasonable level of definition of the employer's requirements at the outset in order for target prices to be set.

Performance criteria, confidentiality matters and employer participation have much to do with decisions to be made on allocation of design responsibility as discussed above. But taken separately, so far as that is possible:

- the ideal choice for a performance contract would be Option A
- the necessary choice for maximum confidentiality may be Option F
- the appropriate choice for employer participation is probably Option E

Operating restrictions

In contracts where there are significant operating restrictions on the contractor either because of the location of the site or because parts of the site contain continuous production facilities or the like, the essential question for contract choice is how well can the restrictions be defined in the tender documents. A secondary question is whether or not the restrictions are likely to be subject to change.

If complete definition of restrictions is possible at tender stage there is no reason why Options A and B should not be used however onerous the restrictions. But if complete definition is not possible, or change is likely, then Options A and B are not suitable because of their inherent inflexibility.

Early start and/or rapid finish

Timing requirements have much to do with the selection of the best main option for any particular contract.

Options A and B, which require the maximum definition of detail at tender stage, have the longest lead times. Options E and F which can commence with minimum definition have the shortest lead times. Options C and D occupy the intermediate position.

As to completion times and how rapidly a finish can be achieved that comes down mainly, in consideration of the main options, as to how well each permits development of the design as the works proceed. That apart there is not much to choose between the options, except possibly that with the cost reimbursable options the employer has greater flexibility in ordering acceleration.

Flexibility in contractual arrangements

As a general rule the employer has more flexibility under cost reimbursable contracts to change not only the detail of his technical requirements but also the detail of contractual arrangements. This follows naturally from the payment mechanism.

One of the more evident and perhaps one of the most important aspects of this flexibility is whether there is the facility for the employer to terminate the contract at will without any suggestion of fault on the part of the contractor. NEC 3 has an elaborate scheme in the section 9 core clauses for dealing with termination and the amounts due on termination. It permits termination at will for all the main options.

Avoidance of disputes

It may seem odd that with a contract such as NEC 3, committed to the cause of avoidance of disputes, it can be suggested that the employer's desire to avoid disputes should find its way into the selection procedure for one of the main options. It might be expected that all options would be equally non-adversarial.

But, in reality, that is not the case. All the main options have common core clauses and a common set of compensation events but that does not stop firm price options A and B being potentially more adversarial than the cost reimbursable options E and F. Nor does it alter the fact that design and build contracts give the contractor less opportunities for making claims than employer designed contracts.

Consequently, if avoidance of disputes is particularly important to the employer, that should be a factor taken into account in the early stages of contract strategy. And it is wholly appropriate that the employer should select the main option with a view to minimising use by the contractor of the compensation event procedures.

Single point responsibility

For some employers the concept of single point responsibility is important enough to influence their entire contract strategy. Principally the matter is one of allocation of design responsibility which in turn works its way into selection of the appropriate main option of NEC 3. So, to take the simplest example, the employer who contracts on a turnkey basis (turn the key and everything is done) will select a design and build contractor; will specify what he requires in performance terms; and will choose Option A.

2.3 Option A – priced contract with activity schedule

Option A is described in NEC 3 as a priced contract with activity schedule. Except for a few changes of detail it generally matches Option A of ECC 2. The activity schedule is defined in clause 11.2(20) as the activity schedule in the contract unless changed in accordance with the contract. There is no definition of Option A beyond this in the contract so to understand what Option A is, and how it differs from the other five main options of NEC 3, it is necessary to look at the clauses of NEC 3 applying particularly to Option A. In total there are fourteen such clauses but for the purpose of defining Option A three are particularly important:

- clause 11.2(27) – the price for the work done to date is the total of the prices for each group of completed activities and each completed activity which is not in a group
- clause 11.2(30) – the prices are the lump sum prices for each of the activities in the activity schedule unless later changed in accordance with the contract
- clause 54.1 – information in the activity schedule is not works information or site information

Section 5 (payment) of NEC 3, clause 50.2, states that the amount due to the contractor is the price of the work done to date. So what can be gathered from the above is that Option A is a lump sum contract in which the lump sum price is broken down into subsidiary lump sum prices for the various activities to be undertaken in providing the works.

There is nothing unusual in this in that a lump sum contract price, whatever the form of contract, is usually supported by a breakdown of the contract price in the form of a schedule to be used either for making interim payments or assisting in the valuation of variations. The difference in NEC 3 is that there is no definition of the contract price and no specific statement to the effect that the contractor's obligation is to provide the works for the contract price. And to further emphasise the significance in NEC 3 of the lump sum prices for activities, changes of prices resulting from the assessment of compensation events are made as changes to the prices of activities.

The legal effects of this are difficult to assess. Perhaps much depends in any particular case on how the form of tender is worded. There is no standard form beyond that provided as a sample form in the Guidance Notes. In this, the contractor offers to provide the works in accordance with the contract data. However, if the form of tender follows too closely the wording of NEC 3 and puts the contractor's offer in terms of lump sum prices for activities then the contract may be held to be for a series of lump sum prices rather than for a single lump sum. Perhaps this is what NEC 3 intends although it is far from obvious what advantage accrues.

But since most parties using Option A of NEC 3 will normally intend to contract on the basis of a single lump sum price for the works it is probably best, for the avoidance of doubt, that the form of tender avoids any confusion and states clearly that the contractor's offer is for a single lump sum. The sample form of tender in the Guidance Notes achieves this by referring to the contract data, which in turn, refers to the 'tendered total of the Prices'.

The activity schedule

The activity schedule was not defined in ECC 2 and it is defined in clause 11.2(20) of NEC 3 only in the circular terms mentioned above. The phrase is used many times throughout NEC 3 but the only indication of what it is in contractual terms is given in clause 54.1 which states that information in the activity schedule is not works information or site information, and in part two of the contract data where it says that if Option A or C is used the activity schedule 'is' . . . and a space is provided for the contractor to state what the activity schedule 'is'.

In practice most users of NEC 3 will understand that the activity schedule is a breakdown of the work to be done under the contract. What may not be so obvious is that under NEC 3 the activity schedule must cover the whole of the contract price and that the contractor's entitlement to interim payments is assessed on the basis of completed activities.

Contractors using ECC 2 soon learned the lesson that the more activities they listed the more regular their interim payments. Thus, listing a bridge abutment as an activity allowed interim payment only when the abutment was wholly completed. But broken down into excavation, piling, blinding concrete, formwork, reinforcement, concrete placing, concrete finishing etc., interim payments became due for each completed operation. One result of this was that activity schedules running into hundreds, sometimes thousands, of items were produced with consequent effects on programmes which, by clause 31.4 of ECC 2 had to show the start and finish of each activity on the activity schedule. This amount of detail then worked its way into the assessment of compensation events.

Clause 31.4 of NEC 3 is written in less precise terms than clause 31.4 of ECC 2. It states that the contractor 'provides information which shows how each activity on the Activity Schedule relates to the operations on each programme which he submits for acceptance'. This may have more to do with programming logic than just start and finish times and it needs to be read in conjunction with clause 31.2 which requires the contractor to show on each programme submitted for acceptance 'the order and timing of the operations which the Contractor plans to do in order to Provide the Works'. But whatever is intended it probably remains the case that the greater the number of activities in the activity schedule, the greater the tasks of re-programming and assessing compensation events.

To counter the problems in ECC 2, some employers adopted the practice of fixing themselves, by instructions to tenderers, the size of the activity schedule. Some may see this as a useful practice to retain when using NEC 3.

Changes in Option A of NEC 3 (from ECC 2)

- New clause 11.2(20) defining activity schedule.
- Revised clause 11.2(22) refers to 'Defined Cost' in place of 'Actual Cost' and refers to the Shorter Schedule of Cost Components in place of the Schedule of Cost Components. This is a change of some significance. See comments in Chapter 15 on the assessment of compensation events.
- Revised clause 31.4 requires information on how each activity in the activity schedule relates to the operations in each programme submitted for acceptance – previously required start and finish of each activity to be shown.
- Revised clause 36.3 relating to acceleration includes a requirement to change key dates.
- Revised clause 54.2 requires the contractor to submit a revised activity schedule if planned changes are such that activities on the activity schedule 'do not relate to' operations on the accepted programme. Was 'so that the activity schedule does not comply'.
- New clause 63.10 relating to price reductions due to compensation events uses part of clause 63.2 from ECC 2 whilst leaving the balance as a shorter clause 63.2 in NEC 3 core compensation event clauses.
- New clause 63.14 states that if the project manager and the contractor agree, rates and lump sums may be used to assess compensation events instead of defined cost. This is another change of some significance. Again, see comments in Chapter 15 on the assessment of compensation events.
- Revised clause 65.4 relates to notifications implementing compensation events.

Note: clause 63.11 in ECC 2 which referred to discretionary use of the Shorter Schedule of Cost Components is not used in NEC 3 – the new clause 11.2(22) having made such use mandatory for main options A and B.

2.4 Option B – priced contract with bill of quantities

Option B of NEC 3 is described as a priced contract with bill of quantities. This is intended to be what is traditionally known as a remeasurement contract. Subject to certain changes of detail in the clauses, Option B is not significantly changed from ECC 2.

The clauses of Option B which identify it as a remeasurement contract are:

- clause 11.2(31) which states that the prices are the lump sums and the amounts obtained by multiplying the rates by the quantities for the items in the bill of quantities, *and*
- clause 11.2(28) which states that the price of the work done to date is the total of the quantity of work completed for each item in the bill of quantities multiplied by the rate plus a proportion of each lump sum as so completed

Not everyone is persuaded, however, that Option B creates a remeasurement contract. There was a long-standing debate as to whether Option B of ECC 2 involved remeasure or simply entitlement to payment by reference to the quantities and rates in the bill of quantities. The drafting changes between ECC 2 and NEC 3 do not resolve the problem.

The background to this unusual debate is that not all contracts in the construction industry where the contract price is founded on a bill of quantities are remeasurement contracts. In many building contracts the function of the bill of quantities is to provide a contract price breakdown and rates for variations. In civil engineering, remeasurement is normal but contracts usually say in express terms that the value of the works is to be determined by remeasurement. What was missing from ECC 2 and arguably is missing from NEC 3 is a clear statement to that effect. Both ECC 2 and NEC 3 define 'the Prices' by reference to 'the quantities for the items in the Bill of Quantities'. And although both define the price for the work done to date in terms of the quantity of the work completed for each item in the bill of quantities, that can be taken as requiring apportionment rather than remeasurement on the basis that the price for the work done to date is concerned with payment rather than prices for final valuation.

The changes that have been made in NEC 3 from ECC 2 may if anything have added to, rather than eliminated, uncertainty on the remeasurement issue. There is a new defined term in clause 11.2(21) which states that the bill of quantities is the bill of quantities as changed to accommodate implemented compensation events and accepted quotations for acceleration. There is also an addition to clause 60.4 which states that a difference between the final total quantity of work done and the quantity stated for an item in the bill of quantities is a compensation event if 'the difference does not result from a change to the Works Information'. Together these might be taken as suggesting that changes in quantities resulting from remeasurement are to be treated as compensation events. The Guidance Notes to NEC 3 take a different view however saying that a change in quantity is not, of itself, a compensation event.

The debate will no doubt go on but it can be resolved for particular contracts if the parties ensure that the form of tender and the form of agreement make clear that the final value of the works is to be determined by remeasurement.

Method of measurement

NEC 3 does not refer to any particular method of measurement. It relies on the employer stating in part one of the contract data which method of measurement is used and whether or not any amendments have been made.

Changes in Option B of NEC 3 (from ECC 2)

- new clause 11.2(21) defining 'Bill of Quantities'
- revised clause 11.2(22) replacing 'Actual Cost' with 'Defined Cost' and replacing the 'Schedule of Cost Components' with the 'Shorter Schedule of Cost Components'
- revised clause 60.4 with new bullet point relating to differences in quantities and changes in the works information and revised bullet point setting the threshold for a compensation event due to change in quantities at 0.5% of the total prices rather than 0.1%
- revised clause 60.5 adding reference to key dates
- revised clause 60.6 referring to division of the work into items in the method of measurement
- new clause 60.7 stating that in assessing a compensation event for correction of inconsistency between the bill of quantities and any other contract document the contractor is assumed to have taken the bill of quantities as correct
- new clause 63.10 relating to price restrictions due to compensation events is part of clause 63.2 from ECC 2 – the balance is left as a shorter clause 63.2 in NEC 3 core compensation event clauses
- revised clause 63.13 stating that if the project manager and the contractor agree, rates and lump sums may be used to assess a compensation event instead of defined cost
- revised clause 65.4 relating to notifications implementing compensation events

Note: clause 63.11 in ECC 2 which referred to the discretionary use of the Shorter Schedule of Cost Components is not used in NEC 3 – the new clause 11.2(22) having made such use mandatory for main options A and B.

2.5 *Target contracts generally*

Target price contracts are versions of cost reimbursable contracts where the reimbursement of cost ceases or reduces when a target price is reached. Con-

tracts where reimbursement ceases altogether at the target price are sometimes called GMP contracts (guaranteed maximum price).

For most target contracts, however, a sliding scale of reimbursement
operates both above and below the target price so that the employer and the
contractor share the financial risks – an arrangement commonly known as
gain/pain share. The contractor, in effect, gains a bonus if he can keep the
actual cost below the target price but he shares the cost when the actual cost
exceeds the target price. So what target price contracts do is to encourage the
contractor to be efficient in the use of resources and economic in placing
purchase and subcontract orders.

For contractors, however, there is a real danger that sight can be lost of the
financial risks of target contracts. Because reimbursement is on a cost plus
basis at the outset and remains that way for much of the contract too little
attention may be given to the impending effects of cost over-runs, in particular to the possibility of having to return money to the employer under the
gain/pain arrangements and to the possibility under some such arrangements that the contract has effectively become guaranteed maximum price.

Target setting

Target price contracts can be used with either contractor's design or employer's design but whichever applies there must be a reasonable definition
of the employer's requirements at tender stage to enable the tenderers to reach
their assessments of the target price. In some cases a performance specification alone is sufficient but in other cases drawings and indicative bills of
quantities are supplied by the employer.

It is not unusual for protracted negotiations to take place before the award
of a target price contract on the precise figure at which the target should be
set. Obviously it is in the contractor's interests to secure the contract at the
highest achievable target price.

Competition

Competition operates between tenders in target price contracts in two
ways:

- Between the fees tendered to cover non-reimbursable costs – principally
  overheads and profit. The fees are usually tendered on a percentage basis
  (to be added to reimbursable cost) but they may be lump sums.
- Between the target prices tendered reflecting the assessments of the various
  tenderers on final actual cost.

In comparing tenders employers use various formulae to analyse the balance
between the different levels of tender fees and target prices but it is not
unknown for employers to fix either the fees or the target prices to simplify
comparisons.

Target price adjustment

For contractors embarking on target price contracts a key question is how restrictive (or how generous) are the permitted adjustments to the target price once the contract is in operation. Clearly, at the very least, there must be upward adjustment for changes and variations which require additional works – otherwise the employer might receive the benefit at no cost. But for such matters as unforeseen ground conditions or other unexpected costs much depends on the policy of risk allocation in the contract – and in that NEC 3 is fairly generous as all compensation events can adjust the target price.

One advantage of NEC 3 target price contracts (Options C and D) over some other target contracts is that they are clear on their policies for target price adjustment. Contractors should beware of straightforward cost reimbursable contracts applied to target price contracts. It is necessary to see what amendments have been made to cover target price adjustments. The standard IChemE *Green Book*, for example, says nothing on unforeseen ground conditions, and does not need to, since all costs are reimbursable. Without some amendment for this in a target price contract the result can be that the contractor ends up taking risks which he never contemplated and were never apparent.

Risk sharing formulae

The simplest arrangement for risk sharing above and below the target price is that each party bears 50% of any cost over-run and each takes 50% of any saving. Most target price contracts, however, have more sophisticated arrangements with sliding scales of risk distribution. Not infrequently there is a cut off point for cost reimbursement at 15% or so above the target price – which effectively creates a guaranteed maximum price (subject only to target price adjustments).

NEC 3 adopts a flexible approach and provides for the employer to enter in part one of the contract data various share percentages against a range of percentage changes from the target price.

Disallowed costs

Even in straight cost reimbursable contracts there are usually some items of cost which are disallowed either because they arise from some specified default or breach on the part of the contractor or because they are not properly substantiated. The contract will normally list those items which are to be regarded as disallowed costs.

With target cost contracts the lists of such items are sometimes more extensive than those for straight cost reimbursable contracts. But this is an area where policies of contracts (and employers) differ considerably – particularly on the question of whether the costs of rectifying defects should be reimbursable or should be disallowed.

NEC 3 applies a common list of disallowed costs to its target cost contracts (Options C and D) and to its cost reimbursable contract (Option E). It does, however, have a more restricted list for its management contract (Option F).

Payment arrangements

The control of costs in cost reimbursable contracts can be extremely complex and time consuming. The amount of paperwork to be processed can be enormous. This is recognised in the IChemE *Green Book* where interim payments each month are made on a combination of estimated costs and incurred costs.

The payment arrangements in NEC 3 however are much the same for cost reimbursable contracts as for firm price contracts. The project manager is required to assess the amount due and to certify the same within one week of each assessment date (clause 51.1). The amount due is the price for work done to date.

For Options C and D the price for work done to date is the defined cost the project manager forecasts will have been paid by the contractor plus the fee. Although an improvement on the position in ECC 2, which referred to costs paid, the project manager still has an ambitious task.

2.6 *Options C and D – target contracts*

Option C is described as a target contract with activity schedule, Option D as a target contract with bill of quantities. The only significant differences between the two are:

- in Option C the target price is based on a lump sum (split into activities) whereas in Option D the target price is based on a bill of quantities
- in Option D the employer takes the risks on changes of quantities (and departures from the method of measurement) and the target price is adjusted according to the final measure

Nowhere in NEC 3 is the phrase 'target price' actually used. 'The Prices' as defined in clauses 11.2(30) and 11.2(31) (lump sums for activities; rates for quantities for bills) are apparently to be taken in Options C and D as the target price. This is a workable arrangement but it is not particularly satisfactory since the target mechanism is not intended to apply individually to either activities or rates and quantities.

The purpose of the activity schedule in Option C and the bill of quantities in Option D is different from the purpose of those documents in Option A and Option B. For Options C and D the documents do not fix amounts due as interim payments. They serve only in the assessment of compensation events (which move the target price) and in calculation of the contractor's share.

Changes in Options C and D of NEC 3 (from ECC 2)

Options C and D of NEC 3 both have a considerable amount of clause re-arrangement, redrafting and new clauses when examined against the detail in ECC 2.

Some common points to note are:

- clause 11.2(25) – costs in preparation for, and conduct of an adjudication or proceedings of a tribunal, are disallowed costs
- clause 11.2(29) – the price of the work done to date is the total defined cost which the project manager forecasts will have been paid before the next assessment date plus the fee
- clause 40.7 – when the project manager assesses the cost incurred by the employer repeating a test or inspection after a defect is found, the project manager does not include the contractor's cost of carrying out repeat tests or inspections
- clause 93.6 – the project manager's assessment of the contractor's share is added to the amounts due to the contractor on termination if there has been a saving, or deducted if there has been an excess

Note also:

- clause 36.5 in ECC 2 which required the contractor to submit subcontractor's proposals to accelerate to the project manager is omitted from NEC 3 – possibly because it is already covered in clause 36.1
- clause 53.5 in ECC 2 which stated that the prices were not reduced if the project manager accepted a proposal by the contractor to change works information provided by the employer so that cost was reduced is omitted from NEC 3 but clause 63.11 is reworded to achieve the same effect
- Options C and D both retain the rules in ECC 2 that the contractor is paid cost plus until completion and that the first assessment of the contractor's share is not made until completion

2.7 *Option E – cost reimbursable contract*

Cost reimbursable contracts put the least financial risk on the contractor and give the employer the least certainty of price. Their chief defect is that they provide no incentive for the contractor to minimise costs and, when the contractor's fee is on a percentage basis, they encourage expenditure. Not surprisingly, cost reimbursable contracts tend to be used only as a policy of last resort and in circumstances when other procurement methods are not appropriate.

Option E of NEC 3 is a straightforward cost reimbursable contract which operates on defined cost plus the percentage fee inserted in part two of the contract data by the contractor.

Comparison of tenders on financial grounds is principally on the various tendered fee levels. Note should, however, also be taken of the particular rates for those parts of the schedule of cost components which tenderers are required to price in part two of the contract data.

Points of change in NEC 3

Particular points to note in Option E are much the same as those listed above for Options C and D except that the target related points have no application in Option E.

2.8 Option F – management contract

A management contract is a cost reimbursable contract where the contractor manages the works but subcontracts all or most of the construction work. Option F of NEC 3 requires that the contractor manages design, provision of site services, construction and installation and that he subcontracts all of these unless the contract data states that he will do some himself.

Changes in NEC 3 include:

- a statement in clause 11.2(24) that defined cost includes the prices for work done by the contractor himself – this was missing from ECC 2
- a statement in clause 11.2(26) that disallowed cost includes payment to a subcontractor for work which the contract data states the contractor will do himself and for the contractor's management
- a new clause 20.5 which states that for work which the contractor is to do himself the project manager and the contractor shall agree price and time changes of any compensation events and, failing such agreement, the project manager decides the changes

Interestingly, Option F is the only one of the cost reimbursable options C, D, E and F which does not list as disallowed cost the costs of preparation for, and the conduct of, adjudication and tribunal proceedings.

2.9 Option W1 – dispute resolution

Option W1 commences with the header note that it is the dispute resolution procedure 'used unless the United Kingdom Housing Grants, Construction and Regeneration Act 1996 applies'. The underlying point of the note is that

Option W1, which generally follows the principles of clauses 90 to 93 of ECC 2, contains procedures and timetables which are not compatible with the requirements of the Act. In particular it stipulates conditions precedent to commencing adjudication which are not compatible with the statutory right under the Act to commence adjudication 'at any time', and it requires the adjudicator's decision to be given within eight weeks of referral rather than four weeks as required by the Act.

But the fact that Option W1 is not compatible with the Act does not fully explain why it should be regarded as the option to be used in contracts which are not subject to the Act, particularly as there is nothing in Option W2 (other than the heading note) which refers to the Act or which makes it suitable only for contracts subject to the Act. In reality Options W1 and W2 provide different approaches to dispute resolution and the use of adjudication. Option W1 encourages prompt notification and adjudication of disputes as part of good management practice and, to facilitate this, the adjudicator will frequently be named in the contract data so that he is on hand to assist as and when required. Option W2 simply provides a statute compliant adjudication procedure. There is no legal or contractual reason why an employer with a contract not subject to the Act should feel constrained to select Option W1 and to avoid Option W2.

Option W1 clauses are similar to those in clauses 90 to 93 of ECC 2 and both sets of clauses contain an adjudication table setting out what disputes can be referred to adjudication and when. An interesting addition to the table in Option W1 is that disputes about a quotation for a compensation event which is 'treated as having been accepted' can be referred to adjudication by the employer. On the face of it this is close to being a contradiction in terms. It seems that a quotation which is 'treated as having been accepted' is treated differently from one which has been accepted.

Another point to note in Option W1 is that it makes clear in clause W1.4(1) that adjudication is a condition precedent to referral to a tribunal (such as arbitration). That was probably intended in ECC 2 also but it was poorly expressed.

For detailed comment on Option W1 see Chapter 19.

2.10 *Option W2 – dispute resolution*

Option W2 commences with the header note 'used in the United Kingdom when the Housing Grants, Construction and Regeneration Act 1996 applies'. By this it means that the adjudication procedure which it contains is compliant with the requirements of the Act. However, there is nothing in Option W2 to stop it being the preferred choice over Option W1 for contracts not subject to the Act. Moreover, there is no reason in law why Option W1 should not be used for contracts subject to the Act. All that then follows is that a party can, if it so wishes, avoid the adjudication provisions of Option W1 and use the statutory adjudication scheme as set down by Regulations.

The adjudication parts of Option W2 broadly follow the provisions of Option Y(UK)2 of ECC 2 issued in 1998 when the Act came into force.

The tribunal clauses of Option W2 are the same as those in Option W1 except that clause W1.4(3) of Option W1 is omitted from Option W2. This clause states if an adjudicator does not notify his decision within the stated time one party may notify the other of his intention to refer the dispute to a tribunal. The reason for the omission is not obvious and it may be a mistake since the clause numbering in part of W2.4 of Option W2 does not follow that in Option W1 in the same manner as elsewhere in NEC 3.

For detailed comment on Option W2 see Chapter 19.

Chapter 3
Secondary option clauses

3.1 Introduction

As was the case with earlier editions of NEC it is not intended that the core of clauses of NEC 3 should cover all the contractual detail necessary for each and every project. Such detail, which will clearly vary from project to project, is to be provided by adding to the core clauses a selection of secondary option clauses. These are not clauses of lesser standing than the core clauses, they are secondary only in the sense that they will normally be considered for inclusion in a contract after the primary decision on which main option to use has been taken. They cover a wide range of important matters and they can significantly alter the balance of risk between the parties.

ECC 2 originally had 14 secondary option clauses lettered G to V so as to follow on from letters A to F used for the main options. Letter Z was to be used for special additional conditions. NEC 3 drops two of those 14 clauses:

- Option U – the Construction (Design and Management) Regulations 1994
- Option V – trust fund

Options U and V both placed financial risks on the employer which went well beyond normal criteria and it is unlikely that they often, if ever, found their way into contracts. They will not be missed.

NEC 3 goes further, however, than simply retaining twelve of the original fourteen clauses. It amends some and adds three new clauses – partnering, limitation of liability, and key performance indicators. The current NEC 3 list, which is numbered X1 to X20 (with numbers X8–X11 and X19 presently excluded) is:

- X1 – price adjustment for inflation
- X2 – changes in the law
- X3 – multiple currencies
- X4 – parent company guarantee
- X5 – sectional completion
- X6 – bonus for early completion
- X7 – delay damages
- X12 – partnering
- X13 – performance bond
- X14 – advanced payment to the contractor

- X15 – limitation of the contractor's liability for design
- X16 – retention
- X17 – low performance damages
- X18 – limitation of liability
- X20 – key performance indicators

Additionally listed as secondary option clauses are:

- Y(UK)2 – Housing Grants, Construction and Regeneration Act 1996
- Y(UK)3 – Contract (Rights of Third Parties) Act 1999
- Z – Additional conditions of contract

Choice of secondary option clauses

Save for the restriction that Option X20 should not be used with Option X12, the employer using either of main options A or B has full choice of the secondary option clauses and can include as few or as many as he wishes. There is not intended to be any duplication or inconsistency between the secondary options to restrict choice and nothing is obviously apparent. However, see the comments later in this chapter on the peculiarities of the damages and the limitation of liabilities options.

With main options other than A and B however there are some restrictions on which secondary options can be used. These are:

- Option X1 – price adjustment for inflation
  Not used with main options E and F
- Option X3 – multiple currencies
  Not used with main options C, D, E and F
- Option X16 – retention
  Not used with main option F

The use of Options Y(UK)2 and Y(UK)3, both of which are related to UK statutes, will normally be restricted to contracts carried out in the United Kingdom and which are subject to the relevant Acts. For Y(UK)2 this will be any contract in the UK subject to the Housing Grants, Construction and Regeneration Act 1996; and for Y(UK)3 any contract subject to the law of England, Wales or Northern Ireland.

Status of secondary option clauses

NEC 3 does not define which documents constitute the contract. Nor does it attempt to set any order of precedence for the various documents forming the contract. It leaves any ambiguities and inconsistencies to be resolved by the project manager under clause 17.1.

This lack of any defined order of precedence together with the unusual 'pick and mix' arrangement of the clauses of NEC 3 may have some unintended effects. One to note is that the usual rule of construction – the particular taking precedence over the general – is unlikely to apply as between core clauses and secondary clauses. So, whereas in a traditional contract special conditions of contract take precedence over standard conditions in the event of ambiguity or inconsistency, the position in NEC 3 appears to be that special conditions included as additional clauses under secondary option Z have no precedence over the core clauses.

To overcome this, employers who see it as a problem should ideally include a clear statement identifying precedence in the contract. An alternative, but perhaps less certain method, would be to keep selected special conditions which are required to have precedence outside the scheme of secondary option clauses.

3.2 Option X1 – price adjustment for inflation

Option X1 is a conventional formula/index based fluctuation clause which allows adjustments to the contract price for inflation. It is used only with main options A, B, C and D. Its use is unnecessary with main options E and F which are fully cost reimbursable. When Option X1 is used the particulars governing the application of the formula and the indices must be included in the contract data.

The only change in Option X1 from the corresponding Option N in ECC 2 is that the term 'Defined Cost' is used in place of 'Actual Cost'.

In the UK the inclusion of price adjustment provisions in construction contracts has diminished in recent years as inflation has stabilised and con- tractors can reasonably predict the risks of rising prices. For some overseas countries however the risks remain uncertain and price adjustment clauses are still regularly used.

Option X1 of NEC 3 has five clauses:

- clause X1.1 – defined terms
- clause X1.2 – price adjustment factor
- clause X1.3 – compensation events
- clause X1.4 – price adjustment Options A and B
- clause X1.5 – price adjustment Options C and D

Good advice on how these clauses operate in practice, together with worked examples, is given in the Guidance Notes for NEC 3.

3.3 Option X2 – changes in the law

Option X2 in NEC 3 is the same as Option T in ECC 2.

The purpose of Option X2 is to place the risks of contract costs and comple- tion times being affected by changes in the law with the employer. Option X2 does this by making changes in the law compensation events. The same effect could probably be achieved by making changes in the law the employer's risk under clause 80.1. They would then come within the scope of compensation event 60.1(14).

Without Option X2 the amount of risk carried by each of the parties on changes in the law depends upon which of the main options is used. Generally the contractor takes the risks on time under all the main options but the risks on price follow the usual rules for the main options.

Clause X2.1 – changes in the law

Clause X2.1 operates only when there is a change in the law of the country in which the site is located and the change occurs after the contract date, i.e. the date on which the contract was made. This is slightly different from some other contracts where changes in the law which occur after the return of tenders are taken into account.

Procedures

Clause X2.1 does not rely expressly on the procedures for the notification and assessment of compensation events set out in section 6 of NEC 3. It states some procedures of its own:

• the project manager may notify the contractor of a compensation event
• the project manager may instruct the contractor to submit quotations
• the prices are reduced for changes which reduce total defined cost

It is not clear if these stated procedures are meant as supplements to the section 6 procedures or as partial replacements. But for contractors the key question is probably: does the eight week notice rule of clause 61.3 apply? The safe answer is to assume that it does.

However one curious, and obviously unintended, effect of applying section 6 procedures rigorously to clause X2.1 is that the contractor is obliged under clause 61.3 to give notice of all changes in the law of the country occurring after the contract date. It is then for the project manager to decide under clause 61.4 whether or not the changes have any effect on cost or completion. This follows from the opening sentence of clause X2.1 which states, 'A change in the law of the country in which the Site is located is a compensation event if it occurs after the Contract Date.'

3.4 *Option X3 – multiple currencies*

The intention of Option X3 is to partially transfer the risk of exchange rate changes from the contractor to the employer. This is not uncommon in overseas contracts. The application of Option X3 is to firm price contracts rather than to cost reimbursable contracts and NEC 3 states that Option X3 should only be used with main options A and B.

Option X3 remains unchanged from Option K of ECC 2 except that in clause X3.1 the phrase 'items and activities' replaces the previous word 'work'. This brings an added measure of precision to the extent of application of the option since by clause X3.1, it is only the 'items and activities' listed in the contract data which are to be paid in a currency other than the currency of the contract.

Clause X3.1 also confirms that the exchange rates used to convert from the currency of the contract to other currencies are to be taken from the publications listed in the contract data. In order to give proper effect to Option X3 it is important that these are reliable publications with regular updates.

Clause X3.2 indicates that the amounts paid in currencies other than the currency of the contract shall not exceed the maximum amounts stated in the contract data and that any excess shall be paid in the currency of the contract. It is, of course, open to the employer to state 'no limit' but where there is a stated maximum it applies to the amount of converted currency not to the amount of currency to be converted.

Care needs to be taken when using Option X3 in conjunction with Option X1 (price adjustment for inflation) to ensure that the indices used for price adjustments do not produce double recovery for exchange rate changes.

3.5 Option X4 – parent company guarantee

Parent company guarantees give a measure of protection to the employer against a subsidiary contracting company's default and/or insolvency.

Because the financial strengths of subsidiary companies are not always reflected in their balance sheets, contracting companies which are subsidiary companies often put forward holding company accounts as evidence of stability. In such circumstances the employer may rightly decide that the security of a parent company guarantee is required in addition to (but sometimes as an alternative to) any performance bond which is specified.

Clause X4.1 requires a contractor owned by a parent company to give a parent company guarantee:

- in the form set out in the works information
- within four weeks of the contract date

Failure to provide the guarantee is a reason for termination under clause 91.2(R12).

Form of guarantee

As with the performance bond the required form of guarantee is to be set out in the works information.

Drafters of the guarantee form should note a potential technical defect in the wording of clause X4.1 in that it refers to the guarantee being given by the company which owns the contractor. This is not necessarily the holding company (the ultimate parent company) within the terms of the Companies Act. Strictly, all that is required under clause X4.1 is a guarantee from a company owning the majority of contracting company's shares.

Apart from numbering there is no change in Option X4 from its equivalent in ECC 2.

3.6 *Option X5 – sectional completion*

Option X5 of NEC 3 remains identical to Option L of ECC 2. However, the introduction of a key dates procedure into NEC 3 puts the operation of Option X5 into a different contractual context to that in ECC 2. In short, under ECC 2 the contractor's obligation was to complete the whole of the works and, providing Option L was included in the contract, any specified sections of the works by stipulated completion dates. Under NEC 3 the contractor has the added obligation to do the work such that specified conditions are met by stipulated key dates.

These conditions can apply to the whole or parts of the works. Presumably, the intention is that any specified conditions should be something short of completion as defined in the contract. But if the employer should choose to specify in the contract data 'completion' as the 'condition' for parts of the works that would seem to have the effect of introducing sectional completion dates into the contract without the use of the sectional completion option.

Such a move, however, might have some unintended consequences. The contractor's liability for failing to meet key dates is simply to pay any resulting costs incurred by the employer whereas the contractor's liability for failing to meet completion dates is to pay delay damages, liquidated or unliquidated, depending on whether delay damages option, Option X7, is included in the contract. And either type of damages can include loss as well as cost.

Such considerations apart, the primary purpose of including Option X5 in an NEC 3 contract is the same as the purpose of including Option L in an ECC 2 contract. It is to allow parts of the works to be called sections of the works such that they qualify for damages for late completion.

Unless Option X5 is used the contractor's obligations to pay liquidated damages for late completion will apply only to the whole of the works. Consequently, Option X5 is one of the more important secondary options for the employer to consider when putting together the contract.

In traditional contracts the problem frequently arises that employers intend partial completion dates to be contractually binding on the contractor but, although they identify the parts, they state liquidated damages only for late completion of the whole of the works. The courts however will not then award either liquidated or unliquidated damages for late completion of the parts. See, for example, the case of *Turner* v. *Mathind* (1986).

The same situation will normally arise under NEC 3 unless it is stated in the contract data that Options X5 and X7 apply and the description, completion date, and delay damages for each section are given.

There is the possibility under NEC 3, because of the lack of precedence of documents and because the project manager is required to resolve ambiguities and discrepancies between documents that in the event of some documents showing sectional completion when the contract data does not, the project manager could give instructions effectively imposing sectional completion requirements. The contractor would have no liability for liquidated damages for late completion of such sections but he would be entitled to a compensation event in respect of the instructions.

Clause X5.1 – sectional completion

In many standard forms of contract the provisions for sectional completion are lengthy and complicated but NEC 3 uses the simple device of stating in clause X5.1 that each reference and clause relevant to the works, to completion, and to the completion date applies, as the case may be, to either the whole of the works or to any section. Where, however, the phrase 'the whole of the works' is used in the conditions of contract, that phrase is not to be taken as applying to sections. Thus when Option X5.1 is used, NEC 3, of necessity, distinguishes between 'the works' and 'the whole of the works'.

Note, however, that to make the NEC 3 arrangement work the total of the sections should not comprise the whole of the works and that delay damages should be stated for all sections and for the whole of the works.

For the possibility of having a combination of liquidated and unliquidated damages for delay under NEC 3 see the comment later in this chapter on Option X7.

3.7 Option X6 – bonus for early completion

Provisions for payment to the contractor of a bonus for early completion are not common in standard forms but ad hoc arrangements for such payments are not unusual. NEC 3 sensibly includes the bonus provisions as a secondary option, Option X6. This is unchanged from Option Q of ECC 2.

Clause X6.1 – bonus for early completion

The drafting of clause X6.1 is comparatively straightforward in that it provides for the contractor to be paid a bonus:

- calculated at the rate stated in the contract data
- for each day from the earlier of
  — completion of the works
  — take-over of the works

until the completion date.

Note however that the only figure to be entered in the contract data is the rate per day for 'the whole of the works'. Therefore, although clause X6.1 on its wording might apply to sections it will probably not do so unless the contract data is extended to include additional figures for sections.

Apportionment

It may be argued that the wording of clause X6.1 implies that there should be apportionment of the daily rate of bonus for the whole of the works when there is early completion or take-over of any part of the works. The basis of such an argument is that since the clause states that the bonus becomes payable from the earlier of 'completion' or 'the date on which the employer takes over the works' and the contract provides for take over of parts of the works then some bonus should be paid when parts are taken over before completion.

For example a situation might arise when 90% of the works are taken over early and put to use by the employer but completion of the whole is not certified by the project manager until the due completion date. How then would the contractor have any entitlement to a bonus without apportionment? The strict legal answer may be that there is no provision for apportionment and the contractor has no entitlement to a partial bonus. But this is hardly in the spirit of the contract.

Effects of delays

Although NEC 3 may be subject to argument on apportionment in its bonus provisions it does appear to have eliminated one of the commonest causes of argument found with bonus provisions in other contracts. That is the question of whether delays for which the employer is responsible, or any delays which give entitlement to extension of time, should be taken into account in calculating the bonus. In some contracts the completion date is fixed for the purposes of calculating the bonus but in others it is not clear how delays should be treated or whether extensions of time apply to bonuses.

In NEC 3 however because the compensation event procedures move the completion date (whether or not an extension of time is required to avoid delay damages) the contractor's bonus entitlement is protected against any delay which is caused by a compensation event.

In the event that acceleration is considered under clause 36.1 of NEC 3 the parties will have to give some thought to how that relates to Option X6.

3.8 Option X7 – delay damages

A contractor who fails to complete by the due date is liable to the employer for damages for breach of contract. Such damages may be either specified in the contract (and are then usually known as liquidated damages) or they may be left to be determined after the breach of contract as general damages (and are then known as unliquidated damages).

Liquidated damages

When damages are liquidated they can be seen either as providing compensation for the employer in lieu of general damages or they can be seen as limiting the contractor's liability for his breach of contract. They serve as both and are regarded in law as an exclusive and exhaustive remedy. See the case of *Temloc* v. *Errill* (1987).

To be enforceable (and not liable to challenge as penalties) any sum specified as liquidated damages must be a genuine pre-estimate of the employer's loss or a lesser sum. And, because the courts have traditionally taken a strict approach to the construction of provisions for liquidated damages, to be effective such provisions must be clear and unambiguous.

Delay damages in NEC 3

The core clauses of NEC 3 are silent on delay damages for completion so unless secondary option X7 for delay damages is included in the contract the legal position is probably, and subject to what is said below on clause 12.4, that:

- the employer retains his common law rights and can sue for the damages he can prove he has suffered as a result of the contractor failing to complete by the due date, *and*
- the contractor is liable for the full amount of those damages unless the contract contains some limitation of his liability

Option X7 is not named a liquidated damages clause but it is clearly intended to operate as such. It requires a rate for damages to be entered in the contract data and the presumption must be that the rate conforms with the rules for liquidated damages. If not, Option X7 is unenforceable and pointless.

An awkward legal question could arise in the event of Option X7 being listed in the contract data as applicable to the contract but no rate being set in the contract data for the delay damages. The question might then be asked – does the inclusion of Option X7 act, in itself, as an exclusion of the employer's common law right to general damages? Or, to put it another way, would an employer by including Option X7 but failing to state a rate for delay damages, forgo his right to any delay damages, liquidated or otherwise?

In the case of *Temloc* v. *Errill* mentioned above, the employer, under a JCT contract, wrote £NIL as the rate for liquidated damages. The Court of Appeal held that the contractual provision for liquidated damages remained valid and therefore the employer had lost his common law remedy of general damages. The case is arguably not applicable to a blank rate entry – as opposed to a £NIL rate entry. But against that the express inclusion of the delay damages option clause might be persuasive of the parties' intention that general damages should be excluded.

In addition to the above there are two matters new to NEC 3 to consider. One is whether the 'entire agreement' referred to in clause 12.4 has any impact on the employer's right to delay damages in the absence of Option X7. The other is whether the clearly expressed condition precedent to entitlement to extension of time in clause 61.3 has any impact on the operation of Option X7. Both matters arise as a result of wording changes in NEC 3 from ECC 2.

If, as discussed in Chapters 1 and 4 of this book, clause 12.4 is an entire agreement of the type which excludes rights not expressed in the contract then without Option X7 it may not be possible for the employer to recover delay damages for late completion.

The new part of clause 61.3 that states that if the contractor does not notify a compensation event within eight weeks of becoming aware of the event he is not entitled to a change in the completion date raises a question, much discussed in legal circles, as to whether in certain circumstances conditions precedent to entitlement to extension of time can effectively invalidate the employer's right to liquidated damages. The question is particularly concerned with delayed completion caused by the employer's breach of contract.

Application to sections

Clause X7.1 of NEC 3 does not expressly mention sections but the intention that Option X7 should apply to sections, if so desired, is evident from the layout of the contract data sheet. This has spaces for the inclusion of rates for delay damages for sections as well as a space for the rate for the whole of the works.

The application of the delay damages provisions in clause X7.1 to sections relies entirely on the effectiveness of Option X5 (sectional completion) in giving the phrase 'the works, completion and completion date', both singular and plural meanings. It remains to be seen what the courts will make of this. They may take the view that the secondary options bolt independently onto the core clauses and are not to be interpreted as relating to one another. If that happens the provisions for liquidated damages for sections in NEC 3 will fail. Until the point is resolved employers concerned over the matter might consider expanding the wording of Option X7 with some express reference to sections.

Combination of delay damages

The prospect was mentioned above in this chapter in the comment on Option X5 (sectional completion) that it might be possible to combine within NEC 3 both liquidated damages for the whole of the works and general (unliquidated) damages for sections or vice versa. In principle there appears to be nothing against this providing there is no double recovery of damages. In *Turner* v. *Mathind* (1986) Lord Justice Parker expressed quite firmly the view that liquidated damages for the whole of the works should not necessarily exclude general damages for sections.

The option structure of NEC 3 seems to lend itself to this arrangement and it could arguably be achieved by including both Options X5 and X7 in the contract and by stating applicable, or not as applicable, as appropriate in the rates entries of the contract data. But, in any event, the new key date procedures in NEC 3 go some way towards providing unliquidated remedies for delay (albeit that only cost is recoverable).

Clause X7.1 – payment of delay damages

The key points of clause X7.1, all of which remain the same as in clause R1.1 of ECC 2, are:

- the contractor pays delay damages
- at the rate stated in the contract data
- from the completion date
- for each day
- until the earlier of:
  — completion, 'and'
  — the date of take-over

Note firstly a small semantic point – the use of the word 'and' where 'or' would seem more appropriate. More importantly, however, note the absence in clause X7.1 of any of the usual conditions precedent to the deduction of liquidated delay damages, e.g.:

- certification of failure to complete on time
- certification that no further extensions of time due
- notification of intention to deduct

It may well be that NEC 3 omits reference to these customary formalities in the interests of simplicity. The consequences however may be anything but simple and they are potentially adversarial. What may have been lost by the terse wording of clause X7.1 is the employer's discretion whether or not to deduct damages to which he is entitled.

The scheme appears to be that under clause 50.2 the project manager assesses the amount due taking into account any amounts 'to be paid by or retained from the Contractor'. The employer then pays the amount due. Hence the employer's loss of discretion. But what of the position if the project manager fails to deduct for damages in his assessment and the damages are not then paid when they become due. Can it then be argued that the employer has waived his right to damages?

Completion and take-over

Note that the project manager 'decides' the date of completion under clause 30.2 and that completion is defined in clause 11.2(2). The question as to whether any such decision is challengeable by the contractor is discussed in Chapter 8.

Clause 35.2 defines the meaning of take-over and clause 35.3 requires the project manager to certify the date on which the employer takes over any part of the works.

Clause X7.2 – repayment of damages

Clause X7.2 deals with repayment by the employer of delay damages when the completion date is changed to a later date. Again this is the same as in ECC 2.

The clause provides that the employer repays the 'overpayment of damages' with interest. The rate of interest is not stated but presumably the interest rate inserted in the contract data and referred to in clause 51.4 is intended to apply. The phrase 'overpayment of damages' suggests only partial repayment but it is unlikely to be so limited in its application.

The final sentence of clause X7.2, 'interest is assessed from the date of payment to the date of repayment and the date of repayment is an assessment date' is difficult to follow. However what it may mean is that interest runs not to the repayment date itself but only to the date of the project manager's assessment of the repayment.

Clause X7.3 – proportioning down delay damages

The delay damages clauses in Option R of ECC 2 were seriously deficient in failing to provide for proportioning down of delay damages when parts of the works were taken over or certified as complete before the whole of the works. The need for proportioning down clauses has long been recognised and they are found in all other well used standard forms. They protect the stated rates of liquidated damages from being declared penalties – the point being that once part of the works is taken over or certified complete the stated rates are usually no longer a genuine pre-estimate of the employer's loss for the remainder. See, for example, the case of *Bramall & Ogden v. Sheffield City Council* (1983).

Clause X7.3 of NEC 3 seeks to remedy the deficiency in ECC 2. It says:

- if the employer takes over a part of the works, delay damages are reduced from the date of taking over
- the project manager assesses the benefit to the employer of taking over the part as a proportion of the benefit to the employer of taking over the whole of the works not previously taken over
- delay damages are reduced in this proportion

The usual rule is that delay damages are reduced in proportion to the value of the works taken over. This is largely an arithmetic or quantity surveying exercise. The benefit rule in clause X7.3 is an interesting departure from the usual rule. The clause gives no guidance as to how the employer's benefit is to be assessed and it is not difficult to visualise endless argument as to how it should be assessed. The principles of assessment are likely to be contentious and similarly the facts.

A basic point which needs to be considered is that stipulated rates of delay damages have to be taken as genuine pre-estimates of loss if they are to stand as valid liquidated damages. Any adjustments to the stipulated rates need therefore to follow some logical and identifiable process to avoid voiding the rates. It is therefore arguable that in assessing the employer's benefit the project manager should only take into account circumstances anticipated at the time the contract was made. However the Guidance Notes to NEC 3 take the opposite view suggesting that only benefits qualifying at the time of calculation of proportioning down should be considered.

Given the potential in the present drafting of clause X7.3 for disputes and differences in applying its 'benefit' rule, many employers may be disposed to amend the clause to bring it into line with the conventional 'value' rule for proportioning down.

3.9 Option X12 – partnering

In June 2001 the promoters of NEC contracts responded to the *Guide to Project Team Partnering* published by the Construction Industry Council by issuing as secondary option X12 of ECC 2, the NEC Partnering Option. This option, re-arranged but otherwise largely unchanged, is now incorporated into NEC 3 as Option X12.

Option X12 is only for use where more than two parties are working on the same project under NEC terms. It does not create a freestanding multi-party contract. It simply supplements the terms of the existing bi-party contracts by introducing some additional responsibilities and it provides a structured mechanism whereby the participants in a project under NEC terms can work together towards common goals. By way of example, if the employer, consultants, main contractor and subcontractors are all engaged under various NEC contracts, all or some may bond together by including Option X12 in their contracts.

Option X12 does not include any remedies or sanctions for breach of its terms. It leaves such matters to be dealt with under the terms of the relevant bi-party contracts. And, for the avoidance of doubt, Option X12 expressly states at clause X12.2(6) 'This Option does not create a legal partnership between Partners who are not one of the Parties in this contract.'

Clause X12.1 – identified and defined terms

In five sub-clauses of definitions, partners are defined as those named in the schedule of partners; own contract is defined as the contract between the two partners including Option X12; core group is defined as the partners listed in the schedule of group members; partnering information is defined as information specifying how the partners work together; and a key performance indicator is defined as an aspect of performance for which a target is stated in the schedule of partners.

Clause X12.2 – actions

The most important sub-clause of clause X12.2 is X12.2(1) which states, 'Each Partner works with the other Partners to achieve the clients objectives stated in the Contract Data and the objectives of every other Partner stated in the Schedule of Partners.' To give effect to this sub-clause, which for the most part speaks for itself, it is essential that the contract data, part 1, of each contract within the partnering group includes a statement of the client's objective.

Sub-clauses X12.2(2) to (5) state the formalities for establishing core groups. Sub-clause X12.2(6), as noted above, confirms that Option X12 does not create legal partnerships outside the contract.

Clause X12.3 – working together

This clause sets out in nine sub-clauses how the partners are to work together on such matters as early warnings, information exchange, and programming of actions. The first sub-clause X12.3(1) repeats the opening exhortation (or obligation if it is such) of NEC 3 to work together 'in a spirit of mutual trust and co-operation'. Sub-clause X12.3(9) is interesting in that it requires a partner to notify the core group before subcontracting any work. This may be intended to ensure that new firms brought into the project are willing to become partners if required. However, this is the type of obligation which, if breached, might have adverse consequences leading to one partner seeking redress from another. Such redress, as explained above, would be confined to the aggrieved partner in direct contract with the defaulting partner, and it would probably have to be obtained by an action for breach of contract, since the standard compensation event for breach of contract works only against a party up the chain – and not down the chain as would be the likely situation here.

Clause X12.4 – incentives

Clause X12.4 concerns the sharing out and payment of bonus targets for achievement of key performance indicators. It is a self-contained scheme independent of secondary option, X20, which states in the heading 'not used with Option X12'. This is explained in the Guidance Notes to NEC 3 as follows: 'The incentive sharing arrangements in Option X12 are sufficiently flexible to cover the payment of different incentives to different Partners, such that Option X20 is unnecessary in contracts when Option X12 is used.' To facilitate this approach Option X12 contains its own definition of a key performance indicator in clause X12.1(5). And it repeats in clauses X12.4(1) and (2) the operational notes found in Option X20.

3.10 Option X13 – performance bond

Option X13 requires the contractor to give a performance bond:

- for the amount stated in the contract data, *and*
- in the form set out in the works information

The bond has to be provided by a bank or insurer which the project manager has accepted.

The wording of Option X13 is identical to that in Option G of ECC 2.

Details of the bond

The contract data states only the amount of the bond. The detailed form of the bond is to be set out in the works information. The difficulties this may cause should not be under-estimated. There is no model form of bond included in the NEC document pack and the model forms produced for use with other standard forms will not readily apply to NEC 3 because of differences in terminology. Special bonds need to be drafted. This is no task for amateurs. The drafting of bonds is a highly specialised business and the legal construction of bonds can perplex even the best lawyers. See, for example, the House of Lords decision in the case of *Trafalgar House* v. *General Surety & Guarantee Co.* (1995) on the much used standard ICE bond.

Type of bond

Bonds differ considerably in their drafting and in the conditions under which they can be called in for payment. At one end of the scale there are 'on-demand' bonds which can be called in without proof of default or proof of loss; at the other end of the scale there are 'performance' or 'conditional' bonds which can only be called in with certification of default and proof of loss.

NEC 3 refers in Option X13 to a performance bond. It is not clear whether this is intended to deliberately exclude the use of on-demand bonds with NEC 3 or whether it is simply general terminology which permits either type of bond.

Acceptance of the bond

Under clause X13.1 the project manager has discretionary power to accept or reject the bank or insurer proposed by the contractor as the provider of the bond. The only stated reason for not accepting the bank or the insurer is that its commercial position is not strong enough to carry the bond. Presumably it is intended that it is the project manager who should be the judge of this commercial position or at least nominally so. But the clause does not actually say this and the project manager will need to act with the greatest caution in rejecting any bank or insurer.

If the project manager is proved to be wrong in his assessment of the commercial position then the stated reason for non-acceptance is invalid and the minimum consequence is that compensation event 60.1(9) applies. Potentially worse is the possibility that the contractor fails to get another bond; that the employer then terminates under clause 91.2(R12); and that is then held by an adjudicator or tribunal to be wrongful termination. It hardly needs to be said that the project manager's liability to the employer might then come under scrutiny.

Provision of the bond

The final sentence of clause X13.1 requires that if the bond is not given by the contract date it is given within four weeks thereof.

The contract date is loosely defined in clause 11.2(4) as the date when the contract came into existence. Clearly the date needs to be positively fixed to give the provision in clause X13.1 effect. And since the only specified sanction in NEC 3 for non-provision of the bond is termination under clause 91.2(R12) there is added need for certainty.

Cost of the bond

Unlike some other standard forms NEC 3 is silent on which party bears the cost of the bond – although ultimately, of course, whatever payment arrangements apply the cost should fall on the employer.

Unless the contract includes a method of measurement which states otherwise the cost of the bond will be deemed to be included in the contract price.

For cost reimbursable contracts the cost of the bond is apparently to be included in the contractor's 'fee'.

3.11 Option X14 – advanced payment to the contractor

This is another secondary option which remains unchanged from ECC 2. Advanced payments to contractors as intended by Option X14 are payments made as a matter of policy or trade custom. They have nothing to do with advanced payments which the contractor may obtain by front loading his activity schedule or bill of quantities.

A common reason for formal advanced payments is that the employer can secure funding at cheaper rates than the contractor; another is that the contractor has heavy early expenditure in procuring expensive plant and materials. Such payments are not uncommon in process and plant industries and in overseas contracts but are less so in UK construction contracts.

The amount

When Option X14 applies the employer's obligation is to pay the amount of advanced payment stated in the contract data (clause X14.1).

The clause is silent as to VAT but the point needs to be clarified in the contract data by writing inclusive or exclusive of any VAT which may be payable.

Payment

Clause X14.2 requires the advanced payment to be made either:

- within four weeks of the contract date, *or*
- within four weeks of receipt by the employer of any advanced payment bond which is required, whichever is the later

Delay by the employer in making payment is stated in the last sentence of clause X14.2 to be a compensation event.

Security for advanced payment

When Option X14 is used the employer should indicate in the contract data whether or not a bond is required as security for the advanced payment.

Under clause X14.2 the bond is to be for the amount of the advanced payment and in the form set out in the works information. The bond is to be issued by a bank or insurer accepted by the project manager.

As with the performance bond a reason for not accepting a bank or insurer is that its commercial position is not strong enough to carry the advanced payment bond. The potential consequences of rejection are similar for both bonds – see the comment in section 3.10 of this chapter.

Repayment

Clause X14.3 requires any advanced payment to be repaid in instalments as stated in the contract data. The contract data deals with this by requiring two entries:

- the first stating when instalments are to commence – by reference to weeks after the contract date
- the second stating whether the instalments are amounts or a percentage of payments due (presumably to the contractor)

Where repayments are stated as amounts it does not automatically follow from clause X14.3 that repayment should only be by way of deductions from interim payments due to the contractor. That may be the broad intention of the scheme but the assessment procedures of section 5 of NEC 3 contemplate the possibility that interim payments may be due from the contractor to the employer.

3.12 Option X15 – limitation of contractor's liability for design

Option X15 of NEC 3 is substantially the same as Option M of ECC 2, in so far that its principal clause limiting the contractor's liability for design to skill and care, clause X15.1, is identical to clause M1.1 of Option M. However, there is in NEC 3 an additional clause in Option X15, clause 15.2, relating to liability for correcting defects which was not in Option M.

It should also be noted that there is in NEC 3 a new option clause, Option X18, dealing with general limitation of contractor's liability. Option 18 however concerns limitation of amounts of liability rather than the basis on which liability is incurred.

Option X15, like the old Option M, remains short on words but difficult to assess as to how it works in practice. It states that the contractor is not liable for defects in the works due to his design so far as he proves that he used reasonable skill and care to ensure that it complied with the works information. Probably nothing more is intended in this than that when the option is used there should be no implied term in the contract that the contractor's liability for his design should be on a fitness for purpose basis.

The probability of such an implied term in design and build contracts was suggested by the House of Lords in the case of *IBA* v. *EMI* (1980). And because it imposes a standard of liability which is potentially higher than the standard of liability carried by professional designers (skill and care) contractors have argued with some success in relation to many standard forms of contract that a clause should be included limiting liability for their design to skill and care. The problem with clause X15.1 of NEC 3, however, is that on its particular wording it is open to various interpretations some of which far from limiting the contractor's liability might actually increase it.

Peculiarities of clause X15.1

Full analysis of the legal effects of the peculiarities of clause X15.1 is beyond the scope of this book but in short the points to note are:

- the clause applies to defects in the works due to the contractor's design rather than to the design itself
- the limitation of liability in the clause applies only to 'Defects' within the meaning of the defined term
- the clause reverses the usual burden of proof applying to negligence so that the burden of proof is put on the contractor to show that he used

reasonable skill and care. Consider the difficulties of this for a contractor where a specialist subcontractor has been involved as the designer and is no longer in business

- the obligation to use skill and care applies only to compliance with the works information – and, for contractor's design, much of this may have been provided by the contractor
- if the works information requires fitness for purpose it is doubtful if clause X15.1 has any effect

An alternative approach

Employers who require nothing more from Option X15 than a simple change in the contractor's liability for his design from fitness for purpose to skill and care would do well to look at the approach of some standard building design and build contracts where it is simply said that the contractor's liability for his design is the same as that of a professional designer.

Liability for defects

Clause X15.2 is new to NEC 3. It states that if the contractor corrects a 'Defect' for which he is not liable it is a compensation event.

There is an implication in this clause, which in itself makes no reference to skill and care or fitness for purpose, that without the inclusion of Option X15 in the contract, the contractor is required to correct defects for which he is not liable without recompense. That is probably not the case but such is the complexity of the wording of NEC 3 on defects that it cannot be excluded.

However, looking at clause X15.2 simply in the context of Option X and limitation of liability for design what it seems to mean is that if the contractor can prove that he used reasonable skill and care in his design he is entitled to recover the time and cost consequences of rectifying defects in the works due to his design. This, if correct, goes well beyond what might normally be expected. It is one thing to say that a contractor's liability for design is not on a fitness for purpose basis but it is very different to say that a contractor should be able to recover the costs of rectifying a defective design undertaken on a skill and care basis. And since the valuation of such costs under the compensation event procedures includes time costs and the fee percentage for overheads and profit, it leaves the employer in a seriously disadvantaged position.

Such is the potential impact of clause X15.2 that it will take a brave lawyer to persuade an employer that Option X15 should be included in the contract.

3.13 *Option X16 – retention*

Provisions entitling the employer to retain a percentage of amounts due to the contractor until the works are completed and any defects period has expired are standard in most construction, process and plant contracts. NEC

3 however makes this a secondary option rather than a core clause and employers need to be careful that it is not inadvertently omitted from the contract.

Option X16 of NEC 3 retains the same wording as Option P of ECC 2 and the same advisory note that it is not for use with main Option F (management contract). The Guidance Notes for NEC 3 suggest that Option X16 is not normally required where Option X13 (performance bond) is used but this is perhaps no more that a speculative suggestion as it is perfectly normal in practice for contracts to contain both retention and performance bond provisions.

Clause X16.1 – deduction of retention

Clause X16.1 deals with the deduction of retention. The first point to note is that the deduction of retention is not intended to commence until the valuations have reached a 'retention free amount'. This is intended to assist the contractor's cash flow in the early stages of the contract.

The retention free amount is to be entered in the contract data. If no such amount is entered, or NIL is entered, the deduction of retention will commence from the first valuation.

The amount of retention is determined by the 'retention percentage' which is entered in the contract data. If this is left blank the employer will have no entitlement to retention. The retention percentage is applied only to the excess above the retention free amount and not to the whole of any valuation.

One aspect of clause X16.1 which may cause some concern to contractors is that retention is apparently held against sums valued for compensation events. This seems to follow from the definition of the price for work done to date. However it is hardly equitable that the employer should be entitled to retention on an amount payable to the contractor in respect of any compensation event which is a breach of contract by the employer. This is not permitted in many standard forms.

Clause X16.2 – release of retention

Clause X16.2 deals with the release of retention. The approach is conventional. Half the retention is released on completion and the remainder on the issue of the defects certificate.

Trust status

There is nothing in Option X16.2 stating that retention is held in trust or requiring the employer to hold retention in a separate bank account. However, see the case of *Wates Construction* v. *Franthom Property* (1991) on the possibility of implied terms that the employer is a trustee and has a duty to safeguard the interests of the beneficiaries (the contractor and subcontractors).

Consider also the effect of the obligation in clause 10.1 for the parties to act in a spirit of mutual trust and co-operation. It is arguable that this extends to an obligation to hold retention money in a trust fund.

3.14 Option X17 – low performance damages

Option X17 of NEC 3 is identical to Option S of ECC 2. It deals with payment by the contractor to the employer of liquidated damages for low performance of aspects of the works when put into use. It should not be confused with the new NEC 3 Option X20 which provides an incentive scheme to the contractor for achieving key performance indicators. Taken together the two options can be utilised to cover both sides of the same coin – the downside being damages for low performance under Option X17; the upside being incentive payments for achieving good performance under Option X20. However, there is no need for this balanced approach and Options X17 and X20 can be used separately.

Clause X17.1 – low performance damages

The essentials of clause X17.1 are:

- a defect must be included in the defects certificate
- the defect must show low performance against a performance level stated in the contract data
- the contractor pays the amount of low performance damages stated in the contract data

Note that the clause applies only to a defect within the scope of the defined term. Thus the defect will have to be measurable by way of some criteria in the works information or in the contractor's design. Also, note that low performance is to be measured against a performance level stated in the contract data. That means there will have to be a careful link between the criteria in the works information and the statements in the contract data.

In practice it will rarely be possible to state low performance damages as simply as the contract data sheet seems to indicate. Amongst the matters commonly subject to performance tests are:

- ability of the works to achieve quoted efficiency
- power consumption
- cost of operating and maintaining the works
- product quantity and quality
- consumption of chemicals
- quantity and quality of effluents
- volume of waste products
- pollution and noise control

Each requires its own parameters and it is not unusual in process and plant contracts for statements on low performance damages to run to many pages of print. As to the mechanism for the payment of low performance damages clause X17.1 is silent. Possibly the rules on payment in section 5 of NEC 3 are intended to apply. But if that is the case note that clause 50.1 is restrictive as to when assessments are made and that the only relevant assessment for low performance damages may be that made four weeks after the issue of the defects certificate.

One aspect of Option X17 which needs some consideration before it is included in any contract is that as a liquidated damages provision it acts not only to provide a remedy to the employer but also as limitation of damages payable by the contractor. Consequently, although Option X17 might appear to be for the benefit of the employer it could in certain circumstances be to the employer's detriment.

3.15 Option X18 – limitation of liability

This is a new secondary option of considerable importance. It introduces various limitations of the contractor's liabilities to the employer and when included in contracts it brings NEC 3 more into line with process and plant contracts than the options in ECC 2 were able to achieve.

Four types of liability are covered:

- clause X18.1 – liability for the employer's indirect or consequential loss
- clause X18.2 – liability for the loss of/or damage to the employer's property
- clause X18.3 – liability for defects due to contractor's design not listed in the defects certificate
- clause X18.4 – total liability for all matters arising under or in connection with the contract other than excluded matters

Clause X18.5 is of general effect and it states that the contractor is not liable to the employer for a matter unless that matter is notified to the contractor before the end of liability date. This is a date to be inserted in the contract data as a date of so many years after completion of the whole of the works.

Clause X18.1 – limitation of liability for indirect or consequential loss

This clause states that the contractor's liability to the employer for the employer's indirect or consequential loss is limited to the amount stated in the contract data. To give the clause effect a legal meaning must be given to the phrase 'indirect or consequential loss'. NEC 3 itself provides no assistance. The matter has, however, come before the courts in both contract and tort cases over the years. In *Croudace Construction Ltd* v. *Cawoods Concrete Products Ltd* (1978), Lord Justice Megan said, 'It is clear that the word "consequential" can be used in various senses. It may be difficult to be sure in some contexts precisely what it does mean. But I think the meaning given to the word in Millar's case is applicable in the present case. It is binding on us as in this case. Even if strictly it were not binding, we ought to follow it. That case was decided in the year 1934. It has stood, therefore, now for more than 43 years. So far as I know it has never been adversely commented upon.' The Millar's case referred to in the passage was *Millar's Machinery Co Ltd* v. *David Way and Son* (1935). From that case it was held in the Cawoods case that losses directly and naturally resulting in the ordinary cause of events from breach of contract were not excluded as 'consequential loss or damage'.

In *F. G. Minter Ltd* v. *Welsh Health Technical Services Organisation* (1980) the Court of Appeal, after considering the Cawoods case, concluded that the term 'direct loss and expense' meant substantially the same as damages recoverable at common law according to the ordinary principles of remoteness of damage under the first limb of the rule in *Hadley* v. *Baxendale* (1854). It seems, therefore, that 'indirect or consequential' loss as a term in a clause for breach of contract is loss falling under the second limb of the rule *Hadley* v. *Baxendale* – and that is sometimes referred to as special loss, being that reasonably within contemplation of the parties at the time they made the contract. As a term in cases for negligence (tort or defect), the meaning of 'consequential' may be somewhat wider.

Frequently references in contracts to 'indirect or consequential' are in exclusion clauses but in NEC 3, the aim of clause X18.1 is not to exclude liability but to limit it. This raises an interesting point. It presupposes that under NEC 3 the contractor may have liabilities to the employer for indirect or consequential losses. There seems to be no way that these can be addressed and assessed under the compensation event procedures. It cannot, therefore, be the case, as is sometimes argued, that the compensation event procedures provide the complete scheme for assessing the parties' entitlements such that common law rights are excluded.

Clause X18.2 – limitation of liability for loss of or damage to the employer's property

This clause states that for any one event the liability of the contractor to the employer for loss of or damage to the employer's property is limited to the amount stated in the contract data. It needs to be considered in conjunction with the insurance provisions in NEC 3, particularly clauses 84.1 and 84.2 which require the contractor to insure for loss of/damage to property. Such insurance is to be to the level set in the contract data.

It is difficult to assess in the abstract whether an employer would wish to set a limit of liability under clause X18.2 greater or less than the insurance cover provided under clause 84.2. But the probability is that pressure for a limit would come from the contractor (specialist contractors are often quite firm on this) and it would be within, rather than above, the insurance cover. Whatever the position, however, neither party should become involved with limitations of liability under clause X18.2 without consulting their insurers.

Clause X18.3 – limitation of liability for defects due design

Clause X18.3 states that the contractor's liability to the employer for defects due to his design not listed in the defects certificate is limited to the amount stated in the contract data. The presumption that by 'his' design is meant the 'contractor's' design is supported by wording in the contract data which refers to the contractor's design.

This is a limitation of liability quite different from that found in Option X15. It deals with financial capping of liability not the basis on which liability is determined. However, it is likely to be of more relevance when the contractor's liability is on a fitness for purpose basis than on a skill and care basis since the risks under fitness for purpose are stricter and come more readily into play.

Note, however, that whatever the basis for liability the limitation in clause X18.3 covers only defects not listed in the defects certificate and it provides no limitation for defects which are so listed but which fall into the category of uncorrected defects within the scope of clause 45.

Clause X18.4 – total limitation of liability

Clause X18.4 is an option clause of potentially great significance. It states that the contractor's total liability to the employer for all matters arising under or in connection with the contract, other than certain excluded matters, is limited to the amount stated in the contract data and that it applies 'in contract, tort or defect and otherwise to the extent allowed under the law of the contract'. The excluded matters are amounts payable by the contractor for loss of/or damage to the employer's property, liquidated delay damages, liquidated low performance damages and the contractor's share under main options C and D.

The significance of the clause can be gathered from the decision in the case of *Strachan & Henshaw* v. *Stein Industrie (UK) Ltd* (1997) which concerned a contract under IMechE/IEE standard form, MF/1, clause 44.4 of which states that the respective rights, obligations and liabilities of the parties as provided for in the conditions are exhaustive of their rights, obligations and liabilities arising out of, under, or in connection with the contract. The Court of Appeal held that the clause was to be taken literally such that not only were common law rights in contract excluded but also claims for misrepresentation as they were claims 'in connection with the contract'.

Clause X18.4 of NEC 3 does not have quite the same excluding effect as does clause 44.4 of MF/1 but it operates in much the same way. If a total limit of contractor's liability is written into the contract that will therefore, save for the specified excluded matters, genuinely be the limit of liability.

One point of difference between clause X18.4 and clause 44.4 of MF/1 worth mentioning is that the MF/1 clause applies to both contractor and employer claims whereas clause X18.4 (and all the other clauses in Option X18) applies only to limitation of the contractor's liabilities. And, following the point made in relation to clause X18.1 above that the wording of Option X18 implies rights to claim damages in contract and in tort, if the contractor seeks to exercise those rights the employer, unlike the contractor, does not have the benefit of limitation of liability.

Clause X18.5 – notification of employer's claims

Clause X18.5 states that the contractor is not liable to the employer for a matter unless it is notified to the contractor before the end of the liability date. This is a date fixed by the employer in the contract data.

Again it is worth noting that the restriction applies only to employer's claims and not to contractor's claims. There is a notice provision in clause 61.7 of NEC 3 stating that the contractor shall not notify compensation events after the defects date but this is not of general application to other claims brought by the contractor in contract and in tort.

Two aspects of clause X18.5 which need to be considered in fixing any 'end of liability date' are firstly, how the clause fits in with liability for latent damage and secondly, how it fits in with statutory limitation or prescription periods. For latent damage, the intention seems to be that the 'end of liability date' is the last date for notifying the contractor of any defects previously latent. As for limitation, it is doubtful that the 'end of liability date' is to be taken as the last date for commencement of legal proceedings. That date will be set by the date any cause of action accrued. This can be a complex matter but some guidance in relation to construction contracts can be drawn from the Court of Appeal ruling in the case of *Henry Boot Construction Ltd* v. *Alstom Combined Cycles Ltd* (2005) where it was held that a contractor's right to payment under standard ICE Conditions of Contract arises when the engineers certificate is issued, or ought to have been issued, and not when the work is done.

Option X18 – generally

The matters dealt with in Option X18 are clearly significant, complex and problematic in their relationship to other clauses of NEC 3. It would be unwise to include Option X18 without taking legal advice.

3.16 *Option X20 – key performance indicators*

This is another secondary option new to NEC 3. It introduces an incentive scheme for the achievement of specified targets. A head note to the option states that it is not used with Option X12.

Clause X20.1 defines a key performance indicator as an aspect of performance by the contractor for which a target is stated in the incentive schedule. This is a schedule to be identified in the contract data.

Clause X20.2 requires the contractor to report at regular intervals on performance against each of the key performance indicators. Clause X20.3 requires the contractor to submit proposals for improving performance if his forecasts are that he will not achieve the specified targets. Clause X20.4 states that the contractor is paid under the incentive schedule only when targets are met or improved upon. Clause X20.5 permits the employer to add new key performance indicators into the contract but debars him from reducing or removing incentives already in the schedule.

On the face of it Option X20 is a straightforward bonus scheme placing no sanctions on the contractor for failing to achieve the specified targets nor any burden on the employer other than to pay for such incentives as are achieved. However, in practice it may prove to be more controversial as bonus schemes often do. One reason for this is that bonuses are frequently a negotiated part of the contract price, not merely manifestations of generosity. Perceived entitlements to bonuses are, therefore, not always given up lightly. Under NEC 3, a contractor deprived of a bonus by actions, inactions or other matters for which the employer is responsible may be disposed to look to the compensation event procedures to see if they provide any remedy. They do not expressly do so but there are numerous events listed in clause 60.1 which might cover the cause of failure to achieve a specified target – failure to provide access, failure to provide something when due, prevention, physical conditions and, not least, breach of contract by the employer, the latter gaining added relevance perhaps by virtue of clause 10.1 and the requirements therein for co-operation. However, attempts to recover a lost bonus through the compensation event procedures will probably fail at the assessment stage since, for compensation events, assessment is concerned only with cost and not with loss. It may be arguable that costs incurred in endeavouring to achieve the bonus target should be assessed but this may be only a partial remedy. If there is to be recovery of loss that may have to be by a claim for damages outside the compensation event procedures.

In the event that key performance indicators are linked with key dates in the incentive schedule any incentive target dates would seem to become moving targets since key dates are treated similarly to completion dates when it comes to extending time through the compensation event procedures.

3.17 Option Y(UK)2 – Housing Grants, Construction and Regeneration Act 1996

In 1998 an addendum to ECC 2 was introduced as a new option clause for contracts subject to the Housing Grants, Construction and Regeneration Act 1996. It was called Option Y(UK)2 and it covered both the payment and adjudication provisions of the Act.

Option Y(UK)2 as it now exists in NEC 3 covers only payments – the adjudication parts of the old Y(UK)2 having being transferred to the new alternative dispute Option, W2.

The payment provisions in Option Y(UK)2 supplement the core payment provisions in section 5 of NEC 3 such that taken together they meet in full the payment requirements of the Act. Clause Y2.1 refers to the Act. Clause Y2.2 refers to the payment dates and states that the project manager's certificate is notice of payment from the employer to the contractor specifying the amount to be paid and the method of calculation. Clause Y2.3 deals with the procedure for withholding payments. Clause Y2.4 states that if the contractor exercises his right to suspend performance under the Act it is a compensation event.

3.18 Option Y(UK)3 – Contracts (Rights of Third Parties) Act 1999

The Contracts (Rights of Third Parties) Act 1999 allows a third party to enforce, in certain circumstance, a term of a contract to which it is, by definition, not a party. It is however permissible to include in contracts clauses limiting or excluding application of the Act.

Thus clause 3(2) of ICE Conditions of Contract, 7th Edition, states that nothing in the contract shall confer or purport to confer on any third party any benefit or right to enforce any term of the contract. Other construction contracts have similar clauses. The aim is to exclude the possibility of such things as:

- contractors suing the employer's professional team (and the reverse)
- employers suing subcontractors (and the reverse)
- subcontractors suing one another
- future owners of the works suing firms and individuals involved in the construction process

Option Y(UK)3 adopts a slightly different approach than ICE 7th Edition stating in clause Y3.1 that a person or organisation not one of the parties to the contract may enforce a term of the contract under the Act only if the term and the person or organisation are stated in the contract data. This has the effect of requiring steps to be taken in compiling the contract to bring the Act into play.

3.19 Option Z1 – additional conditions

Letter Z is reserved for additional conditions drafted specially for a particular contract or included to comply with an employer's standard contractual requirements on such matters as confidentiality, discrimination, prevention of corruption and the like.

The promoters of NEC 3 recommend that additional conditions are kept to the absolute minimum and that they are drafted to match the style of NEC 3 using the same definitions and terminology. That being the case it is disappointing that NEC 3 does not have a greater range of standard secondary options. Some common contractual matters such as assignment, patents, extra-ordinary traffic are not addressed in either the core clauses or the secondary options and there will not be many NEC 3 contracts where the employer does not find it necessary to include additional conditions for these or his own special needs.

Not all employers have the ability or the inclination to draft their additional conditions in the unique style of NEC 3 – concerned, no doubt, in some cases that in doing so they might lose the true intention of an otherwise perfectly straightforward provision. However, incompatibility of drafting may not be a problem of great consequence. There is very little possibility that all the documents in an NEC 3 contract will be written in matching style. In particular, much of the detail needs to be written into the works information including, for example, details of taking-over and performance tests, deliveries of plant, operating manuals and the like. It may be said that such detail should not be included in the works information since the works information is by definition in clause 11.2(19), information which either:

- specifies and describes the works, *or*
- states any constraints on how the contractor provides the works

Taken literally that definition can be argued to exclude the detail of a contractual nature. But the problem is how to fit such detail into the contract if not in the works information. To put the detail into additional conditions is even less attractive.

Chapter 4
Contract documents

4.1 Introduction

Generally NEC 3 retains the characteristics of ECC 2 in its treatment of contract documents. Thus:

- it does not explicitly define the term 'contract' nor does it list the documents forming the contract
- it has no stated order of precedence of documents
- it has no standard form of tender or form of agreement – although samples are included in the Guidance Notes
- it uses contract data forms, part one to be completed by the employer and part two to be completed by the contractor, to provide the specifics for any particular contract
- it uses works information to provide the specifics of the contractor's design and construct obligations for any particular contract

However, steps have been taken in NEC 3 to tighten up the contract by the introduction of two new and potentially very important clauses:

- clause 12.3 – which states that no change to the contract, unless provided for by the conditions of contract, has any effect unless it has been agreed, confirmed in writing, and signed by the parties, *and*
- clause 12.4 – which states that the contract is 'the entire agreement' between the parties

There are various possible explanations for the inclusion of clause 12.3, one being that under ECC 2, it was sometimes taken that the 'spirit of mutual trust and co-operation' referred to in clause 10.1 gave leave for, and perhaps actively encouraged, oral agreements; the other being to clarify a fairly common problem arising under ECC 2 as to the powers of the project manager to act for and bind the employer. More is said on these points in later chapters.

The new clause 12.4, the 'entire agreement' clause, may be intended to reinforce a theme which runs through NEC 3 (and ECC 2 before it) that the parties should treat the contract as combining good project management procedures with complete sets of obligations, liabilities and remedies. Alternatively, it may be intended simply to regulate the status of documents. But whatever the intention, the fact is that stating the contract to be the 'entire agreement' has far reaching implications – not least because there are differing views as to what is meant by an 'entire agreement'.

4.2 *Entire agreements*

Entire agreements should not be confused with entire contracts. Such contracts, which are usually of the lump sum type, are contracts where the contractor's right to payment is dependent upon complete fulfilment of the obligation undertaken. The general rule is that no claim can be made for partial performance in an entire contract. Thus, in the famous case of *Cutter v. Powell* (1795) where the second mate on a ship bound for Liverpool from Jamaica died before the ship reached Liverpool, his widow was unsuccessful in a claim for a proportion of his lump sum wages of 30 guineas. Or, as said by the Master of Rolls in *Re: Hall & Barker* (1878), 'If a man engages to carry a box of cigars from London to Birmingham, it is an entire contract, and he cannot throw the cigars out of the carriage halfway there, and ask for half the money; or if a shoemaker agrees to make a pair of shoes, he cannot offer you one shoe and ask you to pay half the price.' Entire contracts are not commonly found in the construction industry because usually the employer acquires some benefit from the work undertaken by the contractor and the doctrine of substantial performance applies. See, for example, the cases of *Dakin* v. *Lee* (1916) and *Hoenig* v. *Isaacs* (1952) both of which relate to incomplete decorating works. For NEC 3 to be construed as an entire contract the contractor's obligations in the works information would have to be set out in terms which left no doubt as to what was intended and which nullified the standard provisions in clause 45 for uncorrected defects.

Entire agreements are not as easy to describe as entire contracts and the phrase 'entire agreement' does not seem to have a precise legal meaning. At its simplest an entire agreement suggests a contract which is complete as to its terms. But that may mean a contract complete only as to its written terms, or it may mean a contract which is complete to the extent that it excludes all terms other than its written terms and in so doing excludes implied terms and common law remedies.

The distinction can be seen by comparing the terms of the Institution of Chemical Engineers standard form (the *Red Book*) with the terms of the Institutions of Mechanical Engineers and Electrical Engineers standard form MF/1:

- the *Red Book* states in the Form of Agreement:
  '2 – *The Contract as herein before defined constitutes a full statement of the contractual rights and liabilities of the Purchaser and the Contractor in relation to the Works and no negotiations between them nor any document agreed or signed by them prior to the date of the Agreement in relation to the Works shall hereafter be of any contractual effect.*
  3 – *The Purchaser and the Contractor hereby agree that any pre-contractual representations and warranties, whether made orally or in writing, shall be of no legal effect whatsoever, with the result that neither party shall be entitled to found any claim to damages in reliance thereon.'*

- MF/1 states at clause 44.4:
  '*44.4 – The Purchaser and the Contractor intend their respective rights, obligations and liabilities as provided for in the Conditions shall be exhaustive of the rights,*

obligations and liabilities of each of them to the other arising out of, under or in connection with the Contract or the Works, whether such rights, obligations and liabilities arise in respect or in consequence of a breach of contract or of statutory duty or a tortuous or negligent act or omission which gives rise to a remedy at common law. Accordingly, except as expressly provided for in the Conditions, neither party shall be obligated or liable to the other in respect of any damages or losses suffered by that other which arise out of, under or in connection with the Contract or the Works, whether by reason or in consequence of any breach of contract or of statutory duty or tortious or negligent act or omission.'

The application of clause 44.4 of MF/1 was considered by the Court of Appeal in the case of *Strachan & Henshaw Ltd* v. *Stein Industrie (UK) Ltd* and *GEC Alsthom Ltd* (1997). The court held that there was commercial sense in providing expressly for the claims the parties intended to be allowed and excluding all others; that although claims for misrepresentation were not expressly mentioned they were, nevertheless, excluded as claims 'in connection with the contract'; and that clause 44.4 applied even if its effect was to render certain contractual obligations practically unenforceable.

4.3 *Clause 12.4 of NEC 3*

Taken by itself, the statement in clause 12.4 of NEC 3 that the contract is 'the entire agreement' between the parties is not decisive as to its meaning. The position is not helped by the headnote to the contract data forms which says that completion of the data therein is essential to create 'a complete contract'.

Looking at other clauses of NEC 3, it is evident that the compensation event clauses endeavour to bring most contractors' claims for breach of contract into the controlled mechanism of the compensation event procedures. However, notwithstanding the curious wording of the new clause 63.4 which refers to the employer's rights, the compensation event clauses are clearly intended to provide remedies only for the contractor and not for the employer. Moreover, new secondary option X18 which limits liability for indirect and consequential losses presumes that common law remedies are available to the employer.

But, more importantly, the 'entire agreement' or 'complete contract' provisions of NEC 3 are not worded with sufficient force or clarity so as to exclude common law rights and remedies. Perhaps the best that can be said of clause 12.4 is that if the documents forming the contract are listed somewhere, such as in the form of agreement, as being the documents forming the contract, then they, and they alone, will constitute the written aspects of the contract. Perhaps that is all that is intended.

4.4 *Construction of contracts generally*

The courts have laid down certain principles which apply to the construction of contracts. As recently summarised in the case of *Emcor Drake and Scull Ltd* v. *Edinburgh Royal Joint Venture* (2005) these are:

- Specific provisions must be construed in the context of the contract as a whole. If possible, all the provisions of a contract should be given effect.
- A contract must be construed objectively according to the standards of a reasonable third party who is aware of the commercial context of the contract.
- A commercial contract should be given a commercially sensible construction. A construction which produces a reasonable result should be preferred to one which does not.
- Typed elements of a document will normally have priority over standard printed conditions if there is any conflict between them. This rule only applies, however, if the conflict cannot be reconciled using the normal processes of contractual interpretation.
- The court must not substitute a different bargain from that which has been made by the parties.
- In construing a contract the circumstances of formation of the contract can assist in discovering its commercial purposes – this is sometimes referred to as 'the factual matrix'. Courts may have regard to expert or other technical evidence as to the meaning of technical provisions.
- It is not usually helpful to consider evidence on what was said in the course of negotiations.
- Words which have been deleted by the parties prior to signature of a contract should not generally be taken into account as they are not part of the agreement.

4.5 NEC 3 documentation

In a typical NEC 3 contract the following documentation will probably apply – although not all the documents listed here will necessarily become contract documents.

Documents sent to tenderers

- instructions to tenderers
- contract data – part one
- works information including
  - — scope of works
  - — drawings
  - — specifications
  - — other details as appropriate
- site information
- bill of quantities (if appropriate)

Documents submitted with tenders

- form of tender
- contract data – part two

- works information (from the contractor)
- contractor's price – including (as appropriate)
  — activity schedule
  — bill of quantities
  — cost component data
- programme (if required)

Documents making the contract

- letter of acceptance
- form of agreement

Documents submitted post award

- performance bond
- parent company guarantee
- programme

Instructions to tenderers

NEC 3 is silent on the status of instructions to tenderers and it is a matter of policy for individual employers whether or not they are to become contract documents. For the avoidance of doubt a clear statement should be made at the head of instructions to tenderers stating whether or not they are to form part of the contract.

4.6 *Essential contract documents*

As an absolute minimum the essential documents of an NEC 3 contract are:

- contract data – part one – provided by the employer
- the contractor's pricing document
- conditions of contract with
  — main option stated
  — dispute option stated
  — secondary options stated
- works information with input as appropriate from
  — the employer
  — the contractor
- site information – provided by the employer
- contract data – part two – provided by the contractor
- form of tender
- letter of acceptance

This list assumes that the schedules of cost components can be taken as part of the conditions of contract but the point is not entirely certain.

Incorporation of NEC 3 conditions of contract

An important question is whether NEC 3 conditions of contract (the standard core clauses, the dispute resolution options and secondary options) can be incorporated into particular contracts by reference or whether it is necessary in each case for a printed copy of the conditions of contract to be included in the bundle of documents and signed by the parties. The detailing in part one of the contract data of which NEC 3 options have been adopted and the statement that these are the conditions of contract is apparently intended to incorporate the conditions by reference and in many cases the parties will accept this as sufficient.

There is, however, an important legal point to consider. And that is whether it is possible to incorporate an arbitration agreement by reference – even when the arbitration agreement is itself contained in a set of standard conditions. See the Court of Appeal decision in *Aughton* v. *Kent* (1991) which appears to suggest that as a general rule the incorporation of arbitration agreements by reference is not effective. Also note the decision in *Ben Barrett & Son (Brickwork) Ltd* v. *Henry Boot Management Ltd* (1995) following the decision in *Aughton*.

Form of tender

NEC 3 itself does not have a model form of tender although the Guidance Notes do have a sample form of tender. The essentials of a form of tender are:

- that it should constitute an offer from one named party to another
- that it should describe the goods/services/works to be provided
- that it should state the price of the offer (or applicable pricing mechanism)
- that it should state the basis of the offer by reference to the tender documents and conditions of contract

The sample form in the Guidance Notes covers these matters.

Form of agreement

With some standard forms of contract (such as ICE Conditions) completion of a form of agreement is necessary only when the parties intend to execute the contract as a deed – thereby extending the limitation period under English law from six to twelve years. With other standard forms, however, (such as the IChemE contracts) the form of agreement is the definitive document which is evidence of the contract and its contents. It is then an essential contract document.

With NEC 3, because of the potential uncertainty over which documents are to be regarded as contract documents, there is a good case for saying that a properly drafted form of agreement should be used in all cases. The sample form of agreement in the Guidance Notes covers this point by requiring the documents forming part of the agreement to be listed. Without such a list clause 12.4 of NEC 3 is of little purpose.

4.7 Identified and defined terms

NEC 3 uses a system of identified and defined terms which clause 11.1 indicates to be as follows:

- identified terms are terms particular to the contract – such as names and details. These are stated for each contract in the contract data
- defined terms are terms, general to NEC 3 conditions of contract, which are given a particular meaning by definitions in the conditions

The general scheme intended by clause 11.1 is that within the text of NEC 3, identified terms are in italics and defined terms have capital initials. There are, however, some anomalies:

- not all terms with capital initials are defined terms – some such as project manager, supervisor, adjudicator, employer and contractor are in fact identified terms
- not all terms which are identified in the contract data are in italics – note, for example, works information and site information
- not all terms which are effectively defined are treated as defined terms – note in particular, 'compensation event'

4.8 The contract date

Clause 11.2(4) defines the contract date as the date when 'this contract' came into existence. Obviously, the phrase 'this contract' refers, in this context, to a particular contract and not to NEC 3 itself. However in some clauses of NEC 3 the phrase 'this contract' does appear to be a reference to the general text of NEC 3.

References to the contract date

The purposes of references in NEC 3 to the term 'contract date' are principally to set time running for the commencement of certain obligations and to establish base dates relevant to certain compensation events. The references are:

- clause 60.1(12) – compensation event for unforeseen conditions
- clause 60.1(19) – compensation event for prevention
- clause 60.4 – compensation event for remeasurement with bill of quantities
- clause X2 – changes in the law
- clause X4 – provision of parent company guarantee
- clause X13 – provision of performance bond
- clause X14 – advanced payment

NEC 3 however does not use the contract date as the general date for the commencement of all obligations. The contract date, for example, has no contractual link with the completion date (which is set independently in the contract data). For the commencement of some obligations and functions NEC 3 uses other terms:

- the starting date
- access dates

The starting date

The starting date is not a defined term of NEC 3. It is an identified term fixed in part one of the contract data by the employer. Its purpose is principally administrative.

Reference to the starting date is made in the following clauses:

- clause 20.4 – forecasts of total actual cost in options C, D, E and F
- clause 32.2 – submission of revised programmes
- clause 50.1 – fixing assessment dates for payments
- clause 81.1 – contractor's risks
- clause 84.2 – insurance cover
- clause 85.1 – insurance policies of the contractor
- clause 87.1 – insurance policies of the employer
- clause W1.2 – appointment of adjudicator
- clause W2.2 – appointment of adjudicator
- clause X20.2 – key performance indicators

Access dates

Like the starting date the access date is not a defined term but a date fixed by the employer in the contract data. Each access date relates to the commencement of work on part of the site. References to access dates in NEC 3 are:

- clause 30.1 – starting work on site
- clause 31.2 – programming
- clause 33.1 – access to the site
- clause 60.1(2) – compensation event for late access

Note that in ECC 2 the corresponding term for access date was possession date. The change avoids legal complexities which can arise from provisions giving 'possession' of the site or part thereof.

4.9 *Works information*

As with ECC 2 works information is at the heart of NEC 3. Unless it is competently prepared key parts of the contract will be of no application. Works information is defined in the first part of clause 11.2(19) as information which either:

- specifies and describes the works, *or*
- states any constraints on how the contractor is to provide the works

This definition suggests that works information is little more than a specification but to grasp the full extent of the importance of works information see the schedule at the end of this chapter setting out the many clauses with references in the text to the works information. The count runs to forty-five clauses. Not all of these references require the entry of detail in the works information but nevertheless, from examination of those that do, it is clear that works information is much more than the specification for the works.

It is probably of no contractual significance that the works information goes beyond the apparent scope of its definition. But, of course, to any compiler of an NEC 3 contract and to the parties using the contract it is a matter of great significance that all necessary information and detail is included in the contract. These are the matters which need to be considered for each contract:

- clause 11.2(2) – work to be done by the completion date
- clause 20.1   – the works to be provided
- clause 21.1   – extent of contractor's design
- clause 21.2   – particulars of contractor's design to be submitted for acceptance
- clause 22.1   – use of the contractor's design
- clause 25.1   – sharing of the working areas
- clause 25.2   – provision of services
- clause 27.4   – health and safety requirements
- clause 31.2   – works by the employer and others
- clause 31.2   – information to be shown on the contractor's programme
- clause 35.3   – use of part of the works before take over
- clause 40.1   – tests and inspections
- clause 40.2   – materials, facilities and samples for tests and inspections
- clause 41.1   – testing and inspection before delivery
- clause 52.2   – accounts and records
- clause 71.1   – marking of equipment, plant and materials
- clause 73.2   – title to materials from excavation and demolition

- clause X4.1   – parent company guarantee
- clause X13.1 – performance bond
- clause X14.2 – advanced payment
- clause X15.1 – contractor's design

Identifying the works information

Given the range of information which can constitute works information it is essential for the contractor to know what can properly be described as works information. The second part of clause 11.2(19) deals with this. The clause states that works information is either:

- in the documents which the contract data states it is in, *or*
- in an instruction given in accordance with the contract

In part one of the contract data the employer should state which documents his works information is in. And in part two of the contract data the contractor should state which documents the works information for any contractor's design is in.

This rigid scheme for identifying the works information has its obvious drawbacks and it has been the cause of many a problem under ECC 2. A document may be listed as a contract document but then omitted from the listing in the contract data as containing works information. The content of that document is then effectively nullified. The project manager can rectify such a situation under clause 17.1 (ambiguities and inconsistencies) or under clause 14.3 (instructions) but compensation event procedures then apply.

Instructions as works information

As noted above, clause 11.2(19) allows works information to be in an instruction given in accordance with the contract.

Clause 14.3 allows the project manager to give an instruction which changes the works information. So also does clause 18.1 (illegal and impossible requirements) and clause 44.2 (accepting defects). However it is not clear whether these clauses apply only to 'changes' in the works information or whether they apply also to additional information – which then creates new obligations. For example, if there is nothing in the works information requiring the contractor to design parts of the works is the project manager empowered to give instructions which impose design obligations on the contractor? Would such an instruction be a 'change' in the works information or a completely new category of works information? Would such an instruction be an instruction given in accordance with the contract?

There are no certain answers to these questions. But they are important because NEC 3 has none of the usual provisions fixing the scope and limitations of variations which may be ordered under the contract by reference to necessity, desirability or value. All that NEC 3 has is:

- clause 20.1 requiring the contractor to provide the works in accordance with the works information
- clause 11.2(19) stating that works information is information which is in an instruction given in accordance with the contract
- clause 14.3 empowering the project manager to give an instruction which changes the works information

Clearly some practical, if not contractual, limitations have to apply otherwise every NEC 3 contract is completely open-ended so far as the contractor's obligations are concerned. A contract to build a school could theoretically be turned into a contract to build a hospital. No one, of course, would attempt to argue that such an extreme change was valid, but that does not remove the scope for argument on lesser changes.

Perhaps in the course of time the courts will lay down some guidelines on how this aspect of NEC 3 is to be interpreted. Until then, those with a problem with unexpected changes in works information should focus on the word 'information' in clause 11.2(19). Perhaps it is possible to argue that it is simply 'information' in an instruction which constitutes works information and that a bald instruction is not information. Or, put another way, it may be that the project manager can change the information in the works information but not the character of the works information. Much depends on the extent of the project manager's powers and whether, in relation to changing the works information, they are general or restricted – for comment on this see Chapter 5, section 6. See also the comment in Chapter 6, section 3, on the definition in clause 11.2(13) of 'to Provide the Works'.

Works information provided by the contractor

The only works information which the contractor is entitled or required to provide is that relating to his design. In many cases this may be minimal or non-existent. But in other cases, where the contract is fully contractor designed most of the technical input to the works information may be provided by the contractor. This will certainly be the case when the employer states his requirements in performance terms.

Few clauses of NEC 3 expressly recognise that works information provided by the contractor should be treated differently than works information provided by the employer. Those that do are:

- clause 11.2(5) – definition of defect
- clause 60.1(1) – definition of compensation event
- clause 63.8   – assessment of compensation event for ambiguity
- clause X15.1   – limitation of liability to skill and care

But this approach is not without its problems. Consider, for example, clause 18.1 which deals with illegal and impossible requirements in works information. This requires the project manager to give an instruction to change the works information notwithstanding its origin.

Inadequate works information

There is no express obligation in NEC 3 on the employer (through the project manager) to issue additional works information beyond that in the documents identified in the contract data. Consequently it is not absolutely clear how the position on inadequate information is to be resolved. One contractual solution would be the calling of an early warning meeting under clause 16.2 followed by the project manager giving instructions under clause 14.3 (instructions) or clause 18.1 (impossibility). But in the event of this solution failing the contractor might have to rely on there being an implied term in the contract that the employer is obliged to provide all information necessary for the works to be completed.

4.10 *Site information*

Site information is defined in clause 11.2(16) as information which:

- describes the site and its surroundings, *and*
- is in the documents which the contract data states it is in

Unlike its frequent references to works information the text of NEC 3 contains few references to site information. They are:

- clause 54.1 – information in the activity schedule is not site information
- clause 55.1 – information in the bill of quantities is not site information
- clause 60.2 – the contractor is assumed to have taken into account site information in judging physical conditions
- clause 60.3 – if there is inconsistency in the site information the contractor is assumed to have taken account of the physical conditions most favourable to doing the work

Only the last two of these are significant. And their significance derives from compensation event, clause 60.1(12), which comes into effect when the contractor encounters physical conditions within the site which an experienced contractor would have adjudged to have had such a small chance of occurring that it would have been unreasonable for him to have allowed for them.

Unlike the position in ICE Conditions of Contract, there is no express requirement in NEC 3 for the employer to supply all or any of the information he has on the site. Nor is there any express requirement on the contractor to satisfy himself as to conditions on the site.

Importance of site information

The importance of site information depends to a great extent on how much the contractor can rely upon it. For example, can he, or should he, rely on site information to price the work? Can he rely on site information in making claims? Generally incorrect or deficient site information will either affect the design of the works or their construction. If it is the employer's design which is affected, the project manager will have to deal with this by instruction and compensation event. If it is the contractor's design, incorrect site information could give cause for claim under clause 17.1 (ambiguities and inconsistencies) or under clause 60.1(12) (physical conditions). As to construction, and claims under clause 60.1(12), the contractor has the benefit of clause 60.3 whereby ambiguities or inconsistencies in site information are resolved favourably to doing the work.

However, this is a long way from saying that the contractor is entitled to rely on the site information to the exclusion of his own enquires and investigations. And it is certainly not as favourable to the contractor as contracts which expressly require the employer to make available all information which he has on the site.

Identification of site information

The statement in clause 11.2(16), that site information is in the documents which the contract data states it is in may not be of much effect. Any site information provided to the contractor (whether mentioned in the contract data or not) would have to be taken into account under clause 60.2 in assessing compensation events based in site conditions.

Inconsistency within the site information

Clause 60.3 provides that if there is any inconsistency within the site information the contractor is assumed to have taken into account the physical conditions more favourable to doing the work. Note also clause 17.1 which requires the project manager to give instructions resolving ambiguities or inconsistencies in, or between, the documents forming the contract.

Changes in site information

NEC 3 does not allow for any changes in the defined site information. So for contractual purposes the site information is fixed at the time of tender. In practice, of course, there may be changes on the site as the works progress. The employer, for example, may have other contractors installing pipes and the like or additional information on hidden aspects of the site may come to light. The employer may consider it good practice to convey this new information to the contractor and, indeed, may have a duty to do so on safety grounds. The question then is – how does this new information fit into the contractual framework of NEC 3?

In some cases it may be necessary for the project manager to give instructions changing the works information to accommodate this new site information. Without an instruction the contractor may seek to rely on compensation event 60.1(12), but it is questionable if this clause is applicable to supervening events.

4.11 Contract data

Part one of the contract data is provided by the employer – initially to tenderers. It serves the purpose of an appendix to a form of tender in detailing specifics relating to the contract. Part two of the contract data is provided by the contractor – and is returned with his tender. It details specifics relating to his company and his tender. The standard forms incorporated within NEC 3 cover all the necessary entries, but if the forms are used as printed it will be found that more space is required for some of the entries.

It is worth noting that the standard forms for both part one and part two contract data carry, in NEC 3, a head note not found in ECC 2 – 'Completion of the data in full, according to the options chosen, is essential to create a complete contract.' This is an odd note because not all the data entries required by the forms are of the type which would normally be considered as essential to the contract and frequently the entries are not fully filled. For example, employers do not always name 'the Adjudicator' and contractors do not always give details of 'key people'. The consequences of such omissions rarely amounted to much under ECC 2; however, under NEC 3 where clause 12.4 states that the contract is the 'entire agreement' it may be significant if the contract data is insufficient to create a 'complete contract' – whatever that means.

4.12 Schedules of cost components

NEC 3 contains two schedules of cost components:

- the schedule of cost components
- the shorter schedule of cost components

The schedules are stated in their headnotes to form part of the conditions of contract.

The schedules in NEC 3 have been considerably revised, both in their application and their detail from the corresponding schedules in ECC 2. This is likely to be welcomed by users of NEC 3 because the complexity of using the ECC 2 schedules was the cause of much complaint. Nevertheless, it cannot be said that operation of NEC 3 schedules is straightforward, readily understandable and time efficient. Without the benefit of the Guidance Notes to NEC 3 they would remain, for many, incomprehensible.

Purpose of the schedules

In simple terms the schedules provide a division between reimbursable items of cost and the items deemed to be included in the contractor's fee when payments to the contractor are to be calculated on a cost basis.

The application of cost schedules to Options C, D and E is obvious enough. These options are of a cost reimbursable nature. In Options A and B which are essentially firm price contracts the only use of the cost schedules is in the assessment of compensation events – most of which have to be assessed with regard to forecast defined cost.

Neither schedule forms part of the contract when Option F (the management contract) is used. This can be gathered from the definition of 'Defined Cost' in Option F which makes no reference to either schedule, and from the head notes to the schedules, neither of which makes reference to Option F.

Use of the shorter schedule

Under ECC 2 use of the shorter schedule was confined to the assessment of compensation events – and only then when there was either agreement between the project manager and the contractor on its use or when the project manager made his own assessments. Under NEC 3, it is a contractual requirement that the shorter schedule is used with Options A and B, and its use is permissible for the assessment of compensation events under Options C, D and E, if the project manager and the contractor so agree, or when the project manager is making his own assessments.

Differences between the schedules

The main schedule of cost components is a fully detailed schedule under which all costs have to be evidenced except the fee percentages. These are tendered percentages and they cover head office overheads and profit, insurances, taxes, and the like. Because of the amount of detail involved, the process of calculating amounts due by the main schedule requires considerable time and effort. The shorter schedule provides a simpler method of assessment with fewer cost components.

Data provided by the contractor

At tender stage the contractor is required to price only a limited amount of information for the cost schedules. They are not schedules of items to be priced, they are schedules of things to be costed in due course. The few items which are to be priced are detailed in part two of the contract data. Principally, these are the direct fee percentage and the subcontracted fee percentage. These have to cover everything which is not in the priced schedules of cost components. Other items which have to be priced at tender stage are:

● percentages for working area overheads and people overheads – these are to cover miscellaneous on-site overheads

- various rates and charges relating to equipment
- hourly rates and percentages for overheads for costs of manufacture and fabrication outside the working areas
- hourly rates and percentages for overheads for design costs outside the working areas

The various rates and percentages entered by the contractor in the tender do not carry through into the tender total and employers are left to decide for themselves what procedure to adopt to ensure that they are competitive. The common approach is to apply the rates and percentages to notional figures for comparison of tenders. Policies vary on whether or not to inform the tenderers of the amounts of such figures.

Changes from ECC 2

The principal changes between ECC 2 and NEC 3 in the use of, and in the content of, the two schedules of cost components are:

- Compensation events for Options A and B are assessed in NEC 3 using the shorter schedule. This is an important change because assessment is much simpler under the shorter schedule than under the main schedule. Under ECC 2 it was effectively a matter of the project manager's choice as to which schedule was used.
- The main schedule is now only used in Options C, D and E.
- Financing charges are no longer included as cost components under either schedule. Under NEC 3 such charges have to be allowed for in the fee percentages.
- Payments for cancellation charges arising from a compensation event now become recoverable cost components under both schedules.
- Consumables and equipment provided by the contract for the project manager and supervisors staff also become recoverable cost components under both schedules.
- The odd rule in the ECC 2 schedules that people directly employed by the contractor, whose normal place of working was not in the working areas, were not recoverable cost components unless they were working in the working area for a week or more is removed from NEC 3.
- In NEC 3 the main schedule contains a new cost component for the cost of people not directly employed by, but paid by the contractor according to time worked. This appears to relate to labour only subcontractors.
- The main schedule in NEC 3 no longer requires the cost of contractor owned equipment to be calculated by reference to depreciation and maintenance. This is another important change and, to the extent the main schedule is used in the assessment of compensation events, it brings the main schedule closer into line with the shorter schedule.
- All accommodation is now included in both schedules as equipment cost. Again, this is an important change in that it removes the need to make

allowances for accommodation in the percentages for working areas and people overheads.

- Under the shorter schedule, manufacture and fabrication costs are now allowed as the amounts paid by the contractor – previously detailed calculations were required.

Note should also be taken of a major change between ECC 2 and NEC 3 which, whilst not evident in the schedules, is fundamental to cost recovery under the schedules. This is the point that the NEC 3 definition of the 'Fee' in clause 11.2(8) introduces two fee percentages – one for direct work and one for subcontracted work. This removes from the contractor the problem of trying to match his fee percentage (which under ECC 2 was the only fee percentage) with those of his subcontractors.

4.13 *Ambiguities and inconsistencies in the contract documents*

Clause 17.1 of NEC 3 deals with ambiguities and inconsistencies in the contract documents. It requires the project manager or the contractor to notify the other as soon as either becomes aware of any ambiguity or inconsistency in or between the documents forming the contract. The project manager is then required to give an instruction resolving the matter.

At first sight clause 17.1 looks very much like the usual 'ambiguities' clause found in other standard forms. But on closer examination it can be seen to be much wider in its scope than normal. Most 'ambiguities' clauses deal only with matters relating to the construction of the works. They do not normally extend to interpretation (or alteration) of the contract itself.

Clause 17.1, however, is very widely drafted. Taken literally it could lead to absurd results – such as all the questions in this book being landed on the project manager's lap for resolution. But even given a narrow commonsense application the scope of the clause is still worrying. It appears to go well beyond authorising instructions to change the works information. And note that whilst clause 18.1 which deals with illegal and impossible requirements refers to instructions 'to change the Works Information', clause 17.1 makes no direct link to works information. Some thought also needs to be given as to how clause 17.1 fits in with clause 12.3 which effectively precludes the project manager from making changes to the contract. If whatever instruction the project manager gives is not a change in the works information, it is then not a compensation event, but it is likely in some way to change the contract. And even for changes to works information there has to be some concern since the clause appears to put the responsibility of resolving ambiguities and inconsistencies in the contractor's design on the project manager. This cannot be what is intended and project managers would be most unwise to take on the burden of sorting out problems in the contractor's design.

For further comment on clause 17.1 see section 13 of Chapter 4.

4.14 *Schedule of clauses referring to the works information*

1 Common core clauses

Clause 11.2(2) — completion is when the contractor has done all the work the works information states is to be done by the completion date

Clause 11.2(5) — a part of the works not in accordance with the works information is a defect

Clause 11.2(7) — equipment is defined by reference to what the works information does not require to be included in the works

Clause 11.2(19) — definition of works information

Clause 14.3 — the works information can be changed by instruction of the project manager

Clause 18.1 — if the contractor is required by the works information to do anything illegal or impossible the contractor gives notice and the project manager instructs appropriately

Clause 20.1 — the contractor is to provide the works in accordance with the works information

Clause 21.1 — the contractor is to design such parts of the works as stated in the works information

Clause 21.2 — the contractor is to submit for acceptance such particulars of his design as the works information requires
— a reason for the project manager not accepting the design is that it does not comply with the works information

Clause 22.1 — the employer's entitlement to use the contractor's design may be restricted or expanded in the works information

Clause 23.1 — a reason for the project manager not accepting the design of an item of equipment is that it will not allow the contractor to provide the works in accordance with the works information

Clause 25.1 — the contractor is to share the working areas with others as stated in the works information

Clause 25.2 — the employer and the contractor are to provide such services and other things as are stated in the works information

Clause 27.4 — the contractor is to act in accordance with health and safety requirements stated in the works information

Clause 31.2 — the contractor is to show on each programme the work of the employer and others as stated in the works information
— the contractor is to show on each programme any other information which the works information requires

Clause 31.3 — a reason for the project manager not accepting a programme is that it does not comply with the works information

Clause 35.2   – the employer is deemed to take over any part of the works he uses before completion unless the use is for a reason stated in the works information

Clause 40.1   – clause 40 applies only to tests and inspections required by the works information (or the applicable law)

Clause 40.2   – the contractor and the employer are to provide materials, facilities and samples for tests and inspections as stated in the works information

Clause 41.1   – the contractor is not to bring to the working areas plant and materials which the works information requires to be tested before delivery

Clause 42.1   – searching may include doing tests and inspections which the works information does not require

Clause 44.1   – the works information may be changed so that a defect does not have to be corrected

Clause 44.2   – the project manager gives an instruction changing the works information if he accepts that a defect need not be corrected

Clause 45.1   – if the project manager assesses the cost to the employer of having a defect corrected by others and the contractor pays the cost, the works information is treated as having been changed to accept the defect

Clause 45.2   – if the contractor is not given access to correct a defect the project manager assesses the cost to the contractor of correcting the defect, and if the contractor pays this cost the works information is treated as having been changed to accept the defect

Clause 60.1(1)   – an instruction changing the works information is a compensation event unless it is:
                     — a change to accept a defect
                     — a change to the contractor's design at his request or to comply with other works information

Clause 60.1(5)   – failure by the employer or others to work within the times stated in the works information is a compensation event

Clause 60(1)(16)   – failure by the employer to provide materials, facilities and samples for tests as stated in the works information is a compensation event

Clause 63.8   – the assessment of a compensation event which is an instruction to change the works information in order to resolve an ambiguity or inconsistency is made having regard to which party provided the works information

Clause 63.9   – if changes to the works information make descriptions of conditions for key events incorrect, the project manager corrects the descriptions and takes such corrections into account in assessing compensation events

Clause 71.1   – payment for plant and materials outside the working areas is dependent upon the contractor pre-

	paring them for marking as the works information requires
Clause 73.2	– the contractor has title to materials from excavation and demolition only as stated in the works information

2 Clauses in Options A and B

Clause 63.10	– the prices are reduced if a change to the works information is a compensation event which reduces total defined cost

3 Clauses in Options A and C

Clause 54.1	– information in the activity schedule is not works information

4 Clauses in Options B and D

Clause 55.1	– information in the bill of quantities is not works information
Clause 60.4	– a difference between the final total quantity of work and the quantity stated in the bill of quantities is not a compensation event if it results from a change in the works information

5 Clauses in Options C, D, E and F

Clause 52.2	– the contractor is to keep accounts and records as stated in the works information

6 Clauses in Options C, D and E

Clause 11.2(25)	– cost incurred because the contractor did not follow an acceptance or procedure stated in the works information is disallowed cost
	– cost of correcting a defect caused by the contractor not complying with the works information is disallowed cost
	– plant and materials not used to provide the works is disallowed cost unless resulting from a change in the works information

7 Clauses in Options C and D

Clause 63.11   – the prices are reduced if a change in the works information, other than a change proposed by the contractor, is a compensation event which reduces total defined cost

8 Clauses in Option F

Clause 11.2(26)   – cost incurred because the contractor did not follow an acceptance or procedure stated in the works information is disallowed cost

9 Secondary Option clauses

Clause X4.1   – parent company guarantee
   – the contractor gives a parent company guarantee in the form set out in the works information

Clause X13.1   – performance bond
   – the contractor gives a performance bond in the form set out in the works information

Clause X14.2   – advanced payment
   – the bond for advanced payment is in the form set out in the works information

Clause X15.1   – contractor's design
   – the contractor is not liable for defects in his design if he proves that he used reasonable skill and care to ensure it complied with the works information

Chapter 5
Key players

5.1 Introduction

NEC 3 states in various degrees of detail the obligations, duties and powers of the following participants:

- employer
- contractor
- project manager
- supervisor
- adjudicator

Additionally NEC 3 has something to say on subcontractors, suppliers and 'others'. Nowhere, however, does NEC 3 mention the designer as such. His function falls on the employer or on the contractor according to which party is responsible for design.

Most of the text of NEC 3 relating to the above key players is unchanged from ECC 2. However, there is, perhaps, a subtle change in NEC 3 in the relationship between the employer and the project manager in that certain new provisions in NEC 3 suggest a distancing between the employer and project manager not evident in ECC 2. For example, clause 12.3 requiring changes to the contract to be signed by the parties and dispute resolution clauses entitling the employer to challenge quotations for compensation events 'treated as having been accepted'.

The parties

Clause 11.2(1) states simply that the parties to the contract are the employer and the contractor. Both are terms to be identified by name in the contract data. Only the term 'the Parties' is a defined term.

The project manager and the supervisor

These are identified terms and not defined terms. Both the project manager and the supervisor are to be named in the contract data.

The project manager and the supervisor can be replaced by the employer but only after the employer has notified the contractor of the name of any replacement (clause 14.4). There is apparently no need for consultation with the contractor as in some standard forms.

The adjudicator

There is no formal definition in NEC 3 for the adjudicator although from clauses W1.2(1) and W2.2(1) it could be said that the adjudicator is a person appointed under the NEC adjudicator's contract. However, as discussed in Chapter 19 this would not be strictly correct in all situations. Nor is it strictly correct to say that the adjudicator is the person identified in the contract data – as frequently no one is identified and the contract data entry is left blank.

NEC 3 makes one small change from ECC 2 in respect of the adjudicator. It deletes from clause 10.1 the sentence 'The adjudicator shall act as stated in this contract and in a spirit of independence' and replaces it with clauses W1.2(2) and W2.2(2) stating that the adjudicator acts impartially and decides the dispute as an independent adjudicator.

Subcontractors

Clause 11.2(17) makes 'subcontractor' a defined term. Subcontractors are not required to be identified in the contract data but the contractor must submit their names for acceptance by the project manager before their appointment (clause 26.2).

The definition of subcontractor in clause 11.2(17) of NEC 3 differs slightly from that in ECC 2 but it is generally of the same meaning. It states that a subcontractor is:

- a person or organisation
- who has a contract with the contractor
- to construct or install part of the works
- to provide a service necessary to provide the works
- to supply plant and materials which he has wholly or partly designed specifically for the works

The last part of the clause requires some examination. Why should a person or organisation who has supplied plant or materials which he has wholly or partly designed for the works be a subcontractor and not a supplier? The answer, perhaps, is that NEC 3 exercises no control over suppliers. They do not come within the scope of clause 26 on subcontracting and they are not treated in the same way as subcontractors in the schedules of cost components.

Presumably, therefore, the intention of NEC 3 is that suppliers who design specifically for the works should come within its control mechanisms and that is why they are defined as subcontractors. There is, however, a potential difficulty with this. Such firms may have no wish to trade as subcontractors rather than suppliers. And it may be restrictive on the contractor's choice of specialist firms and also on the designers, to insist that they do.

Obligations and responsibilities

It is not intended to provide in this chapter detailed comment on the involvement obligations and responsibilities under NEC 3 of all its participants. Only the employer, the project manager, the supervisor and others are covered in this chapter. For comment on the contractor, on subcontractors and on designers see Chapter 7. For comment on the adjudicator see Chapter 19.

5.2 *Others*

In the execution of most contracts the parties are likely to have dealings with many persons and organisations who are, in a legal sense, remote from the contract itself. The circumstances of such dealings are potentially so varied that standard forms of contract do not usually attempt to state the contractual effects of the dealings. Most contracts rely on the application of the common law rule of prevention that neither party must prevent the other from undertaking the fulfilment of its obligations. And to the extent that either party is responsible for the performance of others the rule extends so that the party with such responsibility becomes responsible for prevention caused by others.

NEC 3 ventures further than most standard forms in setting out the obligations and liabilities of the parties in respect of remote persons and organisations, and in the way it deals with prevention. And to a large extent the employer accepts responsibility for the performance of what is defined as 'Others'.

Definition

Clause 11.2(10) of NEC 3 defines the term 'Others' by exclusion. It states that 'Others' are people or organisations who are not the employer, project manager, supervisor, adjudicator, contractor, or any employee, subcontractor or supplier of the contractor. This is unchanged from ECC 2.

An interesting aspect of the clause is its specific reference to 'any employee' of the contractor. Under the rules for the construction of contracts it may follow that employees of the other categories mentioned in the definition and who are not so specifically excluded are to be taken as 'Others'.

Express references to 'Others'

Except where there are express references to 'Others' in NEC 3, common law rules normally govern their impact on the contract. The express references are as follows:

- clause 25.1   – the contractor is to co-operate with others in obtaining and providing information they need in connection with the works
                          – the contractor is required to co-operate with and to share the working areas with others as stated in the works information
- clause 27.1   – the contractor is responsible for obtaining approval of his design from others where necessary
- clause 27.2   – the contractor provides access to others notified to him by the project manager
- clause 31.2   – the contractor is required to show on his programme the work of others as stated in the works information and dates relating thereto
- clause 60.1(5) – failure by others to work within the times or conditions stated in the accepted programme and/or in the works information is a compensation event if others carry out work on the site not stated in the works information that is a compensation event
- clause 80.1   – loss or damage to plant or materials supplied by others on the employer's behalf is an employer's risk until the contractor receives them
- clause 91.3   – reason for termination of the contract by the employer is that the contractor has substantially hindered others

Application

Common sense is obviously required in the application of these clauses. Taken literally their scope is very wide. For example, the contractor would apparently have to co-operate under clause 25.1 with a journalist sent to write an article on the works and his failure to do so would arguably be grounds for termination under clause 91.3. But this potential absurdity can be avoided by implying a qualification of relevance into the definition of others or by implying a test of relevancy to the application of the clauses.

Note, however, that whereas the impact of others is sometimes specifically defined in NEC 3 by reference to the accepted programme and the works information, the contractual provisions are generally silent on the wider impact of others. One area which may prove to be important is whether they can be brought within the scope of the new provisions on prevention in clauses 19.1 and 60.1(19).

5.3 Actions

The opening clause of NEC 3, clause 10.1, sets the tone for the whole of the contract by requiring the participants to act in a spirit of mutual trust and co-operation. The wording of the clause follows that in ECC 2 except that reference to the adjudicator is excluded. The ECC 2 clause was much debated – as, no doubt, the NEC 3 clause will be. The question is whether the requirement to act in a spirit of mutual trust and co-operation is to be taken as a binding contractual obligation or mere exhortation.

Clause 10.1 – actions

Clause 10.1 states that:

- the employer, contractor, project manager and supervisor 'shall' act as stated in the contract, *and*
- in a spirit of mutual trust and co-operation

Obligation to act

An unusual feature of NEC 3, inherited from ECC 2, is that generally it avoids the convention of using the word 'shall' to indicate obligations. Its style relies on present tense verbs such as 'notifies', 'provides' and 'submits' to convey the intention that an obligation exists. In the first line, however, of the first clause the phrase 'shall act' appears.

The intention appears to be that this 'shall' acts for all following clauses such that a clause 'the Contractor notifies' is to be read as meaning 'the Contractor shall notify'. However, as some lawyers have pointed out, the use of the word 'shall' in one clause and its omission from others could have the effect of casting doubt on how some clauses of the contract are to be interpreted.

Failure to act

Failure by the employer or the contractor to act as stated in the contract is a breach of contract for which there may either be remedies in the contract or at common law.

In NEC 3 the majority of listed contractual remedies are called 'compensation events'. Except that some assessments may be negative and thereby benefit the employer, compensation events are remedies only for the contractor. There are, however, various other express remedies distributed throughout NEC 3 and many of these are available to the employer, e.g. damages for delay, termination, recovery of certain costs, withholding a proportion of payments due. Compared with other standard forms NEC 3 has a wide range of such remedies.

Where there are no contractual remedies and the parties rely on their common law rights a common problem, particularly for the employer, is that proof of loss necessary to recover damages is often difficult if not impossible to establish in respect of some breaches of contract – especially procedural ones. The question of what follows failure by the project manager or supervisor to act as stated in the contract is quite complex. Neither is a party to the contract and as a general rule only the parties have rights and remedies under the contract. However, non-contracting parties can have duties of care and liabilities arising from breach of duty and there is the question applying generally to construction contracts as to what extent the employer warrants the competency and/or fairness of any contract administrator or supervisor appointed by him.

In NEC 3 that latter question is largely avoided by a precise set of rules and remedies. But it is not avoided altogether and for further comment see later in this chapter under 'project manager'.

Mutual trust and co-operation

NEC contracts took a brave step forward, so far as English law is concerned, in expressly including an obligation for the parties to act in 'a spirit of mutual trust and co-operation'.

This is very much a step into the unknown, for as Mr Justice Vinelott said in the case of *London Borough of Merton* v. *Stanley Hugh Leach Ltd* (1985), 'The courts have not gone beyond the implication of a duty to co-operate wherever it is reasonably necessary to enable the other party to perform his obligations under a contract. The requirement of "good faith" in systems derived from Roman law has not been imported into English law.' And twenty years earlier Lord Devlin in his lecture 'Morals and the Law of Contract' had made the telling point that 'If a man minded only about keeping faith, the spirit of the contract would be more important than the letter. But in the service of commerce the letter is in many ways the more significant.'

It is, of course, true that many jurisdictions outside the UK do impose duties of good faith and fair dealing into contracts. But it is questionable whether, when it comes to enforcement, these duties amount to much more than a duty not to act in bad faith. And that, perhaps, is not far removed from the principle well recognised in English law that prevention is a breach of contract.

The difficulty with such admirable concepts as good faith, fair dealing, mutual trust and co-operation is determining what function they are intended to serve. Are they really intended to be legally enforceable – with all the attendant difficulties of proof of breach and proof of loss? Or are they no more than expressions of good intent or warranties to act reasonably?

It is not easy to determine from the wording of clause 10.1 which of the above NEC 3 intends.

If the clause said (which it does not) 'The Employer, the Contractor, the Project Manager and the Supervisor shall act as stated in this contract in a spirit of mutual trust and co-operation' then its purpose would be reasonably clear. It would restrict the rights of the parties, the project manager and the supervisor such that strict application of the contract would be inappropriate and regard would have to be given to application of a test not far dissimilar to one of reasonableness. Although for important matters such as termination where such a restriction would have its greatest effect it is worth nothing that the law may already imply a test of reasonableness. See the Australian case of *Renard Constructions* v. *Minister of Public Works* (1992).

But what clause 10.1 actually says is 'The Employer, the Contractor, the Project Manager and the Supervisor shall act as stated in this contract and in a spirit of mutual trust and co-operation'. There are, therefore, two distinct obligations in the clause:

- to act as stated in the contract, *and*
- to act in a spirit of mutual trust and co-operation

This suggests an intention that the provisions of the contract are to be strictly applied and that there is a further obligation outside the stated provisions which is of separate application. But the problem with this approach is that whilst it might conceivably apply to the employer and to the contractor it is difficult to see how it could apply to the project manager and to the supervisor. Their role is to apply the provisions of the contract.

The debate on the proper legal construction of clause 10.1 will probably run until it is settled in the courts. But in the meantime contractors rather than employers are likely to be the main beneficiaries of any uncertainty. They have more opportunities to capitalise on uncertainty as to whether individual provisions are to be applied in a spirit of mutual trust and co-operation and they are better placed to prove damages in any claim based on failure to do so. And contractors have the benefit of a potential contractual remedy under the compensation event at clause 60.1(18) covering breach of contract by the employer.

5.4 The employer

The role of the employer in NEC 3 is strictly that of a legal party. The employer is not intended to have any direct involvement in the running of the contract, save for a few matters such as dispute resolution and termination, except through the project manager. Two clauses which emphasise this are:

- clause 14.3 – only the project manager may give an instruction which changes the works information, *and*
- clause 21.3 – the contractor is required to obey instructions given only by the project manager or the supervisor

That is not to say however that the employer under NEC 3 has less influence on the running of the contract than with other standard forms. If anything the position is the reverse. The project manager under NEC 3 is clearly the employer's agent for many of his functions and the employer is entitled to exercise more influence on him than would be permissible with a fully independent contract administrator.

Contractual obligations

The primary obligations of the employer in any construction contract are to allow possession of the site to the contractor and to pay the contractor. NEC 3 contains these and a variety of secondary obligations. See the schedule in section 5.5 which follows.

Failure by the employer to comply with any of his obligations is a breach of contract which either entitles the contractor to a compensation event under clause 60 or damages at common law. For further comment on this see Chapter 11 section 5.

A point which was noted by a number of commentators on ECC 2 was the absence of any express obligation on the employer to provide (through the project manager) information additional to that in the works information but necessary for the contractor to complete the works. The same situation applies in NEC 3. The question it poses is whether the employer is bound by an implied term to provide the missing information or whether the contractor has assumed the obligation to fill any gaps himself. The answer will vary according to the facts of each case, but it remains an unsatisfactory aspect of the contract.

5.5 *Express obligations of the employer*

Core clauses

10.1	– to act as stated in the contract and in a spirit of mutual trust and co-operation
14.4	– to give notice to the contractor before replacing the project manager or the supervisor
25.2	– to provide services and other things as stated in the works information
33.1	– to allow access to and use of each part of the site necessary for the work included in the contract, and to do so before the later of the access date and the date for access shown on the accepted programme
35.1	– to take over the works not more than two weeks after completion
35.2	– to take over any part of the works put into use (subject to exceptions)
40.2	– to provide materials, facilities and samples for tests and inspections as stated in the works information
43.4	– to give access to the contractor after take over if needed for the correction of a defect
51.1	– to pay amounts due to the contractor
51.2	– to pay within three weeks of the assessment date or to pay interest on late payment

83.1	– to indemnify the contractor against claims etc. from employer's risks
84.1	– to provide insurances as stated in the contract data
85.3	– to comply with the terms and conditions of insurance policies
90.1	– to notify the project manager giving reasons before terminating
90.2	– to follow the procedures in the termination table when terminating
W1.3(1)/ W2.3(1)	– to notify disputes in accordance with the adjudication table
W1.3(9)/ W2.3(9)	– to proceed as normal until the dispute is decided in adjudication

Option X7 – delay damages

| X7.2 | – to repay any overpayment of delay damages with interest |

Option X14 – advanced payment

| X14.1 | – to make the advanced payment of the amount stated in the contract data |
| X14.2 | – to make the advanced payment within four weeks of the contract date or receipt of the advanced payment bond |

Option Y9(UK) 2 – Housing Grants, Construction and Regeneration Act 1996

| Y2.3 | – to give notice of intention to withhold payment of an amount due |

5.6 *The project manager*

The role of the project manager in an NEC 3 contract is involved and demanding. The contractor and the project manager are intended to work together to see the contract through to completion. And, for the employer, the successful outcome of the contract depends on the competence of the project manager.

The full extent of the project manager's duties can be seen from the schedule in section 5.7 which follows. The list is long by any standards.

Appointment

Some employers have within their organisations persons of sufficient ability and experience to take on the role of project manager and there is nothing in

NEC 3 to prevent in-house appointments. Other employers, through necessity or choice, will appoint an external firm or person as the project manager.

All that NEC 3 requires in contractual terms is that the employer should state the name of the project manager in part one of the contract data and that the employer should not replace the project manager before giving notice to the contractor of the name of the replacement (clause 14.4).

Firm or person

NEC 3 places no restrictions on who or what the project manager should be. Unlike the engineer in the ICE Conditions of Contract he is not required to be a named individual. Nor is he required to be a chartered engineer.

With external appointments the project manager will more often than not be named as a firm – if only to secure the cover of the firm's professional indemnity insurance. But for operational purposes there is much to be said for the identification of a particular person as the project manager.

Delegation

Clause 14.2 permits the project manager to delegate any of his actions. The only formality is that the contractor should be notified. There are no restrictions in NEC 3 on delegation either in regard to which duties and powers can, or cannot, be delegated, or in regard to how many delegates there can be. This can lead to a dangerous division of responsibility and prudent employers will no doubt impose their own restrictions on delegation to avoid being caught by its consequences.

Impartiality and fairness

There is no express requirement in NEC 3 for the project manager to be impartial and much that was written about ECC 2 assumed that it dispensed entirely with the need for impartiality. The proposition was advanced that the project manager was required to concern himself solely with the interests of the employer, for whom he acted as agent, and that it was the task of the adjudicator to step in and resolve any differences with the contractor. Some parts of ECC 2 seemed to support this – most notably, perhaps, the fact that under the disputes resolution procedures the employer had no right to challenge any of the actions of the project manager or the supervisor. This indicated that the actions of the project manager were taken on behalf of the employer. Against this it was noted that there were parts of ECC 2 which did not work if the project manager simply put the interests of the employer before impartiality. For example, the termination provisions required the project manager to issue a termination certificate (or to reject with reasons) on the application of either party. It could not be the case that in considering any application the project manager should put the interests of the employer, who might have been the guilty party, as paramount. And on a more routine scale of decision making such as issuing certificates, valuing compensation events and the like it was difficult to see why the project manager, when exercising his skill and discretion as a certifier or valuer, should be excused the ordinarily legal requirement to act with fairness. Failure to do so would seem to put the employer in breach of the well established implied term that his appointed certifier or valuer should act fairly. And it might expose the project manager to an action in tort from the contractor.

The question of the project manager's duty to act impartially under an ECC 2 based contract came before the courts in the unusual case of *Costain Ltd and Others* v. *Bechtel Ltd* (2005). Costain was part of a consortium of contractors, known as Corber, engaged to carry out part of the Channel Tunnel Rail Link project. Bechtel was part of a consortium engaged to act as project manager. Costain was concerned that Bechtel was deliberately adopting a policy of administering the contract in an unfair and adverse manner. Costain sought interim injunctions restraining the project manager's conduct. A key issue in the case was whether in assessing sums payable to the contractor, the project manager was under a duty to act impartially between the employer and the contractor or merely to act in the interests of the employer. Costain relied on the principles established by the House of Lords in *Sutcliffe* v. *Thackrah* (1974) that a certifier has a duty to act fairly and impartially. Bechtel argued:

- the terms of the contract were specific and detailed and that they conferred no discretion on the project manager – there was, therefore, no need to imply any term on impartiality
- the decisions of the project manager could be challenged in adjudication – thereby excluding the need for an implied term on impartiality
- the position of the project manager under the contract was analogous to that of the project manager in *Royal Brompton Hospital NHS Trust* v. *Hammond* (2002) where the project manager had been specifically employed to look after the interests of the employer
- there were terms in the contract (these were additional conditions) which excluded terms implied by custom

The judge, whilst declining to grant the interim injunctions sought by Costain, expressed the views that:

- the principles of *Sutcliffe* v. *Thackrah* did apply to the contract
- the provisions for adjudication did not affect any duty to act fairly and impartially
- the project manager's position under the contract was not analogous to that in the *Royal Brompton* case.
- the additional conditions excluding terms implied by custom had no impact since the implied duty of a certifier to act fairly and impartially was a matter of law not custom

So much then for the position under ECC 2. The project manager's duty is to act fairly and impartially when acting as a certifier. As to the position under

NEC 3 the same principles apply. If anything, the case for the duty is stronger under NEC 3 because of additional clauses requiring the project manager to assess amounts due from one party to the other.

5.7 *Express duties of the project manager*

Core clauses

10.1 – to act as stated in the contract and in a spirit of mutual trust and co-operation

13.1 – to communicate in a form which can be read, copied and recorded

13.3 – to reply to a communication within the period for reply

13.4 – to reply to a communication submitted or re-submitted for acceptance and to state reasons for non-acceptance

13.5 – to notify any agreed extension to the period for reply

13.6 – to issue certificates to the employer and to the contractor

13.7 – to communicate notifications separately from other communications

14.2 – to notify the contractor of delegation of any actions

16.1 – to give early warning of matters with delay, cost or performance implications

16.3 – to co-operate at risk reduction meetings

16.4 – to record decisions taken at risk reduction meetings, to revise the risk register and to give instructions changing the works information if necessary

17.1 – to give notice of ambiguities or inconsistencies in the documents and to give instructions resolving ambiguities or inconsistencies

18.1 – to give instructions changing the works information in the event of illegality or impossibility in the works information

19.1 – to give instructions stating how the contractor is to deal with prevention events

21.2 – to accept particulars of the contractor's design or to give reasons for non-acceptance

23.1 – to accept particulars of the design of equipment or to give reasons for non-acceptance

24.1 – to accept replacement persons proposed by the contractor or to give reasons for non-acceptance

25.2 – to assess the cost incurred by the employer if the contractor fails to provide services and other things

25.3 – to assess the additional cost incurred by the employer if the contractor fails to meet key dates

26.2 – to accept proposed subcontractors or to give reasons for non-acceptance

26.3 – to accept proposed subcontract conditions or to give reasons for non-acceptance

30.2 – to decide the date of completion and to certify completion within one week of completion

31.3 – to accept the contractor's programme within two weeks of submission or to give reasons for non-acceptance

32.2 – to accept a revised programme or to give reasons for non-acceptance

35.3 – to certify within one week the date when the employer takes over any part of the works

36.1 – to state changes to key dates to be included in any quotation for acceleration

40.6 – to assess the cost incurred by the employer in repeating a test of inspection after a defect is found

43.4 – to arrange for the employer to give access and use to the contractor of any part of the works needed for the correction of defects after taking-over and to extend the period for correcting defects if suitable access and use is not arranged within the defect correction period

44.2 – to change the works information, the prices and the completion date if a quotation for not correcting defects is accepted

45.1 – to assess the cost of having defects corrected by others if the contractor fails to correct notified defects within the defect correction period

45.2 – to assess the costs the contractor would have incurred to correct defects for which he is not given access

50.1 – to assess the amount due for payment at each assessment date and to decide the first assessment date to suit the procedures of the parties

50.4 – to consider any application from the contractor when assessing amounts due for payment and to give the contractor details of how amounts due have been assessed

50.5 – to correct any wrongly assessed amounts due in a later payment certificate

51.1 – to certify payment within one week of each assessment date

61.1 – to notify the contractor of compensation events which arise from the giving of instructions or changing of earlier decisions and to instruct the contractor to submit quotations

61.4 – to decide within one week of notification (or such longer period as the contractor agrees) whether the prices, the completion date and key dates should be changed when the contractor notifies a compensation event and to instruct the contractor to submit quotations

61.5 – to decide whether the contractor did not give any early warning of a compensation event which should have been given and to notify the contractor of his decision

61.6 – to state assumptions for the assessment of compensation events in the event that the effects are too uncertain to be forecast reasonably and to correct any assumptions later found to have been wrong

62.1 – to discuss with the contractor different ways of dealing with compensation events

62.3 – to reply within two weeks to quotations for compensation events submitted by the contractor

62.4 – to give reasons to the contractor when instructing the submission of a revised quotation

62.5 – to extend the time allowed for the submission of quotations and replies if the contractor agrees and to notify the contractor of any agreed extensions for the submission of quotations or replies

64.1 – to assess a compensation event:
— if the contractor has not submitted a quotation within the time allowed
— if the project manager decides the contractor has not assessed the compensation event correctly
— if the contractor has not submitted a required programme
— if the project manager has not accepted the contractor's latest programme

64.2 – to assess a compensation event using his own assessment of the programme:
— if there is no accepted programme
— if the contractor has not submitted a revised programme for acceptance as required

64.3 – to notify the contractor of any assessments made of a compensation event within the period allowed to the contractor for his quotation

65.1 – to implement compensation events by notifying the contractor of accepted quotations or his own assessments

73.1 – to instruct the contractor how to deal with objects of value, historical or other interest

85.1 – to accept policies and certificates of insurance submitted by the contractor or to give reasons for non-acceptance

87.1 – to submit to the contractor policies and certificates for insurances to be provided by the employer

90.1 – to issue a termination certificate when either party gives notice of termination for reasons complying with the contract

90.4 – to certify final payments within thirteen weeks of termination

Option A clauses

36.3 – to change the completion date, key dates and prices when a quotation for acceleration is accepted and to accept the revised programme

54.2 – to accept a revision to the activity schedule or to give reasons for non-acceptance

65.4 – to include changes to the prices, key dates and to the completion date when notifying implementation of a compensation event

Option B clauses

36.3 – to change the completion date, key dates and prices when a quotation for acceleration is accepted

60.6 – to correct mistakes in the bill of quantities

65.4 – to include changes to the prices, to key dates and to the completion date when notifying implementation of a compensation event

Option C clauses

11.2(25)	– to decide disallowed cost
26.4	– to accept proposed contract data for subcontracts or to give reasons for non-acceptance
36.3	– to change key dates, the completion date and prices when a quotation for acceleration is accepted
53.1	– to assess the contractor's share
53.3	– to make a preliminary assessment of the contractor's share at completion
53.4	– to make a final assessment of the contractor's share in the final amount due
54.2	– to accept a revision to the activity schedule or to give reasons for non-acceptance
65.4	– to include changes to the prices and to the completion date when notifying implementation of a compensation event
93.4	– to assess the contractor's share after certifying termination

Option D clauses

11.2(25)	– to decide disallowed costs
26.4	– to accept proposed contract data for subcontracts or to give reasons for non-acceptance
36.3	– to change the completion date and prices and key dates when a quotation for acceleration is accepted
53.5	– to assess the contractor's share
53.7	– to make a preliminary assessment of the contractor's share at completion
53.8	– to make a final assessment of the contractor's share in the final amount due
60.6	– to correct mistakes in the bill of quantities
65.4	– to include changes to the prices, to key dates and to the completion date when notifying implementation of a compensation event
93.5	– to assess the contractor's share after certifying termination

Option E clauses

11.2(25)	– to decide disallowed cost
26.4	– to accept proposed contract data for subcontracts or to give reasons for non-acceptance
36.4	– to change the completion date and key dates when a quotation for acceleration is accepted
65.3	– to include changes to the forecast amount of the prices, key dates and the completion date when implementing a compensation event

Option F clauses

11.2(25) – to decide disallowed cost

26.4   – to accept proposed contract data for subcontracts or to give reasons for non-acceptance

36.4   – to change the completion date and key dates when a quotation for acceleration is accepted

65.3   – to include changes to the forecast amount of the prices, key dates and the completion date when implementing a compensation event

Dispute resolution clauses

W1.3(1) – to notify the employer of disputes relating to quotations treated as having been accepted

W1.3(2) – to notify agreed extensions of the times for referring disputes to adjudication

W1.3(9)/ – to proceed with matters in dispute as though they were not dis-
W2.3(9)   puted until notification of the adjudicator's decision

Secondary option clauses

X7.3   – to assess the benefit to the employer of taking over parts of the works in order to proportion down delay damages

X13.1   – to accept a performance bond or to give reasons for non-acceptance

X14.1   – to accept an advanced payment bond or to give reasons for non-acceptance

5.8 *The supervisor*

One of the unusual features of NEC 3 is the way it separates the functions of contract administration and supervision. It does this not by delegation of powers but by specifying different roles for the project manager and supervisor and by empowering them with independence from each other. The express duties of the supervisor are listed in section 5.9 which follows and from this it can be seen that the supervisor is mainly concerned with the quality of work and defects. There are no significant changes from ECC 2.

Appointment

NEC 3 requires the name of the supervisor to be entered by the employer in part one of the contract data. And like the project manager, the supervisor can either be a firm or a person. There is no express prohibition in NEC 3 on the supervisor and the project manager being the same firm or person and there is no serious procedural difficulty if that is the case. In fact such an arrangement was normal under ECC 2.

Practical difficulties are more likely to arise when the project manager and the supervisor come from different organisations and each takes an uncompromising position on his duties under the contract. An over zealous supervisor can, for example, upset the project manager's plans to put early completion as top priority. And note in particular that although the supervisor issues the defects certificate (clause 43.3), decisions on accepting defects are taken by the project manager (clause 44.1). Note also that the supervisor has no express role to play in the termination procedures set out in section 9 of NEC 3.

Delegation

Under clause 14.2 the supervisor can delegate his duties without restriction providing advance notice is given to the contractor.

5.9 *Express duties of the supervisor*

Core clauses

10.1 – to act as stated in the contract and in a spirit of mutual trust and co-operation
13.1 – to communicate in a form which can be read, copied and recorded
13.3 – to reply to a communication within the period for reply
13.6 – to issue certificates to the project manager and the contractor
40.3 – to notify the contractor of his tests and inspections before they start and afterwards of the results
40.5 – to do tests and inspections without causing unnecessary delay
41.1 – to notify the contractor when plant and materials have passed predelivery tests and inspections
42.1 – to give reasons for searches which are instructed
42.2 – to notify the contractor of defects found
43.3 – to issue the defects certificate
71.1 – to mark equipment, plant and materials outside the working areas for payment purposes

5.10 *Communications*

NEC 3 states in much greater detail than any other standard form of contract (other than ECC 2) how communications between the contractor and the project manager or the supervisor are to be conducted. The requirements are set out in clause 13 but equally important to the contractor is clause 60.1(6) – the compensation event for failure by the project manager or the supervisor to reply to a communication in time.

Note that communication is not a defined term of NEC 3 and that its meaning has to be gathered from the contract.

Clause 13.1 – communications

The main purpose of clause 13.1 appears to be to list those documents/ exchanges which are to be regarded as 'communications'. They are:

- instructions
- certificates
- submissions
- proposals
- records
- acceptances
- notifications
- replies

which the contract requires.

The clause states that these should be communicated in a form which can be read, copied and recorded. This presumably means that they should be in writing. Note that a 'decision' is not listed in clause 13.1 as a matter to be communicated although commonsense suggests that it should be. The explanation for the omission may be that decisions are to be notified and are covered in the clause by 'notifications'.

The final sentence of clause 13.1 'Writing is in the language of this contract' presumably means that all communications are to be written in the language specified in part one of the contract data as the language of the contract.

Clause 13.2 – receipt of communications

Clause 13.2 states that a communication takes effect when it is received. It is not clear how this applies to certificates and the like which are dated by the sender or how evidence of receipt can be monitored. However the reason for making communications take effect when received is obvious enough from clause 13.3 which deals with replies.

Clause 13.3 – period for reply

This clause places an obligation on the project manager, the supervisor and the contractor to reply to communications within the period of reply stated in part one of the contract data. But note that the clause contains two exceptions to the obligation:

- it only applies to communications to which the contract requires a reply
- it does not apply if otherwise stated in the contract

Failure by the project manager or the supervisor to comply with clause 13.3 is a compensation event by clause 60.1(6). There is no stated sanction for failure by the contractor to comply.

The difficulty with clause 13.3 is knowing exactly what is meant by a reply which is required by the contract. Clause 13.4 expressly requires the project manager to reply to communications from the contractor for acceptances but the wording of clause 13.3 suggests that it is intended to be of much wider effect than communications on acceptances.

Clause 13.4 – replies on acceptances

Clause 13.4 deals solely with communications on acceptances. These clearly do require replies within the period for reply. Additionally the clause requires the project manager to state reasons if his reply is not acceptance and requires the contractor to resubmit his communication taking account of the reasons.

Matters falling within the scope of clause 13.4 include:

- clause 15.1   – proposals to add to the working areas
- clause 21.2   – particulars of the contractor's design
- clause 23.1   – particulars of design of equipment
- clause 24.1   – replacement persons
- clause 26.2   – names of subcontractors
- clause 26.3   – conditions of contract for subcontracts
- clause 31.1   – the first programme
- clause 31.3   – regular programmes
- clause 32.2   – revised programmes
- clause 62.3   – quotations for compensation events
- clause 85.1   – insurance policies
- clause X13.1 – performance bond
- clause X14.2 – advanced payment bond

Each of the above clauses has within its own text a stated reason, or reasons, for non-acceptance. Clause 13.4 provides a further general reason for withholding acceptance which applies to all the above – that more information is needed to assess the contractor's submission. Clause 13.8 states that withholding acceptance for a stated reason is not a compensation event.

There is a danger that to avoid the contractor becoming entitled to a compensation event, project managers may be disposed to ask the contractor for further superfluous information. Project managers do not want to be answerable to the employer for compensation events caused by their late replies and, as was experienced under ECC 2, some tactical moves are inevitable in the circumstances.

Clause 13.5 – extending the period for reply

Clause 13.5 provides for the period for reply to be extended. It is for the project manager to formally extend the period for reply but he may only do so when there is agreement with the contractor on the extension before any reply is due.

The wording of clause 13.5 suggests, but it is not completely firm on the point, that any extension of the period for reply is specific to a particular communication and is not of general effect. Since the clause seems to be principally of benefit to the employer in that an extension of the period for reply may save him from the liability of a compensation event the incentive for the contractor to give his agreement to an extension may be correspondingly reduced. But this is, perhaps, a case where failure to give agreement might be breach by the contractor of the obligation to co-operate in clause 10.1 – thereby depriving the contractor of his entitlement to a compensation event.

Clause 13.6 – issue of certificates

Clause 13.6 does no more than clarify the simple point as to who is to be the recipient of certificates. The project manager is to issue his certificates to the employer and to the contractor. The supervisor is to issue his to the project manager and to the contractor. The reason for the supervisor's certificates going to the project manager and not to the employer is the need for the project manager to have those certificates to fulfil his wider role in administering the contract.

Note that the clause applies only to certificates and not to other forms of communication.

Clause 13.7 – notifications

Clause 13.7 deals with notifications. It applies to the contractor, the project manager and supervisor. It states that any notification which the contract requires is to be communicated separately from other communications. The purpose of this is apparently to avoid notifications being overlooked, or lost, in other issues. Compliance with the clause has regularly been raised as an issue in disputes under ECC 2 and it should not be taken simply as an administrative provision of little consequence.

Clauses to which clause 13.7 applies include:

- clause 14.2 – delegation
- clause 14.4 – replacement of the project manager or supervisor
- clause 16.1 – early warning
- clause 17.1 – ambiguities and inconsistencies
- clause 18.1 – illegal or impossible requirements

- clause 31.3 – programmes
- clause 40.3 – tests and inspections
- clause 42.2 – defects
- clause 61.1 – compensation events
- clause 61.3 – compensation events
- clause 61.4 – compensation events
- clause 61.5 – decisions on compensation events
- clause 61.6 – assumptions on compensation events
- clause 62.6 – quotations for compensation events
- clause 64.3 – assessment of compensation events
- clause 64.4 – late assessment of compensation events
- clause 65.1 – implementation of compensation events
- clause 73.1 – discovery of objects of value etc.

Clause 13.7 attracted adverse comment as a generator of paperwork. For example, under clause 61.1 if the project manager gives an instruction he is also required to notify the contractor that a compensation event has occurred and to instruct that a quotation is submitted. It might be sensible to cover these three things in one letter but NEC 3 does not permit that.

Clause 13.8 – withholding an acceptance

NEC 3 takes a direct approach to the reasons for the project manager's actions. It requires reasons to be given and it states which reasons are not compensation events. Clause 13.8 deals with reasons for non-acceptance. It contains two distinct provisions:

- the project manager may withhold acceptance of a submission by the contractor
- withholding for a reason stated in the contract is not a compensation event

The purpose of the first provision of clause 13.8 is presumably to indicate that the project manager may withhold acceptance of a submission for any reason. That generally is the scheme of NEC 3. The purpose of the second provision is not clear. The provision is simply a reflection of clause 60.1(9). Thus, in clause 13.8, NEC 3 provides that withholding for a stated reason is not a compensation event; and in clause 60.1(9) that withholding for a non-stated reason is a compensation event. The problem with this belt and braces approach to drafting is that it brings into question the effectiveness of other provisions which are not treated similarly.

A further problem with clause 13.8 is that it fails to distinguish between reasons based on non-controversial facts and reasons based on what might be controversial opinions. By way of example, stated reasons in clause 31.3 for not accepting a programme include 'it does not show information which this contract requires' and 'the Contractor's plans which it shows are not practicable'. The first of these will generally be a matter of fact; the second is more likely to be a matter of opinion and potentially controversial. And, by way of further example, note the reason in clause X13.1: 'A reason for not accepting the bank or insurance is that its commercial position is not strong enough to carry the bond.' This will almost certainly be a contested reason.

It is not entirely clear what the position is under NEC 3 if the project manager withholds an acceptance for a reason which turns out to be unsustainable on subsequent examination. The consequences could be significant to the contractor in terms of both time and money but there is no obvious contractual remedy. It may be that the project manager's opinion on the validity of a reason cannot be challenged and that the contractor has no remedy even if the project manager can be proved to be wrong. But if that is not the case and if it is possible to open up and review the project manager's withholding action under the dispute resolution procedures of NEC 3, any mistaken action may be a breach for which the employer is responsible. Clearly a project manager needs to be cautious in withholding acceptances.

5.11 *The project manager and the supervisor*

Clause 14 contains in its four sub-clauses a miscellaneous set of provisions under the marginal note 'the Project Manager and the Supervisor' – albeit that the most important of these provisions, clause 14.3 relating to instructions, applies only to the project manager.

Clause 14.1 – acceptance of a communication

This clause states that acceptance by either the project manager or the supervisor of a communication from the contractor or of his work does not change the contractor's responsibility to provide the works or his liability for his design. The broad intention is probably to convey the point found in most standard forms that only the parties themselves and not contract administrators or supervisors have power to change the obligations of the parties. This point is reinforced in the new clause 12.3 of NEC 3.

It is understandable that the contractor should not be relieved of his design liability by acceptances but it is questionable to what extent the generality of the clause is compatible with the requirements in clause 10.1 on mutual trust and co-operation. If the contractor cannot rely on acceptances given by the project manager and the supervisor how much room is left for mutual trust and co-operation? And it is questionable whether it is fully compatible with the notion of the project manager as the employer's agent.

Clause 14.2 – delegation

Clause 14.2 sets out the powers and procedures for delegation by the project manager and the supervisor. As noted in section 5.6 above there are no restrictions on what actions can be delegated or how many delegates there can be.

The difficult question of whether delegation is disposal of authority to someone else or sharing authority with someone else is not directly addressed in clause 14.2 or elsewhere in NEC 3 but the last sentence of the clause, which states that an action by the project manager or the supervisor includes an action by his delegate, may be an indication that power sharing rather than disposal is intended.

Clause 14.3 – instructions

The short and apparently simple clause 14.3 is one of the most important clauses in NEC 3. It states that the project manager may give an instruction to the contractor which changes the works information. The clause may not be instantly recognisable as the variation clause of the contract but that is presumably what it is since there is no other clause in NEC 3 which can be taken as providing for variations. However, the simplicity of the clause must be false. The project manager cannot have an unfettered power to change the works information and thereby change the contractor's obligations. It may be that the only changes the project manager can validly make are those expressly provided for in other clauses of the contract or are incidental in the sense referred to in clause 11.2(13). If so, clause 14.3 is a variation clause of very limited effect. For further comment on this clause see Chapter 4 section 9.

Clause 14.4 – replacements

This clause entitles the employer to replace the project manager or the supervisor simply by giving notice to the contractor.

Most construction contracts have a similar provision but process and plant contracts are generally more restrictive on how replacements are made.

Chapter 6
General core clauses

6.1 Introduction

The common core clauses of NEC 3 commence in section 1 (headed 'General') with nine sets of clauses, numbered 10 to 19, which lay the foundation for the remainder of the contract. These general clauses cover:

- actions – clause 10.1
- identified and defined terms – clauses 11.1 to 11.19
- interpretation and the law – clauses 12.1 to 12.4
- communications – clauses 13.1 to 13.8
- the project manager and the supervisor – clauses 14.1 to 14.4
- adding to the working areas – clause 15.1
- early warning – clauses 16.1 to 16.4
- ambiguities and inconsistencies – clause 17.1
- illegal and impossible requirements – clause 18.1
- prevention – clause 19.1

Comment is given in other chapters of this book on some of the general clauses so the commentary which follows below in this chapter is, for those clauses, no more than supplementary.

The principal changes between ECC 2 and NEC 3 in the general core clauses concern the introduction into NEC 3 of key dates, the risk register, prevention and an 'entire agreement' clause. Other points of change to note are:

- the definition clauses have been re-arranged and re-numbered
- reference to the adjudicator has been omitted from clause 10.1
- the definition of completion has been extended
- the definition of the 'Fee' now has percentages for subcontracted work and direct work
- a new clause 12.3 has been added relating to changes in the conditions of contract
- a new clause 12.4 has been added as an entire agreement clause
- early warning meetings are now referred to as risk reduction meetings
- clause 18.1 of ECC 2 relating to health and safety requirements has been moved from section 1 and repositioned in section 2 as clause 27.4

6.2 *Actions*

Clause 10.1 states that the employer, the contractor, the project manager and the supervisor shall act as stated in the contract and in a spirit of mutual trust and co-operation. For detailed comment on the mutual trust and co-operation aspects of this clause see Chapter 5, section 3.

Meaning of 'actions'

NEC 3 does not define what it means by an 'action'. It would be helpful if it did. It is, for example, fundamental to the operation of Option W1 on the settlement of disputes that 'action' should have a precise meaning. This is because under Option W1 only the contractor may refer disputes about actions of the project manager or the supervisor to adjudication. Or, put another way, the employer is not permitted under Option W1 to dispute actions of the project manager or the supervisor.

On its ordinary meaning an action is performing a task. *The Shorter Oxford Dictionary* gives its first meaning as 'the process or condition of acting or doing'. Clearly the contractor has actions to perform in providing the works and the project manager and the supervisor have actions to perform in fulfilling their duties. The list of items to be communicated in clause 13.1 provides a typical check list of administrative actions:

- instructing
- certifying
- submitting
- proposing
- recording
- accepting
- notifying
- replying

The question is – are disputes about the outcome of actions (opinions/decisions) to be regarded as disputes about actions? In particular, taking perhaps the most arguable points, are disputes about the value of certificates or the assessment of compensation events disputes about actions? If the project manager has followed the procedures of the contract and arrived at an opinion which is different from that of the contractor, is that a dispute about an action?

For further comment on the meaning of 'actions' see Chapter 5, section 3.

6.3 *Identified and defined terms*

Clause 11.1 – terms

This clause states simply that terms identified in the contract data are in italics and defined terms have capital letters.

For comment on this clause see Chapter 4, section 7.

Clause 11.2(1) – the accepted programme

The accepted programme is one of the most important documents in the administration of an NEC 3 contract even though it need not be a formally incorporated contract document. In particular, the accepted programme:

- fixes dates for access to and use of the site (clause 33.1)
- affects amounts due for payment (clause 50.3)
- determines the contractor's entitlements to compensation events (clauses 60.1(2), 60.1(3), 60.1(5))
- governs the assessment of compensation events (clauses 63.3 and 63.7)

Clause 11.2(1) defines the accepted programme as the programme identified in the contract data or the latest programme accepted by the project manager. The latest accepted programme supersedes previous accepted programmes. The purpose of the definition is to ensure that of the many programmes which may be produced and proposed on a project the one which has contractual effect can be readily identified.

The decision as to whether or not a programme should be identified in the contract data, thereby becoming the first accepted programme (or the tender programme as it would ordinarily be called) is a matter for the employer. However, the risks to employers from incorporating tender programmes and method statements into contracts have been well exposed in a number of cases, in particular, in *Yorkshire Water Authority* v. *Sir Alfred McAlpine & Son (Northern) Ltd* (1985); *Holland Dredging (UK) Ltd* v. *Dredging & Construction Co Ltd* (1987); *Havant Borough Council* v. *South Coast Shipping Co Ltd* (1996). Incorporated programmes and method statements can place unintended obligations on the contractor, enabling the contractor to claim variations if things need to be done differently, or to claim impossibility if they cannot be done commercially.

Problems can arise under NEC 3 if the contractor identifies a programme in the contract data even though not required to do so. Such a programme arguably becomes the accepted programme under the definition in clause 11.2(1).

Users of NEC 3, particularly contractors, need to note that NEC 3 retains the rule in ECC 2 that if no programme is identified in the contract data, one quarter of amounts due in interim payments is withheld until the contractor submits a first programme for acceptance (clause 50.3).

Clause 11.2(2) – completion

The meaning of 'completion' is complex and frequently a source of contention in construction contracts – see, for example, the cases of *Emson Eastern Ltd* v. *EME Developments Ltd* (1991); *H W Nevill (Sunblest) Ltd* v. *William Press & Sons* (1981); *City of Westminster* v. *Jarvis* (1970).

Traditionally, building contracts have referred to 'practical completion' whilst civil engineering contracts have referred to 'substantial completion'.

From the various legal cases rules have been developed to fix the meaning of 'practical completion', in particular:

- practical completion means the completion of all the construction work to be done
- the contract administrator may have discretion to certify practical completion where there are minor items of work to complete of a *'de minimis'* nature
- a certificate of practical completion cannot be issued if there are patent defects
- the works can be practically complete notwithstanding latent defects

The meaning of 'substantial completion' in civil engineering contracts is more flexible and generally it is not the *'de minimis'* rule which applies to incomplete work but whatever is acceptable to the engineer. NEC 3 seeks to avoid contention by defining 'completion' rather than by relying on traditional phraseology such as practical completion and substantial completion.

Clause 11.2(2) – definition of completion

Clause 11.2(2) states that completion is when the contractor has:

- done all the work the works information states he is to do by the completion date, *and*
- has corrected notified defects which would have prevented the employer from using the works and others doing their work

The clause then goes on to say that if the work which the contractor is to do by the completion date is not stated in the works information, completion is when the contractor has done all the work necessary for the employer to use the works and for others to do their work. These concluding provisions are new to NEC 3, as is the reference to 'others' in the second bullet point of the clause.

'Not stated in the Works Information'

The change dealing with the situation where the work the contractor has to do by completion is not stated in the works information is readily explained. Many compilers of contracts under ECC 2 failed to realise that, most unusually, they were required to detail in the contract documents precisely what work was to be done in order to achieve completion. Frequently the works information was silent on the matter. That particular problem has now been addressed in NEC 3 – although it remains debatable as to whether defining completion primarily by reference to detail in the works information is a sensible approach.

'Work of others'

The changes relating to the work of others are less readily explained. They appear to defeat the purpose of detailing in the works information the work to be done by completion and they introduce the interesting concept that the contractor's obligations on completion are fixed not only by employer's requirements but also by the requirements of others. Apparently the contractor can have done all the work stated in the works information to be done for completion, he can have corrected all notified defects which would have prevented the employer from using the works, and yet still not be entitled to completion. It is difficult to envisage what sort of works the contractor has to complete to satisfy that part of the clause relating the work of others but, whatever they are, they are presumably the contractor's own incomplete works. From this it seems to follow that completion as derived solely from works information requirements is in the nature of substantial completion rather than practical completion.

'Certification of completion'

By clause 30.2 of NEC 3 the project manager decides and certifies the date of completion. For further comment on this see Chapter 8, section 2. But it is worth noting here that under clause 35 the engineer also certifies the date of take-over of the works, and this is either two weeks after the date of completion or when the employer actually begins to use the whole or parts of the works. Late completion, for the purposes of delay damages under Option X7, is assessed by comparing the date of completion with the date for completion – although, interestingly, proportioning-down of delay damages is assessed by reference to take-over dates. At first sight it might appear that providing the contractor does all the work necessary for the employer to use the works his liability for delay damages stops notwithstanding that operation of the 'work of others' rule in clause 11.2(2) prevents formal completion being achieved. However, if the employer declines to use the works until formal completion neither clause 35 nor the proportioning-down provisions of Option X7 assist the contractor in reducing liability for delay damages as both apply when the employer actually takes over.

The potential for serious disputes under clause 11.2(2) should not be under-estimated.

Clause 11.2(3) – the completion date

Clause 11.2(3) states simply that the completion date is the completion date unless later changed in accordance with the contract. This allows the time for completion to be extended. The clause works because the completion date is both a defined term and an identified term. So the first completion date is entered into the contract data by either the employer or the contractor as appropriate and that date can later be changed through the operation of the contract – which is by the compensation event mechanism or by agreed acceleration.

The completion date is, therefore, the stipulated date at any time 'for' completion, and it is to be distinguished from the achieved date 'of' completion.

Clause 11.2(4) – the contract date

The contract date is defined as the date when the contract came into existence.

For comment on this clause see Chapter 4, section 7.

Clause 11.2(5) – defects

Clause 11.2(5) defines a defect as:

- a part of the works which is not in accordance with the works information, *or*
- a part of the works designed by the contractor which is not in accordance with the law or the design which has been accepted

For comment on this clause see Chapter 9, section 2.

Clause 11.2(6) – the defects certificate

Clause 11.2(6) defines the defects certificate as a list of defects, notified before the defects date but not corrected, or, if there are no such defects, a statement that there are none.

Again see Chapter 9, section 2.

Clause 11.2(7) – equipment

Equipment is defined in clause 11.2(7) as:

- items provided by the contractor, *and*
- used by him to provide the works, *and*
- which the works information does not require him to include in the works

The definition of equipment assists in distinguishing between fixed plant and temporary equipment but it serves mainly in fixing a meaning to the term for the purposes of:

- clause 23.1 – design of equipment
- clauses 70.1 and 70.2 – title to equipment

- clause 72.1 – removal of equipment
- contract data entries
- schedules of cost components

Note that although the definition refers only to 'items provided by the Contractor', clause 26.1 extends the scope to subcontractors by stating that the contract applies as if a subcontractor's equipment is the contractor's. The wording in the last part of the clause – 'which the Works Information does not require' – is obvious enough in its meaning but it is not fully in keeping with the style of NEC 3. In practice the works information is unlikely to have negative requirements other than operating restrictions.

Clause 11.2(8) – the fee

The fee has two functions in NEC 3:

- it applies to all the main options in the assessment of compensation events (clause 63.1), *and*
- it applies to the cost reimbursable valuations of work in main options C, D, E and F. Clause 11.2(8) states, in a definition a little longer and more complex than that in ECC 2, that the fee is the sum of the amounts calculated by applying the subcontractor's fee percentage to the defined cost of subcontracted work and the direct fee percentage to the defined cost of other work. To accommodate this revised definition, part two of the contract data now has entry spaces for:
  — the direct fee percentage
  — the subcontracted fee percentage

Note, therefore, that although there may be many subcontractors, there is only one fee percentage to cover them all. Nevertheless, contractors will welcome the change from ECC 2 where there was no distinction in fee terms between direct work and subcontracted work.

Clause 11.2(9) – key dates

Key dates are new to NEC 3. They are similar to sectional completion dates in that they are set by the employer and are identified in part one of the contract data. The difference is that instead of relating to completion of parts of the works, they relate to conditions (or states of completion) for the whole or parts of the works.

Clause 11.2(9) defines a key date as the date by which the work is to meet the 'Condition' stated. The clause goes on to say that key dates and conditions are as stated in the contract data unless changed later in accordance with the contract.

Key dates are mentioned in the following core clauses of NEC 3:

- clause 11.2(9) – definition
- clause 14.3   – project manager's instructions

- clause 16.1   – early warning
- clause 25.3   – failure to meet key dates
- clause 30.3   – obligation to meet key dates
- clause 31.2   – programmes to include key dates
- clause 36.1   – acceleration
- clause 60.1(4) – compensation event for changes to key dates
- clause 61.3   – notifying claims for changes to key dates
- clause 61.4   – project manager's notifications on claims
- clause 62.2   – contractor's quotations to include key dates
- clause 63.3   – delay to key dates
- clause 63.4   – rights in respect of key date changes
- clause 63.8   – resolving ambiguities or inconsistencies on key dates
- clause 63.9   – correcting description of conditions for key dates

Note also:

- clauses 36.3/36.4 in Options A–F on acceleration
- clause 60.5 in Options B and D on measurement
- clauses 65.3/65.4 in Options A–F on implementing compensation events

Particularly important from the above lists are clauses 30.3 and 25.3 which deal respectively with the contractor's obligations to achieve key dates and the contractor's liability for failure. The latter it should be noted is cost based and not damages based as for late completion.

As might be gathered from the number of references to key dates in compensation event clauses, key dates are extendable in like manner to completion dates under the compensation event procedures. What might not be so obvious is that whilst the project manager has the power to change key dates (clause 14.3), he has only very limited power to change the conditions for key dates. He can only do so by way of correction of a description of a condition under clause 63.9.

A final point to note is that although there is no express reference in the termination provisions of NEC 3 (section 9) to key dates, some of the reasons for termination could arguably extend to failure to achieve key dates.

Clause 11.2(10) – others

Others are defined in clause 11.2(10) as people or organisations who are not the employer, the project manager, the supervisor, the adjudicator, the contractor or any employee, subcontractor, or supplier of the contractor.

For comment on this clause see Chapter 5, section 2.

Clause 11.2(11) – the parties

This clause states only that the 'Parties' are the employer and the contractor. Both terms, being in italics, are to be identified by name in the contract data.

Although only 'the Parties' is a defined term, NEC 3 does, in places, use the singular 'Party' as if it is also a defined term (see, for example, Options W1 and W2).

In process and plant contracts where traditionally the parties are the purchaser and the contractor, purchasers may be reluctant to contract under the title of 'employer' for various administrative reasons. A suitably drafted additional condition substituting 'purchaser' for 'employer' may be a simpler solution than amending the standard NEC 3 conditions.

Clause 11.2(12) – plant and materials

Clause 11.2(12) states simply that plant and materials are items intended to be included in the works.

The key word is probably 'intended' because it indicates that plant and materials do not fall within the scope of the defined term simply by being included in the works. It may well be that some plant and materials, in the ordinary sense of the words, is included in the works – perhaps as temporary works which become incorporated to avoid the costs or difficulties of removal. But these are excluded for the purposes of the definition which is principally to do with title (clauses 70.1 and 70.2); marking for payment (clause 71.1); and the schedules of cost components. Clearly 'plant' as mentioned in the definition does not mean contractor's plant used for constructing the works. Such plant falls under the definition of 'equipment' in clause 11.2(7).

As to precisely which plant and materials are intended to be included in the works, that is to be determined from the works information.

Clause 11.2(13) – to provide the works

NEC 3 avoids conventional terminology such as 'design', 'construct', 'complete', 'maintain' to describe broadly what the contractor undertakes to do. Instead it uses an all embracing term 'to Provide the Works'. Clause 11.2(4) states that to provide the works means:

- to do the work necessary to complete the works in accordance with the contract, *and*
- to do all incidental work, services and actions which the contract requires

The defined term 'To Provide the Works' or the similar terms 'Providing the Works' and 'Provides the Works' are found in the following clauses:

- 11.2(7) – equipment
- 11.2(13) – definition
- 11.2(17) – subcontractors
- 11.2(18) – working areas
- 11.2(19) – works information

- 14.1   – contractor's responsibility for design
- 15.1   – adding to the working areas
- 20.1   – contractor's main responsibility
- 23.1   – design of equipment
- 26.1   – responsibility of subcontractors
- 26.2   – proposal of subcontractors
- 26.3   – acceptance of subcontractors
- 31.2   – programme

The problem with the definition in clause 11.2(13) is that it fails to mention that it is the contractor who is to provide the works. Taken literally it includes by its words 'actions which this contract requires', actions to be performed by the employer, the project manager and the supervisor. Consequently an offer by the contractor in the form of tender or form of agreement 'to provide the works' is not strictly correct.

A point which is perhaps of more importance is whether the phrase 'incidental work' used in the definition can be taken as a restriction on the type of varied work which the contractor can be instructed to perform. See Chapter 4, section 9 for comment on the otherwise apparent lack of any limitations on the amount or type of variations which may be ordered under NEC 3. It may not be unreasonable to say, therefore, that clause 11.2(13) distinguishes between the work necessary to complete the works (as specified at the outset) and incidental work which can be instructed by changes to the works information.

Clause 11.2(14) – the risk register

Risk registers are increasingly being used in the management of major projects. They are jointly compiled by the parties with the aid of their professional teams and are regularly revised and updated. They vary considerably in the number and type of items they cover.

Clause 11.2(14) of NEC 3, which is a clause new to NEC 3, defines the risk register as a register of risks listed in the contract data and risks which the project manager or the contractor has notified as an early warning matter. The clause goes on to say that the register includes descriptions of the risks and descriptions of actions to be taken to avoid or reduce the risks.

The only other clauses in NEC 3 which refer to the risk register are those related to early warnings – clauses 16.1 to 16.4. They require matters for which early warning has been given by the contractor or the project manager to be entered into the risk register; to be considered at risk reduction meetings; and that the risk register be revised to record decisions taken. Apart from putting these managerial and administrative obligations on the project manager and the contractor, the nearest the risk register in NEC 3 comes to creating other obligations and liabilities is in clause 16.4 which states that if a decision on a risk requires a change in the works information, the project manager instructs the change at the same time as he issues the revised risk register. However, it is doubtful if this is intended to be anything more than procedural. It is unlikely that changes to the risk register by themselves are intended to change the substantive obligations and liabilities of the parties.

Clause 11.2(15) – the site

NEC 3 has two defined terms to cover areas used by the contractor in undertaking the works – the site and the working areas. The 'site' is broadly the land (or area) provided by the employer which is identified in a drawing (or by description) in part one of the contract data. The 'working areas' are lands (or other areas) additional to the site identified by the contractor in part two of the contract data or as added to by clause 15.1.

The definition of the 'site' in clause 11.2(15) does little, by itself, to reveal its significance. It states only that the site is:

- the area within the boundaries of the site, *and*
- volumes above and below affected by the work

The significance of the defined term has to be developed from the clauses which use it. In particular:

- clause 30.1 – work not to start on the site until the first access date
- clause 33.1 – the employer to allow access to and use of the site to the contractor
- clause 60.1(12) – physical conditions within the site
- clause 73.1 – objects and materials within the site
- clause 80.1 – risk of use or occupation of the site

Thus it can be seen that the site is an area over which the employer has control which is to be made available to the contractor for the purposes of constructing the works. The employer retains certain responsibilities for the site, however, during the time it is in possession of the contractor.

The employer is required to specify the boundaries of the site in part one of the contract data. There is no obvious provision in NEC 3 for extending the site which raises the question whether it is permissible for a variation (or change in the works information) to be ordered which takes the works beyond the original site boundaries.

Clause 11.2(16) – site information

For comment on the definition of site information in clause 11.2(16) and on site information generally, see Chapter 4, section 9.

Clause 11.2(17) – subcontractors

For comment on the definition of a subcontractor in clause 11.2(17) see Chapter 5, section 1. For comment on subcontractors generally see Chapter 7, section 9.

Clause 11.2(18) – the working areas

Clause 11.2(18) defines the 'Working Areas' as those parts of the working areas which are:

- necessary for providing the works, *and*
- are used only for work in the contract
- unless changed later in accordance with the contract

This is an improved definition from that in ECC 2 which gave no indication of the purpose of the working areas and which hinted only at their geographical extent. What is now evident from the definition in NEC 3 and the entry in part two of the contract data is that the working areas are the site and areas outside the site, designated by the contractor, and which are necessary for, and used only for, providing the works.

The principal purpose of defining the works areas is found in the schedules of cost components where people, equipment, plant and material costs are fixed with reference to costs incurred within the working areas (rather than within the site).

Reference to the working areas is also found in clauses 70 and 71 which deal with title, and entitlement to payment, for equipment, plant, and materials outside the working areas.

Clause 11.2(19) – works information

For comment on the definition of works information in clause 11.2 (19) and on the general importance of the works information in NEC 3 see Chapter 4, section 9.

Clauses 11.2(20) to 11.2(33)

These clauses cover identified and defined terms for particular main options and they relate generally to:

- the prices
- the price for the work done to date
- disallowed cost

6.4 *Interpretation and the law*

Clause 12.1 – interpretation

Clause 12.1 states that, except where the context shows otherwise, words in the singular also mean in the plural, and words in the masculine also mean in the feminine. Neutral clauses of this type are found in many standard forms and rarely present problems. In NEC 3 however care needs to be taken in interpretation of Option X15, sectional completion – see Chapter 3, section 6.

Clause 12.2 – law of the contract

The law of the contract is an identified term to be stated in part one of the contract data. Clause 12.2 merely confirms that the contract is governed by the law of the contract.

The law of the contract is usually called the substantive law, and in the event that no law is stated in the contract, it will normally be the law of the state where the works are performed. However where matters relating to the contract such as dispute resolution proceedings or enforcement proceedings are performed in other states the law governing such proceedings, usually called the procedural law, will not necessarily be the same as the substantive law.

Clause 12.3 – changes to the contract

Clause 12.3, which is new to NEC 3, states that no change to the contract has effect unless it is provided for in the conditions of contract or unless it has been agreed, confirmed in writing, and signed by the parties.

This is potentially a more complex clause than first reading would suggest. It is generally well understood that once a contract has been made its terms cannot be changed except by agreement of the parties or, in exceptional circumstances, by the courts as rectification of a mistake. And, occasionally, statutory laws may come into force which have the effect of adding to, or changing, the terms of the contract. But, such things apart, the parties are bound by the agreement they have made. It may be that the purpose of clause 12.3 is to do no more than restate these basic principles – with the added proviso that all changes must be in writing and signed.

The problems with clause 12.3, however, are that it refers to changes to the contract, not to changes to the conditions of contract; that the contract is not a defined term but a term which encompasses all the documents forming the contract; and that those documents include the works information which is likely to have within it many references to the obligations of the contractor. It is necessary therefore to read clause 12.3 as applying to all the documents forming the contract and not just to the printed conditions of contract.

In most standard forms of construction contract it is easy to recognise the difference between a change to the conditions of contract and a change to the detail or specification of the works – the latter being a change provided for in the conditions of contract by way of a variation order. In NEC 3 changes to the works information take the place of variations but the works information is not confined to detail and specification. Some changes to works information would have the effect of changing the contractual obligations of the parties in much the same way as if they were made by changes to the conditions of contract. In short, it is not always easy to recognise in NEC 3 the distinction between a change to the conditions of contract and a change in the works.

The power of the project manager to change the works information under clause 14.3 of NEC 3 is apparently unrestricted – but see the comment in Chapter 4, section 9 and elsewhere in this book. The true extent of this power is a matter of key importance to the operation of the contract.

Clause 12.4 – entire agreement

Clause 12.4 states only that the contract is the entire agreement between the parties.

Simple as this may seem, this is another clause with potential for complexity. See the comment in Chapter 4, section 3.

6.5 Communications etc.

Clauses 13.1 to 13.8 of NEC 3, all deal with communications. These are covered in Chapter 5 section 10. Clause 14.1 also relates to communications – this is covered in Chapter 5, section 11 as is clause 14.2 on delegation and clause 14.4 on replacements.

6.6 Instructions

Clause 14.3 which states that the project manager may give an instruction which changes the works information or a key date is fundamental to the operation of NEC 3. It serves as the variation clause of the contract. For comment see Chapter 4, section 9, Chapter 5 section 11 and elsewhere in this book.

6.7 Adding to the working areas

The working areas are both a defined term, clause 11.2(18), and an identified term in NEC 3. Their purpose is discussed in section 6.3 above.

Clause 15.1 – adding to working areas

Clause 15.1 provides for adding to the working areas which have been identified by the contractor in part two of the contract data. The wording of the clause in NEC 3 is slightly different from that in ECC 2 but it retains the same intention. The clause states that the contractor may submit a proposal to the project manager for adding an area to the working area and that a reason for not accepting is:

- that the proposed area is not necessary for providing the works, *or*
- that the proposed area will be used for work not in the contract

The most obvious reason for the contractor wishing to add to the working areas is to ensure that resources used in providing the works come within the cost reimbursable scope of the schedules of cost components – either for the purposes of direct payments or the assessment of compensation events. Generally, it seems that apart from design, manufacture and fabrication, resources outside the working areas are to come within the fee.

Another reason could be to permit interim payments to be made for off-site materials etc. without involving the procedures of clause 71.1 (marking equipment, plant and materials outside the working areas). But this might well involve a revision to the activity schedule unless, of course, the contractor has failed to properly identify the working areas in the first place. This does raise the question whether clause 15.1 can be used to rectify an omission in the contract data on the working areas. The answer is that it can. The contract data entry reads, 'The working areas are the Site and . . .'. So even if the contractor leaves the entry blank the works commence with a working area corresponding to the site boundaries.

If the project manager does not accept a proposal for adding to the working areas when that addition is either necessary for providing the works or the additional area will not be used for work not in the contract, that is a compensation event under clause 60.1(9).

6.8 Early warning

One aspect of ECC 2 which attracted much attention and commendation was that it provided for early warning to be given of potential problems. Its operation in practice, which has generally been successful, did much to enhance the status of ECC 2 as a collaborative contract. NEC 3 retains provisions for early warning but they are now integrated with risk reduction matters. Early warning meetings are re-named risk reduction meetings.

Clause 16.1 – early warning notices

Clause 16.1 places an obligation on both the contractor and the project manager to give an early warning notice to the other as soon as either becomes aware of any matter which could:

- increase the contract price
- delay completion, *or*
- delay meeting a key date, *or*
- impair the performance of the works in use

Early warning matters

Clause 16.1 also provides that the contractor 'may' give early warning to the project manager of any other matter which could increase his total costs. The clause goes on to state that the project manager enters early warning matters in the risk register and that early warning of a matter for which a compensation event has previously been notified is not required.

The sort of things which would obviously come within the scope of the mandatory part of clause 16.1 are the discovery of unforeseen ground conditions, materials shortages, design problems, insolvency of key subcontractors and the like. But the clause is so worded that it is clearly more than a mechanism for one party informing the other of its (the other's) faults. It requires confession of the parties' own faults. One of the difficulties of clause 16.1, however is that it suffers from the problem, common to much of NEC 3, of leaving unclear how rigidly its mandatory parts are to be operated. Some degree of common sense and some tests of reasonableness and seriousness must be applied to avoid trivial matters obscuring the true purpose of the provisions.

The additions to clause 16.1 in NEC 3 address three separate matters:

- Discretionary early warning by the contractor of matters which could increase his total cost. The purpose of this is not entirely clear. Under Options C, D, E and F increased total costs could increase the total of the prices and would seem, therefore, to come within the mandatory part of the clause. However, it may be recognition that the mandatory part is worded too strictly and that for cost reimbursable options it is not practicable to require early warning notices for every price increase. In so far that the discretionary provision applies to Options A and B it is, perhaps, simply early warning that the contractor may be looking for claim opportunities or may be running into financial difficulties
- Entry of early warning matters into the risk register. The responsibility for this rests with the project manager. Both mandatory and discretionary matters seem to be included.
- Early warning not required for matters previously notified as compensation events. This remedies a procedural defect in ECC 2 and removes duplication of notices. It raises questions, however, as to whether all compensation events should be entered into the risk register.

Failure to give early warning notice

The sanction on the contractor for failing to give a required early warning notice is found in clause 63.5 relating to the assessment of compensation events. This clause is discussed in detail in Chapter 15. At first reading it appears to suggest that it does not matter whether the contractor gives an early warning or not. But what it presumably intends is that if the contractor does not give a required early warning then the assessment of a compensation event cannot be greater than the assessment which would have followed the notice.

It is worth noting that the obligation on the contractor under clause 16.1 is to give notice 'as soon as' becoming aware of any matter requiring notice. However, in order to apply clause 63.5 to assessments, the project manager must first have notified the contractor under clause 61.5 of his decision that the contractor did not give early warning which 'an experienced contractor could be given'. It is not entirely clear whether the project manager can apply clauses 61.5 and 63.5 to an early warning notice which has been given on the basis that it should have been given earlier. But, if he can, although a contractor may have given notice as soon as becoming aware of a matter, he may still suffer reduced assessments for not having given notice earlier.

There is no express sanction in NEC 3 for failure by the project manager to give early warning. But, acting in the best interests of the employer, the project manager would normally be expected to be conscientious in doing so. Any proven failure by the project manager to give early warning of a matter of which he was aware would potentially be a breach of clause 10.1 (actions) and that would arguably entitle the contractor to damages for breach against the employer or payment under the compensation event in clause 60.1(18) – breach of contract by the employer.

Clause 16.2 – attendance at risk reduction meetings

In appropriate cases early warning notices will be followed by risk reduction meetings. Clause 16.2 allows either the project manager or the contractor to instruct the other to attend such a meeting. The style of the clause is quite peremptory – instructions to attend are given. The consequences of one party finding the instructions inconvenient or impertinent and failing to attend are not addressed.

Clause 16.2 also provides that either the project manager or the contractor may instruct other people to attend if the other agrees. Taken literally, this would be dependent on the project manager or the contractor having it within their power to instruct others to attend. But what it presumably means is that if the project manager and the contractor so agree then either can invite other persons to a risk reduction meeting if they think their presence would be helpful.

Note that the supervisor has no automatic right to attend and, therefore, he can only do so if the contractor and the project manager agree that he can.

Clause 16.3 – risk reduction meetings

Clause 16.3 of NEC 3 is a version of clause 16.3 from ECC 2 expanded to refer to and include for risk reduction. It puts risk reductions meetings on a formal footing by requiring those who attend to co-operate in:

- making and considering proposals on how the effects of registered risks can be avoided or reduced
- seeking solutions that will bring advantage to all affected
- deciding actions to be taken and who will take them
- deciding which risks have been avoided or passed and which can be removed from the register

Clearly the obligation to co-operate only extends to those who are bound by the contract but it does nevertheless raise some interesting questions on whether it really is intended to be an obligation or merely an exhortation. It is, of course, perfectly reasonable that those who attend early warning meetings should co-operate – so far as it is in their interest to do so. And given the obligation in clause 10.1 of the contract for the parties to act in a spirit of mutual trust and co-operation it may be a breach of contract not to co-operate. But there remain difficulties. Consider, for example, a contractor who has been notified by the supervisor that some work is defective. The contractor considers that remedial works will delay completion. The contractor gives an early warning notice and instructs the project manager to attend a risk reduction meeting. The project manager is then to co-operate in seeking a solution which will bring advantage not only to the employer but also to the contractor. The permutations on this theme are endless. And when it comes to defects in the contractor's design the consequences of the project manager being drawn into proposals for rectification need to be very carefully considered. Not least by the project manager – with one eye on his professional indemnity insurance cover.

Clause 16.4 – revision of risk register

Clause 16.4 of ECC 2 required the project manager to record proposals made and decisions taken at early warning meetings. Clause 16.4 of NEC 3 requires the project manager to revise the risk register to record decisions taken at each risk reduction meeting and to issue the revised risk register to the contractor. The clause also states that if the decision needs a change to the works information, the project manager should instruct the change at the same time.

6.9 *Ambiguities and inconsistencies*

Clause 17.1 of NEC 3 is unchanged from ECC 2. It requires the project manager and the contractor to notify the other on becoming aware of any ambiguity or inconsistency in or between the contract documents. The project manager is required to give an instruction resolving the matter.

For comment on clause 17.1 see Chapter 4, section 13.

6.10 *Illegal and impossible requirements*

Illegality and impossibility are difficult subjects which NEC 3 addresses only briefly.

Points to consider are:

- whether the illegality or impossibility is absolute such that it cannot be overcome by any means. The question then is whether the contract is totally frustrated or rendered capable of being only partially performed
- whether the illegality or impossibility is commercial or technical and is capable of being overcome by changes in the design or scope of the works
- whether the responsibility for overcoming illegality or impossibility should rest with the employer or the contractor, a point which largely depends upon which party is responsible for design

Meaning of 'legally or physically impossible'

The meaning of the phrase 'legally or physically impossible' as used in clause 13 of the ICE 4th Edition Conditions of Contract was considered in the case of *Turriff Ltd* v. *Welsh National Water Development Authority* (1980). In that case problems arose with tolerances for precast concrete sewer segments and eventually the contractor abandoned the works on the grounds of impossibility. The employer argued that impossibility meant absolute impossibility without any qualifications and since there was no absolute impossibility the contractor was in breach. The judge declined to accept that impossibility meant absolute impossibility and held that the works were impossible in an ordinary commercial sense.

Responsibility for overcoming illegality or impossibility

At common law, in the absence of express provisions to the contrary, the employer does not warrant that the works can be built. The classic case is *Thorn* v. *London Corporation* (1876) where the contractor was to take down an old bridge and build a new one. The design prepared by the employer's engineer involved the use of caissons which turned out to be useless. The contractor completed the works with a different method and sued for his losses on the grounds that the employer warranted that the bridge could be built to the engineer's design. The House of Lords held that no such warranty could be implied.

Most contracts, however, do have provisions which indicate which party is responsible for overcoming illegality or impossibility. Usually where the employer is responsible for design the contract requires variations to the works to be instructed so that completion can be achieved. Where the contractor is responsible for design the burden of changing the design usually falls on the contractor.

Clause 18.1 – illegal and impossible requirements

Clause 18.1 of NEC 3 requires the contractor to notify the project manager as soon as he becomes aware that the works information requires him to do anything which is illegal or impossible. The clause then states that if the project manager agrees (and by this it presumably means agrees that there is something which is illegal or impossible) the project manager is to give an instruction to change the works information appropriately.

The first point to make is that this is obviously not a frustration clause since it assumes that the contract is capable of being performed. That being the case the clause presumably applies to things which are legally or physically impossible as specified but which can be rectified by change.

The clause does not obviously distinguish between works information provided by the employer and works information provided by the contractor and if there are problems with either the project manager is required to give 'an instruction to change the Works Information'. Note that the wording of the clause is not 'an instruction changing the Works Information'. Such wording would clearly be inappropriate for contractor's design where the problem was in works information provided by the contractor.

The consequence of the project manager giving an instruction to change the works information is compensation event 60.1(1) comes into play. However, that will not always benefit the contractor because if the instruction arises from a fault in his design (even though the fault may not be a defect within the meaning of the contract) clause 61.4 will still prevent any changes to the contract price or completion date.

6.11 *Prevention*

The new clause 19.1 of NEC 3 has the marginal note 'prevention'. However, although so labelled it is not concerned with 'prevention' as normally understood in construction contracts where the term is taken to mean acts or defaults of the employer which prevent the contractor fulfilling his contractual obligations. Such prevention is frequently a matter for consideration in the operation of extension of time and liquidated damages for delay clauses. Clause 19.1 is concerned not with prevention caused by the employer but with prevention arising from matters which have some similarity with those sometimes described as *'force majeure'* or matters beyond the control of the parties.

Force majeure

The expression *'force majeure'* is of French origin. Under the French Civil Code *force majeure* is a defence to a claim for damages for breach of contract. It needs to be shown that the event:

- made performance impossible
- was unforeseeable
- was unavoidable in occurrence and effects

In English law there is no doctrine of *force majeure*. Before 1863 and the case of *Taylor* v. *Caldwell* it was a rule of the law of contract that the parties were absolutely bound to perform any obligations they had undertaken and the fact that performance had become impossible did not provide relief from damages. In *Taylor* v. *Caldwell* a music hall which was to be hired for a concert was destroyed by fire the day before the performance; the court of Queen's Bench held the hirer not liable for damages by implying a term on impossibility of performance.

From this case developed the doctrine of frustration extending the sphere of impossibility to other instances of frustration. On basic legal principles, therefore, it is frustration and not *force majeure* which must be pleaded as a defence in English contract law.

Force majeure does, however, have a place in English law where it is expressly introduced as a contract term – as for example, in MF/1 where it provides grounds for extension of time and termination of the contract.

Contractually based *force majeure* to be effective has to meet the same tests and has to conform with the doctrine of frustration in that there must be no fault attaching to the party using *force majeure* as a defence or a ground for claim. In *Sonat Offshore SA* v. *Amerada Hess Developments Ltd* (1987) a *force majeure* clause entitled Sonat, an oil rig operation, to payment in certain circumstances. The clause applied '. . . when performance is hindered or prevented by strikes (except contractor induced strikes by contractor's personnel) or lockout, riot, war (declared or undeclared), act of God, insurrection, civil disturbances, fire, interference by any Government Authority or other cause beyond the reasonable control of such party . . .'. Arising from the fault of Sonat there was an explosion and severe fire. The Court of Appeal held that '. . . other cause beyond reasonable control . . .' did not include for negligence.

As a general rule, therefore, a party cannot rely on an event constituting *force majeure* within the meaning of such a clause unless it can be shown:

- the occurrence was beyond the control of the party claiming relief
- there were no reasonable steps that party could have taken to avoid or mitigate the consequences of the event

Additionally the courts are disposed to apply to *force majeure* clauses the same guidelines as they apply to the construction of clauses which purport to relieve a party from the consequences of his own negligence.

Beyond the contractor's control

This phrase was given unexpectedly wide meaning by the House of Lords in the case of *Scott Lithgow Ltd* v. *Secretary of State for Defence* (1989). It was ruled that the contractor was entitled to a payment under a provision which included, amongst other things, as grounds for extra payment the phrase 'or any other cause beyond the contractor's control'. Lord Keith said:

> *'Failures by such suppliers or sub-contractors, in breach of their contractual obligations to Scott Lithgow, are not matters which, according to the ordinary use of language, can be regarded as within Scott Lithgow's control.'*

The case concerned nominated specialist suppliers and subcontractors but it may nevertheless have wider applications. Accordingly, many standard forms of contract which originally included the phrase 'beyond the Contractor's control' in relation to payment, extension of time or other matters have been amended to exclude the phrase.

Frustration

At common law a contract is discharged and further performance excused if supervening events make the contract illegal or impossible or render its performance commercially sterile. Such discharge is known as frustration. A plea of frustration acts as a defence to a charge of breach of contract.

In order to be relied on, the events said to have caused frustration must be:

- unforeseen
- unprovided for in the contract
- outside the control of the parties
- beyond the fault of the party claiming frustration as a defence

In the case of *Davis Contractors* v. *Fareham UDC* (1956) Lord Radcliffe said:

> *'Frustration occurs whenever the law recognises that without default of either party a contractual obligation has become incapable of being performed because the circumstances in which performance is called would render it a thing radically different from that which was undertaken by the contract. Non haec in foedera veni. It was not this that I promised to do.'*

In that case a contract to build 78 houses in eight months took 22 months to complete due to labour shortages. The contractor claimed the contract had been frustrated and he was entitled to be reimbursed on a *quantum meruit* basis for the cost incurred. The House of Lords held the contract had not been frustrated but was merely more onerous than had been expected.

Frustration, in the true legal sense of a radical change of obligation, is uncommon in construction contracts. One of the few recorded cases in the UK is *Metropolitan Water Board* v. *Dick Kerr & Co Ltd* (1918) where the onset of World War I led to a two year interruption of progress. It was held that the event was beyond the contemplation of the parties at the time they made the contract and the contractor was entitled to treat the contract as at an end. More recently in a Hong Kong case, *Wong Lai Ying* v. *Chinachem Investment Co Ltd* (1979), a landslip which obliterated the site of building works was held by the Privy Council to be a frustrating event.

Clause 19.1 – prevention

Although the Guidance Notes to NEC 3 state that clause 19.1 is, in effect, a *'force majeure'* clause it is important to note that it is not a conventional *'force majeure'* clause. That is to say, it is not a clause of the type found in many contracts which effectively state the general legal rule that in the absence of express provisions to the contrary, for events beyond the control of the parties, loss lies where it falls. Clause 19.1, taken in conjunction with the compensation event at clause 60.1(19), has the opposite effect. It provides for the employer to bear the time and cost consequences of what it describes as 'prevention'.

Clause 19.1 states that if an event occurs which:

- stops the contractor completing the works, *or*
- stops the contractor completing the works by the date shown on the accepted programme, *and which*
- neither party could prevent, *and*
- an experienced contractor would have judged at the contract date to have had such a small chance of occurring that it would have been unreasonable to have allowed for it, *then*
- the project manager gives an instruction to the contractor stating how to deal with the event

Taken on its own, clause 19.1 does no more than provide a definition and state one of the project manager's duties. But repetition of its definition in clause 60.1(19) makes it a compensation event and repetition in clause 91.7 makes it a specified reason entitling the employer to terminate the contract. These are clearly very important matters and the potential importance of clause 19.1 should not be under-estimated.

For many users of NEC 3 it will be a point of major concern that clause 19.1 defines prevention in terms which are capable of very wide interpretation. A contractor may well be disposed to argue that insolvency of suppliers and subcontractors, that supply of defective materials, that defective work by subcontractors, that defective design by his consultants, that strikes, that accidents and other disturbances, could not have been prevented by either party and that they had such a small chance of occurring that it would have been unreasonable to have allowed for them. The definition goes well beyond what is known in law as *'force majeure'*.

Of particular concern will be the 'small chance of occurring' and the 'unreasonable to have allowed for' tests in the clause. These indicate that even though an event was foreseeable it can still be a clause 19.1 prevention event. They are also difficult tests to examine in dispute resolution proceedings. Apart from the question of which party has the burden of proof for what are, in some respects, negative tests, there are questions as to how properly supportive factual and expert evidence can be assembled.

Another aspect of clause 19.1 which looks troublesome is that it comes into effect either by an event stopping completion of the works or by stopping completion by the date shown on the accepted programme. The clause does not use the defined terms 'Completion' and 'Completion Date' so the meaning of the phrase 'completing the works' is not entirely clear. However, there are clearly two distinct situations when the clause applies: the first being when it is no longer possible to complete the works; the second being when it is no longer possible to complete the works by the planned programme date. The first suggests frustration of the type described earlier in this chapter, the second suggests something well short of frustration. It seems to be concerned simply with delay to completion. But these are very different matters.

Frustration is a rarity in construction contracts, delay is endemic. It cannot be intended that the clause operates for each and every delaying event and questions on when it does operate are likely to turn on the meaning of the word 'stops' in the clause. Does it means stops in an absolute sense such that nothing can be done to overcome the stoppage (or delay to completion) or stops in a lesser sense such that changing plans or increasing resources can avoid the stoppage (or delay to completion)?

Whatever the answers to these questions, the clauses on prevention seem on their face to be a potential gold mine for contractors and a potential minefield for employers. It will be no surprise if they are usually deleted.

Chapter 7
Obligations and responsibilities of the contractor

7.1 Introduction

The words 'obligations' and 'responsibilities' are often used as though they are synonymous. But they are not always the same or interchangeable. An obligation is a burden to be undertaken; a responsibility is a burden to be carried. Thus a contractor may have an obligation to undertake design; he may also have responsibility for design undertaken by others. The difference is obvious.

NEC 3 avoids the word 'obligation' but in section 2 under the heading 'the Contractor's main responsibilities' it does detail a number of obligations. These, however, are by no means the full extent of the contractor's obligations.

Express obligations

The style of NEC 3 in setting out the contractor's obligations is one of its more unusual features. Instead of using the customary word 'shall' to denote an obligation NEC 3 uses, as did ECC 2, present tense verbs such as 'acts', 'notifies', 'obtains'. The word 'shall' appears only in clause 10.1 (actions). But by virtue of the phrase 'shall act as stated in this contract' in that clause it is presumed to operate throughout the rest of the contract.

To find the express obligations of the contractor under NEC 3, therefore, it is necessary to search through the contract for present tense verbs. There are 60 or so applicable to the contractor – the exact number depending upon the particular options used in any contract. They are listed at the end of this chapter under section 7.13 to form a comprehensive schedule of the contractor's express obligations. They are substantially the same as in ECC 2.

Detailed comment in this chapter is only given on section 2 obligations (those in clauses 20 to 27). The remaining obligations are discussed on a clause by clause basis in other chapters.

Implied obligations

Contracts rarely attempt to detail all the obligations of the parties and even with a list of express obligations as long as that in NEC 3 it is usually possible to argue that there are other obligations which should be implied to give the contract business efficacy. Some contracts do specifically exclude implied terms on particular issues and some such as MF/1, do attempt a general exclusion of implied terms by stating that the obligations, rights and liabilities of the parties are only those as expressly stated.

NEC 3 has no general exclusion of implied terms which can clearly be identified as such, although it can be argued that the 'entire agreement' at the new clause 12.4 provides such exclusion. But, in any event, there is very little scope for implied terms on contractor's obligations. This is because NEC 3 relies heavily on detail in the works information to fix obligations. And the contractor's stated obligation in clause 20.1 to 'Provide the Works' (which by definition is comprehensive of the contractor's obligations) is to do so 'in accordance with the Works Information'. This suggests that the contractor's obligations in NEC 3 are mainly those in the works information. This leads to interesting questions on the contractual position under NEC 3 regarding some common obligations under other standard forms on which NEC 3 is silent.

Obligations not stated in NEC 3

To maintain confidentiality

NEC 3 does not contain the provision, commonly found in process and plant contracts for good commercial reasons, that the parties must maintain secrecy and confidentiality about the contract. It may not be possible to imply such a provision so if it is required it is best to include it in the additional conditions under Option Z.

To proceed regularly and diligently

NEC 3 does not directly state any obligation for the contractor to proceed regularly and diligently (or with due expedition and without delay). Nor is there anything in the termination provisions (clause 90), dealing with breach of any such, or similar, obligations. The intention of NEC 3 is to impose discipline on the contractor through the payment scheme, delay damages, and, where included, key dates.

To inspect the site

The usual clause requiring the contractor to inspect the site and to satisfy himself as to the sufficiency of his tender is missing from NEC 3. However it may be that such an obligation can be implied from clause 60.2 which states that in judging physical conditions the contractor is assumed to have taken into account information obtainable from a visual inspection of the site.

To set out the works

There is no express obligation on the contractor in NEC 3 to set out the works. Perhaps it can be argued for construction works that such an obligation is implied from the definition in clause 11.2(13) of 'Provide the Works'. But this is not particularly persuasive for process and plant contracts. To put the matter beyond doubt it is probably best in NEC 3 contracts to deal with setting-out obligations in the works information. This has the added benefit of bringing problems on the accuracy of setting-out information within the scope of the compensation event procedure in so far as the project manager is required to give instructions on interpretation or accuracy of the information.

To perform variations

Most standard forms expressly state the contractor's obligations to perform variations. Some, such as the ICE Conditions of Contract, describe variations as changes being necessary or desirable for the completion or functioning of the works – thereby placing a limit on the scope of the contractor's obligations. Others, like the IChemE forms and MF/1 have financial limits on the value of variations which may be ordered – and also prohibit variations which would prejudice the fulfilment of the contractor's obligations. NEC 3 does not use the word 'variations', nor the increasingly popular replacement word 'changes'. It does not even address the subject of variations directly. Instead it leads towards the contractor's obligation to perform variations by an indirect route:

- the contractor is to provide the works in accordance with the works information – clause 20.1
- the project manager may change the works information by instruction – clause 14.3
- the contractor is to obey the project manager's instructions – clause 27.3

This, however does not address what limitations, if any, apply to the contractor's obligations in respect of variations. The contractor may be able to obtain limitations by using the disputes resolution procedures of the contract but this would be uncertain, time consuming and unsatisfactory as a substitute for a contractual provision. There is, however, a view that far from the project manager's powers to order variations under NEC 3 being near to limitless, they are, in fact, very restricted powers and are confined to making changes in the works information only as expressly mentioned in NEC 3. See Chapter 4, section 9 for comment on this.

To submit interim applications for payment

NEC 3 has a detailed scheme for interim payments to the contractor but, unusually, the contractor's entitlement to payment is not dependent upon his making an application.

To notify on completion

The obligation to decide the date of completion rests with the project manager. There is no obligation on the contractor to notify completion but in the normal course of things he will not be slow in doing so.

To conform to statutes

There is no express obligation in NEC 3 for the contractor to conform to statutes. This, in itself, is not much of a problem since the absence of such a provision does not protect the contractor from unlawful actions. However, in most standard forms the obligation to conform to statutes is accompanied by an obligation to indemnify the employer against claims etc. arising from any breach. This may be covered by the indemnity provisions of clause 83.1 but otherwise it is potentially a serious omission.

7.2 Design obligations, responsibilities and liabilities

As a matter of policy NEC 3 seeks to achieve maximum flexibility on the allocation of design obligations between the parties. The intention is that its standard provisions should be applicable to the entire range of situations between there being no contractor's design and full contractor's design. For any particular contract the extent of the contractor's design obligations is to be determined from the works information.

This is more ambitious than it might at first appear. Other standard forms of contract operate satisfactorily with flexibility in the extent of contractor's design so why not NEC 3?

The difference is that the other standard forms are, in the main, drafted for either employer's design or contractor's design and any flexibility operates within a framework of recognised rules for that type of contract. For example, ICE 6th Edition Conditions of Contract are essentially employer's design and the supervisory role of the engineer in the contract reflects this. The IChemE model forms are essentially contractor's design and the provisions on variations reflect this. NEC 3, however, is drafted to be neutral between the two situations and that presupposes that it is possible for the various provisions of the contract to operate equally well in any situation.

But the potential pitfalls of this approach are only too apparent. Consider, for example, clause 60.3 on unexpected physical conditions. That clause states that if there is inconsistency in the site information the contractor is assumed to have taken into account the physical conditions more favourable to doing the work. Perfectly reasonable, if not perhaps a little generous to the contractor for employer's design and where the contractor is simply building the works. But applied to contractor's design it makes no sense. The essence of sound design is that it should cater for the worst conditions which might be expected, not the best.

Key question on design

Quite apart from the general question raised above on whether a contract can satisfactorily be wholly flexible on design there are three specific key questions which apply to all contracts in which there is some element of design. These are:

- How is the obligation to undertake the design allocated between the parties?
- How is the responsibility for the effectiveness of the design to be allocated between the parties?
- What standard of liability attaches to the party responsible for design? Is it fitness for purpose or the use of reasonable skill and care?

Design obligations under NEC 3

Clause 21.1 of NEC 3 deals with the extent of the contractor's design obligations. It states that the contractor is required to design the parts of the works which the works information states he is to design. This is reasonably clear but see the comment in section 7.4 below on whether a design obligation can be imposed by an instruction changing the works information.

Design responsibility under NEC 3

The intention of NEC 3 is that each party is generally responsible for the design which it undertakes. That follows from the definition of defect in clause 11.2(5) and elsewhere in the contract.

There is no provision in NEC 3 of the type found in the ICE Design and Construct Conditions of Contract and in MF/1 that the contractor is responsible for all the design including that undertaken by or on behalf of the employer. So NEC 3 only provides single point responsibility on design when the works information requires the contractor to undertake either all the design or none of the design.

One possible area of uncertainty on design responsibility is discussed in Chapter 9, section 2 under defects. That arises from the reference in clause 11.2(5) to the contractor's design which the project manager has accepted. Its effect is arguably to transfer design responsibility to the employer.

Design liability under NEC 3

It is generally accepted that in the absence of express provisions to the contrary there is an implied term in design and build contracts that the finished works will be reasonably fit for their intended purpose. See, for example, the case of *IBA* v. *EMI* (1980). The significance of this is that it puts the contractor's liability for his design on a different legal basis from that of a professional designer. The law does not normally imply terms of fitness for purpose into contracts for the supply of professional services. See for example *Greaves Contractors Ltd* v. *Baynham Meikle & Partners* (1975) and many other cases. The duty of a professional designer is to use reasonable skill and care.

In the event of a design failure the difference between the two standards of liability can be critical to the position of the parties. If the contractor's liability is fitness for purpose that is a strict liability and the test for liability is whether the works are fit for their intended purpose. The contractor may have used all reasonable skill and care in his design but if the specified contractual objective is not achieved the contractor will be liable to the employer for damages.

However, if the contractor's liability is limited to skill and care corresponding to that of a professional designer then negligence must be proved to establish breach of duty. And even though design failure may occur the contractor will not be liable if he has used reasonable skill and care.

To relieve the contractor of the higher standard of liability imposed by fitness for purpose some design and build contracts limit the standard of the contractor's design liability to the same as that of a professional designer.

NEC 3 does not have any such limitation of liability in its core clauses and the contractor's liability for his design is almost certainly on a fitness for purpose basis. However, Option X15 does attempt to limit the contractor's liability to reasonable skill and care – although it is arguable that on proper interpretation of its wording it does not actually achieve this. See Chapter 3, section 12 for further comment.

If secondary option X18 (limitation of liability) is included in the contract that may provide certain financial limits on the contractor's liability for his design but this is a different matter than the standard of liability.

7.3 *Providing the works*

Clause 20.1 – obligation to provide the works

NEC 3 avoids the usual lengthy statement of the contractor's general obligations and responsibilities and relies instead on the single short sentence in clause 20.1 stating that the contractor provides the works in accordance with the works information. The key to the effectiveness of this clause lies in the two defined terms 'Provide the Works' and 'Works Information'. The term 'Provide the Works' is defined in clause 11.2(13). It covers both the obligation to complete the works and the obligation to provide whatever is required by the contract. The term 'Works Information' is defined in clause 11.2(19). It specifies and describes the works and details any constraints on the contractor.

Both defined terms are discussed in some detail in Chapter 6 above but the point to be made here (as elsewhere in this book) is that the extent of the contractor's obligations is reliant on the requirements in the works

information. This follows from the simplicity of the wording of clause 20.1 –
and in particular, the words 'in accordance with the Works Information'.
Were it not for the power given to the project manager to change the works
information (clause 14.3) the contractor's obligations under clause 20.1 would
be inadequate in the absence of an express obligation to perform variations
– which the NEC 3 lacks. Clause 20.1, therefore, has to be seen not only as
stating the contractor's obligations to complete the works as originally defined
but also as the starting point of the contractor's obligation to perform
variations.

Note that, by itself, clause 20.1 does not address in any way the matter of
the contractor's entitlement to payment for performance of his obligations.
The clause is not a statement of the type found in some other contracts
that the contractor's price includes for all things necessary to fulfil his obligations. The contractor's entitlement to payment is dependent upon which of
the main options is used for the particular contract.

Clause 20.2 – management obligations

Clause 20.2 applies only in Option F – the management contract. The NEC 3
version of the clause is a considerable improvement on the ECC 2 version
which was ambiguous on the key matter of what work the contractor had to
subcontract and what he could do himself. The NEC 3 clause states firstly,
that the contractor manages his own design, the provision of services and the
construction and installation of the works, secondly, that the contractor is to
subcontract all of these except work which the contract data states that he is
to do himself.

Note that the work the contractor is to do himself is to be stated in the
contract data, and not in the works information as in ECC 2. The entry for
which work the contractor is to do himself is found in the contract data, part
two, form. It seems, therefore, that it is for the contractor to decide what work
he will do himself, not the employer as is the case in some management contracts. The contractor may be restrained, however, from doing too much work
himself as it is to be priced in the contract data as a lump sum or unit-rate
basis for identified activities.

Clause 20.3 – practical implications of design and subcontracting

Clause 20.3 applies in Options C, D, E and F. All are contracts, which are to
some extent cost reimbursable and which assume a close degree of co-
operation and openness between the parties. The clause states that the contractor advises the project manager on the practical implications of the design
of the works and on subcontracting arrangements. Both obligations are aimed
at achieving cost and practical efficiency and are normal for the type of
contract.

Clause 20.4 – forecasts of total actual cost

Clause 20.4, as clause 20.3, applies in Options C, D, E and F. Again it is related to the cost reimbursable nature of the contracts.

The clause requires the contractor to prepare, in consultation with the project manager, regular forecasts of the total defined cost at intervals as stated in the contract data for submission to the project manager. Such forecasts are required from the starting date until completion of the whole of the works. With each forecast the contractor is required to explain any changes from the previous forecast. There is no clear contractual purpose for the forecasts and they appear to be required as management tools for financial awareness and cost control.

7.4 *The contractor's design*

Clause 21.1 – contractor's design

This clause expresses the contractor's obligations for design. It states simply that the contractor designs the parts of the works which the works information states he is to design.

It could be argued from the phrase 'parts of the works' that design by the contractor of the whole of the works is not intended. However, since all the parts constitute the whole it is not thought that the argument has much weight. Of more concern is the argument as to whether design obligations can be imposed on the contractor by instructions from the project manager changing the works information. In many cases such an imposition (if it exists) could be unreasonable and impracticable. It could change the basis of the obligations which the contractor had expected to perform. Such considerations are themselves good arguments against the imposition of design obligations by instruction. A further argument is that clause 21.1 refers to design which the works information 'states' the contractor is to design. And, it can be said, there is a distinction between an instruction changing the works information and an instruction purporting to change that which it 'states'. As to whether an instruction imposing design obligations where no such obligation is stated in the works information is valid there is also the argument the instruction is not changing an obligation in the works information but purporting to add an additional obligation.

One aspect of clause 21.1 which compilers of NEC 3 contract documents should note with care is that it appears to be more concerned with the obligation to design than with responsibility for design. The wording of the clause probably excludes any implication that design obligations fall on the contractor because common-sense interpretation of drawings or instructions suggests that they should. It is, therefore, essential that the works information should state all design obligations and that nothing should be left to chance.

Responsibility for design

As to responsibility for design, the question is not whether the contractor carries responsibility for design which he undertakes (the answer to that is almost certainly that he does) but whether, under the terms of NEC 3 and clause 21.1 in particular, the contractor is responsible for the designs of manufactured products and the like incorporated in the works in the absence of any statement in the works information that he 'designs' those parts of the works. In construction contracts generally implied warranties on fitness for purpose and good quality apply in respect of materials and manufactured products – see for example, the cases of *Young & Marten* v. *McManus Childs* (1969) and *Gloucestershire County Council* v. *Richardson* (1969). However, such warranties can be excluded by express terms. See the case of *Shanks & McEwan (Contractors) Ltd* v. *Strathclyde Regional Council* (1994) in which it was held, in relation to a dispute about defective precast concrete tunnel segments supplied and installed under an ICE 5th Edition contract, that under terms which stated that the contractor was not responsible for design 'unless expressly stated' and there being no such express statement in respect of the tunnel segments, the contractor was not responsible for their design. It can be argued that there is no comparable express exclusion of design liability under NEC 3 and that the usual implied terms remain effective. But that brings into question the meaning of the statement in clause 12.4 that the contract is 'the entire agreement between the parties'. Perhaps one course of action to avoid difficulties with design responsibility is to include a catch-all statement in the works information covering materials and manufactured products.

Clause 21.2 – acceptance of the contractor's design

Clause 21.2 deals with acceptance of particulars of the contractor's design. The clause has three principal elements:

- the contractor's obligation to submit particulars of his design
- reasons for not accepting the design
- prohibition on the contractor from proceeding until the design is accepted

Although clause 21.2 is not expressly limited to design of the permanent works as opposed to the design of the temporary works that limitation can be deduced from clause 23.1 which deals with temporary works albeit that it refers to them as 'Equipment'.

The obligation on the contractor to submit particulars of his design is expressly linked in clause 21.2 to requirements in the works information. In the absence of such requirements the contractor would be entitled to proceed without submitting any particulars for acceptance. That could create difficulties for the project manager in some circumstances but the project manager has the power to remedy the situation by changing the works information (clause 14.3). Such a change would then be a compensation event 60.1(1).

Note that clause 21.2 deals with 'particulars' of the design and not with the contractor's design proposals in a broader sense. Approval of such proposals is a pre-contract function which is formally recognised by the acceptance of the works information provided by the contractor in part two of the contract data and its incorporation into the contract. In the not uncommon event of a dispute arising during construction as to whether the contractor's proposals do fully meet the employer's requirements that is dealt with under NEC 3 by clause 17.1 (ambiguities and discrepancies) and clause 63.8 (assessing compensation events).

NEC 3 does not specify the time for submission of design particulars in any of its clauses or in the standard contract data entries. However in some contracts, for obvious practical reasons, the timescale for the submission of design particulars is important – particularly if there is a technical link with other contracts. In some contracts liquidated damages are specified for late submission of design particulars. In an NEC 3 contract if discipline of this order is required it will have to be introduced through specifications or requirements in the works information, contract data or additional conditions of contract.

NEC 3 does, however, impose a timescale for the project manager to reply to the contractor's submission (clauses 13.3 and 13.4) and the period of reply stated in the contract data. Failure by the project manager to reply in time is a compensation event – clause 60.1(6).

Clause 13.4 requires the project manager to state reasons if his reply to any submission is not an acceptance. The project manager is not restricted in his reasons (clause 13.8) but any reason which is not one stated in the contract is a compensation event – clause 60.1(9).

The only reasons stated in clause 21.2 for not accepting the contractor's design particulars are:

- non-compliance with the works information
- non-compliance with the applicable law

For comment on the implications of acceptance of the contractor's design by the project manager see Chapter 5, section 11.

The prohibition in clause 21.2 on the contractor proceeding with relevant work until his design is accepted is sensible for a variety of reasons – most obviously the avoidance of abortive work.

Clause 21.3 – submission of design in parts

Clause 21.3 states only that the contractor may submit his design for acceptance in parts if the design of each part can be fully assessed. It would be odd if the contractual requirement was otherwise. One of the attractions of contractor's design is the potential for a quick start with the design being finalised as the works proceed.

7.5 Using the contractor's design

Clause 22.1 – employer's use of the contractor's design

Clause 22.1 deals with the employer's right to use the contractor's design for certain purposes. Under the clause the employer may use and copy the contractor's design for any purpose which is either:

- connected with the construction, use, alteration or demolition of the works (unless otherwise stated in the works information), *or*
- is for a purpose stated in the works information

This is a complex legal subject which can easily give rise to disputes on copyright and patents. Most standard process and plant forms are significantly more detailed than NEC 3 and express the employer's rights in terms of restricted licences. A question, for example, which might be asked of NEC 3 is does the phrase in clause 22.1 'any purpose connected with construction, use, alteration, or demolition' cover extensions of the works. The answer to that question it is suggested is probably not but it does indicate the care which needs to be taken by both parties in any statement they make in the contract data relating to use of the contractor's design.

7.6 Design of equipment

Equipment is defined in clause 11.2(7) as items provided by the contractor and used by him to provide the works and which the works information does not require him to include in the works.

In traditional construction contracts such equipment would usually come within the scope of either 'temporary works' or 'contractor's equipment'.

Clause 23.1 – design of equipment

Clause 23.1 states the obligation of the contractor to submit particulars of the design of equipment for acceptance – but only when instructed to do so by the project manager. It also states that reasons for not accepting the design are that the design will not allow the contractor to provide the works in accordance with:

- the works information
- the accepted contractor's design, *or*
- the applicable law

There are some similarities of procedure between clause 23.1 and clause 21.2 (submission of design of parts of the works) in that the project manager can reject a design for any reason. However there are also some notable differences. The first is that clause 23.1 is activated by a project manager's instruction. And that is a communication which imposes on the contractor the obligation to reply within the stated period for reply. The second difference is that there is no prohibition in clause 23.1 on the contractor proceeding with his work until acceptance of the design is received.

This latter point is one of considerable practical importance. It emphasises that the contractor can proceed at his own risk but if he then receives a notice of non-acceptance from the project manager he is obliged by clause 13.4 to resubmit his design taking into account the reasons given for non-acceptance.

7.7 People

NEC 3, as part of its good management strategy, places considerable importance on the quality of key staff employed by the contractor. Firstly, the contractor is required to state in part two of the contract data the names, qualifications and experience of key people. Clause 24 then deals with the contractor's obligations in respect of key people and other employees.

Clause 24.1 – key persons

The first obligation stated in clause 24.1 is that the contractor should employ each key person named in the contract data to do the job described for him or should employ a replacement person accepted by the project manager. It is up to the employer, however, to specify in the instructions to tenderers how many key persons and for what jobs entries are to be made in the contract data. The numbers will obviously depend on the complexity of the project.

Failure by the contractor to employ either named key people or accepted replacements is a breach of contract on the part of the contractor. But, as is often the case with the contractor's breaches of procedural regulations, the employer's remedies are none too apparent. In serious cases the project manager could arguably give an instruction suspending work under clause 34.1 until the breach was remedied – relying on clause 61.4 to prevent the contractor recovering cost and delay as a compensation event. In an extreme case the contractor's breach might be classed as a default under clause 91.2 entitling the employer to terminate.

The second obligation in clause 24.1 is that the contractor shall submit the name, qualifications and experience of each proposed replacement person to the project manager for acceptance. This obligation it is suggested applies only in respect of named key persons and not to other key persons employed by the contractor who are not named in the contract data.

The only reason stated in clause 24.1 for the project manager not to accept a proposed replacement is that his qualifications and experience are not as good as those of the person being replaced. Non-acceptance for any other reason is a compensation event (clause 13.8). It is right that the contractor should not be unduly restricted in who he employs as key persons because regard must be had to such practical matters as staff changes and other workload commitments.

Clause 24.2 – removal of an employee

Clause 24.2 is of wider application than clause 24.1 in that it refers to 'employees' rather than to 'key persons'.

The clause gives the project manager the power to instruct the contractor to remove an employee – but only after having stated his reasons for the instruction. The contractor is obliged to respond such that from one day after the instruction the employee is to have no further connection with the work included in the contract.

The project manager's power here is quite draconian and the clause goes far beyond the usual clause in standard forms relating to the removal of workpeople from site for misconduct or negligence. Firstly, there is no stated restriction on the project manager's reasons. However, unreasonable use by the project manager of his powers would be a breach of clause 10.1 (obligation to act in a spirit of mutual trust and co-operation) and the contractor might then be able to argue for a compensation event under clause 60.1. Secondly, and perhaps of more concern is the timescale for the removal of the employee and the prohibition on his future connection with the contract. Finding a suitable replacement within a day seems a difficult enough burden for the contractor but banning the employee from work connected with the contract, not merely removing him from the site, seems to be going too far.

Any project manager considering exercising his powers under clause 24.2 should give some thought to his potential legal liabilities to the employee concerned.

7.8 Working with the employer and others

Clauses 25.1 to 25.3 of NEC 3 come under the marginal note 'Working with the Employer and Others'. Clause 25.1 is much the same as the corresponding ECC 2 which had the marginal note 'Co-operation'. Clause 25.2 is a repositioned version of parts of ECC 2 clause 33.2 dealing with the provisions of services. Clause 25.3 is completely new to NEC 3. It deals with the employer's right to recover costs incurred by the contractor's failure to achieve key dates.

Clause 25.1

The first sentence of clause 25.1 requires the contractor to co-operate with others in obtaining and providing information which they need in connection with the works. The second sentence requires the contractor to co-operate with others and to share the working areas with them as stated in the works information.

The clause can be read in various ways. Firstly, as three separate obligations – to co-operate with others in obtaining and providing information; to co-operate with others generally; and to share the working areas with others as stated in the works information. Secondly, as the same three obligations but with the obligation to co-operate with others generally being qualified by the concluding words of the clause 'as stated in the works information'. Thirdly, as two obligations – to co-operate with others in obtaining and providing information as stated in the works information, and to share the working areas with others as stated in the works information. Fourthly, as three obligations all qualified by that which is stated in the works information.

Having regard to the compensation event at clause 60.1(5) which applies when the employer or others do not work within the times stated on the accepted programme, or do not work within the conditions stated in the works information, or carry out work on the site which is not stated in the works information, it is clearly important there are no deficiencies in the works information. Perhaps the safest approach therefore to the interpretation of clause 25.1 is to assume the fourth of the above mentioned possibilities.

Clause 25.2

The first sentence of clause 25.2 states an obligation which falls on both parties, namely that the employer and the contractor are to provide services and other things as stated in the works information. The second sentence states that any cost incurred by the employer as a result of the contractor not providing the specified services and other things is to be assessed by the project manager and paid by the contractor.

The extent of the obligation to provide services and things under the first sentence of the clause is apparently restricted only by the content of the works information. And it is probably intended to cover services and things provided to others working on the site as well as services and things the employer might provide to the contractor (or the reverse). On its wording the obligation can even extend to the provision of services and things remote from the site provided that they are stipulated in the works information.

The remedy for non-provision of services and things set out in the second sentence of clause 25.2 applies only to the employer. The contractor's remedy is through the compensation event stated in clause 60.1(3). They are not entirely matching remedies as clause 25.2 is silent as to when the employer's rights materialise whereas clause 60.1(3) links the entitlement to failures by the employer to provide things by dates on the accepted programme. There is also the possibility of a limit on the contractor's financial liability to the employer if secondary option X18 (limitation of liability) is included in the contract.

Clause 25.3

The sole purpose of clause 25.3, which is new to NEC 3, is to provide the employer with a contractual remedy should the contractor fail to achieve the conditions set for key dates. It stands in place of any right the employer might have to sue for breach of contract and is far easier to apply. But, as with clause 25.2, the contractor's liability may be limited if secondary option X18 applies.

Clause 25.3 states:

- if the project manager decides that the work does not meet the condition stated for a key date by the date stated, *and*
- as a result the employer incurs additional cost, *either*
- in carrying out work or the same project, *or*
- by paying others to carry out work in the same project, *then*
- the additional cost which the employer has paid, or will incur, is paid by the employer
- such cost to be assessed by the project manager within four weeks of the date when the condition for the key date is met, *and*
- the employer's right to recover additional costs is his only right in the circumstances

Without a clause such as clause 25.3 the employer would have to rely on his common law rights to sue for damages for breach of contract if conditions for key dates were not achieved. Such an action would not be without its difficulties – particularly if the stipulated conditions could be likened to partial completions and the contract included liquidated damages for late completion. As it is, clause 25.3 in its final sentence, makes clear that it replaces, rather than stands as an alternative to, any damages remedy.

This clear exclusion of common law rights is not found in other clauses in NEC 3 which give the employer rights to recover costs arising from the contractor's defaults – for example, clauses 25.2, 40.6 and 45.1.

An aspect of the introduction of key dates to NEC 3 contracts which needs to be given serious consideration in the preparation of particular contracts is that a high proportion of disputes which find their way to adjudication, arbitration or litigation, are disputes about whether or not completions were achieved by stipulated dates and whether or not they were late completions. The inclusion of conditions for key dates can only increase the potential for disputes, and given that fulfilment of conditions may be even less of an exact science than the fulfilment of completions, and given that a multitude of key dates on any one contract is possible, there is a strong probability that contracts with conditions for key dates will be more dispute prone than those without them.

7.9 *Subcontracting*

The provisions in NEC 3 for the regulation of subcontracting are substantially the same as in ECC 2. They are strict and detailed. Strict, because appointment of a subcontractor for substantial work before acceptance by the project manager is expressly made grounds for termination of the contract (clause 91.2). Detailed, because the provisions extend to control over the terms of subcontracts.

This degree of regulation goes against the trend of other standard forms of contract where the contractor's freedom to subcontract as he thinks fit has been introduced as being in keeping with modern commercial practice. However NEC 3 is designed to suit a variety of procurement options, some of which are cost reimbursable, and it is normal to have strict controls on subcontracting in such contracts.

Nominated subcontracting

NEC 3 does not provide expressly for nominated subcontracting so contractually all subcontractors are to be regarded as domestic subcontractors whether or not they are named or otherwise fixed by the requirements of the works information.

This can create a problem for the main contractor if the terms of business of the named subcontractor cannot be brought into line with those of the main contract. In such circumstances it is suggested that the contractor should seek instructions from the project manager so that changes are made in the works information to accommodate the situation.

Clause 26.1 – responsibility for subcontractors

Clause 26.1 has two provisions. The first confirms the contractor's responsibility under the contract for work which is subcontracted. It does this by stating that the contractor is responsible for performing the contract as if he had not subcontracted. A similar provision is found in most standard forms but it probably is more of a contractual safeguard than of strict legal necessity. Only if there are words in the contract suggesting that the contractor is entitled to some contractual relief for the defaults of his subcontractors can the contractor claim such relief.

The second provision of clause 26.1 states that the contract applies as if a subcontractor's employees and equipment are the contractor's. This is potentially more complex in contractual and legal terms than the first provision. For example, it would seem to give the project manager the right to impose the provisions of clause 24 (people) on subcontractors. And it may have implications on the extent of the contractor's liability for the negligence of a subcontractor's employees.

Clause 26.2 – acceptance of subcontractors

Clause 26.2 deals with the acceptance of subcontractors. The contractor is required to submit the name of each proposed subcontractor for acceptance.

And the contractor is not permitted to appoint a subcontractor until the project manager has accepted him.

The clause does not detail the criteria to be used by the project manager in examining the subcontractor's credentials (e.g. – operates a QA system; has suitable experience; is financially sound) but it merely states that a reason for not accepting a subcontractor is that his appointment will not allow the contractor to provide the works. This will not often be a straightforward matter of fact. More often than not it will be a matter of opinion. Why would the contractor propose a subcontractor who will not allow him to provide the works? So unless the reason for non-acceptance is simply that the proposed subcontractor is not the firm named in the works information and therefore, as a fact, the appointment will not allow the contractor to provide the works in accordance with the contract, or similar clear circumstances apply, there is likely to be a difference of opinion between the contractor and the project manager on the matter. Unless this is resolved by agreement the adjudicator will have to be brought in. But for practical and administrative reasons the contractor may already have been obliged to propose (and appoint) an alternative subcontractor. In such a case the task of the adjudicator would then be to determine if the contractor was entitled to a compensation event for the non-acceptance.

Of course, if the project manager's reason for non-acceptance of a subcontractor is other than the stated reason of not allowing the contractor to provide the works the contractor is entitled to a compensation event under clause 60.1(9).

One aspect of clause 26.2 which may cause some concern is that there is no express exception from the acceptance procedure for minor subcontracts or subcontracts for the supply of plant and labour only.

Clause 26.3 – conditions of subcontracts

Clause 26.3 deals with the conditions of contract for subcontracts. Instead of such conditions being left solely as a commercial matter for the contractor to decide – as is the case with most standard forms (except for certain cost-reimbursable contracts) – NEC 3 imposes a measure of control on the conditions. The contractor is required to submit the proposed conditions of contract for each subcontract to the project manager for acceptance unless:

- an NEC contract is proposed, *or*
- the project manager has agreed that no submission is required

This latter point seems to be a matter for the project manager's absolute discretion.

Clause 26.3 further provides that the contractor shall not appoint a subcontractor until the project manager has approved the conditions. The clause states as the reasons for non-acceptance:

- the conditions will not allow the contractor to provide the works, *or*
- the conditions do not include a statement that the parties to the subcontract shall act in a spirit of mutual trust and co-operation

As discussed there is scope for dispute on what will, or will not, allow the contractor to provide the works. But subcontractors should welcome the employer's concern that subcontracts should include for mutual trust and co-operation. However to the extent that the employer might be seen in law to be taking on some responsibility for the terms of subcontracts, the project manager in exercising his discretion on whether or not to concern himself with the conditions of subcontracts may have to be careful that he does not leave the employer exposed to liability to subcontractors for unfair subcontracts.

Clause 26.4 – contract data for subcontracts

Clause 26.4 applies only in main options C, D, E and F. It extends the control of the project manager over subcontracts so that he is entitled to examine the contract data of proposed subcontracts.

The clause applies when:

- an NEC contract is proposed, *or*
- when the project manager instructs the contractor to make a submission of proposed contract data

The only stated reason for non-acceptance is that the proposed contract data will not allow the contractor to provide the works.

The purpose of this clause is presumably to protect the employer's commercial interests.

7.10 *Other responsibilities*

Four clauses appear in NEC 3 under the marginal note of 'Other responsibilities'. These are:

- clause 27.1 – approval of contractor's design by others
- clause 27.2 – contractor to provide access to work being done
- clause 27.3 – contractor to obey instructions
- clause 27.4 – contractor to act in accordance with health and safety requirements

None of these clauses are new to NEC 3, or substantially changed from ECC 2, but they are re-titled and re-arranged. In particular, clause 27.2 was clause 28.1 in ECC 2; clause 27.3 was clause 29.1; and clause 27.4 was clause 18.1.

Clause 27.1 – approval from others

Clause 27.1 is one of the shortest clauses in NEC 3 but its brevity belies its significance. The clause simply states that the contractor obtains approval of his design from 'Others' where necessary. The danger of the clause is that it does not obviously reveal its intention or its scope. In particular it does not state that the contractor obtains approvals as required by the works information. In other words the clause operates differently from much of NEC 3. However in doing so it leaves the contractor with the responsibility of obtaining all necessary approvals for his design which are required by statute or otherwise.

Contractors taking on design obligations under NEC 3 need to exercise the greatest caution, therefore, as to what approvals are required. The most obvious example is planning consent. In the event of problems on approvals developing various clauses of NEC 3 could come into play. Thus, delay would invoke clause 16.1 on early warning; illegality would invoke clause 18.1.

Clause 27.2 – access to work

This clause states the obligation of the contractor to provide access to the project manager, the supervisor, and others notified by the project manager, to work being done and to plant and materials being stored for the project managers, the supervisor, and others. However, the clause is poorly worded and it is almost certainly intended to apply to access to work and storage of goods and materials of the contractor and subcontractors whether on or off the site, rather than the storage of materials for individuals.

The contractor's obligations are not stated in terms of requirements in the works information and the contractor may have difficulty in recovering costs of requirements he considers to be excessive. Disputes on this could easily develop. For example, the phrase 'provides access' could be argued to extend to an obligation on the contractor to provide telescopic lifting platforms for the supervisor if the supervisor deems it necessary. Alternatively, it could simply mean that the contractor is to allow the supervisor use of access facilities already in place or being used by the contractor.

Clause 27.3 – contractor to obey instructions

Clause 27.3 is one of the most important provisions in NEC 3. It requires the contractor to obey an instruction which is in accordance with the contract which is given to him by the project manager or the supervisor.

The importance of clause 27.3 is that in conjunction with clause 20.1 (providing the works) and clause 14.3 (changing the works information) it provides for variation of the works. It is, however, quite a difficult clause in that it restricts the instructions the contractor is to obey to those given 'in accordance with this contract'. This presupposes, quite rightly, that there may be two types of instructions – those given in accordance with the contract, and those which are not in accordance. The distinction between the two should be obvious to the extent that for an instruction given in accordance with the contract it should be possible, and indeed should be good practice, for the clause of the contract under which it is given to be identified. However, if no such identification is given, or if the instruction is otherwise disputed by the contractor as being in accordance with the contract, two questions emerge – one being, can the contractor refuse to carry out the instruction, or alternatively, can the contractor claim reimbursement for complying with an instruction not given in accordance with the contract?

Various clauses of NEC 3 suggest that the contractor should comply with instructions even if he disputes that they are validly given – in particular clause 10.1 (requirement to act in a spirit of mutual trust and co-operation) and clauses W1.3(9) and W2.3(9) (requirement to proceed as if disputed matter was not disputed). But matters which might weigh more heavily on a contractor's mind would be that by failing to comply he might be in default in failing to provide the works in accordance with the works information, or worse, in default within the scope of termination provisions. As to reimbursement of costs for complying with an instruction later found not to have been given in accordance with the contract, the contractor's entitlement may depend upon whether the instruction can be treated as a compensation event or whether the instruction is so evidently out of order that the contractor can be said to have proceeded at his own risk (and cost). The legal question is: does the employer stand behind all instructions given the project manager or the supervisor or only those instructions given in accordance with the contract? The answer is probably – only the latter.

Clause 27.4 – health and safety requirements

Clause 27.4 requires the contractor to act in accordance with the health and safety requirements stated in the works information.

This clause does not impact on the contractor's obligation to comply with statutory health and safety regulations – whether or not they are stated in the works information. It can, therefore, be taken as applying to non-statutory matters such as the particularised requirements of utilities companies, transport bodies and the like.

7.11 Express obligations of the contractor

Core clauses

10.1 – to act as stated in the contract and in a spirit of mutual trust and co-operation
13.1 – to communicate in a form which can be read, copied and recorded
13.3 – to reply to a communication within the period for reply
13.4 – to resubmit a communication which is not accepted within the period for reply
13.7 – to communicate notifications separately from other communications
16.1 – to give early warning of matters with delay, cost or performance implications

16.3 – to co-operate at risk reduction meetings

17.1 – to give notice of ambiguities or inconsistencies in the documents

18.1 – to give notice of any illegality or impossibility in the works information

20.1 – to provide the works in accordance with the works information

21.1 – to design such parts of the works as stated in the works information

21.2 – to submit particulars of his design for acceptance

23.1 – to submit when instructed particulars of design of items of equipment

24.1 – to employ key persons as stated in the contract data or acceptable replacements. To submit relevant details of proposed replacements

24.2 – to remove any employee on the project manager's instructions

25.1 – to co-operate with others in obtaining and providing information. To co-operate with others and to share the working areas with others as stated in the works information

25.2 – to provide services and other things as stated in the works information and to pay the assessed cost of not providing such services and other things

25.3 – to pay any additional cost incurred by the employer as a result of failure to achieve key dates

26.2 – to submit the names of proposed subcontractors for acceptance

26.3 – to submit the proposed conditions of contract for each subcontract for acceptance

27.1 – to obtain approval of his own design from others where necessary

27.2 – to provide access to the works to the project manager, supervisor and others

27.3 – to obey instructions given by the project manager or the supervisor which are in accordance with the contract

27.4 – to act in accordance with health and safety requirements stated in the works information

30.1 – to do the work so that completion is on or before the completion date

30.3 – to do the work so that the condition stated for each key date is met by the key date

31.1 – to submit a programme for acceptance within the period stated in the contract data

31.2 – to show various details in each programme

32.1 – to show various details in revised programmes

32.2 – to submit a revised programme when instructed to or at intervals as required in the contract data

36.1 – to submit details of assessment with each quotation for acceleration

36.2 – to submit a quotation for acceleration when so instructed or to give reasons for not doing so

40.2 – to provide materials, facilities and samples for tests and inspections as stated in the works information

40.3 – to notify the supervisor of tests and inspections before they start and to notify the supervisor of the results of tests and inspections. To notify the supervisor before doing work which would obstruct tests or inspections

40.4 – to correct defects revealed by tests or inspections and to repeat such tests or inspections

40.6 – to pay the assessed cost incurred by the employer in repeating tests or inspections

42.1 – to carry out searches as instructed by the supervisor

42.2 – to notify the supervisor of defects found before the defects date

43.1 – to correct defects

43.2 – to correct notified defects before the end of the defects correction period

44.2 – to submit a quotation for reduced prices or earlier completion in the event of a change to the works information being considered to avoid correcting a default

45.1 – to pay the assessed costs of having defects not corrected within the defects correction period corrected by others

45.2 – to pay the assessed costs of defects not corrected because access was not given

51.1 – to pay the employer if an interim assessment reduces the amount due from that already paid

61.1 – to put instructions or changed decisions into effect

61.3 – to give notice of any event believed to be a compensation event and to do so within eight weeks of becoming aware of the event

61.4 – to submit instructions for compensation events if instructed to do so

61.6 – to base assessments for compensation events on any assumptions stated by the project manager

62.1 – to submit alternative quotations for compensation events if instructed to do so

62.2 – to submit detail of assessments with quotations for compensation events

62.3 – to submit quotations for compensation events within three weeks of being instructed to do so

62.4 – to submit revised quotations for compensation events within three weeks of being instructed to do so

72.1 – to remove equipment from the site when it is no longer needed

73.1 – to notify the finding of any object of value, historical or other interest

81.1 – to carry risks which are not the employer's risk from the starting date until the defects certificate is issued

82.1 – to make good loss or damage to the works until the defects certificate is issued

83.1 – to indemnify the employer against claims due to contractor's risks

84.1 – to provide insurances as required by the contract

85.1 – to submit insurance policies and certificates for acceptance

85.3 – to comply with the terms and conditions of insurance policies

86.1 – to pay the costs incurred by the employer in covering insurances which are the contractor's responsibility

92.2 – to leave the working areas and remove equipment on termination

Option B

NIL

Options C, D, E, & F

20.3 – to advise the project manager on the practical implications of the design of the works and on subcontracting arrangements

20.4 – to prepare forecasts of the total actual cost for the whole of the works

26.4 – to submit the proposed contract data for each subcontract for acceptance

36.3/36.4 – to submit a subcontractor's proposal to accelerate for acceptance

52.2 – to keep records of costs and payments

52.3 – to allow the project manager to inspect accounts and records

Option F (only)

20.2 – to manage the contractor's design and the construction and installation of the works. To subcontract such design, construction and installation as not stated in the works information to be done by the contractor. To do work not stated in the works information to be subcontracted himself or to subcontract it

Options W1 and W2

W1.2(1)/ – to appoint any adjudicator under the NEC Adjudicator's
W2.2(1)   Contract

W1.3(1) – to notify disputes and to refer to adjudication in accordance with the 'Adjudication Table'

W2.3(1) – to give notice to the employer before referring a dispute to the adjudicator

W1.3(6)/ – to copy to the employer any communication with the
W2.3(6)   adjudicator

W1.3(9)/ – to proceed with matters in dispute as though not disputed until
W2.3(9)   the adjudicator's decision is notified

Option X4 – Parent company guarantee

X4.1 – to give the employer a parent company guarantee in a form set out in the works information

Option X7 – Delay damages

X7.1 – to pay delay damages as stated in the contract data from the completion date until completion or take over

Option X13 – Performance bond

X13.1 – to give the employer a performance bond for the amount stated in the contract data and in the form set out in the works information

Option X14 – Advance payment to the contractor

X14.3 – to repay advanced payments to the employer in instalments as stated in the contract data

Option X17 – Low performance damages

X17.1 – to pay low performance damages as stated in the contract data for defects included in the defects certificate showing low performance

7.12 *Express prohibitions on the contractor*

21.2 – not to proceed with work until the project manager has accepted the design
26.2 – not to appoint a subcontractor without the project manager's acceptance
26.3 – not to appoint a subcontractor without the project manager's acceptance of the terms of the subcontract
30.1 – not to start work on site before the first access date
41.1 – not to bring to the working areas, plant and materials to be tested or inspected before delivery
61.2 – not to put into effect a proposed instruction or a proposed changed decision
90.5 – not to do further work after a termination certificate has been raised

W1.3(2)   – not to refer disputes to adjudication unless notified and referred within the times in the adjudication table

W1.4(1)/   – not to refer a dispute to a tribunal unless it has first been referred
W2.4(1)   to adjudication

W1.4(6)/   – not to call the adjudicator as a witness in tribunal proceedings
W2.4(5)

Chapter 8
Time (and related matters)

8.1 Introduction

Section 3 of NEC 3 entitled 'Time' contains provisions on a variety of important matters, including:

- commencement
- completion
- programmes
- use of the site
- access to the site
- suspension of work (stopping and re-starting)
- take-over
- use before take-over
- acceleration

The principal change from ECC 2 to NEC 3 is that the provisions in NEC 3 relating to completion, programming and acceleration all contain references to key dates. Lesser changes are that NEC 3 refers to 'access to and use of the site' rather than to 'possession of the site'; that the ECC 2 provisions on facilities and services are resited (now to be found in NEC 3 clause 25.2); that the ECC 2 provisions for re-possession of the site are omitted; and that the lengthy list of programming requirements in clause 31.2 is re-arranged. Apart from these changes, section 3 of NEC 3 is much the same as section 3 of ECC 2.

It remains the case that although section 3 is very detailed in the programming requirements it is, compared with other construction contracts, exceptionally brief in its treatment of time related matters generally. It deals with the important matters of commencement and the obligation to complete on time in a single sentence. It leaves other important matters such as sectional completion and delay damages to be dealt with in secondary option clauses. The overall effect is to convey the impression that time related matters under NEC 3 (programming apart) are matters of simplicity. Unfortunately, this is something of an illusion. Ten years of usage of ECC 2 before its replacement by NEC 3 showed that types of disputes on time related matters which plague traditional construction contracts are no less frequent under NEC contracts. Under NEC 3, however, turning to the contract is not much help in resolving such disputes. Such is its economy of wording that the old maxim of the less said the better does not apply here.

Commencement and progress

Particularly conspicuous by their absence are any express requirements in NEC 3 that:

- the contractor should start on or about a particular date
- that the contractor should proceed with due expedition and/or regularly and diligently
- that the contractor should use his best endeavours to prevent or reduce delay

It may be the intention of NEC 3 that compliance with such requirements follows naturally from compliance with the detailed requirements on programming. But, detailed as the programme requirements are, they do not expressly require the contractor to match his progress with his programme. Consequently it is unlikely that the programme requirements of NEC 3 can be taken as imposing binding contractual obligations on commencement and rates of progress. Nor should it be assumed that terms on prompt commencement and regular progress can be implied as a matter of general law if not be expressed. The Court of Appeal decision in the case of *GLC* v. *Cleveland Bridge & Engineering Ltd* (1986) suggests that where there are no express terms on progress they will not be implied and that where the contract simply states the obligation of the contractor to be to finish on time then he is entitled to proceed at his own pace in doing so. Moreover, the absence in NEC 3 of any references to prompt commencement or rates of progress in the termination clauses of section 9 adds to the argument that such terms should not be implied.

It is possible that NEC 3 is intentionally indifferent to the contractor's rate of progress. But that is not readily compatible with the emphasis put on the programme or with the broad policy of the contract on good project management.

Damages for delay

Section 3 of NEC 3 says nothing on the contractor's liability for damages (liquidated or otherwise) for late completion. The contract relies on the inclusion of secondary option X7 for liquidated damages or the application of common law for unliquidated damages.

Sectional completions

Similarly section 3 is silent on sectional completions. For these NEC 3 relies on the inclusion of secondary option X5. Note, however, that some clauses in section 3 do refer to a 'part' of the works – although 'part' is neither a defined term nor an identified term of NEC 3.

When Option X5 is included all references in section 3 clauses to the works, completion and the completion date are to be read in the plural and as applying to sections (clause X5.1).

Suspension of work

NEC 3 does not use the phrase 'suspension of work' nor does it state in any detail the provisions which normally apply to suspensions. It simply gives the project manager powers to instruct the contractor to stop and to restart any work (clause 34.1). The financial implications of such an instruction are dealt with as a compensation event (clause 60.1(4)). Prolonged stoppages (exceeding thirteen weeks) are grounds for termination (clause 91.6).

The contractor is not given under NEC 3 the general right, now common in other construction contracts, to suspend work in the event of late payment but, if the Housing Grants, Construction and Regeneration Act 1996 applies there is a statutory right to suspend, and this is recognised in secondary option Y(UK)2 at clause Y2.4. Note, however, that under clause 91.4 the contractor may terminate the contract if a certified amount is not paid within thirteen weeks.

Take-over

In traditional contracts take-over usually marks the point when responsibility for care of the works passes from the contractor to the employer. And that usually occurs when the contractor achieves completion or when the employer begins to use the works or parts of the works. NEC 3 broadly follows traditional practice in that take-over follows completion or use by the employer but take over in NEC 3 lacks the formality it is given in some other contracts.

Unlike completion, take-over is not a defined term of NEC 3 and its meaning is left to be determined from clause 35. Essentially it is a factual state of affairs which the project manager is required to identify by issuing a certificate. There is no mention in the clause of formal take-over tests and if required they have to be detailed in the works information or in special clauses.

An obvious purpose of identifying take-over in NEC 3 is that after take-over, loss or damage to the works is an employer's risk (clause 80.1). Another is that take-over activates compensation event 60.1(15) which relates to take-over of a part of the works before completion. But examination of the detail of clause 35 shows that it perhaps has a more fundamental purpose in that it allows parts of the works (as well as identified sections) to be treated as contractual entities. However it should be noted that although NEC 3 provides for take-over of parts of the works, unlike most other contracts, it does not provide that defects liability periods commence at take-over. For further comment on this see Chapter 9.

8.2 Starting and completion

Clause 30.1 – starting and completion

Clause 30.1 contains two important and distinct provisions:

- the contractor is not permitted to start work on the site until the first access date, *and*
- the work is to be completed on or before the completion date

The first of these on starting is a prohibition and not an obligation. It relates only to work on the site and it is not intended to deter a start to design work or off-site preparatory production.

Access dates are identified by the employer in part one of the contract data for parts of the site and presumably (although it is by no means certain) the reference in clause 30.1 to 'the first access date' means the first possession date for each part and not merely the first date listed in the contract data.

The brevity of the second provision in clause 30.1 – that completion shall be achieved on or before the completion date – has been touched upon in section 8.1. The provision says nothing on when the work is to commence or whether the contractor is to proceed regularly and diligently. It simply imposes the obligation to complete on time or before. It will, however, apply to sections if secondary option X5 is included in the contract.

One important point which comes out of the provision is the contractor's entitlement to complete early if he is able to do so. However the contractual effect of this can be diluted if the employer exercises his right to state in the contract data that he is not willing to take over the works before the completion date.

Note that the wording used in clause 30.1 in relation to what has to be done before completion is 'does the work' and not 'provides the works'. This is consistent with the part of clause 11.2(2) which defines completion as when the contractor has done 'all the work' which the works information states he is to do by the completion date. Its impact is that clause 30.1 relates only to such work as is expressly required to be completed within the set time and not to the more general obligation of the contractor to provide the works. Where the second part of clause 11.2(2) applies (work the contractor is to do by completion not stated in the works information) completion is when the contractor has done all the work necessary for the employer to use the works and for others to do their work. This also is probably a lesser obligation than providing the works.

For detailed comment on clause 11.2(2) and on the meaning of 'completion' see Chapter 6, section 3.

Clause 30.2 – deciding and certifying completion

This clause, like clause 30.1, also contains two important and distinct provisions:

- the project manager decides the date of completion
- the project manager certifies completion within one week of completion

The true meaning of the first of these provisions is of great contractual significance. On ordinary reading the clause suggests that the parties have agreed that the project manager should decide the date of completion and that is the end of the matter so that it is not open to dispute. However, if it can be said that the project manager's decision is an action within the meaning of clause W1.3(1) (adjudication) or is otherwise not intended to be final then it may be open to dispute. But note that although clauses W1.3(5) and W2.3(4) both expressly empower an adjudicator to open up and review the project manager's actions and inactions neither expressly empowers an adjudicator to open up and review the project manager's decisions.

A further point to consider is that unless the project manager's decision is truly final the reference in clause 30.2 to the decision is superfluous since the obligation to certify completion fulfils by itself all contractual needs.

Quite apart from this important legal question there are some practical aspects of clause 30.2 to be considered. The problem is that the contractor has no entitlement under NEC 3 to apply for the completion certificate, less still an obligation to do so. It is not even clear how the project manager's decision is to be given. Consequently if the contractor and the project manager are in disagreement on whether or not completion has been achieved the contract offers little guidance on procedure. Clause 13 on communications does not appear to take effect. And until the project manager has made his decision he is not in breach of his obligation to certify completion.

There is no provision in the contract for deemed completion and one effect of the second provision of clause 30.2 that the project manager shall certify completion within one week of completion could be to throw into doubt the validity of any certificate overdue by longer than one week. Where there is proven delay in issuing a completion certificate, and backdating may be evidence of this, the contractor may have a remedy under compensation event 60.1(18) – breach of contract by the employer – on the basis that the employer is responsible for the project manager's defaults.

Clause 30.3 – key dates

Clause 30.3, which is new to NEC 3, requires the contractor to do the work so that the condition stated for each key date is met by the key date.

It is not clear if the clause is intended to serve any purpose other than to formally state the contractor's obligation in respect of key dates – which can, in any event, be reasonably derived from clause 11.2(9) (definition of key date) and clause 25.3 (failure to meet a key date). It might be thought that one purpose of the clause is to put key dates on the same contractual footing as sectional completion dates but it is doubtful if this is the case as there is no requirement in clause 30.3, or elsewhere in NEC 3, that the project manager should certify achievement of key dates. However, this may be an unintended omission and for parties wishing to have certification of achievement it needs only minimal redrafting of clauses 30.1 and 30.2 to include for key dates – clause 30.3 is then redundant.

8.3 Programmes

Clause 31.1 – submission of programmes

NEC 3 relies on there being an accepted programme. The contractor may have identified a programme in the contract data in which case that will normally become the first 'Accepted Programme'. Clause 31.1 requires that if there is no such identified programme then the contractor is to submit a first programme for acceptance within the period stated in the contract data. This is a period entered in part one of the contract data by the employer.

The contract does not deal expressly with the position if the project manager finds the programme identified in the contract data unacceptable. It is by definition the accepted programme. Presumably this is a matter to be dealt with before the award of the contract. And, having regard to the contractual effects of the accepted programme, particularly in the obligations it imposes on the employer, assessment of an identified programme is clearly an important pre-contract function for the employer and his consultants.

Note that failure by the contractor to submit a first programme for acceptance (where none is identified in the contract data) entitles the employer to retain one quarter of amounts due as interim payments (clause 50.3).

Clause 31.2 – detail of programme

This clause states the detail to be shown on each programme the contractor submits for acceptance. The amount of detail required by clause 31.2 is comprehensive and it disposes of any notion that a simple programme in bar chart form is adequate for NEC 3. Instead it indicates that the term 'programme' as used in NEC 3 is not a single document but a collection of documents which may include method statements, histograms, bar charts, network diagrams and the like.

The details required are (in the order set out in clause 31.2):

- starting date, access dates, key dates and completion dates
- planned completion dates
- order and timing of planned operations
- order and timing of the work of the employer and others
- dates when the contractor plans to meet the conditions for key dates
- provisions for float, time risk allowances, health and safety requirements, procedures set out in the contract
- dates when the contractor will need access, acceptances, plant, materials and things to be provided by the employer and others, information from others

- method statements for each operation identifying principal equipment and other resources to be used
- other information which the works information requires to be shown

Clause 31.3 – acceptance of programmes

By clause 31.3 the project manager has to respond to submission of a programme within two weeks. The project manager must either accept the programme or state his reasons for not accepting it.

There is nothing in clause 31.3 to indicate whether or not deemed acceptance is intended if the project manager fails to respond within the time allowed. But since late response is a compensation event under clause 60.1(6) a late notice of non-acceptance is probably valid and deemed acceptance, if it occurs at all, probably only occurs when there is no response whatsoever from the project manager. In the event of non-acceptance of any programme the contractor is obliged to resubmit, taking account of the project manager's reasons, within the period for reply (clause 13.4).

Withholding acceptance

Reasons stated in clause 31.3 for not accepting the programme are:

- the plans it shows are not practicable (but note that this applies only to the contractor's plans and not to the plans of the employer and others in so far as they may be in the programme)
- information required by the contract is not shown (this could be either information required by clause 31.2 or by the works information)
- the contractor's plans are not realistically represented (this could be highly contentious)
- it does not comply with the works information (this may mean that the contractor's plans do not comply with the works information or that the programme itself is not compliant)

The project manager can withhold acceptance for reasons other than the above – perhaps to take account of changed circumstances relating to the employer or others – but non-acceptance for a reason other than the stated reasons is a compensation event (clause 60.1(9)). The effects of non-acceptance, other than to resubmit, are related mainly to the assessment of compensation events. Clause 64.2 allows the project manager to make his own assessment if there is no accepted programme. Clause 50.3 on reduced interim payments does not necessarily apply to all non-acceptances since it refers only to submission of a first programme and to the absence of information on that programme.

The contractor is not expressly prohibited by the contract from proceeding in accordance with a non-accepted programme – although in extreme circumstances the consequence could be that the termination procedures of clause 91 might be invoked on grounds that the contractor was substantially failing to comply with his obligations. A less extreme scenario is that the project

manager, unwilling to let the contractor proceed to a non-accepted programme, could give an instruction under clause 34.1 for the contractor to stop
work. That would itself be a compensation event under clause 60.1(4) but not
one entitling the contractor to any extra payment or time if the project manager
decides that the reason for the stoppage was due to a fault of the contractor
(clause 61.4).

Disputes on witholding acceptance

There may even be circumstances where it is appropriate to put a dispute on
non-acceptance of a programme to an adjudicator under Option W1 or W2.
Indeed, it may be inevitable that an adjudicator, called upon to resolve certain
disputes on the assessment of compensation events, is obliged to consider
arguments on the proper programme for the assessment. Such arguments on
the financial relevance of programmes are commonplace in construction
disputes under all standard forms. But with NEC 3, there is added potential
for argument on programmes on a more practical level and some aspects
of this are a cause for concern. For example, the stated reasons for non-
acceptance in clause 31.3 include the project manager taking a view that the
contractor's plans are not practicable or realistic. Arguably that should be a
matter for the contractor to decide and not the project manager.

Note that even if the contractor changes his plans to obtain the project
manager's acceptance of his programme that does not change the contractor's
responsibility (clause 14.1). It might appear from this that the project manager
has power without responsibility but project managers should be aware that
if by their interference in the contractor's plans they cause loss to the contractor, or worse, damage to persons or property, then at least they may render
the employer liable for the financial consequences and again, at worst, render
themselves personally liable.

One interpretation of clause 31.3 which to some extent acts as a brake on
the project manager's control over the contractor's programme is to take the
word 'plans' in a narrow sense so as to exclude the 'provisions' as listed in
the sixth bullet point of clause 31.2. This then excludes from the listed reasons
for non-acceptance supposedly inadequate 'provisions' for float, time risk
allowances, health and safety requirements and other procedures.

Float

With regard to 'float' in the contractor's programme note that by clause 63.3
any delay to the contractor's planned completion as shown on the accepted
programme gives an entitlement to extension of time. So as far as NEC 3 is
concerned the old argument 'who does float belong to?' is firmly settled.
Overall, it belongs to the contractor. This does not mean, however, that float
on an item by item basis is entirely for the contractor's use – such float may
have to be absorbed in re-programming and could, therefore, be said to
belong to the employer.

Clause 31.4 – activity schedules

Clause 31.4 applies only in Options A and C – the contracts with activity schedules. It requires the contractor to provide information showing how each activity on the activity schedule relates to operations on each programme submitted for acceptance. This is a subtle revision of the requirement in ECC 2 which required the contractor to show on each programme the start and finish date of every activity on the activity schedule.

8.4 Revision of programmes

NEC 3, as mentioned above, avoids expressly requiring the contractor to comply with his programme but it ensures that the contractor's programme does not become a redundant document by requiring the contractor to submit revised programmes at regular intervals or as instructed.

Clause 32.1 – revised programmes

Clause 32.1 states that the contractor is to show on each revised programme:

- progress achieved and its effect upon the timing of remaining work
- effects of compensation events and notified early warning matters
- plans for dealing with delays and notified defects
- other proposed changes to the accepted programme

This detail is apparently intended to be additional to the detail required by clause 31.2. The first line of that clause states: 'The Contractor shows on each programme which he submits for acceptance.' Consequently, giving effect to the word 'each', properly revised programmes are likely to be extensive and comprehensive documents – or rather sets of documents.

The requirement for actual progress to be shown is routine as also is the requirement for its effect on the timing of the remaining work to be shown. But note that with NEC 3, planned completion as shown on the accepted programme (which as the works duly progress will be a revised programme) is the base for time related claims in compensation events – so with NEC 3 that base is mobile rather than fixed at commencement.

The requirement to show the effects of implemented compensation events appears to have few contractual implications because, once implemented, compensation events are not reassessed in the light of subsequent events (clause 65.2). However the requirement to show the effects of notified early warnings – which will frequently be compensation events in the course of assessment (or not agreed) may have contractual effects because it is clearly in the contractor's financial interests to underplay events for which he is responsible and to overplay events for which the employer is financially responsible. And bearing in mind that the project manager has only two weeks to respond to the submission of any programme (clause 31.3) he may have insufficient time to fully assess the implications of accepting a revised programme. See in particular the problem discussed under clause 32.2 below on multiple revisions.

The requirement for the contractor to show in revised programmes his plans to deal with delays and to correct notified defects appears to be a requirement to show resources rather than dates.

The final requirement of clause 32.1 that the contractor shall show other changes which he proposes to make to the accepted programme comes close to suggesting that the contractor is not entitled to depart from the approved programme without the project manager's acceptance. But its intention may be no more than to prevent the contractor unilaterally altering the timing of matters which are the employer's responsibility.

Clause 32.2 – submission of revised programmes

Clause 32.2 states the circumstances in which a revised programme shall, or may be, submitted. They are:

- when instructed by the project manager to do so
- when the contractor chooses to do so, *and*
- at the intervals stated in the contract data

See also clause 62.2 requiring a revised programme with quotations for compensation events if the effect of the event is to require alterations to the accepted programme.

In the case of an instruction clause 32.2 requires the contractor to submit his reply within the period for reply stated in the contract data.

Unlike the provision in model form MF/1 there is nothing in clause 32.2 itself to indicate that the contractor should be paid the cost incurred in submitting a revised programme at the project manager's instruction. But arguably a compensation event can be claimed under clause 60.1(1) on the basis that the instruction is a change in the works information. Or the cost may be valued as part of the cost of a compensation event in appropriate circumstances.

The entitlement of the contractor under clause 32.2 to submit a revised programme when he chooses to do so has potentially serious implications for the employer and the project manager with the advancement of computerised programming. Contractors with on-site programmers and estimators can revise their programmes on a regular (if not daily) basis to take account of compensation events and other matters. The burden this throws on the project manager who is obliged to respond to each revision can be immense. But failure to respond is not only a breach of the project manager's duty but it gives advantages to the contractor in the assessment of compensation events.

8.5 Shortened programmes

In the last thirty years or so a great deal has been written and said on the subject of programmemanship and its close relative, claimsmanship. The questions have been to what extent is it possible, or contractually permissible, for a contractor to devise a programme which is to his advantage in claims for extra time and payments.

Most of the debate has focused on the practice adopted by many contractors for perfectly sound commercial reasons of submitting shortened programmes showing completion well within the time allowed in the contract. Contractors see such programmes as necessary if they are to be competitive in tendering; but employers, not without some cause, may see them as props for opportunist claims or as unwelcome redefinement of their own liabilities or obligations.

The Glenlion case

From the decision in the much discussed case of *Glenlion Construction Ltd* v. *The Guinness Trust* (1987) it is clear that a contractor cannot rely on a shortened programme in claims for breach of contract. It is not open to one party to unilaterally change the obligations of the other party after the contract has been made. But *Glenlion* is not directly applicable to claims made under provisions of the contract. For such claims, where shortened programmes are relied on, it is necessary to see what obligations the employer has undertaken in the contract in respect of assisting or permitting the contractor to work to his programme.

Some contracts carefully avoid linking the employer's obligations to the contractor's programme and fix obligations in line with the common law principle of prevention such that the employer must not hinder the contractor from finishing on time. Other contracts, and the IChemE *Red Book* is a good example, do fix the employer's obligations to the contractor's programme.

Shortened programmes in NEC 3

The approach of NEC 3 on the employer's obligations is to fix them either in the works information or, if not so fixed, by reference to the contractor's accepted programme. Clause 60.1 listing the compensation events refers to both. But, in so far as it is left to the contractor to decide his own arrangements and fix his own timescale the NEC 3 approach is likely to encourage rather than diminish the use of shortened programmes.

However, with NEC 3 it is not simply a matter of fixing the employer's obligations which is relevant to the impact of shortened programmes. Another important matter is that the assessment of compensation events is determined by reference to the accepted programme. Contractors under ECC 2 were not slow to see the advantages to be gained by minimising the length of such programmes.

8.6 *Access to and use of the site*

Clause 33.1 of NEC 3 deals with access to and use of the site. In ECC 2, clause 33.1 dealt only with what was called 'possession' of the site. Clause 33.2, which is omitted from NEC 3, dealt with access.

Meaning of access

The Concise Oxford Dictionary defines access as the 'right or means of approaching or reaching'. This clearly indicates that access can mean either the legal permission to enter or the physical needs for entry. Contracts use the term 'access' in different ways with some concerned only with the legal aspects and others concerning themselves also with the physical aspects. The IChemE *Red Book* goes so far as to require the employer to provide access from the nearest road or railway suitable for use by the contractor.

There is no fixed rule for distinguishing between the two types of access but the phrase 'to allow access' as used in NEC 3 suggests the legal meaning whereas the phrase 'to give access' as used in ECC 2 suggests a physical meaning.

Clause 33.1 – access to and use of the site

Clause 33.1 requires the employer to allow the contractor access to and use of each part of the site necessary for the work included in the contract, on or before the later of:

- the access date (which is a date or dates identified in the contract data), *or*
- the date for access shown on the accepted programme

The full impact of clause 33.1 is best seen by considering it in conjunction with other parts of NEC 3, in particular:

- contract data, part one – the employer is to state access dates for identified parts of the site
- clause 25.1 – the contractor is to share the working areas with others as stated in the works information
- clause 33.1 – the contractor is to show access dates on each programme he submits for acceptance
- clause 60.1(2) – failure by the employer to allow access and use as required by clause 33.1 is a compensation event

The first point to note is that by stating access dates for parts in the contract data the employer has the opportunity to dispose of any contention that the contractor is entitled to access and use of the whole of the site from commencement. The second point is that by stating in the works information how the working areas are to be shared with others the employer has the opportunity to dispose of any contention that the contractor is entitled to exclusive use of the site.

If the employer misses these opportunities the contractor may well be able to claim full use and access from commencement and exclusive use – although to succeed on the access and use point the contractor would probably have to show a single date for access on the first programme submitted for acceptance. It may be thought that the phrase 'necessary for the work' in clause 33.1 comes to employer's aid in any claim for full access and use but that phrase is not followed through into the compensation event in clause 60.1(2) and although the project manager can rectify any omission in the works information regarding sharing the site with others, albeit that there is then a compensation event under clause 60.1(1), the project manager has no power to rectify omissions of access dates for parts (clause 12.3).

The second point to note about clause 33.1 is that it requires access and use to be allowed by the 'later' of the access date (or dates) in the contract data or the date (or dates) for access on the accepted programme. This restricts the contractor in the programming of his work but it allows the employer to defer giving access dates and use if the programmed date (or dates) are the later dates. However, there is nothing in clause 32.1 (revising the programme) to prevent the contractor from bringing forward any such later dates in revised programmes and it would be risky for the employer to rely on later programme dates as firm dates for fixing his obligations.

In the event of acceleration under clause 36.1 it would be a matter for the parties to agree how any necessary changes to access dates should be accommodated.

8.7 Instructions to stop or not to start work

Many construction contracts have lengthy and detailed provisions dealing with suspension of work. NEC 3 characteristically deals with the subject in the briefest of terms and without mentioning the word 'suspension' except in secondary option Y(UK)2.

Suspension of work may be either of the contractor's own accord or imposed by instruction of the contract administrator or some authorised external agency. As a general rule contractors are entitled to plan progress as they think fit subject, of course, to recognition of their obligations to complete on time and other contractual obligations requiring compliance with programmes or regular progress. Thus in *Hill* v. *Camden* (1980) it was held on the facts that ceasing work was neither abandonment nor repudiation; and in *Greater London Council* v. *Cleveland Bridge & Engineering Co* (1986) it was held that the contractor was free to programme his work as he felt fit provided he planned to finish on time. Additionally, some contracts permit the contractor to suspend progress in the event of non-payment and for contracts subject to the Housing Grants, Construction and Regeneration Act 1996, there is a statutory right to suspend for non-payment. It is worth noting, however, that at common law the contractor has no implied right to suspend for non-payment, see for example, *Canterbury Pipelines Ltd* v. *Christchurch Drainage Board* (1979) and *Lubenham Fidelities Ltd* v. *South Pembrokeshire District Council* (1986).

Save for the provision in secondary option Y(UK)2 relating to non-payment, NEC 3 does not deal expressly with the contractor's right to suspend. It deals only with the project manager's power to instruct the contractor to stop and start work (clause 34.1) and, by the compensation event in clause 60.1(4), the consequences flowing from any such instruction.

Clause 34.1 – instructions to stop or restart work

Clause 34.1 which is the nearest thing in NEC 3 to a conventional suspension clause states simply that the project manager may instruct the contractor to stop or not to start any work and may later instruct him to restart or start it. The clause itself places no limitations on the project manager's powers and the contractor's remedies for complying with the project manager's instructions are to be found elsewhere in the contract. The clause surprisingly does not require the project manager to state reasons for any instructed suspension.

If the procedures of the contract are properly followed some limitation of the project manager's powers is provided by clause 16.1 (early warning). And since in most cases it is likely that an instruction to stop or not to start work will delay completion, the project manager would seem to be under an obligation to give early warning before giving such an instruction. He would then be obliged to co-operate in making and considering proposals to avoid or reduce the effects at any risk reduction meeting which followed. Another limitation is regard for the employer's financial interests. Any instruction by the project manager to stop or not to start work is a compensation event (clause 60.1(4)). However, if the project manager decides that the event (the instruction) arises from a fault of the contractor and it is the contractor who gives notice of the compensation event there is no change in the prices or the completion date. However, the intention of the contract is probably that the contractor should be compensated for any instruction to stop or not to start work unless it can be proved that default by the contractor is the reason for the instruction.

One aspect of clause 34.1 which should not be overlooked is that by clause 91.6 any instruction to stop or not to start substantial work or all work which remains in effect for thirteen weeks activates rights of termination. The employer may terminate if the instruction is due to a default of the contractor; the contractor may terminate if the instruction is due to a default of the employer; either party may terminate if the instruction is due to any other reason.

Another aspect of clause 34.1 which requires consideration is whether it can legitimately be used by the project manager as a means of ordering omission variations. Strictly, an omission variation should require a change in the works information but note that the wording of clause 34.1 is discretionary and the project manager 'may' give an instruction to restart – he is not obliged to do so. The effect of not giving a re-start order could be to reduce the scope of the work although it is doubtful if this is the intention of the contract.

Instructions to restart

It might be thought that if the project manager gives an instruction to stop work then he has the duty to decide when to instruct a restart. However, insofar that the stoppage instruction is given because of contractor's default that may not follow. In the case of *Crosby* v. *Portland UDC* (1967), best known for recognition of global claims, it was held, under ICE 4th Edition Conditions of Contract, that no term could be implied that the engineer should instigate the lifting of a suspension order given on grounds for which there was no right to time and cost recovery.

8.8 Take-over

General aspects of take-over under NEC 3 are discussed in section 8.1. The particulars are set out in clauses 35.1 to 35.3 which deal respectively with:

- clause 35.1 – take-over and completion
- clause 35.2 – use and take-over of parts of the works before completion
- clause 35.3 – certification of take-over

A point to note on the wording of clauses 35.2 and 35.3 is the use of the phrase 'any part of the works'. Normally this phrase would suggest something less than the whole but in these clauses the phrase appears to mean the whole or any part as applicable.

A further point to note is that clauses 35.1 to 35.3 in NEC 3 were clauses 35.2 to 35.4 in ECC 2. Clause 35.1 of ECC 2 which dealt with return of possession of the site, or part thereof, to the employer on take-over is omitted from NEC 3. This is presumably because the wording change from 'possession' in ECC 2 to 'take-over and use' in NEC 3 eliminates the need to deal with the return of possession.

Clause 35.1 – take-over and completion

Clause 35.1 contains two distinct provisions:

- the employer need not take over the works before the completion date if it is stated in the contract data that he is not willing to do so, *otherwise*
- the employer takes over the works not later than two weeks after completion

The first provision requires a decision to be made by the employer before the award of the contract. It covers the not uncommon situation where an employer perceives no benefit in early completion and does not want to take on, any earlier than planned, care of the works responsibilities. The contractor remains entitled to finish early and remains entitled to have completion certified if he does so but his responsibilities for care of the works continue until the set completion date.

It is unlikely that the provision is intended to take effect other than in the event of early completion. But since neither the provision itself nor the contract data entry mentions completion (both refer to the completion date) it is arguable that it could apply to use before completion – thereby negating the provision in clause 35.2 that the employer is required to take over the works when he begins to use them.

The second provision in clause 35.1 ensures that the contractor is not left with prolonged care of the works responsibilities. It also supports the contractor's right to finish early and it gives the employer two weeks to arrange his own insurance cover.

Clause 35.2 – take-over and use of the works

Clause 35.2 permits the employer to use any part of the works before completion 'has been certified'. It then stipulates that such use is accompanied by take-over except when:

- the use is for a reason stated in the works information, *or*
- the use is to suit the contractor's method of working

It is not clear if any significance is intended by the use of the phrase 'Completion has been certified' in clause 35.2. The word 'Completion' would suffice unless the clause is taken to have a very restricted meaning such that the employer may use the works in between completion and the date when completion is certified.

Note that if the employer has stated reasons for not taking over parts of the works when they are put into use he does so in the works information and not in the contract data. There appear to be no limitations on such reasons but they are probably intended to be of a practical nature. But whatever the stated reasons they are at least settled at the time the contract is made and are hopefully dispute free.

The same cannot be said for the second class of usage exempting the employer from take-over. This is the class described as use 'to suit the Contractor's method of working'. The difficulty here is in deciding whether a distinction should be made between a method of working which includes use which is unavoidable (e.g. in a road improvement scheme or the upgrading of a water treatment works) and a method of working which is solely of the contractor's choosing. It is not unreasonable having regard to the contractor's responsibilities for care of the works and his liabilities for defects that only the latter method of working should apply. But that is not always taken to be the case with similar provisions in other contracts and it is unlikely that everyone will agree that is the case under NEC 3.

Clause 35.3 – certifying take-over

Clause 35.3 requires the project manager to certify the date on which the employer takes over any part of the works within one week of the date of take-over. The certificate is to show the extent of the part of the works taken over.

Where the project manager has certified completion this will not present any problems since by clause 35.1 the date of take-over should not be more than two weeks after the date of completion. Where completion has not been certified the operation of the clause will frequently depend on the project manager's decisions on whether the works have been put into use and whether the exceptions in clause 35.2 apply.

There is no specific remedy in the contract if the project manager fails to certify in accordance with clause 35.3 – although this is, perhaps, another case where compensation event 60.1(18) – employer's breach of contract – might come into play.

8.9 Acceleration

The term 'acceleration' has various meanings according to the contract in which it is used and the circumstances in which it is used. Sometimes it means no more than the mitigation of delay; sometimes it means a formal shortening of the time allowed for completion. NEC 3 uses the term in the latter sense.

Clause 36.1 – acceleration

Clause 36.1 provides principally for acceleration to achieve early completion of the whole of the works. However, when secondary option X5 is included in the contract it can also apply to acceleration of sectional completions. When the contract includes key dates these may have to be changed to match the shortened timescale. The clause states:

- the project manager may instruct the contractor to submit a quotation to achieve completion before the completion date
- the project manager states changes to key dates to be included in the quotation
- the quotation comprises proposed changes to the prices and a revised programme
- the contractor submits details of his assessment of each quotation

Note that the clause does not give the project manager power to instruct acceleration. It gives power only to seek a quotation. Acceleration of the type intended by clause 36.1 involves a change in the obligations of the parties and this can only be by agreement. What is intended, that the contractor can be asked to state his price for taking on a revised contractual obligation and putting in hand the necessary resources?

Although the clause does not deal expressly with acceleration of parts of the works, the parties are probably at liberty, if they so wish, to use the clause for such purposes.

Failure to achieve acceleration

An interesting question which frequently arises in connection with acceleration is what consequences follow failure by the contractor to achieve acceleration after being paid to do so. In NEC 3 the situation appears to be that the contractor becomes liable for delay damages, either liquidated or unliquidated according to whether or not secondary option X7 is included in the contract, and liable for the employer's additional costs in respect of key dates under clause 25.3. There is no provision in NEC 3, however, for the employer to recover monies paid on an accepted quotation. The risk of achieving acceleration is effectively shared.

Clause 36.2 – quotation for acceleration

The clause requires the contractor to submit a quotation when so instructed or to give his reasons for not doing so. Such reasons are to be given within the time for reply as stated in the contract data but it is not wholly clear whether or not the same timescale is intended to apply to the submission of the quotation. There is no sanction in the contract for failure by the contractor either to provide a quotation or to give his reasons. Strictly the contractor would be in breach of contract but it is unlikely that the employer would succeed in a claim for damages. One reason that the contractor might prefer not to submit a quotation is that the contract does not provide for reimbursement of his costs in assembling the quotation. Some other standard forms such as MF/1 do provide for reimbursement.

When the contractor does submit a quotation there may be some question as to whether he is bound by the compilation rules applying to quotations for compensation events. The terminology in clause 36.1 matches that in clause 62.2 and no doubt it would assist the project manager in assessing the quotation for standardisation to apply. However, the imposition of a link between acceleration quotations and compensation event quotations cannot be enforced even if it is intended.

Clauses 36.3 and 36.4 – accepting quotations

Clause 36.3 is found in main options A, B, C and D. It states that when the project manager accepts a quotation for acceleration the completion date, key dates and the prices are changed and the revised programme is accepted.

In short, acceptance of the quotation concludes the formalities of changing the contractual obligations. Clearly it is assumed that the project manager is acting with the full authority of the employer. There is no conflict in this with clause 12.3 since the changes are provided for in the contract.

Clause 36.4 applies to acceptance of quotations for acceleration under main options E and F. It also states that when the project manager accepts a quotation he changes the completion date, key dates and accepts the revised programme.

The difference between this clause and clause 36.3 applying to main options A, B, C and D is that the reference to changing the prices is omitted. This is because options E and F are fully cost reimbursable and the prices are defined in terms of cost.

Chapter 9
Testing and defects

9.1 Introduction

NEC 3 does not attempt to match the detailed provisions on quality, quality control, testing and defects found in other construction, process and plant contracts. As a matter of policy and in the interests of flexibility the detail for individual contracts is left to be supplied in the works information. NEC 3 simply sets out in clauses 40 to 45, which are for the most part unchanged from the ECC 2 clauses, the basic obligations of the parties and the role of supervisor in respect of testing and defects. Perhaps in recognition of the potential dangers of this approach no less than eight pages of the Guidance Notes and eight pages of the Flow Charts are devoted to testing and defects.

The principal danger for users of NEC 3 is that they may not recognise that it is insufficient to specify types of tests and acceptable results in the works information. It may be adequate for many conventional contracts but it will not do for NEC 3 which relies so heavily on what is 'required by the Works Information'. For testing it is necessary to specify in the works information:

- what tests apply
- who undertakes tests
- when tests are to be done
- where tests are to be done
- who provides materials, facilities, samples etc.
- what procedures apply
- what standards apply

The secondary danger is that there may be a temptation to include in the works information extracts from familiar standard forms written in a different style and with a different philosophy from NEC 3. But it may be even more dangerous for individuals to attempt to copy the drafting style of NEC 3. On balance it is probably best to write the works information in straightforward language which is meaningful to the technical people who are going to be concerned with testing and defects.

Types of tests

Unlike other standard forms of contract NEC 3 does not distinguish between different categories of test. Depending on what is required in the works information for any particular contract 'tests' within the meaning of NEC 3 may be:

- tests before delivery
- tests before completion
- tests on completion (or take-over)
- performance tests

The standard provisions in clauses 40 to 45 of NEC 3 apply to all specified tests but this creates the need for great care in the drafting of the works information particularly in regard to role reversal for performance testing. Most contract testing is carried out by the contractor with the employer (or his representative) supervising or observing. As a general rule, however, performance testing is undertaken by the employer because it follows taking-over and the employer is in possession of and in control of the works and is probably using them. The role of the contractor is then to supervise or observe. NEC 3 does not expressly deal with role reversal because it does not mention performance tests in its core clauses. It does mention performance levels in Option X17 (low performance damages), but this does no more than state the contractor's obligation to pay any low performance damages specified in the contract if a relevant defect is included in the defects certificate. Key performance indicators as referred to in secondary option X20 are management related incentives rather than technical criteria.

Role of the supervisor

The principal role of the supervisor under NEC 3 is to monitor quality and performance on behalf of the employer. Consequently most of the references to the supervisor are found in the clauses on testing and defects.

In clauses 40 to 43 it is the supervisor and not the project manager who exercises control over the contractor. It is the supervisor who undertakes the important tasks of notifying defects and issuing the defects certificate. However, in clauses 44 and 45 relating to accepting defects and uncorrected defects, control reverts to the project manager.

To the extent that the supervisor and the project manager act in independent professional capacities there is some potential for conflict in this. On the face of it the project manager alone decides whether or not to accept defects. However there must be a presumption that the supervisor is at least consulted.

Obligations and entitlements

A practical question which frequently arises on construction, process and plant contracts is whether, in the event of the contractor failing in his obligations to undertake tests or remedy defects, the employer is entitled to carry out such work. The contractual answer in most standard forms is YES –

subject to notice being given by the employer and the contractor being given time to remedy the situation. And usually that applies both before and after completion.

NEC 3 does not directly address the issue except in relation to the remedying defects after completion. It is arguable therefore that under NEC 3, the absence of any express entitlement for the employer to act prior to completion prevents him from doing so except at his own risk and expense. However, the sanction on the contractor for his default on testing and defects obligations could in extreme cases be operation of the termination provisions of the contract. But at a more commonplace level sanctions would operate by affecting the amounts in the contractor's entitlements to interim payments.

Defects under NEC 3

NEC 3 uses the word 'defect' with a strictly limited and defined meaning. Essentially it refers only to defects which are in some way the fault of the contractor and for which the contractor is contractually responsible. The contract is generally silent on defects for which the employer is responsible and the intention is probably that the project manager should give instructions dealing with such defects.

There is, perhaps, an assumption in this approach that responsibility for defects can readily be allocated or apportioned. In reality, the opposite is frequently the case. A taxing question for NEC 3 is whether its rigidly structured provisions can accommodate the uncertainties and arguments which are a normal feature of the examination of causation of defects and the making of decisions on their treatment.

Latent defects

ECC 2 did not expressly deal with liability for defects appearing after the issue of the defects certificate – defects generally known as latent defects. That situation is changed in NEC 3 by new wording in clause 43.3 (ECC 2 clause 43.2) stating that the employer's rights in respect of defects not found or not notified are not affected by the issue of the defects certificate. In short this appears to be intended as confirmation that the employer retains his common law rights to sue for breach of contract in respect of latent defects. Such confirmation is probably not needed because there is nothing in NEC 3 (or ECC 2) stating that the defects certificate is conclusive evidence of fulfilment of the contractor's obligations, nor anything expressly excluding the employer's common law rights. See additionally the comment on p. 183 on clause 43.3.

Option clauses

The testing and defects provisions in core clauses 40 to 45 of NEC 3 apply unchanged in all of the main options A to F with the exception that options

C, D and E have an additional clause (clause 40.7) which effectively makes the costs of repeat tests and inspections after a defect is found disallowed costs.

Secondary option clauses which refer to defects (none refer to tests) are:

- Option X15 – limitation of the contractor's liability for design
- Option X16 – retention
- Option X17 – low performance damages
- Option X18 – limitation of liability

Of particular interest is clause X15.2 which is new to NEC 3. It states that if the contractor corrects a 'Defect' for which he is not liable under the contract that is a compensation event. The explanation for this unusual admission that not all 'Defects' are 'Defects' is found in clause X15.1 which states that the contractor is not liable for defects due to his design if he proves that he used reasonable skill and care to ensure that his design complied with the works information. Note, however, that clause X15.2 does not, within its own wording, limit its scope to defects due to design.

9.2 Definitions and certificates

Definition of 'Defect'

Clause 11.2(9) defines the meaning of 'Defect' within NEC 3. A 'Defect' is:

- a part of the works which is not in accordance with the works information, *or*
- a part of the works designed by the contractor which is not in accordance with:
  — the applicable law, *or*
  — the contractor's design which has been accepted by the project manager

This is an interesting definition in two respects. Firstly, it excludes defects due to design for which the employer is responsible. Secondly, it appears to relieve the contractor of responsibility for defects in his own design once that design has been accepted by the project manager – subject to the design being in accordance with the works information.

Defects which are not a 'Defect'

The first point above raises the question of whether the contractor has any obligation to remedy defects which are due to the employer's design. There is nothing in clauses 40 to 45 to cover this but one possible answer is that if it can be said that the defect constitutes damage to the works then the contractor has an obligation to repair under clause 82.1 (repairs).

Another possible answer is that defects which are due to the employer's design are intended to be dealt with by way of project manager's instructions. The contractor is then obliged to comply and make good and the compensation event procedures come into force.

In the event of a dispute on whether or not a defect is or is not a 'Defect' within the contractual definition, questions on the authority of the supervisor to notify the defect and the obligations of the contractor to take any remedial action until in receipt of an instruction from the project manager arise. However, under the dispute resolution procedures of NEC 3 the parties must proceed as if a disputed action is not disputed until the matter in question is settled by adjudication. The contractor would apparently be obliged therefore to remedy the disputed defect on the notification of the supervisor and then to seek recompense through adjudication. In some circumstances the disputed matter might be resolved by tests or searches and use of compensation event at clause 60.1(10) which deals with the situation when searches reveal no contractual 'Defect'.

Note also, in respect of defects which are not a 'Defect', the comment on option clause X15.2 in section 9.1.

Acceptance of the contractor's design

Clause 11.2(5) includes within its definition of a 'Defect' part of the works not in accordance with the contractor's design which the project manager has accepted. Presumably what this means is that if the contractor builds something which is not in accordance with the design he has put forward for acceptance it is categorised as a defect. However, it can be construed as implying that providing the contractor builds to the design which the project manager has accepted he is thereby relieved of responsibility for defects.

It may be possible to dismiss the suggestion of any such relief by reference to clause 14.1 – the project manager's acceptance does not change the contractor's liability for his design. Another argument for dismissal is that design which is defective will not be in accordance with the works information and will therefore be a defined 'Defect' under the first limb of clause 11.2(5). But there may be occasions when this will not hold good – for example, when the works information is written in general terms or as a performance specification or is deficient on matters relating to design.

From the employer's viewpoint it is difficult to see what useful purpose is served by the words 'which has been accepted by the Project Manager' in clause 11.2(5). Employers who are in doubt on the matter should consult their lawyers about possible deletion.

Definition of defects certificate

Clause 11.2(6) defines what is meant by a defects certificate within NEC 3. A defects certificate is either:

- a list of defects that the supervisor has notified before the defects date which the contractor has not corrected, *or*
- if there are no such defects a statement that there are none

At first sight it might appear that the defects certificate is the equivalent of the defects correction certificate under the ICE Conditions of Contract or the certificate of completion of making good defects under JCT terms. But it is not. Those certificates are only issued when the contractor has fulfilled his obligations to make good defects whereas under NEC 3 the defects certificate is issued on a set date as a record of whether or not the contractor has fulfilled his obligations.

Note however that due to the restricted definition of 'Defect' the defects certificate does not cover defects due to the employer's design. Nor, due to its own definition, does the defects certificate cover defects noticed and notified by the supervisor after the defects date.

The definition of defects certificate in its reference to 'a statement that there are none' is not precise as to who should issue this statement or what form it should take. Presumably the intention is that the supervisor should issue a formal document headed 'Defects certificate' which makes the statement. This would seem to follow from clause 43.3 which requires the supervisor to issue the defects certificate. However it is interesting to contemplate what the contractual position might be if, in the event of failure or delay by the supervisor to issue a defects certificate on the required date (a common situation under most standard forms of contract), the contractor himself issues a formal statement that there are no defects.

Effects of the defects certificate

The defects certificate is mentioned in the following clauses of NEC 3:

- clause 11.2(6) – definition
- clause 43.3   – issue of the defects certificate
- clause 50.1   – assessment for payment
- clause 80.1   – employer's risks
- clause 81.1   – contractor's risks
- clause 82.1   – repairs
- clause 84.2   – insurance cover
- clause X16.2   – retention
- clause X17.1   – low performance damages
- clause X18.3   – limitation of liability

The purpose of the defects certificate as indicated by these clauses is to put on record the state of the works at the date at which the contractor's entitlement to make good defects expires. It is not to be taken as a certificate of confirmation of fulfilment of the contractor's obligations. However the effect of the defects certificate is similar to that in other standard forms in that it triggers the release of the final tranche of retention money and sets the date for expiry of various obligations.

A point to note is that it is the date of issue of the defects certificate which is generally the effective date in the above listed clauses and the implication from clause 43.3 is that the certificate will be issued by the supervisor immediately it becomes due.

Defects date

The defects date is not a defined term of NEC 3. It is not even a fixed date. It is a date to be determined principally from a period entered by the employer in part one of the contract data. That period indicates how many weeks after completion of the whole of the works the defects date occurs. Thus, instead of stating in the usual manner that there is a defects liability period of six months or twelve months after completion, NEC 3 arrives at a similar position by reference to its defects date. If, by operation of the compensation event procedure, the time for completion of the works is extended then the defects date is correspondingly adjusted.

The defects date has three principal express purposes in NEC 3:

- under clause 42.2 it sets the date until which the contractor and the supervisor are obliged to notify each other of 'defects' which they find
- under clause 43.3 it sets (with some adjustment for the last defect correction period) the date for issue of the defects certificate
- under clause 61.7 it sets the final date for notification of a compensation event

But what the defects date also does, although not expressly stated, is that it sets (again with some adjustment for the defect correction period) the period within which the contractor is entitled to access to the site to remedy his own defects. This can be implied from the obligation to remedy defects stated in clause 43.2.

Defect correction period

The phrase 'defect correction period' as used in NEC 3 has a wholly different meaning from the identical phrase used in the ICE Conditions of Contract and such phrases as 'defects liability period' and 'maintenance periods' used in other standard forms.

In NEC 3 the defect correction period is a period (or periods) of weeks entered in part one of the contract data by the employer to indicate how long the contractor is given to remedy 'defects' after completion. It is not the whole of the period from completion to the defects date. There is no definition in NEC 3 to this effect but it can be deduced from the wording of clause 43.2. That clause states the contractor's obligation to correct notified 'defects' before the end of the defect correction period and states that the period begins at completion for defects notified before completion. Note that whereas under

ECC 2 the contract data form allowed only one entry for the defects correction period, NEC 3 allows for multiple entries.

9.3 Tests and inspections

Clause 40.1 – tests and inspections

This brief clause does no more than define the scope of clause 40. It states that clause 40 only governs tests required by the works information 'or' the applicable law. In ECC 2 the word 'and' was used – thereby unintentionally limiting application of the clause.

However, even with the new wording of clause 40.1 it is apparent that clause 40 overall is intended to be restricted in its operation to specified or statutory tests. So although it evidently does not apply to tests and inspections which the contractor carries out for his own purposes, less evidently it is of no application to testing required by the employer but not stated in the works information. This emphasises the need for comprehensive testing and inspection requirements to be detailed in the works information.

The project manager does have the power to change the works information (clause 14.3) and therefore can issue instructions for additional or varied tests. But these will then be treated as compensation events (clause 60.1(1)). The supervisor, however, has no express power to change the works information and accordingly has no obvious power to order additional or varied tests.

Clause 40.2 – materials, facilities and samples

Clause 40.2 is another brief clause. It simply confirms the obligations of the contractor and the employer to provide materials, facilities and samples for tests and inspections as stated in the works information.

The only point to note is that yet again these obligations take effect only to the extent that they are detailed in the works information. So unlike the position in most other standard forms there are no fixed obligations on either party in respect of certain categories of tests and inspections.

Clause 40.3 – notifications

Clause 40.3 deals with notifications of intentions to test and inspect and notification of results. It also confirms the power of the supervisor to watch any test by the contractor.

Both the contractor and the supervisor are required to notify each other before commencing tests or inspections and to notify each other of results afterwards. There could be some argument on whether 'results' means simply pass or fail or whether it means full records. There should be no argument however on whether the notifications need to be in writing. Clause 13.1 requires all notifications to be in writing.

With regard to tests or inspections which the supervisor is to carry out clause 40.3 expressly requires the contractor to give notice before doing work which would obstruct the tests or inspections. Failure by the contractor would be a breach of contract but the employer's remedy is not immediately apparent. The supervisor could arguably give instructions to uncover under clause 42.1 (searching and notifying defects) but neither the project manager nor the supervisor has the express power to order the contractor to break out premature work (or even to break out patently faulty work).

There is however one firm sanction to encourage the contractor to give timely notice and that is the proviso in clause 60.1(10) – the compensation event for searching. The proviso makes it clear that the compensation event does not operate if the contractor gave insufficient notice of doing work obstructing a required test or inspection.

The final provision in clause 40.3 that the supervisor may watch any test done by the contractor might appear to be superfluous as an obvious implied term but at least it puts the matter beyond doubt. Additionally it can perhaps be taken as giving the supervisor the right to attend off-site tests and the entitlement to the necessary facilities to observe on-site tests.

Clause 40.4 – repeat tests and inspections

This is a short clause which in most contracts would be straightforward in its application and free from complication. It states that if a test or inspection shows that any work has a defect the contractor is to correct the defect and repeat the test or inspection.

The problem with NEC 3 is that 'defect' has a restricted meaning and tests and inspections are only those required by the works information (or statute). The clause is not therefore of general application to defective work. It is of application only to a category of defect revealed in a particular way.

In some circumstances where the clause does actually apply there may be practical or financial reasons for the contractor to propose that the defect should not be corrected. Clause 44.1 (accepting defects) then comes into play. For comment on this see section 9.7. The contractor would also be obliged to give an early warning notice under clause 16.1 if the defect could delay completion or impair the performance of the works.

Clause 40.5 – the supervisor's tests and inspections

Clause 40.5 deals with the possibility that the supervisor's tests and inspections may cause delay to the works or delay to payments due to the contractor. The clause should be read in conjunction with clause 60.1(11) which classes as a compensation event a test or inspection done by the supervisor which causes unnecessary delay.

Clause 40.5 commences by stating that the supervisor shall do his tests and inspections:

- without causing unnecessary delay
- to the work, *or*
- to a payment which is conditional upon a test or inspection being successful

It then states that:

- a payment which is conditional upon supervisor's test or inspection being successful becomes due
- at the later of the defects date, and the end of the last defect correction period, *if*
- the supervisor has not done the test inspection, *and*
- the delay is not due to the contractor's fault

The first difficulty with clause 40.5 is a practical one. How is an unnecessary delay to be distinguished from a necessary delay and who is to decide? The second difficulty is a contractual one. Does the compensation event at clause 60.1(11) cover both situations envisaged in clause 40.5 – delay to work and delay to payment? The third difficulty is understanding why, if the supervisor has not done tests and inspections which have to be done before certain payments become due, these payments then only become due at the later of the defects date and the end of the last defect correction period. This seems unfair to the contractor as regards cashflow even if the contractor can utilise clause 60.1(11) to claim a compensation event.

Clause 40.6 – costs of repeat tests and inspections

Clause 40.6 relates to costs incurred by the employer where tests or inspections have to be repeated after a defect is found. The clause states that the project manager assesses the cost incurred and the contractor pays the amount assessed.

Similar clauses are found in process and plant contracts but rarely in construction contracts. However, such clauses normally refer to the employer's costs in observing or supervising the contractor carrying out repeat tests. Clause 40.6 seems to apply to tests carried out by the employer – but this may not be the intention.

It is unlikely that the intention of clause 40.6 is that it should be applied to any serial testing which might be thought necessary after the discovery of a defect. But, taking a broad view of the meaning of 'repeated', it could be argued that the clause contemplates and covers such testing.

9.4 *Testing and inspection before delivery*

Clause 41.1 – delivery of plant and materials

Clause 41.1 is a prohibitive clause of a type common in process and plant contracts. It is aimed at ensuring that all specified off-site tests and inspections are undertaken before delivery of plant or materials. The clause states that the contractor shall not bring plant and materials to the 'Working Areas' until the supervisor has notified the contractor that they have passed tests or inspections required by the works information. 'Working Areas' is a defined term of NEC 3 and it includes both the site and any additional areas to be used by the contractor and detailed in part two of the contract data.

The clause is somewhat unusual in that instead of the contractor notifying the supervisor that tests and inspections have been passed the position is reversed and it is for the supervisor to notify the contractor. It might be implied from this that the clause only applies to tests and inspections which the works information requires to be carried out by the supervisor. But that would seriously emasculate the clause since the majority of pre-delivery tests and inspections are carried out by specialist subcontractors and suppliers.

However there is clearly a danger in the supervisor taking on the burden of notifying the contractor that tests and inspections have been passed (and accordingly plant and materials are fit for delivery) if he, the supervisor, has not been responsible for those tests and inspections.

Obviously the clause can be applied without too much difficulty to tests and inspections carried out by independent agencies engaged by the employer since the supervisor can then take on the role of examining results before they are passed to the contractor. However for tests carried out by the contractor, his subcontractors or his suppliers, it is difficult to find any meaning in the clause other than that the contractor should supply the supervisor with results and should then await the supervisor's consent to commence delivery.

9.5 Searching and notifying defects

Clause 42.1 – instructions to search

This clause empowers the supervisor to instruct the contractor to search for defects. The supervisor is required to give his reasons for the search with his instruction. 'Searching' is not a defined term in NEC 3 but clause 42.1 lists various actions which come within the scope of searching for the purposes of the clause. These include:

- uncovering, dismantling, re-covering and re-erecting work
- providing facilities, materials and samples for tests and inspections done by the supervisor
- doing tests and inspections which the works information does not require

Clause 42.1 of NEC 3 is more restricted in its scope than its counterpart in ECC 2. It confines the supervisor's power to instructions 'to search for a "Defect"'. The ECC 2 clause gave the power to instruct searches generally. By the definition in clause 11.2(5) a 'Defect' is something for which the contractor is responsible. However, if there is a problem which requires searches to be undertaken it may not be apparent until they are complete which party carries responsibility for the problem.

Note that the definition of 'Defect' in clause 11.2(5) includes 'a part of the works which is not in accordance with the Works Information'. This can include work covered up without due notice. It is possible, therefore, for the supervisor to use clause 42.1 to order uncovering of such work. If this happens the compensation event in clause 60.1(10) may come into play – 'The Supervisor instructs the Contractor to search for a "Defect" and no Defect is found unless the search is needed only because the Contractor gave insufficient notice of doing work obstructing a required test or inspection.' Much will then depend on what constitutes 'insufficient notice' and that will lead back to the level of detail specified in the works information on notices and covering-up.

A further point to consider is that as clause 42.1 is confined in its scope to searches for defined 'Defects' there is an apparent gap in NEC 3 for investigating defects of a wider range – including, for example, defects arising from design for which the contractor is not responsible. The only obvious way to deal with the problem is for the project manager to take over from the supervisor and to issue instructions to search as a change to the works information. Clause 27.3 is only of assistance for instructions given in accordance with the contract – and the supervisor has limited power to give such instructions.

The final parts of clause 42.1 which extend the meaning of 'searching' to include the provision of facilities, etc. and doing tests and inspections which the works information does not require appear to operate as an extension of the supervisor's powers, including ordering things which amount to changing the works information. However, to the extent that the supervisor has this power it is again only operable in connection for searches for defined 'Defects' and it is not a general power. Moreover use of the power has the potential for bringing into play the compensation event in clause 60.1(10).

Clause 42.2 – notification of defect

Clause 42.2 deals with the notification of defects. It requires both the supervisor and the contractor to notify each other as soon as either finds any defects. The only change from the corresponding ECC 2 clause is the addition of the 'as soon as' requirement.

The clause is unusual compared with provisions in other contracts in that it expressly places a contractual obligation on the contractor to give notice of his own defects. But within the framework of NEC 3 this is understandable and is in keeping with the early warning procedure.

Note that it is only defined defects which have to be notified under clause 42.2 and not defects in the wider sense. When the contractor finds a defect he has to form a judgment as to whether it is a defect for which he is responsible (a Defect) or a defect due to employer's design or some other cause which places it outside the definition of defect. He then has to decide whether to give notice under both clause 16.1 (early warning) and clause 42.2 (notifying defects) or just under clause 16.1 for defects for which he considers he is not responsible. The danger for the contractor in giving notice under clause 42.2 without first considering the cause of the defect is that it could be taken as an admission of responsibility for the defect.

For the supervisor there is no obligation (or any power) to give early warning notice under clause 16.1 in the event of discovery of a defect due to employer's design. That obligation rests with the project manager. There must therefore be an implied procedure that the supervisor liaises with the project manager on early warnings.

One practical aspect of the notice requirements of clause 42.2 which may cause some concern is that, like other requirements in NEC 3, they are expressed as always binding – without regard to the scale or importance of the matters involved. Taken literally, clause 42.2 could lead to an endless stream of written notices between the supervisor and the contractor for every minor infringement of the specification as the works proceeded. Given the possibility of such a situation the contractor might well be inclined to argue that a defect cannot exist as such until the works are offered up as complete. Such an argument is not obviously at odds with the definition of defect in clause 11.2(5). Nor is it wholly at odds with the opening words of clause 42.2 which say 'until the defects date' – if that is read as applying to a period from completion until the defects date. Moreover it is an argument which fits in well with the provisions in clause 43.2 for the correction of defects.

9.6 Correcting defects

NEC 3 deals only with the correction of 'Defects' as defined in clause 11.1(5). It does not address defects which are not the contractor's responsibility. There are two changes from ECC 2. Clause 43.1 from ECC 2 is split into clauses 43.1 and 43.2 in NEC 3 and there is an extra provision in clause 43.3 of NEC 3 aimed at protecting the employer's rights in respect of latent defects.

Clause 43.1 – obligation to correct

The clause states only that the contractor corrects a 'Defect' whether or not the supervisor notifies him of it.

The purpose of the reference to the supervisor is not wholly clear. It may be an indicator that the clause applies only after completion. It would certainly appear to go without saying that the contractor is required to correct known defects for which he is responsible before completion. He would not be able to achieve completion without doing so. And there would be very little weight in any argument that the contractor was not obliged to correct defects known before completion unless notification was given by the supervisor.

As to defects occurring or discovered after completion it is normal in most contracts for the contractor to be given notice, if only for the practical reason that he may not otherwise know about them. Clause 43.1 appears to suggest that the NEC 3 takes a different approach but when it comes to clause 45.1 (uncorrected defects) it can be seen that there is an express sanction only for failure to correct notified defects. Perhaps this provides another explanation for the reference to the supervisor in the opening sentence in clause 43.1, namely that, not only the supervisor but also other persons such as the project manager and the employer may give notice of defects after completion.

Clause 43.2

The first sentence of clause 43.2 states that the contractor corrects notified defects before the end of the defect correction period. That period, as indicated in the second sentence of the clause, begins at completion for defects notified before completion – and for defects notified after completion it begins when they are notified.

What this means is that the contractor is put under an obligation to correct notified defects after completion within whatever relevant timescale is stated as the defect correction period in part one of the contract data. This is a sensible arrangement which will be welcomed by most employers. Note that although clause 43.2 does not use the word 'relevant' it can be implied from the defects correction period.

For defects which are not notified the position as indicated above is not clear. Clause 43.1 imposes an obligation on the contractor to correct them – but clause 43.2 does not provide any particular timescale. However there is no sanction in the contract for failure to correct such defects (clause 45.1 applies only to notified defects) and they cannot be included in the defects certificate. As to the timing for the correction of defects before completion, that is left to the contractor. But it is subject always to the discipline imposed by clause 11.2(2) which states that completion is when the contractor has done all the work required and has corrected notified defects which would have prevented the employer from using the works.

Clause 43.3 – issue of defects certificate

Clause 43.3 of NEC 3 contains two distinct provisions:

- the supervisor is required to issue the defects certificate at the later of the defects date or the end of the last defect correction period
- the employer's rights in respect of defects not found or notified are not affected by the issue of the defects certificate

Unlike some standard forms of contract the supervisor is not given a period of grace within which to issue the certificate. The requirement is that it should be done on the due day.

Delay in issue of the certificate would leave the employer open to a claim for damages based on prolonged risk carrying by the contractor under clauses

81, 82 and 84 and possibly late release of retention under secondary option
X16. However, as discussed in section 9.2, an NEC 3 defects certificate is
wholly different from a conventional defects correction certificate and there
is no reason why there should be any of the usual delay (due to arguments
on outstanding remedial works) in the issue of the certificate.

The second part of the clause states that the employer's rights in respect
of a defect which the supervisor has not found or notified are not affected by
the issue of the defects certificate. This is apparently intended to protect the
employer's rights to damages for latent defects but it is questionable whether
there is anything in NEC 3 which would take away these rights – other than
by way of limitation of liability if secondary option X18 applies. The definition
of defects certificate at clause 11.2(6) cannot be read as applying to latent
defects and there is nothing in NEC 3 expressly excluding the employer's
common law rights.

An alternative view of the second part of clause 43.3 is that it is concerned
not so much with truly latent defects but with defects which the supervisor
for whatever reason may have failed to find and notify. In short, the clause
may be saying that the employer retains his rights in respect of all defects,
whether latent or patent, which are not included in the defects certificate.

Clause 43.4 – access for correcting defects

Clause 43.4 covers the contractor's entitlement to access to and use of the
works after they are taken over in order to correct defects. The project manager
is required to arrange access and use and the employer is required to give
access and use as necessary. The defects correction period begins when these
have been provided.

Note that the wording of the clause is slightly different from that in clause
43.3 of ECC 2 where the period for correcting the defect was extended. In
NEC 3 it is the start of the defects correction period which is delayed.

A question to consider is whether the contractor should be compensated
for delayed access and use and possibly delay in issue of the defects certificate.
There is no compensation event dealing with delay in the issue of the certificate and the contractor might have difficulty in arguing breach of contract.

9.7 *Accepting defects*

Clause 44.1 – proposals to accept defects

Clause 44.1 is a useful practical provision which addresses the possibility of
acceptance of a defect if the contractor and the project manager so agree. The
clause simply permits either to propose to the other that the works information should be changed so that the defect does not have to be corrected.

There is no mention in the clause of the supervisor. This is presumably
because any agreement which follows from the clause is effectively an agreement between the parties (with the project manager acting for the employer)

and because any agreement will require a change in the works information and only the project manager is empowered to make such a change (clause 14.3). However, it can be expected that the supervisor will have a behind the scenes involvement in the process.

There is nothing in clause 44.1 to indicate when it can be put into operation and it would seem to operate both before and after completion.

Clause 44.2 – acceptance of defects

Clause 44.2 details the procedure for the acceptance of a defect. Providing the parties are prepared to consider the change, the contractor submits a quotation for reduced prices or earlier completion and, if accepted, they are changed accordingly.

The first step is that both the contractor and the project manager must indicate that they are prepared to consider the change. The question is – are either under any obligation to consider the change? The answer is far from simple. It is easy to say that the employer is entitled to strict performance to the works information and will consider nothing less. However, common law will not necessarily support this: see, for example, the House of Lords decision in *Ruxley Electronics v. Forsyth* (1995). And in any event the contractual provisions taken as a whole indicate a different position.

In NEC 3 the first relevant contractual provision is that found in clause 10.1 – the parties are obliged to act in a spirit of co-operation. Not being prepared to even consider a proposal from the other party would possibly be a breach of this. The second relevant provision is in clause 45.1 (uncorrected defects) which implies that the contractor is liable for the full correction cost of any defect whether or not the correction is actually made by the employer. This is potentially so severe that it also leads to the probability that the employer is obliged to consider proposals made under clause 44.1.

Assuming that the contractor and the project manager are prepared to consider proposals for change and that the contractor submits a quotation for reduced prices or an earlier completion date which is acceptable then, when the project manager accepts the quotation he gives an instruction to change the works information, the prices and the completion date accordingly. Note that under clause 60.1(1) such an instruction is expressly not a compensation event.

In the event of a dispute on the acceptability of the contractor's quotation that might well be a matter which could properly be referred to adjudication given the overall ethos of NEC 3 and the points mentioned above.

9.8 Uncorrected defects

NEC 3 deals with uncorrected defects firstly by considering the position when access to correct is given but no timely action is taken (clause 45.1), and secondly by considering the position when access is not given (clause 45.2). ECC 2 dealt only with the first of these.

Clause 45.1 – uncorrected defects with access given

The provisions of clause 45.1 can be broken down as follows:

- if the contractor is given access to correct a notified defect
- but has not corrected it within its defect correction period
- the project manager assesses the cost to the employer of having the defect corrected
- the contractor pays this amount
- the works information is treated as having been changed to accept the defect

In broad terms, the clause is similar to the type of clause found in every construction, process and plant contract entitling the employer to recover the cost of making good uncorrected defects. On strict interpretation of its wording, however, it may be far more onerous on the contractor than other standard forms. The point to note is that the contractor is not simply liable for the cost incurred in correcting the defect – as is the normal position. Under clause 45.1 the contractor is liable to pay an assessed cost – whether or not that proves to be the actual cost. And, since there is no reference to incurred cost, the contractor appears to be liable to pay the assessed cost whether or not the employer actually incurs any cost. Note in particular here the change of wording in clause 45.1 from that of clause 40.6 which does refer to the project manager assessing the cost 'incurred' by the employer.

The implications of this for the contractor are quite alarming. In the most extreme case he could be liable for the estimated replacement cost of the whole of the works for some minor infringement of the works information – such as building the works marginally, but inconsequentially, out of position. At common law, following the *Ruxley Electronics* decision mentioned in section 9.7, such a liability no longer exists (if it ever did) and it is surprising to find the liability in a contract as progressive as NEC 3.

In the event of a dispute on the matter it is questionable if the adjudication procedures of NEC 3 would be of assistance to the contractor, other than in respect of the particulars of the assessment – the employer would simply be enforcing the terms of the contract. But relief could perhaps be gained against oppressive use of the clause by reliance on clause 10.1 of the contract – which requires the employer to act in a spirit of mutual trust and co-operation. In the event of clause 45.1 being operated simply because the defect had not been corrected within the defect correction period, albeit that the contractor might have taken steps to put in hand the correction, or might even be engaged upon the correction, the potential impact of clause 10.1 would be particularly apparent.

Clause 45.2 – uncorrected defects with access not given

This new clause provides:

- if the contractor is not given access to correct a notified defect before the defects date

- the project manager assesses the cost to the contractor of correcting the defect
- the contractor pays this amount
- the works information is treated as having been changed to accept the defect

The principles behind this clause follow the general legal position that if the employer takes it on himself to rectify defects within the specified defects liability period thereby depriving the contractor of his right to make good his own defects, the employer will be able to recover as damages, not the full amount of his expenditure, but only the amount of cost that the contractor would have incurred in rectifying the defects. See, for example, the case of *Tomkinson & Sons Ltd* v. *The Parochial Church Council of St. Michael* (1990).

Contractors, however, may not be too pleased with a situation where, under clause 45.2 they may be deprived of access but end up liable to pay an amount assessed by the project manager.

Access and use

A final point to note in respect of clauses 43 to 45 is the changing terminology. Under clause 43.4 the contractor is to be allowed 'access to and use of a part of the works' needed to correct a defect. Under clauses 45.1 and 45.2 the reference is to 'access' only.

Chapter 10
Payments

10.1 Introduction

Section 5 is the main body of core clauses of NEC 3 dealing with payments. Its provisions are grouped under three headings:

- clause 50 – assessing the amount due
- clause 51 – payment
- clause 52 – defined cost

These clauses, however, are only part of the payment scheme of NEC 3. Much of the detail is found in the core clauses applicable to particular main options, including:

- clause 11 – defined terms for:
  — the prices
  — the price for work done to date
  — defined cost
  — disallowed cost
- clause 53 – the contractor's share
- clause 54 – the activity schedule
- clause 55 – the bill of quantities

Also relevant, if included in the contract, are certain secondary options, in particular:

- Option X1   – price adjustment for inflation
- Option X3   – multiple currencies
- Option X14   – advanced payments
- Option X16   – retention
- Option Y(UK)2 – Housing Grants, Construction and Regeneration Act 1996

In addition to the contract clauses the following entries in the contract data have to be noted:

- in contract data part one provided by the employer:
  — the starting date
  — the currency of the contract
  — the assessment interval
  — the interest rate
  — the payment period (if not three weeks)

— the method of measurement (for Option B)
— share percentages (for Option C or D)
— exchange rates (for Option C, D, E or F)
— indices details (for Option X1)
— currency details (for Option X3)
— bonus details (for Option X6)
— advanced payment details (for Option X14)
— retention details (for Option X16)
- in contract data part two, provided by the contractor:
  — the activity schedule (for Option A or C)
  — the bill of quantities (for Option B or D)
  — the tendered total of prices (for Options A, B, C or D)
  — fee percentages
  — cost component details

Essentials of the payment scheme

Although there are different payment mechanisms for each of the six main options some common characteristics can be extracted which define the essentials of the NEC 3 payment scheme. These are:

- assessments of amounts due are made at not more than five week intervals (contract data)
- certification is within one week of each assessment date (clause 51.1)
- payment is due within three weeks of each assessment date, unless stated otherwise (clause 51.2)
- interest is due on late certification, under-certification or late payment (clauses 51.2 and 51.3)

Amounts due

The rules for calculating amounts due for both interim and final payments vary according to the main option used. In short, excluding specific adjustments, the amounts due are as follows:

Option A – priced contract with activity schedule

- interim amounts – the total of prices for completed activities
- final amount – the total of the prices of the activities

Option B – priced contract with bill of quantities

- interim amounts – the quantities of completed work at bill of quantity rates and proportions of any lump sums
- final amount – remeasured value of the work in accordance with the bill of quantities

Option C – target contract with activity schedule

- interim amounts – defined cost plus fee
- final amount – tendered price as the activity schedule plus or minus the contractor's share

Option D – target contract with bill of quantities

- interim amounts – defined cost plus fee
- final amount – remeasured value of the work in accordance with the bill of quantities plus or minus the contractor's share

Option E – cost reimbursable contract

- interim amounts – defined cost plus fee
- final amount – defined cost plus fee

Option F – management contract

- interim amounts – defined cost plus fee
- final amount – defined cost plus fee

Peculiarities of the payment scheme

Although much of NEC 3 payment scheme is conventional there are some peculiarities which should be noted.

Perhaps the most important of these from the employer's viewpoint is that the burden of assessing the amount due falls squarely on the project manager – and he carries this burden whether or not the contractor submits an application for payment (which he is not obliged to do). For Option A assessment of the amount due is a straightforward matter of deciding which activities have been completed and the project manager's burden is comparatively light. For the other main options, however, particularly those where interim payments are based on costs paid or incurred, the assessment process can be time consuming and complex. And since the project manager is only allowed one week (clause 51.1) to make his assessment he is likely to need plentiful support staff or the services of a professional quantity surveying firm. These expenses fall directly on the employer.

Other peculiarities to note are:

- retention is not automatic; it applies only when secondary option X16 is incorporated
- interim payments suffer a 25% deduction until a first programme is submitted for acceptance (clause 50.3)
- there is no provision to stipulate a minimum amount for interim payments
- there is no reference to a final certificate; nor is any certificate given special contractual status

Changes from ECC 2

NEC 3 retains most of ECC 2 provisions on payment without change. It also retains the overall schemes for payment for the various main options. The provisions necessary to bring the schemes into compliance with the Housing Grants, Construction and Regeneration Act 1996 remain in secondary option clause Y(UK)2.

There are some changes, however, which need to be noted, in particular:

- Provision is made in clause 11.2(8) of NEC 3 for separate fee percentages for direct and for subcontracted work. This relieves a serious problem which existed in ECC 2 which allowed only one fee percentage to be stated.
- The term 'Defined Cost' is used throughout NEC 3 in place of the ECC 2 term 'Actual Cost' which was patently a misnomer.
- The price for the work done to date in main options C, D and E of NEC 3 is calculated by reference to the defined cost the project manager 'forecasts will have been paid by the Contractor before the next assessment date' whereas in ECC 2 it was the actual cost 'which the Contractor has paid'. This relieves another serious problem in ECC 2 which effectively required the contractor to operate on a negative cashflow basis under these options.
- Disallowed cost in main options C, D and E of NEC 3 includes 'preparation for and the conduct of adjudication or proceedings of the tribunal'. This seems to be recognition that dispute resolution is now a bigger business than was contemplated when ECC 2 was introduced in 1995. Oddly, such cost is not disallowed under Option F of NEC 3.
- Interest under clause 51.4 of NEC 3 is to be calculated 'on a daily basis'. ECC 2 was silent on this.
- Clause 50.1 of NEC 3 extends the period for regular assessments but it does not include for assessments to be made after completion when an amount is corrected or when a payment is made late.

In addition to the above there are significant changes in the two schedules of cost components and the manner in which they can be used. For detailed comment see Chapter 4, section 12 but note, in particular, that under main options A and B of NEC 3 all compensation events are to be assessed using the shorter schedule of cost components.

10.2 *Assessing the amount due*

Clause 50.1 – assessment procedure

Clause 50.1 commences by requiring the project manager to assess the amount due at each assessment date. It then continues by stating when assessment dates occur.

The significance of the obligation on the project manager to assess the amount due is mentioned above. However, note that by clause 50.4 if the contractor does make an application for payment the project manager has to consider it in his assessment. Note also that by clause 51.1 the project manager is required to issue his certificate within one week of the assessment date.

The first assessment date is decided by the project manager 'to suit the procedures of the Parties' but it must not be later than 'the assessment interval after the starting date'. In the contract data (but not in the written conditions) it is indicated that the assessment interval should be not more than five weeks – so the first assessment date should never be more than five weeks after the starting date (a date fixed by the employer in the contract data).

The phrase 'to suit the procedures of the Parties' suggests that the project manager should take into account the views of both parties – but sometimes, of course, there are differences, with the employer concerned with regularising payment dates and the contractor concerned with internal management accounting dates.

The second part of clause 50.1 stipulates the timing of assessments after the first assessment date. It states that later assessments occur:

- at the end of each assessment interval (this is stated in the contract data)
- until four weeks after the supervisor issues the defects certificate, *and*
- at completion of the whole of the works

Under NEC 3, clause 50.1, there is however no provision for further assessments after completion when an amount is corrected or when a payment is made late as was the case in ECC 2. This, however, should not be a problem as under NEC 3 the requirement for later assessments continues until the defects certificate is issued whereas under ECC 2 it was only until completion.

The assessment after the issue of the defects certificate is probably intended to be the assessment which will lead to what is normally called the final certificate. The involvement of the contractor in this is not specifically stated but applying clause 50.4 suggests that if the contractor wants to have his say in the final assessment he must put in his final account before the last assessment.

Clause 50.2 – the amount due

Clause 50.2 describes in general terms the amount due. It is:

- the price for work done to date, *plus*
- other amounts to be paid to the contractor, *less*
- amounts to be paid by or retained from the contractor

Additionally the clause states that any tax which the law requires the employer to pay to the contractor 'is included in the amount due'. The wording of this is a little unfortunate because on one interpretation it could mean that the contractor's prices are inclusive of VAT whereas what it presumably means is that the prices are exclusive of VAT. The phrase 'is included' in the last sentence of the clause is better read as 'is to be included'.

But even given that meaning there is still an administrative problem to overcome on value added tax in that, unless the employer operates an approved self billing system, value added tax only becomes due on receipt of a VAT invoice. In practice therefore it will be normal for the project manager and the contractor to liaise so that the contractor's certificate is accompanied by a matching VAT invoice.

For comment on the detail of the amounts due under the various main options see sections 10.5 to 10.10.

Clause 50.3 – failure to submit programme

Clause 50.3 is an unusual provision which penalises the contractor if he delays in submitting a first programme for acceptance.

The clause provides that:

- if no programme is identified in the contract data, *then*
- one quarter of the price for work done to date is retained in assessments of amounts due, *until*
- the contractor has submitted a first programme for acceptance showing all the information required by the contract

Note that the retained amount applies only to the price for work done to date and not to other components of the amount due. Note also that the deduction is made at the assessment stage by the project manager so the certificate itself is for the reduced amount. In the not improbable situation that the contractor and the project manager are in dispute as to whether the submitted programme shows all the information which the contract requires it seems to be open to the project manager to make the deduction leaving the contractor to seek adjudication if dissatisfied.

Some commentators have suggested that the clause may be challengeable in law as a penalty clause and that it may not be enforceable. As far as interim payments are concerned it is questionable whether the argument would succeed because the provision is, in effect, an agreed precedent to a contractual entitlement rather than a form of liquidated damages for breach. However, if a situation arose where a complying first programme was never submitted and the clause was used (as appears possible) to reduce the final contract price by 25% that might well be a penalty.

Finally, it is worth noting that clause 50.3 does not necessarily lead to an accepted programme coming into place early in the contract. Clause 31.3 states four reasons for not accepting a programme but clause 50.3 refers to only one – lack of information. So the motivation for submitting a programme which is acceptable on the other grounds is not to be found in clause 50.3. For that the contract relies on clause 64.2 – the assessment of compensation events.

Clause 50.4 – assessing amounts due

Clause 50.4 contains two useful provisions. Firstly, if the contractor submits an application for payment on or before the assessment date the project manager is required to consider the application when making his assessment. Secondly, the project manager is required to give the contractor details of how an amount due has been assessed.

Clearly if the contractor only submits his application on the assessment date itself that leaves the project manager with very little time (one week under clause 51.1) to consider it. But, it is possible that for commercial reasons (maximising the amount due) and contractual reasons (maximising the potential for interest) the contractor may be disposed to submit his application as late as permissible.

The requirement for the project manager to give details of his assessment appears to be a stand alone provision which is applicable whether or not the contractor has made any application. However, it might have been better if this requirement had been put in clause 50.1 and if some timescale had been attached.

Clause 50.5 – corrections of assessments

Clause 50.5 states only that the project manager corrects any wrongly assessed amount due in a later certificate. But the clause may not be as simple as it seems.

The question is – who decides whether an amount has been wrongly assessed? Obviously there is no problem if the wrong assessment is confirmed by an adjudicator but, short of involving an adjudicator, it is none too obvious how the reality of a wrong assessment can be established or how the project manager can be obliged to admit to making a wrong assessment. In most cases, wrong assessments, or alleged wrong assessments, will automatically be corrected in later certificates without there being any admission of an earlier wrong assessment. So if the purpose of the clause is to establish the contractor's right to interest under clause 51.3 it may not be too effective.

On a point of detail note that any wrongly assessed amount becomes due 'in a later payment certificate'. The contractor does not appear to have an entitlement (other than interest) to correction in the 'next' certificate.

10.3 Payments

Clause 51.1 – certification

The provisions of clause 51.1 can be summarised as follows:

- the project manager is required to certify payment within one week of each assessment date

- the first payment is the whole amount certified (subject to any retentions)
- subsequent payments are changes in amounts due from certificate to certificate
- if the change is a reduction the contractor pays the employer
- when the change is an increase the employer pays the contractor
- payments are made in the currency of the contract (as specified in the contract data) unless otherwise stated (i.e. Option X3 on multiple currencies applies)

Note that strictly the project manager does not certify amounts due (except in the first certificate) but only changes in amounts due. The terminology may lead to some confusion but most project managers will as a matter of good practice issue certificates showing both amounts due and changes in amounts due.

The requirement for the contractor to pay the employer for any change reducing the amount due is proper in principle but its application in NEC 3 is arguably more onerous than normal. This is because by clause 51.2 the contractor must make the payment within three weeks or pay interest on late payments whereas most contracts leave overpayments to be settled in the final certificate.

Clause 51.2 – time for payment and interest on late payment

Clause 51.2 of NEC 3 combines the provisions of clauses 51.2 and 51.4 of ECC 2. It does so by dealing with both late payment and late certification.

The first provision of the clause requires payment on each certificate within three weeks of the assessment date or within such other time as may be stated in the contract data.

As the project manager is allowed one week from the assessment date to certify (and will probably need all of that) the employer has effectively two weeks from certification to payment. If the project manager over-runs his time in certifying that cuts into the employer's time since the payment time is linked to the assessment date and not to the date of certification.

The second part of clause 51.2 provides for interest on late payment in the event of either late payment of a certified amount or in late payment because the project manager does not issue a certificate which he should issue. Interest is to be calculated for the period between the due payment date and the actual payment date and is to be included in the assessment following the late payment. Interest is apparently payable without application by the entitled party and it is apparently up to the project manager to ensure that his assessments include for interest when appropriate. The interest rate is that fixed by the employer in part one of the contract data – which is to be a rate not less than 2% above a specified bank rate. Clause 51.4 confirms that interest is to be calculated on a daily basis and compounded annually.

An interesting aspect of clause 51.2 is that it treats with equality payments due from either party to the other. Nowhere does it mention the employer or the contractor. Generally it will, of course, apply to payments from the employer to the contractor but it is not inconceivable, since by clause 50.2 amounts due are net amounts, that on occasions amounts will be due from the contractor to the employer. If such amounts are certified and paid late, the employer will be entitled to interest. And even if the project manager in breach of his obligations fails to certify such amounts the employer will still, theoretically, be entitled to interest.

Clause 51.3 – interest on corrected amounts

Clause 51.3 provides for interest on amounts corrected in later certificates. The clause appears to be unusually strict in its application because it states that interest is paid on the correcting amount if a certificate is corrected either:

- by the project manager in relation to
  — a mistake, *or*
  — a compensation event
- or following a decision of an adjudicator or disputes tribunal

The reference in the clause to 'mistake' could be interpreted as applying to a mistake by the contractor as well as to a mistake by the project manager. This may not be the intention but since it is the responsibility of the project manager to assess amounts due on certificates without any obligatory input from the contractor, any correction to a certificate will appear at face value to arise from a mistake by the project manager – whether by a mistake of law or a mistake of fact.

There may occasionally be circumstances where the contractor has obstructed the project manager from making a correct assessment, perhaps by the non-disclosure of records or non-compliance with the accepted pro-gramme, and where the contractor cannot argue that the circumstances con-stitute a mistake but otherwise it is difficult to see how corrections can avoid attracting interest.

The reference in clause 51.3 to corrections for compensation events is not wholly clear in its purpose. It may simply be intended that if compensation events are revalued then interest accrues from the original valuation. But the intention may be much wider such that interest runs from the first certifica-tion date after a compensation event is claimed until certification of the proper value. This would be not far removed from giving the contractor an automatic right to financing charges on claims.

Interest under clause 51.3 is calculated as for clause 51.2 and it runs from the date of the incorrect certificate to the date of the corrected certificate.

Clause 51.4 – rate of interest

The interest rate applicable throughout NEC 3 is an identified term fixed by the employer in part one of the contract data. The data entry stipulates that the interest rate shall be not less than 2% above a specified bank rate.

Clause 51.4 states that interest is to be calculated at the identified rate on a daily basis and is to be compounded annually.

10.4 Defined cost

'Defined cost' is a defined term found in:

- clause 11.2(22) for Options A and B
- clause 11.2(23) for Options C, D and E
- clause 11.2(24) for Option F

Although defined cost only forms the full basis of the contractor's entitlement to payment under the cost reimbursable options E and F, it is of considerable importance in options A and B for the assessment of compensation events and in options C and D for compensation events and cost sharing calculations.

Clause 52.1

Clause 52.1 states certain matters common to usage of defined cost. The first provision of the clause states that all the contractor's costs not included within defined cost are deemed to be included in the fee. In other words the contractor must allow in the fee percentages which he tenders in part two of the contract data for all costs not expressly covered within the definition of defined cost.

The second provision of clause 52.1 stated that defined cost includes only:

- amounts calculated using rates and percentages stated in the contract data, and other amounts
- at open market or competitively tendered prices with deduction of all discounts, rebates and taxes which can be recovered

The application of this provision is not free from practical difficulties but it goes some way towards protecting the employer from the excesses which sometimes tarnish cost plus contracts.

10.5 Payments – main option A

The following core payment clauses are particular to main option A – the priced contract with activity schedule:

- clause 11.2(20) – definition of activity schedule
- clause 11.2(22) – definition of 'Defined Cost'
- clause 11.2(27) – definition of price for work done to date
- clause 11.2(30) – definition of the prices

- clause 54.1   – the activity schedule
- clause 54.2   – revision of activity schedule
- clause 54.3   – reasons for not accepting the activity schedule

Clause 11.2(20) – definition of activity schedule

This is a clause new to NEC 3. It states simply that the 'Activity Schedule' (as a defined term) is the activity schedule (identified in the contract data) unless later changed in accordance with the contract. Its purpose is to allow the phrase 'Activity Schedule' to be used as a defined term in other clauses of the contract. And when so used it is then the current activity schedule which is referred to.

Clause 11.2(22) – defined cost

Defined cost for Options A and B is defined as:

- the cost of components in the shorter schedule of cost components
- whether subcontracted or not
- excluding the cost of preparing quotations for compensation events

The first part of the clause restricts recovery on cost basis to the items detailed in the schedule of cost components. The second part of the clause referring to subcontracted work highlights a point which is not too obvious from the schedules of cost components. This is that for Options A and B the contractor cannot simply put forward subcontract invoices as evidence of defined cost. Subcontractor costs are to be calculated with reference to the rules of the shorter schedule of cost components in the same manner as the contractor's costs. However, under NEC 3, the contract data does provide for a separate fee percentage to be applied to subcontractor costs.

The final part of clause 11.2(22) stating that defined cost excludes the cost of preparing quotations for compensation events is a surprising provision to find in NEC 3 which is promoted as being a fair contract. Since many compensation events arise from defaults for which the employer is responsible and some are expressly breach of contract provisions the contractor should be able to recover the costs he incurs. This is particularly so where the contractor is instructed to prepare quotations or alternative quotations for proposed changes which are not later instructed.

Under ECC 2 the corresponding provision generated much resentment amongst contractors and considerable ingenuity went into efforts to recover the costs of preparing quotations for compensation events. In some cases these costs ran into huge sums. One interesting line of argument was to the effect that it could be implied from the provision that compensation events would be few and far between and where there were multiple compensation events there was breach and the costs of preparing quotations were recoverable under clause 60.1(18) – the compensation event for breach of contract.

Clause 11.2(27) – price for work done to date

The defined term 'the Price for Work Done to Date' governs the amount the contractor is due to be paid (clause 50.2) at both interim and final stages. The definition for the price for work done to date is the total of the prices:

- for each group of completed activities, *and*
- each completed activity which is not in a group
- which is without defects which would delay following work or which would be covered immediately by following work

It is up to the contractor how he forms his activity schedule and whether or not he shows grouping of activities. The contractor has to keep in mind that only completed groups of activities or completed single activities attract entitlement to interim payment. There is no contractual advantage to the contractor in grouping activities together but the disadvantage is obvious enough.

The reference to defects in the price for work done to date is worded so as to permit a certain level of defects to be tolerated without prejudicing the contractor's right to payment.

Note that activities which are not included in the activity schedule do not come within the scope of the definition of 'Prices' in clause 11.2(30) and therefore are not within the scope of 'the Price for Work Done to Date' in clause 11.2(27). Consequently omitted activities never attract a right to payment and are deemed to be covered in the listed activities.

Clause 11.2(30) – definition of the prices

The prices are defined as:

- the lump sum prices
- for each of the activities in the activity schedule
- unless changed later in accordance with the contract

The definition suggests that a contract let under main option A is a contract for a collection of various activities with individual lump sum prices rather than a straightforward lump sum price contract. For comment on this see Chapter 2, section 3.

The phrase 'unless later changed' ensures that the definition of the prices remains valid from tender to completion. But note that the changes are to be 'in accordance with this contract' and they do not extend to other changes of the lump sum price or prices which may be agreed between the parties.

The activity schedule

For general comment on the activity schedule see Chapter 2, section 3.

Clause 54.1 – information in the activity schedule

The purpose of clause 54.1 which states only that information in the activity schedule is not works information or site information is apparently to ensure that the activity schedule does not acquire unintended contractual effect in respect of the obligations of the parties.

Clause 54.2 – changes to the activity schedule

In order to maintain the integrity of the payment system for Option A which relies on the identification of completed activities and the integrity of the scheme for assessment of compensation events NEC 3 needs compatibility between the activity schedule and the accepted programme.

Clause 54.2 requires the contractor to submit a revised activity schedule to the project manager for acceptance:

- when he changes a planned method of working
- at his discretion
- such that the activities on the activity schedule do not relate to operations on the accepted programme

It is not wholly clear why clause 54.2 is confined to changes in methods of working made at the contractor's 'discretion'. Changes imposed on the contractor by compensation events are just as likely to affect the activity schedule. Perhaps it is assumed that these changes are already incorporated into the accepted programme via the compensation event procedures.

Clause 54.3 – reasons for not accepting a revised activity schedule

Clause 54.3 states three reasons for the project manager not accepting a revision of the activity schedule:

- the revision does not comply with the accepted programme
- the changed prices are not distributed reasonably between the prices
- the total of the prices is changed

This final reason stated here provides confirmation, if it is needed, that the total of the prices in the original activity schedule is the total contract price (subject, of course, to contractual adjustments).

The consequences of not accepting a revised activity schedule are to leave payments and compensation events to be valued in accordance with the previous activity schedule.

10.6 *Payments – main option B*

The core clauses particular to main option B – the priced contract with bill of quantities – are:

- clause 11.2(21) – bill of quantities
- clause 11.2(22) – definition of defined cost
- clause 11.2(28) – definition of the price for work done to date
- clause 11.2(31) – definition of the prices

Clause 11.2(21) – definition of bill of quantities

This is another clause new to NEC 3. It states that the 'Bill of Quantities' (as a defined term) is the bill of quantities (identified in the contract data) as changed to accommodate implemented compensation events and accepted quotations for acceleration. Its purpose is similar to that of clause 11.2(20) found in Option A – namely to allow the phrase 'Bill of Quantities' to be used as a defined term in other clauses of the contract. However, it is not entirely clear why its wording differs from that of clause 11.2(20) in referring to compensation events and acceleration.

Clause 11.2(22) – defined cost

This is the same clause as used for Option A – for comment see the preceding section.

Clause 11.2(28) – the price for work done to date

The price for work done to date is stated in clause 11.2(28) as:

- the quantity of completed work for each bill of quantities item multiplied by the appropriate rate, *and*
- such proportion of each lump in the bill of quantities as is completed

The clause states further that completed work 'in the clause' means work without defects which would either delay or be covered by immediately following work. The phrase 'in this clause' is presumably intended to emphasise that 'completed work' as mentioned in the clause for payment purposes is not to be taken as completed work for other contractual purposes.

Clause 11.2(31) – definition of the prices

The prices are defined as:

- the lump sums, *and*
- the amounts obtained by multiplying the rates by the quantities for the items in the bill of quantities
- unless changed in accordance with the contract

The traditional approach in bill of quantities contracts is to refer to rates and prices – with rates applying to remeasured items and prices to lump sums. NEC 3 takes an unusual approach and defines prices so that a rate times a quantity is regarded as a price.

10.7 *Payments – main option C*

The following payment core clauses are particular to main option C – the target contract with activity schedule:

- clause 11.2(20)   – definition of activity schedule
- clause 11.2(23)   – definition of defined cost
- clause 11.2(25)   – definition of disallowed cost
- clause 11.2(29)   – definition of the price for work done to date
- clause 11.2(30)   – definition of the prices
- clause 50.6   – assessing the amount due
- clauses 52.2 & 52.3 – records of defined cost
- clauses 53.1 to 53.4 – the contractor's share
- clauses 54.1 to 54.3 – the activity schedule

Clause 11.2(20) – definition of activity schedule

This is the same clause as found in Option A – for comment see section 10.5.

Clause 11.2(23) – definition of defined cost

In ECC 2 'Actual Cost' was defined fairly simply as amounts due to subcontractors for work which was subcontracted, plus the costs of components in the schedules of cost components for work not subcontracted, less disallowed costs. The definition in clause 11.2(23) of NEC 3 of the replacement term 'Defined Cost' is less concise because of the inclusion of a list of five items, all deductions which the contractor may have made against subcontractors, which need not be taken into account in totalling the amounts due to subcontractors. These are:

- retentions
- payments to the employer for failures to meet key dates

- correction of defects after completion
- payments to others
- supply of equipment etc. included in the charge for overhead cost

The reason for the inclusion of these items in the clause is stated in the Guidance Notes to NEC 3 to be to avoid double deduction from the contractor's account. It appears that some project managers under ECC 2 interpreted 'amounts due to subcontractors' too literally. But apart from the new list of non-qualifying deductions, defined cost under NEC 3 is the same as actual cost under ECC 2 in being subcontractor costs plus direct costs less disallowed costs.

An interesting point of note is that whereas defined cost under clause 11.2(22) which applies to Options A and B expressly excludes the costs of preparing quotations for compensation events, clause 11.2(23) which applies to Options C, D and E has no such exclusion. It can reasonably be taken therefore that the costs of preparing quotations under these options are valid elements of defined cost.

The major difference between clauses 11.2(23) and 11.2(22), however, is that subcontractors invoices can form part of defined cost under clause 11.2(23). Another significant difference is that the definition of defined cost under clause 11.2(23) expressly excludes disallowed costs. This difference results from the respective uses of defined cost under Options A and C. Under Option A defined cost is considered only in the assessment of compensation events – questions of disallowed cost should therefore not arise. Under Option C the price for the work done to date is based on defined cost. Therefore, that which is not chargeable to the employer needs to be excluded.

Clause 11.2(25) – disallowed cost

Disallowed costs under clause 11.2(25) of NEC 3 are essentially the same as those under ECC 2 but there are a few points of difference:

- Clause 11.2(25) excludes the disallowed cost of paying a subcontractor more for a compensation event than included in a quotation or assessment. Although, on its face, it seems reasonable that this should be disallowed, and that no doubt was why it was included in ECC 2, the reality is that under Options C, D and E to which clause 11.2(25) applies the contractor is obliged to pay the subcontractor on a cost basis if the subcontract is also under Option C, D or E.
- Clause 11.2(25) adds 'supplier' to 'subcontractor' for cost which should not have been paid.
- Clause 11.2(25) qualifies plant and materials not used with 'unless resulting from a change to the works information'.
- Clause 11.2(25) adds as a new item of disallowed cost 'preparation for and conduct of an adjudication or proceedings of the tribunal'.
- Clause 11.2(25) changes correcting defects caused by the contractor not complying with a 'requirement' in the works information to not complying with a 'constraint' in the works information.

The full list of items of disallowed cost in clause 11.2(25) is:

- costs not justified by accounts and records
- costs which should not have been paid to subcontractors or suppliers
- costs incurred because the contractor did not follow an acceptance or procedure in the works information or did not give an early warning
- costs of correcting defects after completion
- costs of correcting defects caused by not complying with a constraint in the works information
- plant and materials not used to provide the works – after allowing for reasonable wastage and unless resulting from a change in the works information
- resources not used to provide the works or not taken away when requested
- preparation for and conduct of adjudication or tribunal proceedings

Most of these are straightforward in principle even if open to argument on their application in particular circumstances. However, what may cause some surprise is that the costs of correcting defects before completion are apparently not disallowed unless the defects are caused by the contractor not complying with a constraint in the works information. Thus, amongst other things, defects caused by the contractor's design can apparently be corrected at cost – which raises questions on the suitability of using Option C (and other cost reimbursable options) with contractor's design.

Clause 11.2(29) – definition of the price for work done to date

This clause states that the price for work done to date is the defined cost which the project manager forecasts will have been paid by the contractor before the next assessment date plus the fee.

Clause 11.2(30) – definition of the prices

This is the same clause as for Option A – for general comment see section 10.5. However, it is important to note that the prices have far less contractual importance in Option C than in Option A. In particular in Option A the prices form the foundation of the price for work done to date (which governs the final contract price) whereas in Option C the prices play no part in the price for work done to date and only affect the final contract price through calculations of the contractor's share (clause 53).

Clause 50.6 – assessing the amount due

Clause 50.6 deals with the situation when payments for actual cost are made by the contractor in a currency other than the currency of the contract.

The clause provides that in such circumstances the amount due to the contractor is calculated by reference to the currency of the cost but for calculation of the fee and the contractor's share payments are converted to the currency of the contract.

Clause 52.2 – records of defined cost

In keeping with the cost reimbursable aspect of Option C clause 52.2 requires the contractor to keep records of his defined cost including, and expressly:

- accounts of payments of defined cost
- records showing payments made
- records relating to compensation events for subcontractors
- other records and accounts as stated in the works information

Clause 52.3 – inspection of records

Clause 52.3 provides that the contractor shall allow the project manager to inspect the records at any time within working hours. Since it is the project manager's obligation to assess amounts due to the contractor this is clearly an essential provision.

The contractor's share

For any contractor considering entering into a target cost contract one of the key questions is what are the potential risks and rewards arising from excesses or savings on the target cost. For general comment on this see Chapter 2, section 5.

Some target cost contracts have very simple formulae for fixing the contractor's and the employer's shares of excesses and savings. NEC 3 has an incremental scheme generally the same as that in ECC 2 which requires the employer to state in the contract data (in percentage terms) ranges of deviation from the target cost and corresponding share percentages.

Clause 53.1 – calculating the share

Clause 53.1 of ECC 2 was commonly regarded as a masterpiece of obfuscation. It remains unchanged in NEC 3. The Guidance Notes to NEC 3 helpfully provide at page 66 a worked example of how the clause is to be understood.

Clause 53.2 – payment of the share

This clause appears to do little more than state the obvious – namely, that the contractor is paid his share of any saving and that he pays his share of any excess. But the clause may be necessary since in the event of excess the contractor will have been overpaid under the rules of NEC 3 and the obligation to repay his share of the excess needs to be clearly stated.

Clause 53.3 – preliminary assessment of the share

Clause 53.3 requires the project manager to make a preliminary assessment of the contractor's share at completion of the whole of the works. The assessment is made using the project manager's forecasts for the final price for the work done to date and the final prices (which are the tender prices adjusted for compensation events and the like). This share is to be included in the amount due 'following' completion of the whole of the works. This probably means that the contractor's share is included in the assessment made 'at' completion under clause 50.1.

Note that as NEC 3 does not provide for interim assessments of the contractor's share before completion the contractor is fully reimbursed on a cost basis up to completion. In this respect the NEC 3 is significantly different from target contracts of the type where the target mechanism operates in part as a guaranteed maximum price and where payment cuts off when this is reached.

Clause 53.4 – final assessment of the share

The final assessment of the share is made using the final price for work done to date and the final total of the prices. This share is included in the final amount due – so, unless there are complications, it should be included in the amount certified after the issue of the defects certificate.

Proposals for reducing defined cost

Missing from NEC 3 is a clause corresponding to clause 53.5 of ECC 2 which provided that if the project manager accepted a proposal by the contractor to change the works information so as to reduce actual cost, the prices were not reduced. This allowed the contractor to keep any benefit by way of increased share.

The activity schedule

In Option C, the activity schedule serves a different purpose than in Option A. Whereas in Option A, the activity schedule is used to assess interim payments, in Option C the activity schedule is used only in the assessment of compensation events and in detailing the total of the prices for the calculation of the contractor's share.

Clauses 54.1 to 54.3 – activity schedule

These are the same clauses as used in Option A – see section 10.5 for comment.

10.8 Payments – main option D

The payment core clauses particular to main option D – the target contract with bill of quantities are:

- clause 11.2(21)   – definition of bill of quantities
- clause 11.2(23)   – definition of defined cost
- clause 11.2(25)   – definition of disallowed cost
- clause 11.2(29)   – definition of the price for work done to date
- clause 11.2(31)   – definition of the prices
- clause 11.2(33)   – definition of 'The Total of the Prices'
- clause 50.6   – assessing the amount due
- clauses 52.2 and 52.3 – records of actual cost
- clauses 53.5 to 53.8   – the contractor's share

Clauses 11.2(21) and 11.2(31) are common to Options B and D. For comment see section 10.6. Clauses 23, 25, 29, 50.6, 52.2 and 52.3 are common to Options C and D – for comment see the previous section.

Clause 11.2(33) is a definition used solely in Option D. It introduces as a defined term 'The Total of the Prices', and describes this as:

- the quantity of work completed for each item in the bill of quantities multiplied by the rate, *and*
- a proportion of each lump sum proportioned to the completed work covered by the item

This is in fact the definition of the price for the work done to date found in clause 11.2(28) of Option B and the sole purpose of repeating it in Option D under a new number seems to be to facilitate expressions of, and perhaps calculation of, the contractor's share. So much can be gathered from the renumbering of clauses 53.1 to 53.4 in Option C as clauses 53.5 to 53.8 in Option D and the replacement of the phrase 'the total of the Prices' in Option C with the phrase 'the Total of the Prices' in Option D.

Note that bill of quantities in Option D serves the same purpose as the activity schedule in Option C and it is not used for assessing interim payments.

10.9 Payments – main option E

The following payment core clauses are particular to main option E – the cost reimbursable contract:

- clause 11.2(23)   – definition of defined cost
- clause 11.2(25)   – definition of disallowed cost

- clause 11.2(29)   – definition of the price for work done to date
- clause 11.2(32)   – definition of the prices
- clause 50.7   – assessing the amount due
- clauses 52.2 and 52.3 – records of actual cost

Because main option E is a fully cost reimbursable contract it does not include clauses relating to the contractor's share or to either an activity schedule or a bill of quantities. Accordingly, no further comment is required here. Clauses 11.2(23), 11.2(25), 11.2(29), 52.2 and 52.3 common to Options C and D, have been considered earlier.

Clause 11.2(32) – definition of the prices

The prices are defined simply as the defined cost plus the fee.

There is no significance in the use of the term 'Prices' as opposed to 'Price'. It seems to be used simply to achieve compatibility with other clauses of the contract.

Clause 50.7 – assessing the amount due

This clause is similar to clause 50.6 used in Options C and D for dealing with payments made by the contractor in currencies other than the currency of the contract except that it omits the reference in clause 50.6 to the contractor's share.

10.10 Payments – main option F

The payment core clauses particular to main option F – the management contract are:

- clause 11.2(24)   – definition of defined cost
- clause 11.2(26)   – definition of disallowed costs
- clause 11.2(29)   – definition of the price for work done to date
- clause 11.2(32)   – definition of the prices
- clause 50.7   – assessing the amount due
- clauses 52.2 and 52.3 – records of defined cost

From the above list only clauses 11.2(24) and 11.2(26) differ from the clauses also applicable to main option E.

Clause 11.2(24) – definition of defined cost

The difference between the definition of defined cost in clause 11.2(24) and the definition found in clause 11.2(23) which applies to Options C, D and E is that for work done by the contractor himself, clause 11.2(24) refers to 'the prices', whereas clause 11.2(23) refers to the costs of components in the schedules of cost components.

Clause 11.2(26) – definition of disallowed cost

The differences between the definition in clause 11.2(26) of disallowed cost and the definition in clause 11.2(25) applicable to Options C, D and E are firstly that clause 11.2(26) omits the reference in clause 11.2(25) to:

- the costs of correcting defects
- the costs of plant and materials not used to provide the works
- the costs of resources not used to provide the works or not taken away when requested

This suggests that there is less disallowed cost under Option F than under the other cost reimbursable options but that is not intended to be the case.

Normally all the work in Option F will be subcontracted as packages on lump sum prices and each subcontractor will be responsible for correcting his own defects at his own cost. Only if the contractor does some of the work himself will the omitted items of disallowed costs be of any significance.

Other differences are:

- clause 11.2(26) does not include as disallowed cost preparation for and conduct of adjudication and tribunal proceedings
- clause 11.2(26) includes as disallowed cost payment to a subcontractor for work which the contract data states the contractor will do himself or payment to a subcontractor for the contractor's management.

Chapter 11
NEC 3 compensation event schemes

11.1 Introduction

Since first introduced in 1991 the compensation event schemes of NEC contracts have been the most discussed and the most disputed parts of the contracts. This is not surprising given that they aim to cover all claims from the contractor for extra time and money and to do so with procedures which are a radical departure from traditional methods of assessing extensions of time, valuing variations and quantifying claims. It will, however, be a disappointment to many users of NEC 3 contracts that the opportunity seems to have been missed in the latest revisions to fully address and to simplify the most obvious complexities of the schemes.

Some changes have been made, but overall, and irrespective of whether they turn out individually to be for better or for worse, they leave in place procedures which are time consuming and expensive to operate, unsuitable for multiple claim situations, and as likely to be abandoned by the parties as unworkable as sometimes happened under ECC 2.

Theory and reality

The problems of the compensation event schemes can best be seen by comparing the theory of their design with the reality of their operation. As emphasised in the Guidance Notes the fundamental objectives of NEC contracts are good management and minimisation of the incidence of disputes. The management of compensation events is described as being an example of these objectives. This is what is then said:

> 'A principle of the ECC is that, when such an event occurs, the Project Manager, acting on behalf of the Employer and in communication with him, should, whenever possible, be presented with options for dealing with the problem from which he can choose, directed by the interests of the Employer.
>
> The ECC is designed to ensure that the Contractor will be unaffected financially by the choice that the Project Manager makes. To achieve this, the Contractor prepares a quotation for the valuation of compensation events that is based upon a forecast of the impact which the change or problem will have upon his cost of carrying out the work – as forecast by him at the time the event is assessed. Where, as is often the case, alternative ways of dealing with the problem are possible, the Contractor prepares quotations for different ways of tackling the problem.

The Project Manager selects one on the basis of which will best serve the interests of the Employer. Criteria for such selection can include lowest cost, least delay or best finished quality, or any combination of these.'

The first difficulty which springs out from the above, and it is a major difficulty in many NEC contracts, is that compensation events are not rare events or occasional events as seems to be implied by the above but common events, frequently running into hundreds of events. They are the only mechanism in the contract for increasing prices and extending time whether by large amounts or by small amounts. Not surprisingly they are well used. The standard assessment procedure however requires detailed calculations, supported by programmes of forecast effects. These can be time consuming both in their preparation by the contractor and consideration by the project manager even when infrequent. When frequent they can collapse the system by overload – one particular problem being that the accepted programme which acts as the base for the calculations cannot always be updated as fast as the compensations events are flowing in for assessment.

A second major difficulty with the theory of the schemes is the presumption that generally the project manager will be active in recognising compensation events and in seeking quotations from the contractor. The reality is often otherwise. Sometimes this is because the project manager is reluctant to accept the existence of a compensation event – a common example being refusal to accept changes in the works information as changes on the basis that they are merely design development. Sometimes it is because the project manager is nervous about seeking quotations which might prove to be, after the event, more beneficial to the contractor than to the employer and because of this the project manager would prefer the compensation event to be valued retrospectively on actual cost rather than prospectively on forecast cost. Changes in NEC 3 attempt to deal with this latter problem by strengthening the status of the contractor's quotations, whether or not they are requested by the project manager, by creating a new category of status called 'quotations treated as having been accepted'. Oddly, by other changes in NEC 3 they are not treated as having been accepted because they can be disputed by the employer.

A third difficulty with the theory and practice of compensation events is the presumption that the contractor will be free to price risk into quotations for compensation events in much the same way as in tenders. When the contractor is so free he may well make money out of compensation events. The contract then is likely to be dispute free and said to have worked well. For many years that was the case under traditional process and plant contracts with quotation based valuation of variation provisions. Under ECC 2, however, it was commonplace for project managers to reject quotations because they considered them too costly and because they believed, wrongly it is suggested, that the assessment system allowed them to make their own assessments if they thought fit – thereby completely nullifying the quotation system on which the contract was founded. That problem has not been directly addressed in the NEC 3 changes.

11.2 Changes in NEC 3 (from ECC 2)

Terminology

NEC 3 uses the phrases 'access to and use of a part of the Site' and 'access date' in place of the ECC 2 phrases which referred to possession and the possession date.

NEC 3 refers to 'Defined Cost' rather than to 'Actual Cost' as in ECC 2.

Key dates

The new provisions in NEC 3 for key dates to be stated (if so required) are reflected in the compensation event clauses – with provisions for changes to key dates in much the same way as changes to completion dates.

Amendments to listed events

Clause 60.1(5) – previously this compensation event arose only when the employer or others did not work within the times on the accepted programme or within the conditions stated in the works information. The new clause also applies when the employer or others carry out work on the site which is not stated in the works information. This is a substantial widening of the scope of the clause.

Clause 60.1(12) – an additional sentence states that only the difference between the physical conditions encountered and those which it would have been reasonable to allow for is taken into account in assessment of a compensation event. This clarifies a point, sometimes disputed under ECC 2, as to whether the assessment should cover all costs arising from an event or only excess costs.

Clause 60.1(13) – in like manner to the above, an additional sentence states that only the difference between actual weather conditions and 'ten year' conditions is to be taken into account in assessment of a compensation event.

Clause 60.1(17) – the words ' about a compensation event' replace 'about the nature of a compensation event'.

Clause 60.2 – to the phrase 'In judging the physical conditions' is added 'for the purpose of assessing a compensation event' – thereby eliminating the possibility that the clause might be taken to be of wider scope than intended, for example, in design.

Clause 60.4 – applies to main options B and D only. A new sentence is added clarifying the point that 'a compensation event for changes between final quantities and billed quantities does not arise under the clause if the difference results from a change in the works information. The overall percentage price change necessary to trigger a compensation event under the clause, which was stated as 0.1% in ECC 2, is increased to 0.5%.

Clause 60.6 – applies to main options B and D only. The compensation event for correction of mistakes in the bill of quantities is extended from departures 'from the rules for item descriptions' to departures from the 'division of the work into items in the method of measurement'.

Clause 60.7 – applies to main options B and D only. States that in assessing a compensation event which results from inconsistency between the bill of quantities and another document, the contractor is assumed to have taken the bill of quantities as correct.

Additional listed events

Clause 60.1(19) – a new clause which brings the circumstances described as 'prevention' in the new clause 19.1 into the compensation event regime.

Clause X15.2 – applies only if secondary option X15 limiting the contractor's liability for design is included in the contract. States that it is a compensation event if the contractor corrects a defect for which he is not liable under the contract.

Amendments to notification clauses

Clause 61.1 – the new clause requires the project manager to notify a compensation event 'at the time of giving the instruction or changing the earlier decision' whereas previously in ECC 2 it was 'at the time of the event'.

Clause 61.3 – the old clause stated that the contractor notifies a compensation event 'if it is less than two weeks since he became aware of the event'. It was much debated as to whether this was a time-barring clause. The new clause resolves the matter by stating, 'If the Contractor does not notify a compensation event within eight weeks of becoming aware of the event, he is not entitled to a change in the Prices, the Completion Date or a Key Date unless the Project Manager should have notified the event to the Contractor but did not.' This is clearly intended to be time-barring but questions remain as to its effectiveness.

Clause 61.4 – the old clause is extended so that if the project manager has not notified his decision as to whether or not a claimed event is a compensation event which requires assessment within one week, or such longer period as may be agreed, the contractor may notify the project manager of his failure and if the project manager does not reply within two weeks, the contractor's notification is treated as acceptance by the project manager and as an instruction to submit quotations.

Amendments to quotation clauses

Clause 62.1 – the wording allowing the project manager to instruct the contractor to submit alternative quotations is changed from 'based upon different ways of dealing with the compensation event which are practical' to 'after discussing with the Contractor different ways of dealing with the compensation event which are practical.'

Clause 62.2 – the sentence 'If the programme for remaining work is affected by the compensation event, the Contractor includes a revised programme in his quotation showing the effect' in the old clause is replaced in the new clause by 'If the programme for remaining work is altered by the compensation event, the Contractor includes the alterations to the Accepted Programme in his quotation.'

Additional quotation clause

Clause 62.6 – this important new clause sets out in some detail the circumstances by which a contractor's quotation can become treated as accepted as a result of the project manager's failures to reply to submitted quotations.

Amendments to assessment clauses

Clause 63.1 – the new clause contains the added provision 'The date when the Project Manager instructed or should have instructed the Contractor to submit quotations divides the work already done from the work not yet done.'

Clause 63.2 – the old clause stated that if the effect of a compensation event was to reduce total actual cost the prices were not reduced except as stated in the contract. It then continued with a rule as to how this was to apply. The new clause contains only the part stating that prices are not reduced except as stated in the contract. The applicable rules are now found in the clauses particular to main options A to D.

Clause 63.3 – the new clause contains an added provision to the effect that delay to a key date is assessed by reference to delay to the date shown on the accepted programme.

Clause 63.8 – this clause replaces clause 63.7 of ECC 2 with considerably briefer wording as to how compensation events arising from instructed changes in the works information made to resolve ambiguities or inconsistencies are to be assessed. The overall effect remains unchanged – interpretation is to be favourable to the party which did not provide the relevant works information.

Additional assessment clauses

Clause 63.4 – this new clause states, somewhat enigmatically in respect of the employer, that the rights of the employer and the contractor to changes to the prices, completion dates and key dates are their only rights in respect of the compensation event.

Clause 63.9 – this new clause requires the project manager to correct descriptions for key events if made necessary by changes to the works information and to take the correction into account in assessing the compensation event for the change to the works information.

Clause 63.10 – this is a new clause found only in main options A and B. It deals with reduced prices.

Clause 63.11 – this is the corresponding clause on reduced prices for main options C and D.

Clause 63.14 – this clause contains a potentially very useful new provision. It states that if the project manager and the contractor agree, rates and lump sums may be used to assess compensation events instead of defined cost. It appears in main option A as clause 63.14 but it is also to be found in main options B and D at the bottom of clause 63.13. It is not included in option C, E or F.

Omitted assessment clauses

An important point to note in respect of assessment changes between ECC 2 and NEC 3 is that clause 63.11 of ECC 2 which appeared in main options A to E is omitted from Options A and B of NEC 3 and is now only found in Options C to E as renumbered clause 63.15. The clause says that if the project manager and the contractor agree, the contractor assesses a compensation event using the shorter schedule of cost components and that the project manager, in his assessments, may use the shorter schedule of cost components. The reason the clause is omitted from NEC 3 Options A and B is that the new definition of defined cost for those options at clause 11.2(22) states that defined cost is the cost of components in the shorter schedule.

Amendments to project manager's assessment clauses

Clause 64.1 – the third bullet point to the new clause adds failure to submit 'alterations to a programme' to the matters permitting the project manager to assess a compensation event when the contractor has not submitted a programme with his quotation.

Clause 64.2 – this clause contains the same added wording for situations where there is no submitted or accepted programme.

Additional project manager's assessment clause

Clause 64.4 – this provides that if the project manager does not assess a compensation event within the time allowed, the contractor may notify the project manager, and failing reply within two weeks, the contractor's quotation is treated as having been accepted by the project manager.

Amendment to implementation clause

Clause 65.1 – the old clause is restructured and contains the added provision that a compensation event is implemented when a contractor's quotation is treated as having been accepted by the project manager.

11.3 *Outline of procedures*

In summary NEC 3 compensation event procedures work as follows:

- Certain events are stated in core clauses 60.1 to 60.7 to be compensation events. Other events are stated in secondary options X2, X14 and X15 to be compensation events. Additional events may also be stated by the employer in the contract data.
- The project manager is required to notify the contractor of compensation events arising from instructions or the changing of earlier decisions. The contractor is required to notify the project manager within eight weeks of other events or events not notified by the project manager.
- The contractor is required to submit quotations for compensation events showing both time and money implications. He may be required to submit alternative quotations. A revision of the accepted programme must be submitted with each quotation if there are time or disruption implications.
- Quotations for changes to the contract price are based on assessments of defined cost incurred or forecast to be incurred.
- In circumstances where the project manager does not reply to a quotation within a stipulated period a quotation is treated as having been accepted.
- The project manager is permitted to make his own assessment if the contractor does not submit his quotation on time or if the contractor's programme is not in order or if he (the project manager) decides that the contractor's assessment is incorrect.
- In circumstances where the project manager does not accept a quotation but fails to make his own assessment within a stipulated period, the quotation is treated as having been accepted.
- The project manager is required to notify the contractor when a quotation is accepted or his own assessment is made. The contract price and the times for completion and key dates are changed accordingly.

11.4 Defining a compensation event

NEC 3 lists the events it states to be compensation events but it does not define what a compensation event is. The contractual function of a compensation event is left to be derived from the provisions of the contract.

Clause 62.2 is helpful. This states that quotations for compensation events comprise proposed changes to the prices and any delay to the completion date and key dates. Clause 65.1 adds to this by stating that the project manager implements each compensation event by notifying the contractor of the quotation he has accepted or his own assessment. So clearly a compensation event is an event which can lead to an increase in the contract price and/or an increase in the time for completion or changes to key dates.

However, not all compensation events which occur necessarily lead to either. Clause 61.4 indicates that there is no change to the contract price or the time for completion or key dates if the compensation event arises from the fault of the contractor or if it has no effect on actual cost or completion.

It would seem, therefore, that a compensation event is a listed event which, if it occurs, allows for changes in the contract price or times for completion or key dates providing it does not arise from a fault of the contractor.

11.5 Compensation events as exclusive remedies

A question of key importance in the analysis of NEC 3 is whether or not its compensation event procedure provides an exclusive and exhaustive scheme for dealing with the contractor's claims. Or, put another way, does the procedure exclude the contractor's common law rights to damages for breach of contract?

There can be little doubt that when the NEC was first produced its promoters thought or hoped that they had devised a scheme which would fully cover the contractor's entitlements to extra time and money and which would eliminate end of contract claims – particularly global claims. That message was fairly well paraded. And when the promoters realised that the list of compensation events in the first edition of NEC did not fully cover the employer's possible defaults they revised the list for the second edition and included an event covering the employer's breach of contract.

In NEC 3 there are further signs of the intention to make the compensation event procedure exclusive and exhaustive of the contractor's rights. There is a new clause 63.4 which states that the rights of the employer and the contractor to changes to the prices, to the completion date, and to key dates are their only rights in respect of a compensation event. When this is combined with the new clause 12.4, which states that the contract is the entire agreement between the parties, the intention in respect of the contractor's contractual rights is obvious enough even if the reference in clause 63.4 to the employer's rights is less obvious in its intent.

Nevertheless, doubts remain both of a general and particularised nature as to whether NEC 3 achieves exclusion of the contractor's common law rights. To do so clear words are needed – see the decision in *Hancock* v. *Brazier* (1966). The wording of clause 63.4, however clear on the contractual rights, is far less clear on common law rights. And since the new secondary option X18, limitation of liability, apparently applies only to limitation of liability in damages claims, albeit the employer's claims, it cannot be said in general terms that clause 63.4 is an exclusion of common law rights clause.

Further points which go against the proposition that NEC 3 excludes the contractor's common law rights are:

- the contractor's entitlements under the compensation event procedure are rigidly prescribed by timing and administrative requirements
- the amounts recoverable under the compensation event procedure can fall short of the amounts due as damages for breach of contract even when properly assessed and with adequate risk allowances, and are subject to retention if Option X16 is included in the contract
- the contractor is required to forecast at his own expense the costs of the employer's breaches of contract and his recovery is limited to his forecast
- by clause 83.1 each party indemnifies the other against claims, proceedings, compensation and costs due to an event which is at his risk
  – compensation event assessments do not necessarily provide such indemnity
- the permitted time for making compensation event claims is only a fraction of normal limitation/prescription periods.

It remains to be seen what view the courts will take on the matter but unless and until a decision emerges, the parties and adjudicators may be disposed to follow the approach taken in *Milburn Services Ltd* v. *United Trading Group (UK) Ltd* (1995) where the absence of express works excluding the common law right to damages for breach seems to have been an important factor in the decision to regard the contractual scheme as supplementary to, but not in substitution of, common law rights.

One final point which does need to be made is that even if the contractor's common law rights to damages are preserved in NEC 3 as a matter of law, those rights are enforceable only in respect of breach of contract claims and not in respect of pure contractual entitlements. So, in so far that the list of compensation events contains both items of breach and items of entitlement (e.g. unforeseen ground conditions), any claims in respect of the latter can only be pursued under the compensation event procedure.

11.6 *Fairness of the compensation event procedures*

One of the major surprises which comes out of analysis of the compensation event procedures is that far from excelling as schemes which are fair to the contractor as the promoters of NEC 3 suggest, they place more risks on the contractor than other standard forms of construction contracts. This may not have been the intention of the draftsmen but by putting the risk of inadequate forecasting on the contractor and by combining the scheme for the valuation of variations with the scheme for the valuation of the employer's breaches of contract there is considerable potential for the contractor to lose money in circumstances where normally cost recovery would be regarded as a fair outcome.

Other risks to consider are:

- the contractor's risk of losing his rights under the notice requirements
- the contractor's risk that the amount of assessed defined cost recovered will be less than true defined cost – a risk to which the contractor is highly vulnerable under main options A and B

11.7 *Unusual features of the compensation event procedures*

In addition to the matters discussed above there are two further points which deserve a brief mention in this introduction to the compensation events.

The first point comes out of clause 65.2 which states that the assessment of a compensation event is not revised if a forecast upon which it is based is shown by later recorded information to have been wrong. One effect of this appears to be that NEC 3 adopts what is known as the first-in-line approach to causative events. Thus, if there is a delaying event for which the contractor is entitled to be paid and that event is overtaken by a delaying event for which the contractor is responsible, the contractor continues to be paid for the first event even though he is no longer suffering loss as a result of that event.

The second point comes out of clause 63.3. This states that a delay to the completion date is assessed as the length of time that planned completion is later than planned completion shown on the accepted programme. In short, the contractor owns overall the float in his programme and extensions of time are assessed with regard to the programme and not with regard to the time for completion.

Chapter 12
Listed compensation events

12.1 Introduction

Clause 60.1 lists nineteen compensation events which are intended to apply to all the main options. Clauses 60.2 and 60.3 provide clarification of some of the events but do not add to the list.

Clauses 60.4, 60.5 and 60.6 are compensation events applicable only to NEC 3 contracts with bills of quantities – main options B and D.

The secondary options list five more compensation events:

- clause X2.1 – a change in the law occurring after the contract date
- clause X12.3(6) – change in partnering information
- clause X14.2 – delay by the employer in making an advanced payment
- clause X15.2 – correction by contractor of a defect for which he is not liable
- clause Y2.4 – suspension of performance under HGCR Act 1996

There is a space in part one of the contract data for the employer to list additional compensation events. However, there are no clauses in the contract covering the incorporation of such additional events and it is questionable if they do become incorporated.

Listed events

In summary the listed events are:

- clause 60.1(1) – changes in works information
- clause 60.1(2) – late access/use of site
- clause 60.1(3) – late provision of specified things
- clause 60.1(4) – stopping/suspension of work
- clause 60.1(5) – late/additional works
- clause 60.1(6) – late reply to communications
- clause 60.1(7) – finding of objects of interest
- clause 60.1(8) – changes of decisions
- clause 60.1(9) – withholding of acceptances
- clause 60.1(10) – searches for defects
- clause 60.1(11) – tests or inspections causing delay
- clause 60.1(12) – physical conditions

- clause 60.1(13) – weather conditions
- clause 60.1(14) – employer's risk
- clause 60.1(15) – take-over before completion
- clause 60.1(16) – failure to provide materials etc.
- clause 60.1(17) – correction of assumptions
- clause 60.1(18) – breach of contract by employer
- clause 60.1(19) – prevention
- clause 60.4 – final quantity differences
- clause 60.5 – increased quantities causing delay
- clause 60.6 – correction of mistakes in bill of quantities
- clause X2.1 – changes in the law
- clause X12.3(6) – changes in partnering information
- clause X14.2 – delay in making advanced payment
- clause X15.2 – correction of a defect not contractor's liability
- clause Y2.4 – suspension under HGCR Act 1996

12.2 Omissions from the listed events

Conspicuously absent from the listed compensation events are failure by the project manager or the supervisor to act in accordance with the contract and late supply of information to the contractor. However, these may be covered by other listed events.

Thus, if the employer is taken to have full responsibility for the performance of the project manager and the supervisor then any failures by them to act in accordance with the contract will be breaches of contract by the employer and covered by clause 60.1(18). Late supply of information may come within the scope of clause 60.1(3) – the employer not providing something he is required to provide by the date in the accepted programme, or under clause 60.1(1) – changes to works information.

12.3 Works information related events

Under ECC 2 it was overwhelmingly the case that claims for compensation events and disputes arising from compensation events were mostly linked to the first of the listed compensation events – changes to the works information. It is unlikely that this will change under NEC 3. All the significant factors which applied in ECC 2 remain in place in NEC 3. In particular, works information remains the basis of the contractor's obligation in providing the works (clause 20.1) and the task of assembling works information adequately covering all the requirements of the numerous clauses of NEC 3 referring to works information remains as onerous as ever. Added to that, as Kipling once observed, things change slowly in the building industry and the concept that every construction detail should be finalised and all constraints, restraints and the like identified, before a contract is made is still a long way from universal acceptance or implementation. This may not matter much with construction contracts which cater for post-tender design development and drip feeding of information to the contractor without any automatic rights of claim but under NEC 3 it matters to the point that it can make or break satisfactory operation of the contract.

Clause 60.1(1) – changes to the works information

Clause 60.1(1) states that an instruction given by the project manager changing the works information is a compensation event unless it is a change:

- made to accept a defect, *or*
- is a change to the works information provided by the contractor for his design made either at the contractor's request or to comply with works information provided by the employer

At first sight this appears to be the equivalent of the usual clause in standard forms providing that all variations shall be valued, but on closer examination it is far wider than that. Save for the stated exceptions, it makes any instructed change to the works information a compensation event and it is not restricted to changes in the works.

Points to consider in respect of clause 60.1(1) are:

- what is works information
- what constitutes change
- what if there is change but no instruction

Works information is discussed in some detail in Chapter 4 but an important point of note for the purposes of clause 60.1(1) is that works information is a defined term – clause 11.2(19). This is the starting point for examination of the compensation event. The definition is interesting because it not only says what works information is (information which specifies, describes or states constraints) but it also says where the information is to be found – in documents where the contract data states it is or in an instruction.

From the definition it can be deduced that anything by way of specification, description or constraint which is additional to that to be found in the documents listed in the contract data constitutes a change in the works information. This may come as an unpleasant shock to those wedded to the old practice of issuing a preliminary or tender set of drawings for pricing purposes and a construction set after the award of contract – sometimes referred to as design development. So also to those who, by choice or circumstance, provide any information post-award. By way of simplistic example, it has long been customary to issue details of paint colours as the works progress – the drawings and specification showing surfaces to a particular finish and paint quality. When, under NEC 3, along comes the eventual instruction for red, black or whatever colour of paint, the works information then changes – from paint to red paint (or whatever) – and a compensation event has arisen. Of course, it may be said that such a change has no effect on cost and therefore the project manager will rule, should a claim for a compensation event be made, that prices and dates should not be changed. To which the contractor may say that he has a surplus stock of black paint which he was entitled to use in the absence in the works information of any specified colour and the change to red paint will involve him in extra costs of purchase and delay in procurement.

Works information not listed

A not uncommon problem relating to change in the works information under ECC 2 was inadvertent omission from the list in the contract data of all the sources of the works information – with the effect that although the contractor might not be lacking any information, having been provided with a full set of documents, not all the documents would have the status of works information. Claims relating to this type of situation may well bring in discussion on clause 10.1 of the contract – the parties to act in a spirit of mutual trust and co-operation, but there is an argument, not without some merit, that when tendering the contractor will rightly give most attention to those documents listed as providing works information.

No instructed change

As to the position when there is no instruction from the project manager changing the works information this is to some extent dealt with in clause 63.1 which divides 'the work already done' from 'the work not yet done' according to when the project manager instructed or should have instructed a quotation – and, by clause 61.1 this should be at the time of giving the instruction. Thus when there is no instruction at the time of the change, and this may be because the project manager does not agree or recognise that there is change, the position can be retrospectively restored either by a change of view of the project manager or a decision of an adjudicator.

But if it should be said that clause 60.1(1) is of limited application and that it only applies in strict accordance with its wording – i.e. where the project manager gives an instruction, there are two alternative lines of thought. One, that on its wording the definition of works information at clause 11.2(19) creates a deemed instruction. The other that failure by the project manager to issue an instruction can be taken as employer's breach for the purpose of the compensation event at clause 60.1(18).

Note that if the project manager permits a change in the contractor's design at the contractor's request that is not a compensation event. So arguably if the contractor can make savings in his design he takes the full benefit of the savings (at least under Options A and B) since there is no obvious mechanism in the contract for valuing the change.

12.4 Employer's default events

This section covers:

- clause 60.1(2) – late access/use of the site
- clause 60.1(3) – late provision of specified things
- clause 60.1(5) – late/additional works
- clause 60.1(16) – failure to provide materials etc.
- clause 60.1(18) – breach of contract

Clause 60.1(2) – late access/use of the site

Under this clause it is a compensation event if the employer:

- does not allow access to and use of the site, *by*
- the later of its access date, *and*
- the date shown on the accepted programme

This is slightly different from the corresponding ECC 2 clause which dealt only with possession of the site. The NEC 3 clause links back to the employer's obligations as stated in clause 33.1 (see Chapter 8, section 6 for comment).

Clause 60.1(2) is concerned, principally, with late fulfilment of the employer's obligations rather than with total failure. However, in the event of total failure it might suit the contractor to claim under the clause rather than to seek redress under clause 60.1(18) for employer's breach or under the termination provisions – of which R19 (instruction not to start work due to employer's default) seems the most appropriate.

Clause 60.1(3) – late provision of specified things

Under this clause it is a compensation event if the employer fails to provide something which he is contractually required to provide by the date shown for providing it in the accepted programme.

There is the potential problem of dates being brought forward by the contractor in revised programmes which thereafter become the accepted programmes. This is a problem for the project manager to control but note that bringing dates forward is not a stated reason under clause 31.1 for not accepting a programme.

The expression 'does not provide something' used in the clause is potentially wide in its application and could extend to failure to provide physical things or failure to provide information necessary for the construction of the works. It all depends upon what is shown on the accepted programme.

The clause 60.1(3) compensation event is linked expressly to dates in the accepted programme. But if, as a matter of fact, the employer is required to provide something which is necessary to the contractor's performance and there is a failure of provision by the employer that will be a breach of contract irrespective of whether or not it is mentioned in the accepted programme.

This is covered by the compensation event in clause 60.1(18) or, for certain types of things, by other compensation events. Note, in particular clause 60.1(16) relating to things for testing and inspections.

Clause 60.1(5) – late/additional works

This clause provides a compensation event, if

- the employer or others
- do not work within the times shown on the accepted programme, *or*
- do not work within the conditions stated in the works information, *or*
- carry out work on the site not stated in the works information

The provision in the final bullet point of the clause relating to work not stated in the works information is new to NEC 3. It considerably extends the scope of the clause because whereas under the ECC 2 clause defaults were related to what was stated in the works information, under the NEC 3 clause they are also related to what is not stated in the works information.

This may be particularly important in relation to the work of others. Under the ECC 2 clause the employer took responsibility for the performance of others – but only to the extent that they did not work within the times and conditions shown on the accepted programme and works information. The position under NEC 3 is that if others (or the employer) do work not stated in the works information that is a compensation event. In effect the employer undertakes to give the contractor exclusive possession of the site except as stated otherwise in the works information. That is consistent with clause 25.1 which states that the contractor shares the working areas with others as stated in the works information.

As with other compensation events which fix the contractor's entitlement by reference to what is shown on the accepted programme, there is with clause 60.1(5) a potential problem if the contractor seeks to bring forward dates relating to the obligations of the employer and others when submitting revised programmes for acceptance.

Clause 60.1(16) – failure to provide materials etc.

Under this clause it is a compensation event if the employer fails to provide materials, facilities and samples for tests and inspections as stated in the works information.

The obligation for the employer to provide such things is found in clause 40.2 which is worded to include both the employer and contractor. However, whereas the contractor's remedy for the employer's breach is listed as a compensation event, the employer's remedy for the contractor's breach is recovery of any cost incurred under clause 25.2.

In the event of late provision of materials, facilities etc. stated in the works information (as opposed to non-provision) but where there is no specified requirement, either in the works information or in the accepted programme, the contractor's remedy can arguably be claimed under clause 60.1(16) or clause 60.1(18) – employer's breach. Clause 60.1(3) is probably too firmly linked to obligations relating to dates on the accepted programme to be of relevance.

Clause 60.1(18) – breach of contract by the employer

A breach of contract by the employer which is not one of the other compensation events in the contract is stated in clause 60.1(18) to be a compensation event.

This is obviously intended to be a catch-all clause for unspecified breaches of contract. An identical clause was introduced into the second edition of the NEC (ECC 2) to cover omissions in the first edition. These omissions led to the possibility of time being put at large by unspecified breaches of contract (since no provision existed for extending the time for completion for such breaches) and to the realisation that claims based on unspecified breach fell outside the scope of the compensation event procedure.

The problem with clause 60.1(18) is that as worded it is obviously not a true reflection of the intention of the parties. What it effectively says is that all breaches of contract by the employer are compensation events. But this is not consistent with other clauses of the contract which have their own remedies for the employer's breaches – e.g.:

- interest for late payment under clause 51.3
- payment on termination under clause 93.2

However, this is not fatal to the operation of clause 60.1(18) and for the contractor the clause offers a contractual remedy for breach which is potentially very wide in its scope. Thus, under ECC 2, clause 60.1(18) was much used for claims by contractors based on alleged deficiencies in the project manager's performance and for late supply of design information. For the employer the clause could be seen as a general limitation of liability to assessments as made under the compensation event procedure. That could have the effect of excluding the employer's liability for consequential losses and providing the contractor with a poorer remedy than common law damages. Whether or not the clause is effective in doing that depends upon whether or not it excludes the contractor's common law rights – which is doubted.

12.5 *Employer's risk events*

Clause 60.1(14) provides that an event which is an employer's risk as stated in the contract is a compensation event.

The employer's risks are detailed in clause 80.1 and can broadly be described as:

- general – use of the works, unavoidable loss or damage
- loss or damage of employer supplied goods
- war, riots and similar non-insurable events
- loss or damage after take-over
- loss or damage after termination
- additional risks as listed in the contract data

For comment on these see Chapter 17, section 2.

It is not entirely clear what purpose clause 60.1(14) serves unless it is solely to provide for extension of time. By clause 83.1 each party indemnifies the other against claims and costs due to an event which is at his risk so the financial consequences of an employer's risk occurring would already seem to be covered – albeit that the remedy under clause 60.1(14) might not exactly match that under clause 83.1 because of the method of assessing compensation events.

Another point to note about clause 60.1(14) is that for certain events of serious consequence it overlaps with the compensation event in the new clause 60.1(19) – which covers what NEC 3 describes as prevention but what might more widely be described as *force majeure*. But, whichever clause applies, not all employers will be happy to pay the contractor's costs for events which, under most standard forms of contract, would attract the rule that loss (or cost) lies where it falls.

12.6 *Project manager/supervisor related events*

The events covered in this section all expressly relate to actions, or lack of actions, of the project manager or supervisor. They are:

- clause 60.1(4) – stopping/suspension of work
- clause 60.1(6) – late reply to communications
- clause 60.1(7) – finding of objects of interest
- clause 60.1(8) – changes of decisions
- clause 60.1(9) – withholding of acceptances
- clause 60.1(10) – searches for defects
- clause 60.1(11) – tests or inspections causing delay
- clause 60.1(15) – take-over before completion
- clause 60.1(17) – correction of assumptions

Clause 60.1(4) – stopping/suspension of work

Under this clause it is a compensation event if the project manager gives an instruction to stop or not to start any work or to change a key date.

The project manager's powers to give such instructions are found in clause 34.1 (stopping and starting) and in clause 14.3 (changes to key dates). For comment on these clauses see Chapter 8, section 7.

The wording of clause 60.1(4) does not fully match the wording of clause 34.1 which, in addition to giving the project manager power to stop or not to start any work, also gives the power to later instruct restart or starting. In the event of the project manager ordering a suspension of work three categories of claim are likely to arise – stoppage/demobilisation costs, standing time/ prolongation costs, and restart/remobilisation costs. Whether all of these can be put together and claimed under clause 60.1(4) is debatable because on its wording the clause only covers the first category. However, as there are no other listed compensation events covering what is usually called suspension of work it is probably intended that clause 60.1(4) should apply to everything arising from the initial instruction to stop or not to start work. But note that clause Y2.4 of secondary option Y(UK)2 does simply state that suspension is a compensation event.

If, as may well be the case, instructions are given under clause 34.1 because of some default on the part of the contractor, the provisions of clause 61.4 come into play and the contractor may have no entitlement to assessment of the compensation event.

Regarding key dates it is important to note that clause 14.3 only empowers the project manager to instruct changes to the date, not to the conditions to be met by the date. The most likely explanation therefore for the inclusion in clause 60.1(4) of reference to key dates is to provide compensation for acceleration costs if a key date is brought forward – the delay effects of compensation events generally being covered by clauses 62.2 and 63.3 which require delay costs to be included in quotations.

Clause 60.1(6) – late reply to a communication

Failure by the project manager or the supervisor to reply to a communication from the contractor within the time stated in the contract is a compensation event under clause 60.1(6).

Under traditional forms of contract this is not normally a ground for claiming extra cost or loss and expense. Employers using in-house project managers or supervisors may be inclined to delete it from the contract but for externally appointed project managers or supervisors it is a powerful incentive to perform to the contract.

The question is often asked – what is the corresponding remedy for the employer if the contractor fails to reply to a communication within time? The answer is probably that in some cases the contractor prejudices his rights under the contract but that apart the employer has no remedy unless he can prove damages and is prepared to invoke use of the disputes resolution procedures of the contract to pursue his claim.

Clause 60.1(7) – objects of interest

Under clause 73.1 the project manager is required to instruct the contractor what to do with objects of value, historical or other interest, found within the site. Under clause 60.1(7) any such instruction is a compensation event.

Both clauses are open to abuse if taken literally since neither indicates what constitutes an object of value.

Clause 60.1(8) – changing a decision

A change by the project manager or the supervisor of a decision previously communicated to the contractor is a compensation event under clause 60.1(8).

The intention and application of this clause is somewhat obscure. It uses the word 'decision' which is a word used very sparingly in NEC 3. A 'decision' is not even listed in clause 13.1 as one of the things to be communicated in writing.

The question is – does the clause apply only to the narrow range of 'decisions mentioned in the contract' or is the word 'decision' to be given wider meaning so that the clause can encompass, for example, reversals of instructions?

If the clause is given the wider application it may have the effect that any relaxation granted to the contractor by the project manager or the supervisor as a change of heart on earlier insistence of compliance in full by the contractor of his obligations is a compensation event. The acceptance of defects is dealt with under clause 44.2 so any relaxation on that front has its own mechanism for settlement but for other issues any revocation by the project manager or the supervisor could potentially involve the employer in financial liability.

Clause 60.1(9) – withholding of acceptances

Under this clause, withholding by the project manager of an acceptance for a reason not stated in the contract is a compensation event – unless the withheld acceptance is of a quotation for acceleration or for not correcting a defect.

This clause emphasises the power of the project manager to withhold acceptance for any reason – subject to the employer being liable for any delays or costs arising unless the reason is a stated reason.

Project managers will wish to avoid imposing unnecessary liabilities on the employer and accordingly they need to be particularly careful in the wording of any non-acceptance to ensure that it conforms exactly (if that is the project manager's intention) with the wording of the chosen stated reason for non-acceptance.

Clause 60.1(10) – searches for defects

An instruction by the supervisor for the contractor to search for a defect is a compensation event under clause 60.1(10) if no defect is found, unless the search is needed because the contractor gave insufficient notice of doing work which obstructed a required test or inspection.

The position under clause 60.1(10) is similar to that in traditional contracts where the contractor is liable for the cost of searches if he covers up work without giving proper notice or his work is found to be defective.

Clause 60.1(11) – tests or inspections causing delay

Any test or inspection done by the supervisor which causes unnecessary delay is a compensation event under clause 60.1(11). The obligation of the supervisor to do his tests and inspections without causing unnecessary delay is stated in clause 40.5.

A potential problem with this compensation event is in distinguishing between a necessary delay and an unnecessary delay and in deciding whether the event applies only to the time taken in carrying out the tests or inspections or whether it also applies to the consequences of their findings.

Clause 60.1(15) – take-over before completion

Under this clause certification by the project manager of any part of the works before both completion of the works and the completion date is a compensation event.

There are two important points to note here. The first is that premature use of the works (or any part) is not itself the compensation event. The trigger for the compensation is certification of take-over. The second point is that after the completion date has passed the take over of part of the works before completion is again not the compensation event.

This latter point suggests that the employer is entitled to take over and use parts of the works after the completion date (i.e. when the contractor is in culpable delay) without incurring any liability to the contractor. Indeed at the time the employer may well be collecting liquidated damages from the contractor for late completion.

Clause 60.1(17) – correction of an assumption

Correction by the project manager of an assumption about a compensation event is itself a compensation event under clause 60.1(17).

The reason for the inclusion in the list of compensation events of this particular event is to reconcile two other clauses of the compensation event procedure which would otherwise be in conflict, those being:

- clause 61.6 which permits the project manager to state assumptions on which forecasts for assessments of compensation events are to be based
- clause 65.2 which states that an assessment is not revised if a forecast is shown by later information to have been wrong

Clearly clause 61.6 could not operate fairly without the compensation event in clause 60.1(17).

Note that the wording of clause 60.1(17) is slightly different in NEC 3 from ECC 2 which referred to assumptions about the nature of a compensation event when it probably meant assumptions about the effect. This problem has been removed.

For comment on how this clause applies in respect of overstated assumptions see Chapter 14, section 2.

12.7 *Physical conditions*

In this section three clauses are considered:

- clause 60.1(12) – compensation event for physical conditions
- clause 60.2 – judging physical conditions
- clause 60.3 – ambiguity or inconsistency in site information

Clause 60.1(12) – physical conditions

Under clause 60.1(12) it is a compensation event if the contractor encounters physical conditions which are:

- within the site
- not weather conditions
- conditions which an experienced contractor would have judged at the contract date to have such a small chance of occurring that it would have been unreasonable to have allowed for them

The clause concludes with a provision, new to NEC 3, that it is only the difference between physical conditions encountered and those it would have been reasonable to take into account which is to be taken into account in assessing the compensation event. This is patently an assessment matter rather than an identification matter and its inclusion in the clause is presumably on grounds of particularity – although a similar provision is now found in clause 60.1(13) in respect of weather conditions. Although the provisions in both clauses serve useful purposes in clarifying, at least in principle, what is recoverable by way of compensation, they seem to establish by their particularised placement in the text of the conditions an assessment rule that cannot then be applied to other compensation events. In practical terms, it is by no means easy to establish when it has been accepted that the contractor has encountered physical conditions which it would have been unreasonable to have allowed for, what it would have been reasonable for the contractor to have allowed for.

Returning to the generality of clause 60.1(12) it is the rule of many contracts that employers take the risk of unforeseen ground conditions on the site. There is an element of fairness in this in that the employer has probably had more opportunity to discover the nature of the site than the contractor has had when tendering for the contract. And there is an element of commercial logic in that it may be cheaper for the employer to pay for what does happen than to pay for what might happen – assuming the contractor will price the risk if he is left to carry it. So clause 60.1(12) is not unusual in its principles. Its wording, however, deserves careful attention.

Firstly, note that it applies when the contractor encounters 'physical conditions'. This is significant for two reasons. One is that the clause is not restricted to ground conditions; the other is that the phrase 'physical conditions' as it applied in a similar provision in the ICE 5th Edition Conditions of Contract has been considered by the courts and given an unexpectedly wide meaning. The Court of Appeal in the case of *Humber Oil Trustees Ltd* v. *Harbour and General Public Works (Stevin) Ltd* (1991) held that the term 'physical conditions' is not restricted to tangible matters and that it can also apply to a transient combination of stresses. In that case the contractor's chosen methods of working unexpectedly collapsed and the only rational explanation was that the ground had behaved unpredictably. The employer was found liable for the contractor's costs. In short, the transfer of risk to the employer when the phrase 'physical conditions' is used may be much greater than when the phrase 'ground conditions' is used. It is certainly the case that since the *Humber Oil* decision was published, ground conditions claims are frequently made by reference to effect, rather than by identification of the cause. Thus it is said, for example, the ground collapsed, the piling rig could not make progress, or the tunnel boring machine stopped.

The second point to note is that clause 60.1(12) applies to conditions which are 'not weather conditions' and it is not restricted to conditions which are not 'due to' weather conditions as is the case in some other contracts. Consequently, weather related conditions such as floods arguably qualify as compensation events under NEC 3.

Test for entitlement

The test for the operation of clause 60.1(12) is unusually worded. It is based on what a notional experienced contractor would have judged as having such a small chance of occurring that it would have been unreasonable to have allowed for it. This is a probability test rather than an unforeseeability test and it raises questions as to whether it is intended to be technical, commercial or a combination of both. It is not the type of test which a project manager will usually be competent to judge – although that task falls on him under clause 61.4. In adjudications and arbitrations the parties often seem to be at a loss as to what discipline of expert/opinion evidence to call to support their respective positions.

One aspect of the test which requires some thought is to which party would it be 'unreasonable' if the contractor does allow for physical conditions which have only a small chance of occurring. Could any fault be attributed to a contractor who does 'unreasonably' allow for such conditions and could he have any liability to the employer for doing so? The point is raised because the question of whether the contractor has actually allowed for the physical conditions does not necessarily come into the compensation event test, and the contractor may not be debarred by the assessment rules from recovering the actual cost of dealing with the compensation event whether or not he has already included for it.

Some employers may be disposed to exclude clause 60.1(12) as a compensation event leaving the risks of physical conditions to be carried by the contractor. Some may follow the practice of inviting alternative tender prices with and without an unforeseen conditions clause in the contract.

There is certainly a case for excluding such clauses from contractor designed contracts on the general principle that risks should be apportioned to the party best able to control them and in recognition of the problem that once it has been accepted that the contractor's design does not work because of unforeseen conditions, the employer's liability can become open-ended. However, if the reason for excluding unforeseen conditions clauses is to obtain better certainty of price, employers should be mindful that in excluding such clauses they increase their exposure to misrepresentation claims if the contractor can find fault with the site information provided by the employer.

Clause 60.2 – judging physical conditions

Clause 60.2 supports clause 60.1(12) by stating the factors the contractor is assumed to have taken into account in judging physical conditions. These are:

- the site information
- publicly available information referred to in the site information
- information obtainable from visual inspection of the site
- other information which an experienced contractor could reasonably be expected to obtain

The opening sentence of the clause expands on the wording of the ECC 2 clause by stating that the judging is 'for the purpose of assessing a compensation event'. The ECC 2 clause was capable of misinterpretation as to its scope.

One effect of clause 60.2 is that the contractor is entitled to rely on site investigation reports and the like provided by the employer in the site information. However, the contractor effectively has his own obligations under the clause and these preclude the contractor from relying entirely on the site information. It can be contentious as to what other information an experienced contractor could reasonably have been expected to obtain pre-tender – and, insofar that the clause relates back to the contractor's knowledge at the contract date, it is his pre-tender knowledge and not his post-tender knowledge which is important. It is not unusual in dispute proceedings for the parties to engage highly eminent geologists to give expert opinion evidence on ground conditions but it is frequently questionable what relevance this has to the information which should have been obtained by an experienced contractor when tendering. The best opinion evidence of that is usually evidence given by another experienced contractor.

A point to note about clause 60.2 and NEC 3 generally, is that the contractor is not deemed to have carried out his own pre-tender site investigations. If it is required that the contractor should carry out such investigations the contract requires some modification.

Clause 60.3 – inconsistency in site information

Further support to clause 60.1(12) is given in clause 60.3 which states that if there is ambiguity or inconsistency within the site information the contractor is assumed to have taken into account the physical conditions more favourable to doing the work.

It is arguable whether or not this needs to be said since there is a rule for the legal construction of contracts (the *contra proferentum* rule) which says that in the event of ambiguities in documents the contract is construed least favourably to the party which put forward the documents. However, the danger of clause 60.3 is that it appears to go much further than the *contra proferentum* rule and it arguably overrules clause 60.2. Thus, if there is an inconsistency in the site information, that inconsistency, and not the four factors listed in clause 60.2, apparently governs what the contractor is assumed to have taken into account.

A further problem with clause 60.3, as discussed in Chapter 7 section 2, is that it appears to be wholly contrary to the contractor's duty to use reasonable skill and care when he is responsible for design unless prominence is given to the closing words of the clause 'favourable to doing the work'.

12.8 *Adverse weather*

NEC 3 retains as a compensation event under clause 60.1(13) weather, which by comparison with ten year records or assumed values stated in the contract data, is regarded as adverse weather.

The corresponding compensation event was not well received by employers under ECC 2 and it was frequently deleted. Although it is customary to allow extensions of time for delays caused by exceptional adverse weather it is not customary for the employer to pay the costs arising. Nor is it particularly logical that an employer should. Firstly, the employer has no control over the situation if it occurs; and secondly, the impact of an exceptional weather claim on the costs of a singular project cannot be averaged out by an employer in the same way that a contractor can average out the impact of such costs over numerous projects and numerous years.

The wording of clause 60.1(13) does not of itself lead to identification of the compensation event. The clause needs to be read in conjunction with the contract data, part one, entries for the compensation event. These state:

- the place where weather is to be recorded
- the weather measurements to be recorded
- the location of the historic weather records
- assumed values where there are no historic records

The clause as then read provides for a compensation event if the recorded weather over a calendar month, experienced before the completion date for the whole of the works, at the place stated in the contract data, exceeds the ten year average or stated assumed value.

Particular points to note are:

- a short, sharp spell of bad weather does not necessarily trigger a compensation event – it is the weather over a calendar month which is considered
- the compensation event does not apply to weather encountered by the contractor when working after the completion date – sometimes stated as when the contractor is in culpable delay. There is a potential problem in this insofar that clause 61.3 requires prompt notification of compensation events but awards of extension of time are themselves frequently delayed

Note also that the NEC 3 version of clause 60.1(13) explains that only the difference between recorded weather and baseline weather is taken into account when assessing a compensation event. Under ECC 2, which did not have this explanation, contractors were prone to claiming their entire weather related costs and time.

12.9 *Prevention*

Clause 60.1(19) introduces a new compensation event into NEC 3. For reasons explained in the commentary on clause 19.1 (prevention) in Chapter 6 section 11, it is likely to be a controversial compensation event. Put simply, if a prevention event such as described in clause 19.1 occurs it is likely to be a compensation event and the employer carries the time and cost consequences. Because of its potential scope, and because the events it covers are in the nature of *force majeure* and not normally solely at the employer's risk, it is likely that many employers will require its deletion.

Clause 60.1(19) – prevention

The clause states as a compensation event, an event which:

- stops the contractor completing the works, *or*
- stops the contractor completing by the date shown on the accepted programme

- and which neither party could prevent
- and which an experienced contractor would have judged at the contract date to have had such a small chance of occurring that it would have been unreasonable to have allowed for it
- and which is not one of the other compensation events

A presumption can be read into the clause, because of inclusion of the reasonable allowance test, that the stoppage events can include foreseeable events. This is likely to encourage imaginative use of the clause where it is left in the contract.

12.10 Measurement related events

This section covers four clauses found in main options B and D only, all relating to measurement of the works by bill of quantities:

- clause 60.4 – final quantity differences
- clause 60.5 – increased quantities causing delay
- clause 60.6 – correction of mistakes in bill of quantities
- clause 60.7 – assessment of events resulting from inconsistencies

For reasons which are obvious bills of quantities should not be used for contracts with contractor's design unless the contract is amended to make the contractor responsible for their accuracy.

Clause 60.4 – final quantity differences

NEC 3 permits tendered rates in bills of quantities to be changed if the measured quantities differ from those billed. The applicable rules are however quite complex.

The wording of clause 60.4 is not of the clearest order and the comparison it draws between the final total quantity of work done and the quantity stated for an item is presumably to be read as the final measured quantity for an item compared to the billed quantity for the same item.

Assuming that to be the case then a compensation event occurs when:

- the difference does not relate to a change in the works information
- the difference causes the actual cost per unit quantity to change, *and*
- the measured value of the item involved is significant to the extent that it is more than 0.5% of the tender sum

The clause expressly confirms that if the actual cost per unit is reduced then the affected rate is reduced. The intention, perhaps, is that the employer should benefit if there is an increase in quantities which reduces the costs of production. But it is not clear how this takes effect. It is unlikely that the contractor would notify a compensation event in such circumstances and the project manager has no obvious power to do so.

Where, as will often be the case, the contractor has subcontracted much of the work, the application of the clause is very much a theoretical exercise based on calculations of the defined cost rather than actual cost. If this produces a windfall for the contractor that apparently is his good fortune.

Where there are quantity changes resulting from changes in the works information the intention seems to be that the cost and time implications are dealt with under clause 60.1(1).

The timing of notification and assessment of a compensation event under clause 60.4 is more likely to follow completion than to precede it, but note that by clause 61.7 notification must be before the defects date.

Clause 60.5 – increased quantities causing delay

By clause 60.5 a difference between the measured quantity of work for an item and the billed quantity which delays completion or the meeting of a key date is a compensation event.

This is considerably more straightforward than clause 60.4. In effect the employer warrants the accuracy of the quantities in the bill of quantities insofar as the contractor's obligations to complete on time and/or by key dates are concerned.

The assessment of a compensation event under clause 60.5 seems to follow the general assessment rules of clause 63.1 rather than the particularised rules of clause 63.13 such that, although it is delay which triggers the event, both time and cost are recoverable.

Clause 60.6 – correction of mistakes in the bill of quantities

By clause 60.6 the project manager is required to correct mistakes in the bill of quantities which are:

- departures from the rules for item descriptions or division of items in the method of measurement, *or*
- are due to ambiguities or inconsistencies

The clause states that each such correction is a compensation event which may lead to reduced prices.

The intention of this clause is probably no more than to follow the rule that the contractor prices the bill of quantities produced by the employer for tendering and the employer accepts responsibility for any mistakes in the format of the billing. This may require the addition and measurement of additional items.

There is no express exclusion in the clause for mistakes in the contractor's rates, but presumably only mistakes which are due to ambiguities or inconsistencies in the bill of quantities or other contract documents stand to be corrected under the clause – although on its wording it could be taken to be of greater effect.

Since the project manager has an obligation to correct mistakes it may be that he also has the obligation to notify the compensation event. However, the contract is not clear on the point and it may be best for the contractor to assume that discovery of a mistake should be notified in the same way as for other compensation events.

It is not thought that the reference in the clause to reduced prices means that each correction may only lead to reduced prices. It is probably no more than a link with clause 63.2 which states that prices are not reduced except as stated in the contract.

Clause 60.7 – assessment of compensation events resulting from inconsistencies

Clause 60.7 is new to NEC 3. It states that:

- in assessing a compensation event which results from correction of inconsistency
- between the bill of quantities and another document
- the contractor is assumed to have taken the bill of quantities as correct

The wording of this clause confirms that the correction of mistakes in clause 60.6 caused by inconsistencies is not confined to inconsistencies within the bill of quantities. It is not clear, however, why clause 60.6 refers to ambiguities and inconsistencies and clause 60.7 refers only to inconsistencies.

This seems to be another clause where the employer comes close to warranting the accuracy of the bill of quantities. It appears to go against the usual rule that the contractor's obligations are derived from the drawings and the specification and not from the bill of quantities. If it does, the potential implications are profound. Consider, for example, the case of a bridge with two abutments but, by mistake, only one is billed. The constructed quantities will be double the billed quantities – that will be corrected in the measure. But is the contractor to get an extension of time and prolongation costs under clause 60.5 simply for doing work obviously in the contract? Perhaps so.

12.11 Secondary option clause events

This section covers five clauses in secondary options which provide entitlement to compensation events:

- clause X2.1   – changes in the law
- clause X12.3(6) – changes in partnering information
- clause X14.2   – delay in making advanced payment

- clause X15.2   – correction of a defect not contractor's liability
- clause Y2.4   – suspension under HGCR Act 1996

Clause X2.1 – changes in the law

This clause provides:

- a change in the law of the country in which the site is located which occurs after the contract date is a compensation event
- the project manager may notify the contractor of the change in the law and instruct him to submit quotations
- the prices are reduced if the effect of the change in law is to reduce total defined cost

This is an important clause in those contracts into which it is incorporated. It places significant risk on the employer and, on long running contracts, can give rise to a multitude of claimable events.

Note that it is the law of the country of the site which applies, not the law of the contract (if that is different).

Clause X12.3(6) – changes in partnering information

This clause states that an instruction given by the core group to the partners changing the partnering information is a compensation event which may lead to reduced prices.

Clause X14.2 – delay in making advanced payment

This clause makes late payment of an advanced payment by the employer which is provided for under the contract a compensation event.

No details are stated in the clause as to how the event is to be notified or assessed and presumably it follows the general rules of NEC 3 – thus permitting the contractor to claim both time and money.

Clause X15.2 – correction of a defect not the contractor's liability

The clause states simply, 'If the Contractor corrects a Defect for which he is not liable under this contract it is a compensation event'.

It would seem logical for this to be the case whether or not Option X15 is incorporated into the contract. The explanation for inclusion of clause X15.2 into a secondary option is probably because the draughtsmen only envisage there to be a 'Defect' for which the contractor is not liable when clause X15.1

applies – and the contractor's liability for his design is limited to reasonable skill and care.

Clause Y2.4 – suspension under HGCR Act 1996

The Housing Grants Construction and Regeneration Act 1996 permits the contractor to suspend performance in certain circumstances of late payment. The Act however does not go into the detail of who bears the consequential costs.

Clause Y2.4 provides in the simplest of terms that if the contractor exercises his right to suspend performance under the Act that is a compensation event.

Chapter 13
Notifying compensation events

13.1 Introduction

Clauses 61.1 to 61.7 of NEC 3 set out detailed requirements for the notification of compensation events. These are important clauses because the contract aims to make notification a condition precedent to entitlement and a condition subject to time-bars.

Under ECC 2 the corresponding clauses were much discussed as to their intent and their effectiveness. No court decisions were given resolving the various contentious points and it was left to individual adjudicators and arbitrators to reach their own conclusions. Some supported the views put forward in the Guidance Notes, others held the provisions to be too poorly drafted to eliminate on procedural grounds claims which were otherwise perfectly valid. For parties in dispute on notification issues it was something of a lottery as to what decision they received. NEC 3 endeavours to correct this unsatisfactory situation with significantly changed wording to two of the clauses.

Changes in NEC 3

The two significant changes referred to above are found in clauses 61.3 and 61.4:

- clause 61.3 is amended such that the uncertainly stated obligation to notify a compensation event within two weeks in ECC 2 is replaced in NEC 3 by a more clearly stated eight week time-bar
- clause 61.4 has additional provisions entitling the contractor to take the initiative if the project manager fails to deal properly with compensation event notifications and introducing the concept of deemed acceptances and instructions

Changes of lesser significance in the notification clauses are:

- references to key dates are included in clauses 61.3 and 61.4
- 'Defined' cost replaces 'Actual' cost in clause 61.4
- clause 61.1 requires the project manager to notify the contractor of a compensation event arising from an instruction or changed decision 'at the time of giving the instruction or changing the earlier decision' whereas in ECC 2 it was 'at the time of the event'

13.2 Notifications by the project manager

The project manager is expressly required to notify compensation events under clause 61.1 – but that clause refers only to compensation events arising from instructions or changed decisions. The presumption seems to be that for all other compensation events it is for the contractor to decide and notify whether or not there is an event or default which is claimable.

Whilst this may seem to be less than an even-handed approach in that it apparently allows the project manager to remain silent on employer's defaults, regard must be had to clause 16.1 which requires both the contractor and project manager to give early warning notice as soon as either becomes aware of any matter which could increase the prices or delay completion. This clearly includes matters which are, or could become, compensation events. Additionally, it may be arguable that the project manager's duties under clause 10.1 requiring him to act in a spirit of mutual trust and co-operation extend to warning the contractor to give notifications of other events of which he (the project manager) is aware.

Further points to consider are that for some compensation events the burden of action falls on the project manager without the need for an instruction and for others there appears to be no need for notification by the contractor. Thus, under clause 60.6, found in Options B and D, the project manager is required to correct certain mistakes in the bill of quantities and any such correction is stated to be a compensation event. And suspension under option Y(UK)2 is stated to be a right which is a compensation event.

It seems therefore that the project manager has greater duties in the notification of compensation events than is evident from clause 61.1. But whether or not this is correct it would be unwise for a project manager to assume that acting strictly to the letter of clause 61.1 is always in the employer's best interest. The point is developed elsewhere in this chapter in relation to the time-bar provisions in clause 61.3 that the employer may lose his rights to liquidated damages for late completion if the cause of delay is the employer's responsibility and no compensation event is notified.

Clause 61.1

Clause 61.1 provides:

- for compensation events which arise from the project manager or the supervisor
  — giving an instruction, *or*
  — changing an earlier decision
- the project manager notifies the contractor
  — of the compensation event
  — at the time of giving the instruction or changing the earlier decision

- the project manager instructs the contractor to submit quotations
  — unless the event arises from the fault of the contractor, *or*
  — quotations have already been submitted
- the contractor puts the instruction or changed decision into effect

The compensation events which expressly arise from giving an instruction are those which refer in their description to an instruction. Thus:

- clause 60.1(1) – instruction changing the works information
- clause 60.1(4) – instruction to stop or not to start or to change a key date
- clause 60.1(7) – instruction dealing with object of interest
- clause 60.1(10) – instructions to search

However, it will often be the case that other compensation events will arise from, or be directly related to, a project manager's instruction. For example:

- clause 60.1(2) – access/use of site restrictions
- clause 60.1(3) – non-provision of things by the employer
- clause 60.1(15) – take-over of part of the works
- clause 60.1(18) – employer's breach
- clause 60.1(19) – prevention
- clause X15.2   – correction of defect for which the contractor is not liable

It is a matter of some importance, having regard to the condition precedent/time-bar provisions in clause 61.3, as to whether clause 61.1 applies in such cases – thereby requiring the project manager to notify compensation events and to instruct quotations. See the comment on clause 61.3 overleaf.

As to the detail of clause 61.1, it requires good administrative arrangements for the project manager to give substantive instructions, to notify compensation events and to instruct quotations all at the same time without breaching the requirements in clause 13.7 for separate communications. Many project managers use pro-forma systems to avoid such difficulties and to generate conformity of style and practice.

An interesting aspect of the wording of clause 61.1 is the way in which it relates the phrase 'fault of the contractor' only to the need to instruct quotations. The phrase does not appear to have any bearing on the obligation of the project manager to notify a compensation event. The consequence of this is that the project manager is in breach of duty if he fails to notify a compensation event arising from an instruction or changed decision even if the instruction or changed decision results from fault of the contractor.

The final sentence of clause 61.1 requiring the contractor to put instructions and changes in decisions into effect seems at first sight to duplicate the obligation already found in clause 27.3. However, what it probably indicates is that in respect of instructions which are relevant instructions for the purposes of clause 61.1, the contractor is not obliged to put into effect his obligation under clause 27.3 until he has notification of a compensation event under clause 61.1. In short, on receipt of an instruction of the type changing the works information or the like the contractor can demand, and await, notification of a compensation event before proceeding.

For comment on the quotation aspects of clause 61.1 and on clause 61.2 which also concerns quotations, see Chapter 14.

13.3 *Notifications by the contractor*

The principal clause of NEC 3 governing notifications of compensation events by the contractor is clause 61.3. As noted in section 13.2 above the clause apparently puts on the contractor the burden of notifying all compensation events not notified by the project manager. And insofar that NEC 3 endeavours to restrict the contractor's entitlements to additional time and money to the assessment of notified compensation events this is obviously a burden of great importance. So although some compensation events such as those arising from remeasurement of the works under Options B and D might seem to take effect without formal notification, and notwithstanding the difficulties of the clause as discussed below, the clause should be strictly followed by contractors wishing to preserve their entitlements.

Clause 61.3

The clause has two distinct sets of provisions – those stating the contractor's obligations to give notice and those stating the consequences of failure to give notice. The first set, when read in conjunction with clause 61.4 which refers to notified compensation events, indicates that giving notice is a condition precedent to entitlement to the benefits of a compensation event; the second set imposes a time-bar on late notices.

The provisions of the first set can be broken down as follows:

- the contractor notifies the project manager
- of an event which has happened, *or*
- which he expects to happen
- as a compensation event, *if*
  — the contractor believes the event is a compensation event, *and*
  — the project manager has not notified the event to the contractor

It should be noted that these provisions, and other provisions which follow in clause 61.3 and clause 61.4, appear to make a significant distinction between an 'event' and a 'compensation event'. An event for the purposes of these clauses is not itself a compensation event but something which may give rise to a compensation event. This is a different drafting approach than used in clause 60.1 where it is stated that certain events are compensation events.

The opening words of clause 61.3 'The Contractor notifies the Project Manager' is presumably to be taken as an obligation given the wording style of NEC 3 and the use of the discretionary phrase 'the Contractor may notify' in other clauses such as clause 61.4. Failure to notify is strictly, therefore, not only failure to comply with a condition precedent but also a breach.

The contractor's obligation is to notify not only events which have happened but also events which he expects to happen. The latter, which might, for example, relate to adverse weather expected as a result of weather forecasts, raises interesting questions as to what happens if the compensation event procedure is followed through, the contractor provides a quotation which is accepted, the compensation event is implemented, but the event never happens. The answer is probably that the project manager gets blamed by the employer for accepting the quotation and/or for not using the assumption provisions of clause 61.6. A more general point of interest is that under clause 61.3 the contractor is not expressly confined to notifying only listed compensation events. In the event that the contractor notifies a non-listed event that is to be dealt with by the project manager under clause 61.4.

'the Contractor believes'

Under Clause 61.3 the contractor is only required to notify an event as a compensation event if he believes it is a compensation event. The intention of this is reasonably clear but it is not without its complications. Belief is essentially an individual's state of mind and this is a difficult subject when considered in connection with legal or contractual matters. It is questionable if there is such a thing as corporate belief but if there is it is probably something to be examined by reference to facts, such as the content of reports, minutes and correspondence rather than by interrogation of individual members of the corporate body. Perhaps words such as 'if the Contractor wishes to claim the event as a compensation event' would better state what seems to be intended.

Timing requirements

The second set of provisions in clause 61.3 deals with timing requirements for notices. These provisions can be summarised as:

- if the contractor does not notify a compensation event
- within eight weeks of becoming aware of the event
- he is not entitled to a change in the prices, the completion date or a key date
- unless the project manager should have notified the event to the contractor but did not

These provisions are obviously intended to act as a time-barring mechanism and, if it is the case that the contractor's only entitlements to extra time and money are those found in compensation events, then they are obviously very important provisions. Unless and until the courts decide how they operate they deserve, and will no doubt get, close examination of their detail.

This part of the clause retains the distinction between 'the event' and a 'compensation event' found in the opening part of the clause. The timing requirement is for notifying the compensation event whereas the obligation is to notify the event. The intention seems to be that notification of an event is obligatory and notification of a compensation event is discretionary – subject to timing requirements and consequences of non-compliance. However, if this is correct, the timing requirements do not apply to notification of the event itself.

The potential importance of this lies in the next part of the clause which specifies the timing requirement for a compensation event as being 'within eight weeks of becoming aware of the event'. Thus it is not the event which sets time running but the contractor's awareness of the event.

Contractor's awareness

The difficulties in determining in any particular situation when it can properly be said that the contractor becomes aware of an event are considerable. Firstly, who or what, for the purposes of the clause is 'the Contractor'. Is it the board of directors, a director, the site manager, or any employee?

Questions of this sort usually come before the courts on criminal matters or statutory related matters and if any generalisation can be drawn it is that managerial knowledge is required to establish company knowledge. In *Bolton Engineering* v. *Graham & Sons* (1956), it was said by Lord Denning that 'the state of mind of these [directors and managers] is the state of mind of the company and is treated by the law as such'. The second difficulty is establishing what is meant, in the context of clause 61.3, by the phrase 'of becoming aware of an event'. It will no doubt sometimes be argued under NEC 3, as it was under ECC 2, that the contractor, at management level, did not become aware that events had occurred until financial reports indicated losses, and specialist contractual and legal advice identified the events as compensation events. Whether or not this is a good argument or a bad argument probably depends on the circumstances of the particular case but it does illustrate the type of problems to be faced in applying the awareness test.

It also further illustrates the wording complications in clause 61.3 arising from the distinction between the 'event' and the 'compensation event'. Time runs from awareness of the event. The obligation to notify the event does not arise until the contractor believes the event is a compensation event. By that time the eight week period for giving notice may have expired. Moreover, in some cases it will not be immediately obvious, or even readily obvious, whether an event will lead to a compensation event. For example, the date of encountering adverse ground conditions (if this is to be described as the event) may be well in advance of the date of establishing whether it would have been reasonable for the contractor to have allowed for such conditions (the compensation event). And similarly whether prevention (as an event) will delay completion (as a compensation event) may not be known, or forecastable, within the eight weeks allowed in clause 61.3.

These are difficult and complex issues but see the comment under clause 61.4 (p. 249) on the potentially more difficult issue of who is to decide them.

'not entitled to a change'

The stated effect in clause 61.3 of the contractor not notifying a compensation event within eight weeks of becoming aware of the event is that he is 'not entitled to a change in the Prices, the Completion Date or a Key Date unless . . .'

The gravity of this potential loss of entitlement is, as regards changes in the prices and/or extra money, dependent to some extent on whether or not NEC 3 is to be construed as excluding the contractor's common law rights of damages from breach. For comment on this see Chapter 11, section 5. But whether or not common law rights are excluded clause 61.3 is clear enough in its wording to exclude contractual rights. One aspect of this, and it is an aspect which may have some bearing on the loss of common law rights question, is that for compensation events there is effectively a limitation (or prescription) period of only eight weeks.

The loss of entitlement to change in respect of time/completion date is potentially as much a problem for the employer as it is for the contractor. It is well established as a general principle of English law that unless a contract provides for extension of time to cover delays for which the employer is responsible, and there is such delay, any liquidated damages clauses in the contract for late completion will be unenforceable. See, in particular, the case of *Peak Construction* v. *McKinney Foundations* (1970).

English law is less clear, however, on the position which applies when there are provisions for extensions of time but they are subject to time-bars – as in NEC 3. There is no recorded English case on this. There are however some overseas decisions which bear on the matter. In particular, the Australian case of *Gaymark Investments* v. *Walter Construction* (2000) in which the Supreme Court declined to allow an employer to recover liquidated damages for delays of its own making notwithstanding the contractor's failure to comply with notice provisions. The Australian case of *Abigroup Contractors* v. *Peninsula Balmain* (2002) had a similar outcome, but the South African case of *Group Five Building* v. *Minister of Community Development* (1993) was to the opposite effect. There is an interesting Scottish case, *City Inns* v. *Shepherd Construction* (2003) which also appears to reach an opposite decision but that case concerned the contractor's obligation to respond within a set period to instructed variations and, by virtue of the concluding words of clause 61.3 (project manager's duty to notify) it is doubtful if it is of application to NEC 3.

Perhaps of more application to NEC 3 is the general principle of English law that clear and express provisions are required to contradict the presumption that a party to a contract should not be able to benefit from its own breach – *Alghussein Establishments* v. *Eton College* (1988).

Overall the position is one of uncertainty and there is something to be said for amending clause 61.3 such that the conditions precedent/time-bar elements do not extend to the employer's breaches. Consideration of this principle inevitably brings into question the clarity, or lack of it, in clause 61.3.

'unless the Project Manager should have notified the event'

The final part of clause 61.3 stating that the contractor is not entitled to a change 'unless the Project Manager should have notified the event to the Contractor but did not' does much to diminish the overall impact of time-barring effect of the clause. It may similarly diminish notice as a condition precedent. The explanation for this is that in practice the majority of compensation events are likely to arise from events which the project manager should have notified. Most will be for instructions given, or which should have been given, changing the works information.

There is therefore no time-bar in NEC 3, other than that found in clause 61.7 stating that compensation events are not notified after the defects date, in respect of claims for additional works and variations and other classes of events which the project manager should have notified but did not. Such claims it seems can, subject to clause 61.7, be presented as and when it suits the contractor. This does not, of itself, give the contractor free reign to present global or total cost claims at the end of the contract but the reality is that if a substantial bundle of compensation events has to be assessed by the project manager, an adjudicator or an arbitrator, at the end of contract, the complexities of the contractual assessment procedure may well lead to adoption of a total cost solution.

Employers will rightly look to their project managers to ensure that they are not landed with end-of-contract claims but, if experiences under ECC 2 are anything to go by, employers will not welcome over-indulgence by their project managers in recognising the need to notify compensation events and to call for contractor's quotations.

A particular drafting point to note about the concluding part of clause 61.3 is that it uses the words 'unless the Project Manager should have notified the event'. Clause 61.1, however, uses the words 'the Project Manager . . . notifies the compensation event'. Since there is no express obligation in NEC 3 for the project manager to notify 'events', other than 'compensation events', it is probably intended that the notification referred to in clause 61.3 is that referred to in clause 61.1. But if that is not the case the 'unless' provision in clause 61.3 is of very wide scope.

13.4 *Project manager's response to notifications*

Clause 61.4 of NEC 3 contains sets of provisions detailing the duties of the project manager in respect of notifications of events believed by the contractor to be compensation events. In short, the project manager is required to decide and notify the contractor whether or not a notified event requires assessment as a compensation event and, if he considers that it does require assessment, to instruct the contractor to submit quotations. If the project manager fails to notify his decision and further fails to respond to notification from the contractor of the same, the notified event is treated as an accepted compensation event and there is a deemed instruction to submit quotations.

The clause is interesting not only in what it says but also in what it does not say. Conspicuously absent from the clause is any power of the project manager to decline to deal with a notified event on the grounds that the notification is out of time. The position appears to be that the project manager is required to decide on all notified events. If this is correct, assessment of notified events proceeds whether or not the timing requirements of clause 61.3 have been fulfilled. It is then for the employer to dispute the contractor's entitlements to any assessed extra time or money through the dispute resolution procedures in the contract relying on clause 61.3. There is some logic in this approach. It ensures that assessments of all notified events are promptly made whereas if it was open to the project manager to decline to deal with notified events on timing grounds and the notifications were subsequently found to be in time the opportunity for timely assessments would be lost and complex retrospective and theoretical assessments might be necessary. Additionally, the approach avoids drawing the project manager into the difficult belief and awareness tests in clause 61.3.

Clause 61.4 – notification of decisions

The first set of provisions in clause 61.4 details the rules for the project manager's decisions on notified events. These are:

- if the project manager decides that an event notified by the contractor
  — arises from a fault of the contractor
  — has not happened or is not expected to happen
  — has no affect on defined cost, completion or meeting a key date
  — is not one of the compensation events stated in the contract
- the project manager notifies the contractor of his decision that the prices, completion date or key dates are not to be changed
- if the project manager decides otherwise he notifies the contractor and instructs him to submit quotations

It should be noted that clause 61.4 applies only to events notified by the contractor. The procedure for events notified by the project manager is stated in clause 61.1. It should also be noted that the clause refers to events notified by the contractor and not to compensation events so notified.

'fault of the Contractor'

The first consideration for the project manager's decision is whether the event arises from a 'fault of the Contractor'. This seems to be a test of limited application. The compensation events as listed are for the most part expressions of the potential faults or actions of the project manager, the supervisor or the employer. It is possible to envisage circumstances where the contractor might be the cause or contributory cause of some of the events listed as compensation events but for others it is difficult to do so.

The clause does not deal with the possibility of contributory or partial fault and it is not clear whether the test for consideration is, 'arises solely from fault of the Contractor', or, 'arises in part from the fault of the Contractor'. But even if the project manager has the power to apportion liability (which is doubted) he does not have any obvious power to apportion assessment.

'is not expected to happen'

The power of the project manager to decide whether or not an event notified by the contractor is one which he (the contractor) expects to happen is not an event expected to happen is an interesting expression of supremacy of the views of the project manager over those of the contractor. The contract does not deal expressly with the situation which applies if the project manager is wrong and the event does happen. The contractor would not be obliged to re-serve his notice and presumably it would stand to be assessed retrospectively along with the added compensation event under clause 60.1(8) for the project manager changing his decision.

'has no effect'

The power of the project manager to decide before even reaching the assessment stage that a notified event has no effect on defined cost, completion or meeting a key date does not sit easily with the general purpose of clause 61.4 which is to decide liability not quantum. Precisely how, and on what information, the project manager is to reach his decision is not clear.

'is not one of the compensation events'

If the project manager decides that the event notified by the contractor is not one of the compensation events stated in the contract it seems reasonably clear from clause 61.4 that the project manager has no power to deal with it other than to give notice that it will not be assessed for time and money changes. It follows that if the contractor submits claims outside the evident scope of the compensation event procedures these are not claims which the project manager can decide either as to liability or quantum.

Clause 61.4 – failure to notify decision

The second set of provisions in clause 61.4 deals with the situation which applies if the project manager defaults in notifying the contractor of his decision on a notified event. They state:

- if the project manager does not notify his decision within either one week or such longer period as the contractor agrees
- the contractor may notify the project manager of this lack of notification
- failure by the project manager to reply to this reminder within two weeks
- is treated as acceptance by the project manager that the event is a compensation event, *and*
- is treated as an instruction to submit quotations

This is another clause placing a heavy burden on the project manager. It may, for example, be impossible for the project manager to form a considered view within one week of whether physical conditions have been encountered which it would have been unreasonable for an experienced contractor to have allowed for at the contract date. But, be that as it may, unless the contractor agrees otherwise, the project manager has effectively to decide within one week whether or not the contractor has in principle, a valid claim. Having once decided in favour of the contractor there is no obvious way of going back for the project manager – unless it is that the compensation event at clause 60.1(8) which refers to changes in decisions contemplates both positive and negative changes.

Failure by the project manager to reply within the stipulated two weeks of reminder by the contractor has the potentially serious consequence of treating a notified event as a compensation event. That entitles the contractor to submit quotations which then have to be considered. On the face of it that would seem to leave the project manager in a difficult position, however since the dispute resolution procedures of NEC 3 expressly allow the employer to refer disputes about quotations for compensation events treated as having been accepted to adjudication, the project manager and the employer may consider it preferable in some circumstances to have a treated acceptance rather than a notified acceptance.

Other points

Some points of clause 61.4 relate to procedures for quotations and these together with clauses 61.5 and 61.6 which also relate to procedures for quotations are considered in Chapter 14.

13.5 *Last date for notification of compensation events*

Clause 61.7 of NEC 3 states briefly that a compensation event is not notified after the defects date.

The defects date is not a defined term of NEC 3 but is a date determined for any particular contract by reference to the number of weeks after completion of the whole of the works entered by the employer in part one of the contract data. It corresponds to the date which in traditional construction contracts might mark the end of the maintenance or defects correction period. It will frequently be six months or twelve months after completion.

It is not unusual in traditional standard forms to find provisions fixing an end date for the submission of contractual claims – although usually a period of three months or longer is allowed after the end of the maintenance/defects correction period to allow for preparation of the final account. The rule in NEC 3 is, however, a stricter rule both in timing and potential effect. It allows no extra time after the defects date and by the inclusion of employer's breaches of contract in the list of compensation events it endeavours to prevent application of the normal limitation/prescription periods for bringing claims for breaches of contract. For further comment in this see Chapter 11, section 5, but note, however, that even if clause 61.7 is effective under English law it may not be effective under some foreign law jurisdictions which do not give contractual provisions precedence over statutory limitation periods.

Chapter 14

Quotations for compensation events

14.1 Introduction

Quotation is not a defined term of NEC 3 but from clause 62.2 it can be seen to be a proposal from the contractor for changing the contract price or extending the contract time.

One of the most important characteristics of NEC 3 is that the contractor should have the opportunity to submit quotations for the assessment of compensation events. Another is that assessments should be based on the contractor's quotations except in circumstances where the contractor fails to follow the contractual rules. This was also the scheme in ECC 2 but it was not very well expressed and it failed to deal with the not uncommon situation that the contractor was not given the opportunity to submit quotations either because the project manager did not acknowledge or did not wish to acknowledge that compensation events had occurred, or because he preferred to assess compensation events retrospectively on the basis of costs incurred rather than by accepting forward looking quotations. NEC 3 endeavours to rectify that situation with drafting changes which emphasise the primacy of the quotation system.

Principal changes from ECC 2

In summary the principal changes in NEC 3 from ECC 2 relating to quotations are:

- clause 61.4 is extended with provisions for deemed instructions to the contractor to submit quotations
- clause 62.1 is amended to require the project manager to discuss matters with the contractor before instructing alternative quotations
- clause 62.6 (which is new to NEC 3) provides for quotations to be treated as accepted if the project manager defaults in following the contractual rules for instructing quotations
- clause 64.4 (which is also new to NEC 3) provides for quotations to be treated as accepted if the project manager defaults in following the contractual timing rules for assessing compensation events

The overall effect of these changes is that whereas under ECC 2 no evident status was attached to a quotation which had not been instructed or accepted by the project manager, under NEC 3 deemed instructions and acceptances occur in stipulated circumstances.

NEC 3 clauses referring to quotations

For full understanding of how the NEC 3 system of quotations for compensation events works it is worthwhile noting the many references in the contract to such quotations:

- clause 11.2(21) — the bill of quantities is changed to accommodate accepted quotations for acceleration – applies to Options B and D only
- clause 11.2(22) — defined cost excludes the cost of preparing quotations for compensation events – applies to Options A and B only
- clause 36.1 — the project manager may instruct the contractor to submit a quotation for acceleration
- clause 36.2 — the contractor submits his quotation for acceleration or gives his reasons for not doing so within the period for reply
- clause 44.2 — the contractor may submit a quotation for reduced prices or earlier completion for changes to the works information to avoid correction of a defect
- clause 60.1(17) — the project manager's notification of correction to an assumption (to be used in a quotation for a compensation event) is itself a compensation event
- clause 61.1 — the project manager instructs the contractor to submit quotations when giving an instruction for a compensation event or when changing an earlier decision
- clause 61.2 — the project manager may instruct the contractor to submit quotations for a proposed instruction or a proposed change of decision
- clause 61.4 — the project manager instructs the contractor to submit quotations for an event notified by the contractor as a compensation event unless he decides the prices, the completion date and key dates are not to be changed – failure by the project manager to reply to notification by the contractor that he [the project manager] has not dealt with notification of a compensation event is treated as an instruction to submit quotations
- clause 61.5 — the project manager notifies the contractor when he instructs him to submit quotations if he decides that the contractor did not give early warning of the event

- clause 61.6   – the project manager states the assumptions to be made in quotations if he decides the effects of a compensation event are too uncertain to be forecast reasonably

- clause 62.1   – the project manager may instruct the contractor to submit alternative quotations

- clause 62.2   – quotations comprise proposed changes to the prices and any delay to the completion date or to key dates assessed by the contractor

- clause 62.3   – the contractor submits quotations within three weeks of instruction and the project manager replies within two weeks

- clause 62.4   – the project manager can only instruct the contractor to submit a revised quotation after explaining his reasons for doing so

- clause 62.5   – the time for the contractor submitting quotations and for replies by the project manager can be extended by agreement

- clause 62.6   – if the project manager does not reply to a quotation within time and after notification of this by the contractor the project manager does not reply within two weeks, the quotation is treated as having been accepted

- clause 63.1   – for the purpose of assessment of compensation events the date when the project manager instructed or should have instructed the contractor to submit quotations divides the work already done from the work not yet done

- clause 64.1   – the project manager assesses a compensation event if the contractor defaults under the contractual rules for the submission and acceptance of quotations

- clause 64.3   – the project manager notifies the contractor of his assessment within the time allowed to the contractor for submission of his quotation

- clause 64.4   – if the project manager does not assess a compensation event within the time allowed and does not reply to notification of this by the contractor within two weeks, the quotation proposed by the contractor is treated as having been accepted

- clause 65.1   – a compensation event is implemented when the project manager notifies the contractor of acceptance of a quotation or when a quotation is treated as having been accepted

- clause 65.2   – the assessment of a compensation event is not revised if a forecast (the basis of the quotation) is shown by later information to have been wrong

- clause W1.3(1)   – the employer may refer to adjudication a dispute about a quotation which is treated as having been accepted
- clauses W1.3(5) and   – the adjudicator may alter a quotation which is W2.3(4)   treated as having been accepted

14.2 *Instructions to submit quotations*

Clause 61.1

The starting point of the compensation event assessment procedure, for events arising from the project manager giving an instruction or changing an earlier decision, is found in clause 61.1. This provides that:

- at the time of giving an instruction or changing an earlier decision the project manager notifies a compensation event
- the project manager also instructs the contractor to submit quotations
- unless the event arises from a fault of the contractor
- or quotations have already been submitted
- the contractor puts the instruction or changed decision into effect

Comment on the notification aspects of clause 61.1 and the concluding provision requiring the contractor to put instructions and changed decisions into effect is given in Chapter 13, section 13. As to quotations the first point of interest in clause 61.1 is that the project manager's obligation to instruct the submission of quotations is not expressly stated as being at the time of the instruction and/or changed decision. However, the words 'He also instructs the contractor to submit quotations' are perhaps indicative that notification of a compensation event and instruction of quotations are to be simultaneous. If, however, the project manager notifies a compensation event without instructing quotations the consequences are potentially serious. Clause 61.3 and 61.4 are by-passed because the event has already been notified; and clauses 62.3, 62.4, 62.5, 62.6 are of no effect unless and until the contractor chooses to submit a quotation of his own accord. In short, by notifying a compensation event but not instructing quotations, the project manager leaves the assessment of the compensation event completely open as regards timing. The situation can probably be rectified by the project manager belatedly instructing quotations but the rule in clause 63.1 for retrospective quotations then applies – and these, by their nature, will normally be favourable to the contractor.

The situation that applies when the project manager declines to instruct quotations because he considers the event arises from a fault of the contractor is different in that presumably there will be no notification of a compensation event. Clause 61.3 and 61.4 do then take effect and the order of the contract is maintained.

Two further interesting aspects of clause 61.1 are that it refers throughout to 'quotations' in the plural and it contemplates that 'quotations have already been submitted'. The reference to 'quotations' may be simply to ensure that the clause is properly linked to other clauses of NEC 3 which do deal with quotations in the plural. It is doubted that there is any intention that there should always be multiple quotations under clause 61.1. But, in any event, clause 12.1 confirms that words in the plural also mean the singular.

As to quotations already submitted these are not obviously dealt with in any of the clauses which follow clause 61.1 except for clause 61.2. It may be that they relate to circumstances where assessment of the consequences of an event is agreed between the project manager and the contractor before any instruction or changed decision or to the circumstances covered by clause 61.2. In those cases the quotation will stand to be treated as an accepted quotation. However, if there is no such agreement or application of clause 61.2, it is not clear what status attaches to a quotation 'already given'. Unless it can be brought within the scope of an 'instructed' quotation it is questionable whether the project manager can reject it. For further comment on this see section 14.4.

Clause 61.2

This clause provides:

- firstly, that the project manager may instruct the contractor to submit quotations for proposed instructions or changed decisions, *and*
- secondly, that the contractor does not put a proposed instruction or changed decision into effect

The purpose seems to be to obtain prices for something which may or may not happen rather than to obtain up-front prices for something which it is known is going to happen. But, whether or not that be the case, once the project manager has obtained quotations and then gone on to give firm instructions or changed decisions based on the proposals it seems reasonable to assume, although it is not so stated in the contract, that the quotations are to be treated as accepted quotations. If the project manager has concerns on the acceptability of the quotations but finds himself obliged to give instructions or changed decision it would be sensible to bring out these concerns before taking actions which would bring clause 61.1 and other clauses of the contract into play.

One aspect of clause 61.2 which is likely to cause concern, as it did under the corresponding clause in ECC 2, is that, under Options A and B, the cost of preparing quotations is excluded from defined cost. The Guidance Notes to NEC 3 seek to explain this by referring to the need to retain certainty of prices but, apparently recognising the injustice, then suggest that the rule will not always be followed. Technically, the contractor would be in breach of clause 27.3 in failing to comply with an instruction to submit quotations for the project manager's proposals without payment but it would be difficult for the employer to prove loss since if the proposals advance to instructions, with or without prior quotations, there are contractual mechanisms for dealing with them. Perhaps clause 61.2, insofar that it concerns proposals for things which may or may not happen, needs to be read in close conjunction with the requirements in clause 10.1 for mutual trust and co-operation rather than in accordance with the strict payment provisions of the contract. But if that fails the parties should note an oddity in the wording of clause 61.2. It does not actually refer to quotations for compensation events, proposed or otherwise. It refers to quotations for proposed instructions or proposed changed decisions. Strictly interpreted, the rules for the assessment of compensation events by reference to defined cost, may have no bearing on clause 61.2.

Clause 61.4

Whereas clause 61.2 deals with the submission of quotations for compensation events which the project manager has notified, clause 61.4 deals with the submission of quotations for events notified by the contractor. Those parts of the clause relating to the notification of compensation events are considered in Chapter 13, section 5. The parts now considered are those relating to quotations for compensation events. The relevant provisions are:

- if the project manager decides that an event notified by the contractor is a compensation event which requires to be assessed he instructs the contractor to submit quotations
- if the project manager does not decide whether or not there is such a compensation event within one week of the contractor's notification
- and if the contractor notifies the project manager of this failure
- and if then the project manager does not reply within two weeks
- the contractor's notification is treated as an instruction to submit quotations

In short, clause 61.4 requires that the project manager must instruct quotations for notified events he accepts as compensation events and if he fails to do so, after reminder by the contractor, there is a deemed instruction to submit quotations.

An important interpretive point of clause 61.4 is whether, in reaching his decision on whether or not to instruct the contractor to submit quotations, the project manager can go beyond the four stated reasons for not doing so stated in the clause. See the discussion in Chapter 13, section 5 on this point. If it is the case that he cannot, which seems likely, then the project manager is bound to instruct quotations whether or not he considers the contractor's notification of the event to be time-barred.

Clause 61.5 – failure to give early warning

The early warning scheme of clause 16 is intended to be more than simply persuasive and failure by the contractor to comply with its notice provisions is taken into account in assessing compensation events.

Clause 61.5 commences the procedure for this by requiring the project manager to notify the contractor if he decides that the contractor did not give an early warning which an experienced contractor could have given. The project manager is to notify his decision to the contractor when he instructs him to submit quotations.

The purpose of the latter provision is perhaps to indicate that the project manager has only one opportunity to raise alleged lack of early warning and that he cannot notify the contractor after he has instructed him to submit a quotation.

See also the comments on clauses 16.1 and 63.5 in Chapter 6, section 8.

Clause 61.6 – assumptions on effects

Having regard to the speed at which the notification and quotation procedures for compensation events are intended to operate it is essential that some provision is made for uncertainty of effects. Clause 61.6 does this, but not perhaps as generously as contractors would prefer, because only the project manager is allowed to make assumptions on the effects of compensation events which are correctable.

The clause provides that:

- if the project manager decides that the effects of a compensation event are too uncertain to be forecast reasonably
- he states assumptions about the event in his instruction to the contractor to submit quotations
- the assessment of the event is based on these assumptions
- if any assumption is found to be wrong the project manager notifies a correction (and compensation event 60.1(17) then applies)

The full implications of this clause can only be seen by reference to clause 65.2 which states that the assessment of a compensation event is not revised if a forecast is later shown to have been wrong. This makes clear that the contractor takes this risk of inadequacy of his quotations. If the contractor perceives that he is at risk by the uncertainty of effect of a compensation event he will accordingly load his quotation so as to minimise that risk. The project manager may then see the employer as being at risk of paying over the odds and may see himself as vulnerable for having permitted it.

Some project managers using ECC 2 adopted a policy of generally stating assumptions. They did this as a precautionary measure to retain some element of cost control. Their concern was that the provisions for the non-acceptance of quotations and assessments for compensation events might not extend to challenging the contractor's assumptions and might be limited to challenging only his calculations. This was probably a correct analysis of the contract – see the comment which follows on clause 64.1.

14.3 *Instructions for alternative quotations*

The proper outcome of the early warning requirements and risk reduction meetings of clauses 16.1 and 16.3 of NEC 3 will often be consideration of alternative ways of dealing with compensation events. Clause 62.1 which provides for alternative quotations can be taken as reflecting this – as, to a lesser extent can clause 61.2, considered in section 14.2.

Clause 62.1

The intent of clause 62.1 of NEC 3 is the same as that of clause 62.1 of ECC 2 but the wording is different in that the NEC 3 clause commences with the pre-condition, 'After discussing with the contractor different ways of dealing with the compensation event which are practicable.' Whether or not this is referring to discussions at risk reduction meetings the provision is fully in keeping with the spirit of the contract.

Once the pre-condition is met, the clause provides that:

- the project manager may instruct the contractor to submit alternative quotations
- the contractor submits such quotations as required
- the contractor may submit quotations for other methods which he considers practicable

Although the clause refers to 'different ways' and the 'other methods' which suggests that it is intended to deal principally with practical alternatives it may be wide enough to permit different combinations of price and time for the same method. Used in this way it would act as a supplement to clause 36.1 which provides for acceleration in that the employer could effectively purchase the contractor's right to more time by agreement.

As with clause 61.2 the expense of submitting the quotations is left with the contractor under main options A and B.

On its wording clause 62.1 looks as though it can only be activated by the project manager but it is possible that taken together with the provisions in clause 16.3 for proposals at risk reduction meetings the contractor may be able to activate it of his own accord.

14.4 Submission of quotations

The principal clauses dealing with the submission of quotations are clauses 62.2 and 62.3.

Clause 62.2

Clause 62.2 starts with the important statement that quotations for compensation events comprise proposed changes to the prices and any delay to the completion date and key dates assessed by the contractor.

Taken by itself this would suggest that it is a delay beyond the completion date which has to be assessed and included in a quotation. But note the wording of clause 63.3 which clarifies what is meant in clause 62.2 and makes clear that it is a delay to completion which is to be assessed.

Clause 62.2 continues with the requirement that the contractor is to submit details of his assessment with each quotation and if the programme for the remaining work is altered by the compensation event the contractor is to include the alterations to the accepted programme in his quotation.

The amount of detail required depends not only on the scale of the compensation event involved but also on which of the schedules of cost components is used for assessment. However, whichever schedule is used the accepted programme (or its revision) is the key to the assessment since the defined cost basis for assessment relies on cost components and duration times.

It is worth noting a few apparently minor drafting changes in the NEC 3 clause which may, in practice, be rather more than minor. Firstly, NEC 3 uses the word 'altered' instead of the ECC 2 word 'affected' in respect of the effect on the remaining work and the programme. Secondly, NEC 3 requires alterations to the 'Accepted Programme' to be included in the quotation – whereas in ECC 2 it was a 'revised' programme which was to be included. The change from 'affected' to 'altered' could be seen as attempting to minimise, if not to exclude, the inclusion of disruption costs in a quotation. The change from 'revised programme' to 'Accepted Programme' has the potential to cause serious difficulties where there are frequent and multiple compensation events. In such situations the accepted programme may provide a static base for any rapid series of successive quotations – with inevitable duplication of effects and costs in the quotations. For example, if event 1 causes time to extend over a holiday break and events 2, 3 and 4 are all delaying events and all occur shortly after event 1 and before the accepted programme used in quotation 1 is changed, all four quotations are likely to repeat the same holiday break time and cost effects.

Clause 62.3

Under clause 62.3 the contractor is required to submit quotations within three weeks of being instructed to do so. The project manager is required to reply within two weeks of the submission. These are tight times but note the possibility of agreement of an extension under clause 62.5.

Failure by the contractor to submit his quotations on time entitles the project manager to make his own assessments (clause 64.1). The consequences of failure by the project manager to reply in time which were less than clear in ECC 2 are now clearly set out in the new NEC 3 clause 62.6.

Clause 62.3 does not leave it to the project manager to decide what type of reply he should give to the contractor's quotation. The clause restricts his reply to:

- an instruction to submit a revised quotation
- acceptance of the quotation

- notification that a proposed instruction or changed decision will not be given
- notification that he will be making his own assessment

Of these the least certain in its intention and application is the first one – an instruction to submit a revised quotation. Clause 62.4 requires the project manager to explain his reasons for asking for a revised quotation but it says nothing as to what those reasons might be. For comment on this see below. For comment on the powers of the project manager to make his own assessments see Chapter 15, section 10.

Clause 62.4 – instruction to submit a revised quotation

Clause 62.4 supports clause 62.3 which permits the project manager to instruct the contractor to submit a revised quotation. Clause 62.4 makes clear that he can exercise this power only after explaining his reasons for doing so. One valid reason might be the project manager's belated use of clause 61.6 to state assumptions on the effects of the compensation event. More questionable would be the project manager's attempts to substitute his own assumptions without the use of clause 61.6 and/or to substitute his own risk allowances for those of the contractor.

The contractor is required to submit his revised quotation within three weeks (as in clause 62.3). But the clause 62.5 provision allowing for time to be extended by agreement appears to apply to revised quotations as well as to original quotations.

One aspect of clause 62.4 which is not too clear is whether it can be used on a repeat basis. It probably can if only because the consequences of not being able to do so would be over advantageous to the contractor.

Clause 62.5 – extending the time for quotations

By clause 62.5 the project manager is permitted to extend the time allowed for the contractor to submit quotations and for his own replies if he and the contractor agree to any extension before the submission or reply is due. The project manager is required to formally notify the contractor of any extension agreed.

14.5 *Status of the contractor's quotations*

As noted elsewhere in this book a major difference between NEC 3 and ECC 2 is the emphasis NEC 3 puts on the contractor's right to submit quotations for compensation events and the status of those quotations. The need for change arose because the provisions of ECC 2, although almost certainly drafted with the same intentions as now evident in NEC 3, did not cater for the possibility that the project manager, by inertia or intent, could completely undermine the basic principle that the assessment of compensation events should be based on the contractor's quotations. In particular it was sometimes said with dubious circularity, that quotations not instructed had no status and that the contractor had no right to submit quotations – only a duty to do so when instructed.

The new provisions in NEC 3 which aim to correct this situation are found in clauses 61.4, 62.6 and 64.4. They can be summarised as follows:

- clause 61.4 – failure by the project manager to timeously respond to notification by the contractor of a compensation event is treated as a deemed instruction to submit quotations
- clause 62.6 – failure by the project manager to timeously reply to a quotation submitted by the contractor is treated as acceptance of the quotation
- clause 64.1 – failure by the project manager to timeously assess a compensation event after finding some fault in the contractor's quotation is treated as acceptance of the contractor's quotation

Project manager's power to reject quotations

The question of whether the project manager can reject the contractor's quotations at will and carry out his own assessments has not been clearly dealt with in NEC 3. Problems potentially remain with the provision in clause 64.1 which allows the project manager to assess a compensation event if he decides that the contractor has not assessed the event correctly in a quotation.

The identical provision in ECC 2 was sometimes used by project managers to substitute their own assessments in place of the contractor's quotations with the effect that discouraged contractors saw little point in submitting quotations which were destined for rejection from the outset. There are, however, good arguments for saying that the project manager has only limited powers for assessing compensation events and only limited power to decide that the contractor has not assessed a compensation event correctly.

The first point is that the contract expressly restricts the power of the project manager to make his own assessment to four stated default situations. The project manager has no general power to make his own assessments.

The second point is that any decision by the project manager as to whether the contractor has or has not made a correct assessment in his quotation has to have regard to the entire contractual scheme for assessments and quotations. The best place to start is probably with clause 65.2 at the back end of the procedure, 'The assessment of a compensation event is not revised if a forecast upon which it is based is shown by later recorded information to have been wrong.' In short, the contractor takes the risks of the forecasts he makes in his assessments for quotations. It is commercially improbable that the contract intends that the contractor should be bound by the forecasts made by the project manager. But, in any event, the contract expressly provides at clause 61.6 for the project manager to state assumptions for forecasts if he so wishes and for those particular forecasts to be corrected through clause 60.1(17), if eventually found to have been wrong.

The correct approach for a project manager concerned that he has received a quotation based on incorrect forecasts is not to embark on his own forecasting, relying on clause 64.1, but to state assumptions under clause 61.6 for a revised quotation under clause 62.3. As to risk allowances, these are regulated by clause 63.3 to matters which have a significant chance of occurring but again there is no commercial sense in the contractor being bound by the project manager's assessment of risk. Again the proper approach would be for the project manager to call for a revised quotation.

Taking an overall view of the compensation event provisions it is difficult to escape the conclusion that the only valid grounds for the project manager deciding that the contractor has not assessed a compensation event correctly, and not instructing revised quotations, is when the contractor has declined to follow the assessment rules in clause 63.1. On that view assessments by the project manager are a fall-back provision and not an alternative to the quotation system.

Chapter 15
Assessment of compensation events

15.1 Introduction

The rules for the assessment of compensation events in ECC 2 were clearly not designed in the expectation that they would be regularly used. Such was their complexity and so time consuming and expensive their operation that it was not unusual, for low value items, for the costs of assessment to exceed the value of the compensation event. The draftsmen of the contract were apparently of the view that compensation events would be rare events with no more than a handful or so on any one contract.

This was a serious miscalculation. It overlooked two key aspects of the system – one being that all time and money changes, however minor, were subject to application of the compensation event assessment rules, the other being that any change to the works information, again however minor, was a compensation event.

The result was that the number of compensation events on many contracts ran into dozens, multiples of hundreds, and sometimes more. Not infrequently the system broke down under overload. Faced with such difficulties project managers and contractors often sought sensible alternatives or modifications of the rules for assessing compensation events such as batching, time-grouping, establishing schedules of rates, and excluding items below a certain value level from the full procedural rigours of the system.

Expectations were high that NEC 3 would address the well known difficulties of the ECC 2 rules and would contain revisions and new provisions for the assessment of compensation events which would be user-friendly, economical to operate, and safe from collapse.

Regrettably the changes made fall well short of what is required. There are some very welcome improvements such as increased use of the shorter schedule of cost components and, for Option A, the use by agreement of rates and lump sums. But the basic problems remain and may even have been worsened by some of the changes. Compensation events are still assessed by reference to their effect on the work already done and forecast cost of work still to be done rather than by reference to their work contract. There is something to be said for the rationale of this in that when properly applied it picks up delay and disruption costs for each event, but the downside is the amount of programming and cost calculating involved in the process.

The points of concern on the NEC 3 revisions are that by fixing the start date for the work still to be done as the date when quotations should have been instructed they increase the amount of artificial prospective analysis, and by stipulating that assessments are based on the accepted programme they increase the possibility of cost duplication in successive quotations. A point of more general concern is that the new clause 12.3, which requires the parties to agree any change in the conditions of contract, appears to prevent the project manager from relaxing the assessment rules in the interests of good project management. In connection with this it is worth noting the following extract from the Guidance Notes to NEC 3 which, whilst sensibly recognising the problem, illustrates a solution which is not contractually compliant without agreement under clause 12.3.

> *'If several minor compensation events occur within a short period, it can be counter-productive to produce a revised programme for each one – particularly as the status of quotations for earlier ones will not yet be finalised. Some project managers have adopted a procedure where all the compensation events notified in one month are considered in one revised programme.'*

15.2 Changes from ECC 2

The principal changes from ECC 2 to NEC 3 in relation to assessments are as listed below:

Core clauses

- clause 11.2(8)   – addition of fee percentage for subcontracted work
- clause 60.1(12) – only the difference between physical conditions is taken into account in assessing a compensation event
- clause 60.1(13) – only the difference between weather measurements and actual weather data is taken into account in assessing a compensation event
- clause 62.2   – programmes submitted with assessments are to show alterations to the accepted programme
- clause 63.1   – the date when the project manager instructed or should have instructed quotations divides the work already done from the work not yet done
- clause 63.2   – prices are not reduced except as stated in the contract
- clause 63.3   – delays affecting key dates are assessed by reference to the accepted programme
- clause 63.4   – rights of the employer and contractor to change prices, the completion date or key dates are their only rights in respect of a compensation event
- clause 63.8   – ambiguity or inconsistency is resolved in favour of party which did not supply the works information
- clause 63.9   – corrections of descriptions for key dates are taken into account in assessing compensation events
- clause 64.1   – the project manager assesses a compensation event if required alterations to a programme are not included in a quotation

- clause 64.2   – the project manager assesses a compensation event if required alterations to a programme are not submitted for acceptance
- clause 64.4   – if the project manager does not assess a compensation event within the time allowed the contractor's quotation is treated as having been accepted
- clause 65.1   – a compensation event is implemented when a contractor's quotation is treated as having been accepted

Main option clauses

- clause 11.2(22) – defined cost is the cost of the components in the shorter schedule of cost components (Options A and B only)
- clause 60.7   – assessment of a compensation event relating to inconsistency between the bill of quantities and another document is made on the assumption that the contractor has taken the bill of quantities as correct (Options B and D only)
- clause 63.10   – the prices are reduced if the effect of a compensation event relating to a change to the works information or to correction of an assumption is to reduce total defined cost (Options A and B only)
- clause 63.11   – the prices are reduced if the effect of a compensation event relating to a change in the works information (other than a change to works information provided by the employer which the contractor has proposed and the project manager has accepted), or to correction of an assumption, is to reduce total defined cost (Options C and D only)
- clause 63.13   – revised rules for assessment of changed prices for compensation events (Options B and D only)
- clause 63.14   – if the project manager and the contractor agree, rates and lump sums may be used to assess a compensation event instead of defined cost (Option A only)

15.3 *General assessment rules*

The assessment rules of general application in NEC 3 are found in clauses 61.6, 62.2, 63.1 to 63.7 and 65.2. They can be summarised as follows:

- clause 61.6 – assumptions about compensation events can be made by the project manager – the contractor is to base his assessment on these assumptions
- clause 62.2 – quotations for compensation events comprise proposed changes to the prices and delays to the completion date or to key dates as assessed by the contractor

- clause 63.1 – changed prices to be assessed as the effect of the compensation event on actual defined cost of work already done and forecast defined cost of work not yet done
- clause 63.2 – prices are not reduced except as stated in the contract
- clause 63.3 – delay is assessed by reference to the accepted programme
- clause 63.4 – the rights of the parties to changed prices, completion dates and key dates, are their only rights in respect of compensation events
- clause 63.5 – if the contractor does not give early warning, compensation events are assessed as if he had
- clause 63.6 – assessments include time and risk allowances for matters with a significant chance of occurring
- clause 63.7 – assessments assume the contractor reacts competently and properly and extra cost and time are reasonably incurred
- clause 65.2 – assessment of a compensation event is not revised if a forecast on which it is based is shown by later recorded information to have been wrong

Clause 61.6 – assumptions about compensation events

Clause 61.6, which needs to be read in conjunction with clause 60.1(17), is a useful clause permitting the project manager to state the assumptions on which the contractor's assessments for quotations are to be made. If the assumption turns out to be wrong the project manager is obliged to notify a correction. The compensation event at clause 60.1(17) then comes into play. For further comment on this clause see Chapter 12, section 6.

Clause 62.2 – quotations for compensation events

This clause, when read in conjunction with clauses 63.1 and 63.3, effectively states a general rule that the contractor's quotations are to be time and cost assessments made under the rules of the contract. For further comment on this clause see Chapter 14, section 4.

Clause 63.1 – changes to the prices

Clause 63.1 is one of the most important clauses in NEC 3 as it establishes the basic rules for changes to the prices – and under NEC 3 changes to the prices are the only way for the contractor to obtain entitlement to more money. In short, the rules as set out in the clause can be re-stated as:

- changes to the prices are assessed as the effect of the compensation event, *on*
- actual defined cost and/or forecast defined cost plus the fee, *and*

- the date when the project manager instructed or should have instructed the contractor to submit quotations divides actual defined cost from forecast defined cost

These rules apply to the assessment of all compensation events except where the contract provides otherwise or allows alternatives. Important clauses in this respect are:

- for Option A – clause 63.14 allowing rates and lump sums to be used if the project manager and the contractor agree
- for Options B and D – clause 63.13 which provides for changes to the bill of quantities and which also states that rates and lump sums may be used to assess a compensation event if the project manager and the contractor agree

It is not entirely clear why Option C lacks the alternative of using rates and lump sums by agreement.

'effect of the compensation event'

These words, as stated in the opening sentence of clause 63.1, have a major impact on the way the assessment system of NEC 3 operates. They require assessments to include not only for direct costs but also for delay and prolongation costs. In doing so they eliminate entitlement to separate delay and disruption claims and, if the system is operated as intended, they eliminate the possibility of end-of-contract global claims. This is a significantly different approach to that used in traditional construction contracts where extra works are valued by reference to bill rates and delay and disruption costs are separately assessed.

To determine the effect of a compensation event as required by clause 63.1 a comparison has to be made between the cost to the contractor of completing the work with the compensation event included and the cost without it. This is a far more elaborate exercise than simply valuing additional work. It involves detailed planning and programme revisions and costing out fully resourced programmes.

'actual Defined Cost'

The intention of NEC 3 is, and was under ECC 2, that the contractor should not lose out financially from compensation events. As the Guidance Notes explain, 'No compensation event for which a quotation is required is due to the fault of the Contractor or relates to a matter which is at his risk under the contract. It is therefore appropriate to reimburse the Contractor his forecast additional costs (or actual costs if the work has already been done).' On the face of it, it would seem that the contractor is protected from loss except for loss arising from erroneous forecasts or inadequate risk allowances.

However, that is not quite the case. Defined cost is not actual cost, and 'actual Defined Cost' is only defined cost which has been incurred – as opposed to that which is forecast. It is not actual cost. To find out what 'Defined Cost' is it is necessary to examine the definitions of the term for each of the main options A to F. By way of example, Option A states at clause 11.2(22) – 'Defined Cost is the cost of components in the Shorter Schedule of Cost Components whether work is subcontracted or not excluding the cost of preparing quotations for compensation events.' And what that means is that the contractor cannot use subcontractor invoices as representing cost. A position which also applies in Option B but not in Options C to F. Consequently for Options A and B, the contractor's cost records may be of little assistance in determining actual defined cost and the contractor is put to the expense of undertaking theoretical analysis. When this is combined with the rule that excludes the costs of preparing quotations for compensation events there can be no assurance that the assessment system provides full reimbursement of costs.

'forecast Defined Cost'

Preparing forecasts of defined cost can be a costly exercise involving planners, programmers, estimators and quantity surveyors. It can also be a risky exercise because by clause 65.2 inadequate forecasts cannot be revised or revisited. Contractors do not have a free hand, however, to load their forecasts to avoid the possibility of any loss – they are constrained by the assessment rules requiring them to link assessments to programmes (clause 62.2) and allowing them to include only for matters which have a significant chance of occurring (clause 63.6).

'the resulting fee'

Under NEC 3 the fee has, by definition in clause 11.2(8), two components – the subcontracted fee percentage and the direct fee percentage. This is a considerable improvement on the position in ECC 2 which allowed only one component.

'date for the division of work'

The new provision in clause 63.1, stating that the date when the project manager instructed or should have instructed the contractor to submit quotations is the date which divides the work already done from the work not yet done, raises more questions than it answers. It may prove to be one of the most difficult provisions of NEC 3 to apply. One problem is that it appears to preclude the practice, commonplace under ECC 2, of agreement between the project manager and the contractor that all compensation events should be valued on known costs after the event. This disposed of arguments about the contractor's quotations and protected both the project manager and the contractor from the embarrassment that an inaccurate forecast could bring to one or the other. Another problem is that it appears to be of general effect such that any retrospective assessment, such as might arise from late acceptance that an event was a compensation event or an adjudicator's decision to that effect, would be substantially on a forecast basis – albeit that the forecasting would be undertaken after the event.

Clause 63.2 – reduction of prices

In NEC 3 this clause states only that if the effect of a compensation event is to reduce total defined cost, prices are not reduced except as stated in the contract. The corresponding ECC 2 clause went on to say that if the effect of the compensation event was to reduce total actual cost and the event was a change in the works information or correction of the project manager's assumption about a compensation event, then the prices were reduced.

The explanation for the difference between the two clauses is that NEC 3 states the reductions that are permissible in clauses particular to the various Options A to F. Thus, clause 63.10 of Options A and B states the above-mentioned part of ECC 2 clause 63.2. Permitted reductions to the same effect are also found in clause 63.11 of Options C and D.

Additionally, clauses 60.4 and 60.6 of Options B and D permit reductions for compensation events relating to quantities. Clause X2.1 of secondary option X2 (relating to changes in the law) also allows for reductions.

The most commonly encountered reduction events are those covered by clauses 63.10 and 63.11. They are what might be described as omission variations. Under ECC 2 they frequently attracted dispute as to whether the fee element of the reduction should be to the employer's or to the contractor's benefit.

Strict reading of the clauses suggests that the benefit is to the employer but there is potential injustice in that it assumes savings by the contractor which have no relation to the composition of his tender. Taken to the extreme the contractor could end up owing money to the employer for large scale deductions of work. Perhaps the argument put by the contractors that they should receive the fee element as compensation for omission variations has some merit.

Clause 63.3 – delay to completion

The first part of clause 63.3 states that any delay to the completion date is assessed as the length of time that, due to the compensation event, planned completion is later than planned completion shown on the accepted programme. For contractors this is a particularly important clause. It indicates that the contractor's entitlement to an extension of time for completion is

judged by reference to the date of planned completion on his accepted programme. Any assessed delay beyond that date caused by a compensation
event is added to the formal contract time for completion by adjusting the
stated completion date. Thus if the contractor has terminal float in his programme he retains that float.

The second part of clause 63.3 is new to NEC 3. It relates to key dates and
states that a delay to a key date is assessed as the length of time the planned
date for meeting a key date is later than the date shown on the accepted programme due to a compensation event. In short, it is again the accepted programme which fixes the basis of assessment.

Clause 63.4 – rights of the parties

This is an interesting new clause which states that the rights of the parties to
change the prices, completion dates and key dates are their only rights in
respect of a compensation event.

So far as the contractor is concerned the purpose of the clause is apparently
to indicate that for events which qualify as compensation events he has no
cost or time remedies except through the compensation event procedures.
The purpose of the clause as regards the employer is obscure.

On its wording, however, the clause may not achieve anything. It is essentially circular since the only rights in respect of a compensation events are
changes to the prices, completion dates and key dates and nothing obviously
useful is added by saying these are the rights.

Clause 63.5 – failure to give early warning

Clause 63.5 states the sanction on the contractor for failing to give early
warning of a compensation event. The clause states that:

- if the project manager has notified the contractor of his decision
- that the contractor did not give an early warning
- which an experienced contractor could have given
- the event is assessed as if the contractor had given early warning

At first reading it appears that if an event is assessed 'as if the Contractor had
given early warning' it does not matter whether the contractor gave early
warning or not. But obviously the intention of the clause must be the
opposite.

In practice, however, applying the clause with this latter intention could
lead to some surprises. It may be the expectation that the contractor will
suffer because of his default of not giving early notice – but that does not
follow, particularly having regard to clause 65.2 which bars revision of assessments that this will be the result.

Clause 63.6 – time and risk allowances

Clause 63.6 can be seen as supporting clauses 63.1 and 63.3 which require 'the effects' of a compensation event to be assessed. It expressly permits assessments to include for risks of cost and time. The clause states:

● the assessment of the effect of a compensation event
● includes cost and time risk allowances
● for matters which have a significant chance of occurring
● and are at the contractor's risk

Some matters such as materials wastage, downtime due to inclement weather and other routine estimating allowances should be relatively non-controversial. More sophisticated allowances such as provision for excesses on damage claims may attract closer examination and argument. The big issues, however, are delay, disruption and winter working. It is up to the contractor to show that they have a 'significant' chance of occurring.

The intention of the words which conclude clause 63.6 'and are at the Contractor's risk under this contract' is not immediately obvious. The clause would seem to work perfectly well without the words. When applied to the main options with a cost reimbursable element they seem to throw some uncertainty on whether risks should be allowed for in whole or in part. They may be included simply to make the point, if it needs making, that the contractor should not include in his assessment for employer's risks.

Clause 63.7 – assumptions on reactions

Clause 63.7 states certain restrictive assumptions applied to assessments. Namely:

● that the contractor reacts competently and promptly
● that additional cost and time are reasonably incurred
● that the accepted programme can be changed

The first two of these are commonsense measures designed to protect the employer against the contractor's inefficiencies. They correspond broadly to the rules for the assessment of damages. The third point in the clause, the reference to the accepted programme, is an indication that the contractor is expected to change his programme if that is practicable but that begs the question – what is the position if the accepted programme cannot be changed? Consider, for example, a programme which is fixed by external restraints such as railway track possessions. Is the contractor's entitlement in such circumstances to be paid the actual costs of working to the fixed programme or is he entitled to the notional costs of working to a changed programme? The latter would have some logic in that the contractor would be paid the costs of a notional extension of time instead of being paid his acceleration costs.

Clause 65.2 – no revision for later information

Clause 65.2 is brief but very important. It states that the assessment of a compensation event is not revised if a 'forecast' upon which it is based is shown by later 'recorded' information to have been wrong.

In short an assessment which is accepted stands as valid even if the assumptions in the forecast on which the assessment is based are later proved to be wrong. Or put another way, the contractor stands the risks of his forecasts. He may lose out financially or make a surprise windfall. But what has been achieved is a measure of certainty on the amount of money to change hands and the amount of time to be awarded.

Note that by using the word 'forecast' in relation to what may or may not have been wrong, the clause leaves open the possibility of a revision of an assessment which is shown to be wrong in its calculations.

One aspect of the corresponding clause under ECC 2 which attracted debate was whether it conferred absolute finality on forecasts, and if it did whether this applied to forecasts made by the project manager as well as to those made by the contractor. It was argued that if the contractor, rightly or wrongly, took on the burden of assessing a compensation event it would be inequitable if an adjudicator was barred from rectifying inadequacies or errors in the project manager's forecasting. The point illustrated the difficulties of the project manager putting himself in the shoes of the contractor. See section 15.5 for further comment.

The significance of the word 'recorded' in the last line of the clause is not fully understood. The clause states a barring provision. Qualifying 'later information' by 'recorded' could therefore suggest limitation and not enhancement of application of the clause. Possibly what it means is that no account is to be taken in any re-assessment of information which was not available at the time of the assessment.

15.4 *Particular assessment rules*

In addition to the general assessment rules found in clauses 63.1 to 63.7 and in clause 65.2, NEC 3 contains assessment rules particular to certain events and situations and/or related to particular options. Not all of these come under the marginal note 'assessing compensation events' and some are to be found attached to the description of a compensation event. The full list is:

- clause 60.1(12) – adverse physical conditions
- clause 60.1(13) – adverse weather conditions
- clause 60.2   – judging physical conditions
- clause 60.3   – site information
- clause 60.7   – bill of quantities – Options B and D
- clause 61.6   – project manager's assumptions
- clause 63.8   – resolving ambiguity or inconsistency
- clause 63.9   – description of conditions for key dates

- clause 63.12 – changes to the activity schedule – Options A and C
- clause 63.13 – changes to the bill of quantities – Options B and D
- clause 63.14 – use of rates and lump sums – Option A
- clause 63.15 – use of shorter schedule of cost components – Options C, D and E
- clause X1.3 – price adjustment for inflation – secondary option X1

Clause 60.1(12) – adverse physical conditions

The clause makes clear that only the difference between the conditions encountered and those it would have been reasonable to have allowed for is taken into account in assessing a compensation event.

Clause 60.1(13) – adverse weather conditions

In like manner this clause makes clear that it is only the difference between actual conditions and ten year conditions which is taken into account.

Clause 60.2 – judging physical conditions

This clause states how physical conditions are to be judged for the purpose of assessing compensation events.

Clause 60.3 – site information

The main purpose of clause 60.3 which deals with ambiguity or inconsistency within site information is probably to assist in determining whether or not there is a compensation event, but on its wording it may have an impact on assessment.

Clause 60.7 – bill of quantities

This clause, which applies only to Options B and D states that in assessing a compensation event which results from correction of an inconsistency between the bill of quantities and another document the contractor is assumed to have taken the bill of quantities as correct. For comment on this clause see Chapter 12, section 10.

Clause 63.8 – ambiguity or inconsistency

Clause 17.1 requires the project manager to give an instruction resolving any ambiguity in or inconsistency between the documents in the contract. This is a general requirement which covers both employer and contractor provided documents. The probability is that any instruction given will change the works information but the possibility is that the fault will not always be the employer's.

Clause 63.8 deals with this by stating how compensation events which are instructions to change the works information to resolve an ambiguity or inconsistency are to be assessed. It follows a legal rule for the construction of contracts (the *contra proferentum* rule) in allowing the most favourable interpretation of the documents to be given to the party which did not create the ambiguity or inconsistency. Accordingly, the clause provides that if the employer produced the works information which is at fault, the compensation event is assessed with an interpretation in favour of the contractor. If the contractor produced the works information the effect of the compensation is assessed with an interpretation in favour of the employer.

The clause appears to go a little further than traditional contractual provisions to the same effect in that, taken with clause 63.2 and other clauses which allow for reductions in the contract price for changes in the works information, it may give the employer rights to what are, in effect, contractual rights of counterclaim for faults in works information provided by the contractor. Alternatively, or additionally, it permits the project manager to instruct the contractor to perform the works to the highest standards that his (the contractor's) documents suggest without the employer taking on liability for any extra costs.

Clause 63.9 – description of conditions for key dates

This clause, which is new to NEC 3, provides:

- if a change to the works information
- makes the description of a condition for a key date incorrect
- the project manager corrects the description
- the correction is taken into account in assessing the compensation event changing the works information

The clause does not itself distinguish between works information provided by the employer and that provided by the contractor. But when read in conjunction with clause 60.1(1) which deals with compensation events arising from changes in the works information it probably applies only to works information provided by the employer.

Clause 63.12 – changes to the activity schedule

Clause 63.12 applies only to main options A and C. It states that assessments for changed prices for compensation events are in the form of changes to the activity schedule.

This is a curious and unusual arrangement but one in keeping with the NEC 3 approach to lump sum contracts in that the contract apparently recognises the components of the lump sum as individual contract prices. Amounts due on claims and variations are strictly not added directly to the contract price but are first added to items in the activity schedule. The purpose of this apportionment seems to be to maintain the integrity of the interim payment scheme, however, under ECC 2 it was frequently not undertaken.

Clause 63.13 – changes to the bill of quantities

Clause 63.13 of NEC 3 is a restructured and extended version of clause 63.9 of ECC 2. It applies only to Options B and D. Its two key provisions are:

- assessments for changed prices for compensation events are in the form of changes to the bill of quantities
- if the project manager and the contractor agree, prices and lump sums may be used to assess a compensation event instead of defined cost

These were the only provisions in clause 63.9 of ECC 2. The extended clause 63.13 of NEC 3 explains how changes to the bill of quantities are to be made. In summary, it states:

- for work not yet done and for which there are items in the bill of quantities the changes are changed rates, changed quantities or a changed lump sum
- for work not yet done for which there are no items in the bill of quantities the changes are new priced items compiled in accordance with the method of measurement – unless the project manager and the contractor agree otherwise
- for work not already done the change is a new lump sum item

Clause 63.14 – use of rates and lump sums – Option A

Clause 63.14 of Option A provides that if the project manager and the contractor agree rates and lump sums may be used to assess a compensation event instead of defined cost. The same provision appears in clause 63.13 of Options B and D.

Clause 63.15 – use of shorter schedule of cost components

This clause, which appears in Options C, D and E permits the use of the shorter schedule of cost components for the assessment of compensation events if the project manager and the contractor so agree. Additionally, it entitles the project manager to make his own assessments using the shorter schedule.

Provisions to this effect were included in Options A and B of ECC 2 but as assessments under Options A and B of NEC 3 now require the use of the shorter schedule they no longer appear in those options.

Clause X1.3 – price adjustment for inflation

Clause X1.3 of secondary option X1 states how price adjustment for inflation is applied to the assessment of compensation events. In short, defined cost is adjusted by reference to base date levels.

15.5 *The project manager's assessments*

Clauses 64.1 to 64.4 of NEC 3 set out the circumstances in which the project manager may make his own assessments of compensation events; the procedures for doing so; and the consequences of procedural default. Clauses 64.1 to 64.3 remain largely unchanged from ECC 2 but clause 64.4 is a new clause by which, if the project manager does not make his assessments in the time allowed, the contractor's quotations become treated as accepted.

One of the most contentious aspects of ECC 2 was whether the project manager had broad ability or only very restricted ability to undertake his own assessments. There were two main issues. One was whether the project manager could make his own assessments in circumstances where he had failed to instruct the contractor to submit quotations. The other was whether the project manager could decide that the contractor had not assessed a compensation event correctly in a quotation simply because he disagreed with the contractor's assumptions and/or risk allowances.

The background to the first of these issues was that it was arguable under ECC 2 that the contractor's quotation had no status unless instructed. Project managers wishing to avoid use of the quotation system were able to exploit this by not instructing quotations and then claiming the right to make their own assessments. This was almost certainly misunderstanding or abuse of the ECC 2 system but, whatever the arguments, they carry no weight in the NEC 3 system which could not make clearer the contractor's right to submit quotations. If the project manager fails to instruct quotations under NEC 3 the status of the contractor's quotations is confirmed.

The second issue is not addressed in NEC 3 and arguments are likely to remain as to the meaning of 'has not assessed the compensation event correctly' as it appears in clause 64.1. But so far as disagreements on assumptions are concerned, it cannot be right for the project manager to substitute his own assumptions for those of the contractor in assessments which are not capable of being revised when there is the facility in the contract for the project manager to state assumptions for assessments which can be revised. As for disagreements on risk allowances there is obviously a balance to be struck between the commercial interests of the contractor and exploitation of the employer. But these can be dealt with by the project manager instructing revised quotations rather than by undertaking his own assessments.

Clause 64.1 – project manager's assessment

Clause 64.1 enables the project manager to assess a compensation event:

- if the contractor has not submitted his quotation and assessment in time
- if the project manager decides that the contractor has not assessed the event correctly (and no instruction to submit a revised quotation has been given)
- if the contractor has not submitted with his quotation a programme, or alterations to a programme, which the contract requires
- if when the quotation is submitted the project manager has not accepted the contractor's latest programme for a reason stated in the contract

It may be arguable whether the clause requires the project manager to act or simply empowers him to do so but the broad intention of the clause appears to be that the project manager can, and must, intervene in the assessment process if its rules are not being followed. However, as discussed above, there is nothing in the clause permitting the project manager to make his own assessment simply because he disagrees with the assumptions made by the contractor in his assessment. The clause appears to be concerned with the mechanics of assessment and not with the logic of assumptions.

Clause 64.2 – assessment of programme

Clause 64.2 supports clause 64.1 by allowing the project manager to make his assessment of a compensation event by reference to his own assessment of the programme for the remaining work when:

- there is no accepted programme
- the contractor has not submitted a programme or alterations to a programme for acceptance as required

Such a power might be implied into clause 64.1 but the fact that it is expressed separately in clause 64.2 suggests that clause 64.1 is concerned more with the project manager's power to act on default by the contractor rather than with the way the power is exercised.

Clause 64.3 – notification of the project manager's assessments

If the project manager makes an assessment of a compensation event under clause 64.1 he is required by clause 64.3 to notify the contractor and to give details of the assessment within the same period allowed to the contractor for submission of a quotation (three weeks under clause 62.3). The period starts when the need for the project manager's assessment becomes apparent. The consequences if the project manager fails to comply with the timescale are set out in clause 64.4.

Clause 64.4 – failure by project management to assess

Clause 64.4 is new to NEC 3. It provides:

- if the project manager does not assess a compensation event within the time allowed the contractor may notify the project manager to this effect
- if the contractor has submitted more than one quotation he states in his notification which quotation he proposes should be accepted
- if the project manager does not reply within two weeks the contractor's notification is treated as acceptance of the contractor's quotation by the project manager

This clause has already been mentioned previously in this book as being the last step in the process whereby the contractor's quotation becomes treated as accepted – see, for example, Chapter 14 section 5.

An interesting aspect of the clause is that whilst it deals with the default situation of no reply by the project manager within two weeks, it does not indicate what reply the project manager might be expected to make, or permitted to make, if he has failed to assess a compensation event. It may be that he is permitted to belatedly make an assessment – subject to operation of the compensation event at clause 60.1(6) for late reply. But any reply to the effect that he is going to make an assessment in the course of time would seem to be entirely contrary to the general intentions of the contract. It may, therefore, be that the only reply which has the effect of stopping the contractor's quotation being treated as accepted, is a reply which contains the project manager's assessment.

15.6 *Implementing compensation events*

NEC 3 expresses the process of changing the contract price, extending the time for completion or changing key dates as 'implementing' compensation events. The phraseology is odd since by clause 60.1 compensation events are stated to be various actions, circumstances or breaches and in the ordinary meaning of words they are not capable of being implemented once they have occurred.

Clause 65.1 – implementing compensation events

The wording of clause 65.1 of NEC 3 differs from that of the corresponding clause in ECC 2 and is undoubtedly clearer in its meaning. The clause states that a compensation event is implemented when:

- the project manager notifies acceptance of the contractor's quotation, *or*
- the project manager notifies the contractor of his own assessment, *or*
- the contractor's quotation is treated as having been accepted

Other clauses of NEC 3 which refer to the implementation of compensation events are clauses 65.3 and 65.4.

Clause 65.3 – changes to forecast amounts

Clause 65.3 applies only to main options E and F – the two fully cost reimbursable options. It supports clause 65.1.

The clause states that the project manager includes the changes to the forecast amounts of the prices and the completion date in his notification to the contractor implementing a compensation event. This appears to be a reference to the forecast which the contractor is obliged to prepare under clause 20.4 but whatever its meaning it highlights a fundamental question – what purpose does the compensation event procedure serve in fully cost reimbursable contracts?

Clause 65.4 – change to prices and the completion date

Clause 65.4 applies to main options A, B, C and D.

It states that the project manager includes the changes to the prices, to the completion date, and to key dates, which he has accepted or assessed in his notification implementing a compensation event. Again this is no more than detail supporting clause 65.1.

15.7 *Other financial remedies*

Not all the financial remedies available to the parties under NEC 3 are covered by the compensation event provisions. NEC 3 also provides other remedies under various clauses to both the employer and to the contractor – although mostly to the employer. These are:

- clause 25.2   – costs incurred by the employer as a result of the contractor not providing services and other things as stated in the works information are assessed by the project manager and paid by the contractor
- clause 25.3   – additional costs incurred by the employer as a result of the contractor not achieving conditions for key dates are assessed by the project manager – the employer's right to recover these costs is his only right in the circumstances
- clause 36.3/36.4 – when the project manager accepts a quotation for acceleration he changes the prices, the completion date and key dates accordingly

- clause 40.6   – costs incurred by the employer in repeating a test or inspection after a defect is found are assessed by the project manager and paid by the contractor
- clause 44.2   – if the project manager accepts a quotation for reduced prices to avoid correcting a defect, the prices and the completion date are changed accordingly
- clause 45.1   – if the contractor is given access but does not correct a defect within defect correction period the project manager assesses the cost to the employer of having the defect corrected and the contractor pays this amount
- clause 45.2   – if the contractor is not given access to correct defects before the defects date the project manager assesses the cost to the employer of correcting the defects and the contractor pays this amount
- clause 51.3   – if an amount due is corrected in a later certificate interest on the correcting amount is paid
- clause 53.2   – the contractor is paid his share of the saving; the contractor pays his share of the excess – Options C and D only
- clause 83.1   – each party indemnifies the other against claims, proceedings, compensation and costs due to an event which is his risk
- clause 85.4   – amounts not recovered from an insurer are borne by the party for events at its risk
- clause 86.1   – if the contractor does not submit a required insurance certificate, the employer may insure and the cost is paid by the contractor
- clause 87.3   – if the employer does not submit a required insurance certificate, the contractor may insure and the cost is paid by the employer
- clause 90.4   – payments due on termination are paid within three weeks of the project manager's certificate
- Option X7   – delay damages
- Option X17   – low performance damages

Note also, Option X18 on limitation of the contractor's liability to the employer.

Chapter 16
Title

16.1 Introduction

Section 7 of NEC 3 deals with title to equipment, plant and materials, and other objects of value or interest. With the exception of a minor wording change in clause 73.1 section 7 is unchanged from ECC 2.

NEC 3 avoids the ambitious provisions of many standard forms of contract which purport to give the employer title to anything he has paid for or anything the contractor has brought onto site. Instead NEC 3 sensibly goes no further than passing to the employer 'whatever title the Contractor has'.

This may concern some employers who want to be assured that payment for plant and materials secures ownership and that equipment brought onto site for the construction of the works (e.g. false work and scaffolding) cannot be removed until it has served its purpose. Such concern is understandable but it is better addressed by the realistic provisions of NEC 3 and firm discipline by the project manager and the supervisor in checking the contractor's title rather than by the misleading and ineffective assertions to title of some contracts.

The problem with such contractual assertions, which NEC 3 recognises, is that they operate only between the employer and the contractor and they do not diminish the legal rights to title of third parties or override statutory rules in the event of insolvency. They may give comfort to the employer by their appearance but when things go wrong and conflicting claims to title emerge then the full complexity of the law of ownership is revealed. See, for example, the Court of Appeal ruling in the case of *Cosslett (Contractors) Ltd* v. *Mid Glamorgan County Council* (1997) concerning a contract under ICE Conditions of Contract, 5th Edition.

It is beyond the scope of this book to comment in detail on the law of ownership except to say that amongst the complexity one firm rule has remained clear and withstood the passage of time. That is the rule in *Appleby* v. *Myers* (1867) which states that 'Materials worked by one into the property of another become part of that property.' In short, title passes to the employer as against the contractor when plant and materials are incorporated into the works. However, note that there is a distinction between goods fixed and goods merely on site as illustrated by the case of *Dawber Williamson* v. *Humberside County Council* (1979) where a roofing subcontractor successfully sued the employer for the value of roofing slates, paid for by the employer when brought onto site, but not fixed at the time the main contractor went into liquidation.

16.2 Employer's title to equipment, plant and materials

Clause 70.1 – title outside the working areas

Clause 70.1 provides that whatever title the contractor has to equipment, plant and materials:

- which is outside the working areas, *and*
- has been marked by the supervisor as for the contract, *then*
- that title passes to the employer

The purpose of this clause is quite modest – simply to state the change of title effected by marking. The clause says nothing about the obligation or the entitlement to mark (for that see clause 71.1) nor anything about the contractor's rights (if any) to payment consequent upon marking – for comment on that see section 16.3 below.

Note, that the clause refers to the 'working areas' and not to the 'site'. This maintains compatibility with the schedules of cost components.

Clause 70.2 – title within the working areas

Clause 70.2 deals with equipment, plant and materials brought within the working areas. It provides that whatever title the contractor has passes to the employer. The clause further provides that title passes back to the contractor when equipment, plant and materials are removed from the working areas with the project manager's permission.

The transfer of title under this clause is automatic and is not dependent on marking by the supervisor. Nor is it expressly made dependent on payment or any right to payment. This raises interesting questions on whether the transfer of title, particularly with respect to the contractor's equipment, is intended to be permanent or temporary. For example, if the contractor becomes insolvent is the employer entitled only to retain title to the equipment until completion of the works or can the employer sell the equipment after completion and retain the proceeds notwithstanding any claim on the equipment by a receiver or liquidator? The answer to this may be found in clause 92.2 (termination) which states that the employer 'may use' any equipment to which he has title. This suggests that the transfer of title, at least for equipment, is intended to be only temporary.

In so far that parts of the working areas are outside the boundaries of the site the employer's hold on items to which he acquires title may be somewhat precarious. The employer can secure his site to protect his hold on items to which he claims title but the working areas outside the site may be beyond his control.

Note that the reversal of title to the contractor under clause 70.2 only occurs when removal of equipment, plant and materials from the working areas is with the project manager's permission. There is no express obligation in NEC 3 to seek permission for removal and no obvious prohibition on removal without permission. However, the potential problem for the contractor is that if he does not seek permission for removal title remains with the employer and the consequences of this could be unpredictable.

The consequences of the project manager refusing to give permission for removal are also unpredictable. This situation is not expressly covered in the contract as a compensation event and a claim by the contractor for breach of contract would be difficult to sustain.

16.3 Marking equipment, plant and materials

Clause 71.1 supports clause 70.1 in detailing the circumstances in which equipment, plant and materials outside the working areas are to be marked.

Clause 71.1 – marking equipment

The clause provides that the supervisor marks such equipment, plant and materials if:

- the contract identifies them for payment, *and*
- the contractor has prepared them for marking as the works information requires

The dual aspects of this clause cause some difficulties of interpretation. The intention of the clause, taken together with clause 70.1, appears to be that if the employer wants to obtain title to equipment, plant or materials before it is brought within the working areas then he must pay for the privilege and in return the contractor must allow the relevant items to be marked as the property of the employer by the supervisor. Alternatively, if the contractor wants to obtain the benefit of payment for off-site equipment, plant and materials then he must allow them to be marked and concede the transfer of title.

What is not clear is where, and by which party, the identification for payment is to be made and whether the requirements in the works information are intended to be procedural or item specific. What, for example, is the position if the contractor in his activity schedule or bill of quantities identifies off-site items for payment but the works information is silent on marking? Is that to be taken as an indication that the employer does not intend to pay for off-site items or merely an administrative omission in the works information which can be corrected by the project manager?

These are points the parties would do well to clarify before they sign their contract.

16.4 Removing equipment

Construction contracts traditionally include clauses requiring the contractor to clear the site on completion and to remove items belonging to the contractor. Such clauses may not be strictly necessary since the obligations can probably be implied as integral and essential parts of proper performance.

NEC 3 does not have the usual clearance of site on completion clause but in clause 72.1 it does deal with removal of the contractor's equipment.

Clause 72.1 – removal of equipment

The clause requires the contractor to remove equipment from the site when it is no longer needed – unless the project manager allows it to be left in the works. Note that in this clause the obligation is expressed, quite rightly, as to remove from the site and not from the working areas.

The obligation is stricter than that found in most contracts in that it may take effect before completion. However, if the contractor is in breach it would take exceptional circumstances for the employer to have a legal remedy – and there is nothing in the contract to suggest that the employer has the right to effect the removal himself.

One example of exceptional circumstances could be where contractor's equipment which is no longer needed for the works is obstructing the employer's use of his premises. Perhaps then the employer could exercise his right to terminate under clause 91.3 (reason R14).

16.5 Objects and materials within the site

Clause 73.1 – articles of interest

Clause 73.1 contains four distinct provisions:

- the contractor has no title to an object of value or historical or other interest found on the site
- the contractor is required to notify the project manager when such an object is found
- the project manager is required to instruct the contractor how to deal with the object
- the contractor is not permitted to move the object without instruction

This is the equivalent of a typical 'antiquities' clause and in principle it is perfectly sound. Unfortunately the wording of the clause exhibits a tendency running through NEC 3 of imposing unqualified obligations without regard to practical applications. The problem is who is to decide whether a thing is of value or interest – the project manager or the contractor. If it is the project manager, and the contractor takes clause 73.1 literally, work will stop every time a coin, bone or fossil is found. Obviously the clause must be given some commonsense level of application. The losers, if the contractor does decide to take the clause literally, will be the employer who will foot the bill for compensation event claims under clause 60.1(7) and the project manager who will be run off his feet.

For practical reasons it may well be appropriate for the project manager to delegate his powers under clause 73.1 to the supervisor.

Clause 73.2 – title to materials

NEC 3 addresses directly a point of some uncertainty in many contracts – who owns materials taken off the site? If the phrase 'take away and dispose' is found in the specification or method of measurement it is reasonable to assume that the contractor is given title and is entitled to retain the proceeds of any sale. In other cases there can be uncertainty.

Clause 73.2 of NEC 3 settles the matter by providing that the contractor has title to materials from excavation and demolition only as stated in the works information. It follows from this that if the works information is silent on title to materials (and it is a point which can easily be missed) then title remains with the employer. That could cause complications in relation to the contractor's obligations to dispose of surplus materials; to the employer's liabilities in respect of such materials even after they have left the site; and to adjustments to the contract price in respect of any resale value.

In most cases, however, giving the contractor title will be a better option than the employer retaining title. A general statement in the works information that the title of all surplus materials taken off site passes to the contractor will probably be sufficient to achieve this.

Chapter 17
Risks and insurances

17.1 Introduction

Section 8 of NEC 3 deals with the allocation of risks and the insurance of risks. These are far from straightforward matters. Risks and liabilities may seem easy enough to apportion on paper but the law reports are full of complex cases which expose the difficulties of drafting contractual provisions which readily identify the risk carrier when disaster strikes.

The case of *The National Trust* v. *Haden Young Ltd* (1993) which concerned the destruction of Uppark House by fire resulting from the negligence of subcontractors working on the roof is a classic example. The court held, amongst other things, that under a JCT Minor Works form of contract a clause imposing an obligation on the employer to insure in the joint names of the employer and the contractor neither expressly nor by implication included an obligation to insure in respect of subcontractors.

Professional advice

Given the difficulties with insurance matters it is understandable that project managers or other professionals with a technical background are sometimes inclined to leave such matters to others they regard as better equipped to look after the employer's interests. This is sound policy to the extent that a project manager or similar should always ensure that the employer receives the best professional advice. But in so far that a project manager may have, by the terms of his appointment, a general duty to advise the employer on all contractual matters the project manager should not assume that the employer has of his own accord recognised and understood the obligations and implications of the contract. To do so is to invite a charge of negligence.

In the case of *William Tomkinson & Sons Ltd* v. *The Parochial Church Council of St. Michael in the Hamlet* (1990), again on a JCT Minor Works contract, it was held that an architect who failed to advise the employer of certain risks and the need to insure against them was in breach of his duty of care.

Risks generally

Standard forms vary in the extent to which they identify and deal with particular risks. The employer's responsibility for his own property and its contents is one area of significant variance. But generally matters to be considered include:

- damage to the works prior to taking-over
- damage to the works after taking-over
- faulty materials and workmanship
- thefts and vandalism
- design defects
- damage to the employer's property
- damage to third party property
- consequential losses from damage
- injuries to the contractor's employees
- injuries to the employer's employees
- injuries to third parties

Some of these can be grouped together for drafting purposes.

Allocation of risks

The strategy which underlies most standard forms is that risks should be allocated to the party best able to control them. Thus taking-over of the works by the employer is usually seen as a watershed in respect of the works. Up to that time the contractor has care of the works and is generally responsible for damage whereas afterwards the employer becomes responsible – subject to the proviso that the contractor is responsible for any damage he causes whilst remedying defects.

Responsibility for damage or injury to third parties usually follows the cause but damage to the employer's property is the employer's risk in some contracts.

The contractor is almost invariably responsible for the quality of work and carries the risks of faulty workmanship and materials. Responsibility for defective design generally falls on the party which undertook the design but that is not always the case.

Excepted risks

Excepted risks, or the employer's risks as they are called in some contracts, are those risks which are expressly excluded from the contractor's responsibility. Typically they include:

- acts or omissions of the project manager, employer or his servants
- use or occupation of the works
- damage which is the inevitable or unavoidable consequence of the construction of the works
- war, riots and similar non-insurable events

Broadly the excepted risks fall into three categories:

- fault or negligence of the employer
- matters under the control of the employer
- matters not the fault of either party

The logic of the first two categories is obvious enough. The argument for the third category, where it applies, is that the employer is the party better able to carry the risk.

Limitations on liability

Some contracts place limitations on the liability of the contractor to the employer for his acts and defaults. Such limitations however apply only between the contractor and the employer and they do not protect the contractor against third party claims.

Insurances generally

Certain insurances are required by law – for example, motor insurances and employer's liability. In addition construction contracts invariably impose insurance requirements on one or both parties to ensure that funds are available to meet claims and to facilitate the completion of the works.

Some forms specify only the insurances which the contractor must carry. Other forms place obligations to insure on both parties.

Common insurance provisions

The common insurance provisions of construction contracts are:

- the contractor is responsible for care of the works until completion
- the contractor must insure the works to their full replacement cost
- the contractor must indemnify the employer against claims for injury to persons or damage to property
- the contractor must insure against that liability

Other insurance provisions

According to the amount of detail in the insurance clauses of particular contracts other provisions may cover:

- approval of insurers
- production of documentary evidence
- minimum levels of cover
- maximum levels of excess
- the employer's rights if the contractor fails to insure

- professional indemnity
- joint insurances

Professional indemnity for consultants

Employers who engage consultants as designers almost invariably require that they have professional indemnity insurance.

Where the contractor is responsible for design, either in-house or through consultants, it might appear on the face of it to be no concern to the employer whether or not professional indemnity insurance is maintained. However, it is not always seen that way and it is not uncommon for such insurance to be required as a safeguard of financial security.

For cover where consultants are the designers there are two problems. Firstly, there is the point that professional indemnity insurance is usually on a claims made basis so that the cover is only effective in respect of the year in which the claim is made. Thus once a policy lapses there is no cover for past work. Consequently a contractual requirement for such insurance needs to be drafted to ensure that cover is maintained for the legal limitation period rather than merely the construction period as for other insurances.

Secondly, there is the problem that the legal responsibility of a professional designer is limited at common law to the exercise of reasonable skill and care and his professional indemnity cover is usually similarly limited. A claim on a fitness for purpose basis will have no access to such insurance.

Contractor's in-house design

Contractors who undertake in-house design can insure against the negligence of their own designers. The cover is usually defined as being in respect of a negligent act, error or omission of the contractor in performance of his professional activities. The need for such insurance arises because a contractor's all risks policy usually excludes design entirely or limits the indemnity to damage caused by negligent design to third party property or construction works other than those designed.

An ordinary professional indemnity policy does not cover the contractor against the problem of discovery of a design fault before completion. At that stage there is no claim against the contractor as there would be against an independent designer. To overcome this contractors usually seek a policy extension giving first party cover. In effect this amounts to giving the construction department of the contractor's organisation a notional claim against the design department.

For an interesting case revealing the complexities of in-house design claims see *Wimpey Ltd* v. *Poole* (1984) where the contractor sought to prove its own negligence in order to recover remedial works costs from its insurers.

Insurance terminology

Insurance clauses in contracts often use phrases which are not particularly clear in themselves but which have particular meanings to insurers. For example:

- subrogation – this is the legal right of an insurer who has paid out on a policy to bring actions in the name of the insured against third parties responsible for the loss
- waiver of subrogation – an agreement by one party's insurers to give up its rights against another party
- joint names – insurance in joint names provides both parties with rights of claim under the policy and it prevents the insurer exercising his rights of subrogation one against the other
- cross liability – the effect of a cross liability provision in a policy is that either party can act individually in respect of a claim notwithstanding the policy being in joint names (without such a provision liability between joint names is by definition not between third parties and is not covered)
- all risks – an all risks policy does not actually cover all risks since invariably there will be exceptions. However, the effect of an all risks policy is to place on the insurer the burden of proving that the loss was caused by a risk specifically excluded from cover. In contrast, under a policy for a specified risk it is the insured who must prove that his loss was caused by the specified risk

Risks and insurances under NEC 3

NEC 3 generally allocates risks and requires insurance cover in accordance with conventional principles. However, it has some differences from traditional construction contracts. In particular the contractor's risks are defined by reference to those risks which are not detailed as employer's risks; the contractor's obligations for care of the works extend to the issue of the defects certificate and do not end at completion; the employer may acquire insurance obligations under the contract.

There are no significant changes from the insurance provisions of ECC 2.

17.2 Employer's risks

Clause 80.1 of NEC 3 sets out the employer's risks. The contractor's risks are not specifically detailed and are stated only in general terms in clause 81.1 to be those not carried by the employer. Accordingly, for the allocation of risk when an incident occurs reference has to be made to the detail of clause 80.1.

Clause 80.1 – employer's risks

Clause 80.1 lists the employer's risks under six groupings which can be broadly described as:

- general – i.e. use of the works, unavoidable loss or damage, employer's fault
- loss or damage of employer supplied goods
- war, riots and similar non-insurable events
- loss or damage after take-over
- loss or damage after termination
- additional risks as listed in the contract data

These risks which in most construction contracts are described as the excepted risks apply, as appropriate, to both care of the works and to third party liabilities.

General employer's risks

Clause 80.1 commences by detailing a general set of employer's risks. These are claims, proceedings, compensation and costs payable due to various specific causes for which the employer accepts responsibility.

- The first of these general causes is: 'use or occupation of the Site by the works or for the purpose of the works which is the unavoidable result of the works'.

The wording here is anything but clear. The words used do not relate naturally to one another and the arrangement does not assist in producing an obvious meaning. Perhaps it means simply this: that if claims arise from the use of the site for the construction of the works and the damage caused is unavoidable then the employer meets such claims. Or put another way, the employer indemnifies the contractor in respect of use of the site. It is unlikely that this particular employer's risk extends to the employer's use of the works – that is covered in a later item in the list of risks (loss or damage to the parts of the works taken over by the employer).

- The second of the general causes is: 'negligence, breach of statutory duty or interference with any legal right by the Employer or by any person employed by or contracted to him except the Contractor'.

In short, under this provision, the employer takes the risk of claims arising from his own negligence, breach or interference; or from that of others for whom he is responsible.

- The third of the general causes is: 'a fault of the Employer or a fault in his design'.

This is potentially wide ranging in its scope but its application as between the employer and the contractor is more likely to be through the compensation event procedures than through insurance provisions.

Loss or damage to employer supplied goods

This risk applies to plant and materials supplied by the employer or others on his behalf until the contractor has received and accepted them. It is a risk which in most circumstances is so obviously the employer's risk that it is not normally stated. But given the definition of plant and materials in NEC 3 the risk as stated in clause 80.1 might extend well beyond normal circumstances and arguably to such things as materials on site for earthworks – which, if correct, has interesting implications.

Non-insurable events

As is customary in construction contracts the employer takes the risk of loss or damage to the works from war and other generally non-insurable events. The list is conventional with only pressure waves obviously missing. Some contracts do include *force majeure* with a definition of *force majeure* which covers events beyond the control of the parties.

Note, in relation to the reference to 'strikes, riots and civil commotion not confined to the Contractor's employees' by clause 26.1 the contract applies as if a subcontractor's employees are the contractor's.

Loss or damage after take-over

This is an important employer's risk because clause 35.2 states that the employer takes over parts of the works when he begins to use them. Therefore this risk relates to the employer's use of the works both before and after they are completed.

It should be noted, however, that there are stated exceptions to the take-over requirement in clause 35.3 and there are stated exceptions to the employer's liability in clause 80.1. One such exception which may attract some attention is that the employer may state a reason in the works information for not taking over parts of the works when he begins to use them. This could become a device whereby the employer does not take the risks of loss or damage to the parts of the works he has put into use.

The exception in clause 80.1 relating to the 'activities of the Contractor on the Site after take over' may also attract some attention. This is placed in the clause as though it indicates some fault on the part of the contractor. But note that by clause 82.1 the contractor is obliged to repair the damage to the works until the defects certificate whether or not he is responsible. The contractor may, for example, be on site to repair vandal damage after take-over. It is questionable whether in such circumstances the contractor should be responsible for loss or damage to the works unless he is in some way at fault.

Loss or damage after termination

This risk falls naturally on the employer once the contractor has left or been expelled from the site.

Additional employer's risks

It is not unusual, particularly in large projects or for projects where there will be many contractors on the site, for the employer to carry additional risks and to take out comprehensive project insurance. This can reduce the potential for disputes and it avoids duplication of insurance premiums. Additional risks are to be stated by the employer in the contract data.

In the event of there being a project insurance policy care should be given to the way it deals with legal costs of disputes between and/or involving the parties. The cover provided by the policy can rapidly be used up if it includes each and every parties' costs of legal proceedings.

17.3 *Contractor's risks*

As noted above, NEC 3 avoids the usual practice of detailing the contractor's risks and stating the employer's risks as exceptions. It details the employer's risks and places all other risks on the contractor.

Clause 81.1 – contractor's risks

The clause is brief. It states simply that from the starting date until the defects certificate has been issued the risks not carried by the employer are carried by the contractor.

The clause as drafted may cause some concern to contractors and their insurers in that the risks extend until the defects certificate. Any reduction of risk after take-over or completion can only be determined from analysis of the employer's risks. This is significantly different from the approach of most standard forms.

17.4 *Repairs*

The manner in which contracts express the contractor's obligations to 'make good', 'maintain' or 'repair' the works after completion can be of the greatest importance if defects or damage arises.

The usual position in construction contracts is that the contractor has an obligation during the defects correction period, or defects liability period (whatever it is called), to make good defects and damage for which he is responsible and he has an entitlement to enter the site to do so. The burden of proof establishing the contractor's responsibility is normally with the employer. In some process and plant contracts the contractor's obligation to make good defects and damage during the liability period is more widely drawn and the burden of proof may be on the contractor to show that he is not responsible. NEC 3 appears to take the latter approach.

Clause 82.1 – repairs

This clause provides that:

- until the defects certificate has been issued
- and unless instructed otherwise by the project manager
- the contractor promptly
- replaces loss of, and repairs damage,
- to the works, plant and materials

Perhaps this clause would be better placed in section 4 of NEC 3 with defects rather than in section 8 with risks and insurance. But placed as it is it carries two important provisions, the second of which follows from the first:

- the contractor has obligations to replace loss of and to repair damage to the works until the defects certificate is issued irrespective of the cause
- the risk lies with the contractor unless he can show that it is an employer's risk

The clause is silent as to how and on what basis the contractor is to be paid for repair works which are not his responsibility. It may be that compensation event 60.1(14) (employer's risk) is intended to apply but procedures for assessing compensation events are hardly applicable after completion. There is in any event a potential timing problem in that a compensation event may not be notified after the defects date (clause 61.7) whereas the defects certificate can be issued after the defects date (clause 43.3).

17.5 *Indemnity*

Clauses 83.1 and 83.2 are conventional indemnity provisions.

Clause 83.1 – indemnity

This clause provides simply that each party indemnifies the other against claims etc. due to an event which is his risk.

Clause 83.2 – contributory reduction

The liability of each party for his own risk is reduced in proportion to the other party's contribution to the event responsible for the claims etc.

17.6 *Insurance cover*

NEC 3 conveniently tabulates the insurance cover to be provided by the contractor. The core clauses put no express obligation on the employer to insure against his risks but the employer is required to provide insurance cover if he has stated in the contract data that he will do so.

Clause 84.1 – provision of insurances

This requires:

- the contractor to provide insurances as stated in the insurance table, except insurances to be provided by the employer as stated in the contract data
- the contractor to provide additional insurances as required by the contract data

Clause 84.2 – the insurance table

The opening provisions of clause 84.2 which tabulate the insurances the contractor is to carry are important:

- the contractor's insurances are to be in joint names
- the insurances are to cover events which are the contractor's risk
- the insurances are to give cover from the starting date to the issue of the defects certificate

Note that because the contractor's insurances need only to cover his own risks, damage to the works from the employer's negligence is not covered by the insurances.

The insurance table provides that:

- insurance of the works, plant and materials is to be for replacement cost
- insurance of the contractor's equipment is to be for replacement cost
- third party cover is to be for the amount stated in the contract data for any one event with cross liability
- cover for the contractor's employees is to be for the greater of the amount required by the applicable law or the amount stated in the contract data

17.7 Insurance policies

Clauses 85.1 to 85.4 deal with the details for inspection, approval and compliance with insurance policies.

Clause 85.1 – submission of policies

This clause, which is slightly modified from its counterpart in ECC 2, requires the contractor to submit his policies and certificates of insurances to the project manager for acceptance:

- before the starting date, *and*
- on each renewal date until the defects date

The certificates are to be signed by the insurer or insurance broker. The only stated reason for not accepting the policies and certificates is that they do not comply with the contract. Rejection for any other reason is a compensation event – clause 60.1(9).

Clause 85.2 – waiver of subrogation

Insurance policies (and this would seem to include the employer's stated insurances as well as the contractor's) are required to include waiver of subrogation rights by the insurers against directors and employees of all insured except where there is fraud.

Clause 85.3 – compliance with policies

This clause simply states that the parties are to comply with the terms and conditions of the insurance policies.

Clause 85.4 – unrecovered amounts

This clause makes the point that amounts recovered from insurances do not act as limits of liability. It states that amounts not recovered are borne by the parties causing the risk.

17.8 Contractor's failure to insure

Clause 86.1 – contractor's failure to insure

Clause 86.1 provides that if the contractor does not submit required insurance certificates the employer may insure a risk which the contractor is required to insure, and the cost of the insurance to the employer is then to be paid by the contractor.

17.9 Insurance by the employer

Clauses 87.1 to 87.3 provide for the contractor to have similar rights in respect of insurances to be provided by the employer as the employer has in respect of insurances to be provided by the contractor.

Clause 87.1 – submission of policies

This clause matches clause 85.1 in requiring the project manager to submit the employer's policies and certificates to the contractor for acceptance.

Clause 87.2 – acceptance of policies

This clause qualifies the significance of acceptance by the contractor of the employer's policies and certificates by stating that acceptance does not change the responsibility of the employer to provide insurances as stated in the contract data.

Clause 87.3 – failure by the employer to insure

This clause matches clause 86.1 in permitting the contractor to insure in the event that the employer fails to insure, the cost in this instance being paid by the employer to the contractor.

Chapter 18
Termination

18.1 Introduction

The circumstances by which any contract may come to a premature end can be broadly categorised as:

- termination – by agreement of the parties
- frustration – arising from events beyond the control of the parties
- determination – based on the default of one of the parties

Most standard forms of contract have something to say on some or all of these matters. But no matter how simply or straightforwardly the wording appears to be expressed the reality is that ending a contract prematurely is rarely simple or straightforward. More often than not it is highly contentious, uncertain in its outcome and painful in its consequences. If it has to be done, ending a contract is a job for lawyers, not for laymen. Not least because even the terminology used is a layman's nightmare.

Terminology

Some contracts use the phrase 'termination of the contract' to cover all types of premature ending; some use the phrase 'determination of the contract'; others refer to 'determination of the contractor's employment under the contract'. But the terminology itself is not decisive of the process as this extract from the 11th edition of Hudson's *Building and Engineering Contracts* shows:

> 'A very varied terminology has been used both judicially and in commerce to describe the process by which a party, unilaterally and by his own action, brings a contract to an end before it has been fully performed either by himself or the other party. Thus forfeiture, determination, termination, renunciation, rescission (and even repudiation when applied to the action of the innocent party in ending the contract), have been variously used in the cases and elsewhere. In context the different descriptions should generally be regarded as synonymous, with no significant differences of consequential effect.'

NEC 3 uses only the phrase 'termination' and within that phrase it covers what is described above as 'frustration' and 'determination'.

Termination at common law

The ordinary remedy for breach of contract is damages but there are circumstances in which the breach not only gives a right to damages but also entitles the innocent party to consider himself discharged from further performance. This is usually a breach so serious that it goes to the heart of the contract. Sometimes it is called a 'fundamental' breach.

In such circumstances the innocent party has the legal right to terminate the contract at common law and is not reliant on a contractual right to terminate.

Termination under contractual provisions

To extend and clarify the circumstances under which termination can validly be made and to regulate the procedures to be adopted, most standard forms of contracts include provisions for termination. Many of the grounds for termination in standard forms however are not effective for termination at common law. Thus failure by the contractor to proceed with due diligence, failure to remove defective work and subcontracting without consent are often to be found in contracts as grounds for termination. But at common law none of these will ordinarily be a breach of contract sufficiently serious to justify termination.

The commonest and the most widely used express provisions for termination relate to insolvency. Again at common law many of these are ineffective and even as express provisions they are often challenged as ineffective by legal successors of failed companies.

The very fact that grounds for termination under contractual provisions are wider than at common law leads to its own difficulties. A party is more likely to embark on a course of action when he sees his rights expressly stated than when he has to rely on common law rights. This itself can be an encouragement to error. Some of the best known legal cases on termination concern terminations made under express provisions but found on the facts to be lacking in validity.

In *Lubenham Fidelities* v. *South Pembrokeshire District Council* (1986) the contractor terminated for alleged non-payment whilst the employer concurrently terminated for failure to proceed regularly and diligently. On the facts, the contractor's termination was held to be invalid. But in *Hill & Sons Ltd* v. *London Borough of Camden* (1980), with a similar scenario, it was held on the facts that the contractor had validly terminated.

Parallel rights of termination

Some contracts expressly state that their provisions, including those of termination, are without prejudice to any other rights the parties may possess. That is, the parties have parallel rights – those under the contract and those at common law – and they may elect to use either.

Other contracts, including NEC 3, are silent on the issue but the general rule is that common law rights can only be excluded by express terms. Contractual provisions, even though comprehensively drafted, may not imply exclusion of common law rights.

The point came up in the case of *Architectural Installation Services Ltd* v. *James Gibbons Windows Ltd* (1989) where it was held that while a notice of termination did not validly meet the timing requirements of the contractual provisions, nevertheless there had been a valid termination at common law. However, in the case of *Lockland Builders Ltd* v. *John Kim Rickwood* (1995) the Court of Appeal held that an express term in the contract limited the scope of common law rights. It was said that although express termination clauses and common law rights can exist side by side, the common law right only arises in circumstances where the contractor shows a clear intention not to be bound by the contract.

Legal effects of termination

In construction contracts, termination is often expressed as 'termination of the contractor's employment under the contract' as though to emphasise that the contract itself is not terminated and that some of its provisions, particularly those for assessing amounts due and dispute resolution, remain in force.

In relation to arbitration provisions and provisions limiting liability for negligence such wording is probably superfluous since those provisions survive independently of the main contract – see the House of Lords' decision in the case of *Heyman* v. *Darwins* (1942). By contrast provisions for liquidated damages may not survive termination – see the case of *Bovis Construction (Scotland) Ltd* v. *Whatlings Construction Ltd* (1994). For other provisions the wording of the contract is likely to be decisive.

NEC 3 in its termination provisions sets out in some detail certain procedures and assessments which survive termination. This, itself, probably reduces the scope for implying that other provisions should also survive.

Termination under NEC 3

Termination under NEC 3 can best be described as termination by numbers. The contract has twenty-one numbered reasons for termination; four numbered procedures for termination; and four numbered methods of calculating amounts due on termination. A table is included in clause 90.2 to show how the various reasons, procedures and amounts due relate.

But although the termination scheme of NEC 3 is elaborate and unusual in its presentation it is not for the most part unusual in its content. However, a distinctive feature of the NEC 3 scheme is that it permits the employer to terminate for any reason above and beyond the twenty-one numbered reasons.

In other words, the employer has the contractual right to terminate at will. Or, as some would say, the contract has a 'convenience' clause.

Changes from ECC 2

NEC 3, unlike ECC 2, allocates the whole of section 9 of its core clauses to termination. In ECC 2, for what appeared to be numbering reasons, termination clauses were grouped with dispute resolution clauses. However, apart from the cosmetic change the only differences of note between the termination provisions of NEC 3 and ECC 2 are:

- clause 90.1 – NEC 3 uses the words 'if either party wishes to terminate the Contractor's obligation to Provide the Works' whereas the ECC 2 wording was 'if either party wishes to terminate'
- clause 90.1 – NEC 3 requires the terminating party to notify both the project manager and the other party whereas ECC 2, somewhat oddly, required only that the project manager be notified
- clause 90.2 – the termination table in NEC 3 differs slightly from that in ECC 2 because of a few changed reason and procedure reference numbers
- clause 90.4 – NEC 3 requires payment on termination to be made within three weeks of the project manager's certificate – a provision lacking in ECC 2
- clause 91.5 – the corresponding clause in ECC 2 (clause 95.5) entitled either party to terminate for prolonged effects of war or radioactive contamination (exceeding 26 weeks) or if released under the law from further performance of the whole of the contract. Clause 91.5 of NEC 3 contains only the 'release under the law' provision
- clause 91.7 – this clause, which is new to NEC 3, repeats much of the wording of clause 19.1 (prevention) and clause 60.1 (19) (compensation event for prevention). It allows the employer (but not the contractor) to utilise prevention, as defined in NEC 3, as grounds for termination
- clause 92.1 – NEC 3 refers only to the employer completing the works whereas ECC 2 referred also to the employment of other people to do so
- clause 92.2 – in NEC 3, part P3 of this clause is extended to require the contractor to remove equipment from the site after any use by the employer
- clause 93.2 – NEC 3 omits from amounts due on termination what was in ECC 2 referred to as amount A5 (that itself being half of A4)

18.2 *Summary of NEC 3 termination provisions*

Termination certificate

Termination is commenced when the project manager issues a termination certificate – which he is obliged to do at the request of either party if the reason given complies with the contract (clause 90.1). Once the termination certificate is issued the contractor does no further work (clause 90.5).

Reasons for termination

The stated reasons for termination include:

- insolvency of either party – reasons R1 to R10
- specified contractor's defaults – reasons R11 to R15
- non-payment by the employer – reason R16
- release under the law – reason R17
- prolonged suspension – reasons R18 to R20
- prevention/*force majeure* – reason R21

In addition to the stated reasons the employer (but not the contractor) can terminate for 'any reason' (clause 90.2).

Action on termination

On termination the employer is entitled to complete the works or employ others to do so. The contractor leaves the site either by instruction or by his own choice. The employer retains and may use any plant and materials to which he has title. The employer's rights to use the contractor's equipment depend upon the reason for termination and apply only where there is insolvency or other default by the contractor (applying P3 from clause 92.2 to the termination table in clause 90.2).

Amount due on termination

Within thirteen weeks of termination the project manager is required to assess and certify the amount due to or from the contractor (clause 90.4). Payment is due within three weeks of the project manager's certificate (clause 90.4).

The amount due is determined by reference to the reason for termination but in all cases it includes as a base amount (A1) which in simple terms is the valuation of the work at termination. To this is added or deducted according to the reason for termination one or more of the following:

- the forecast cost of removing equipment – A2
- the forecast costs of completion – A3
- the fee percentages applied to the uncompleted work

The minimum amount due applies when the reason for termination is contractor's insolvency or default and is the valuation at termination less the cost of completing. The maximum amount applies when the employer terminates for a reason not stated in the contract and is the valuation at termination plus the contractor's costs of removing his equipment plus the fee percentages applied to the uncompleted work.

18.3 *Termination for 'any reason'*

The inclusion in NEC 3 of the provision in clause 90.2 permitting the employer to terminate for any reason is probably to ensure that the contract is acceptable to employers with a genuine need for a 'convenience' clause on state, security or exceptional commercial grounds. But the inclusion raises complex legal questions on which there is little legal authority.

If it is open to the employer to terminate for any reason he chooses then it appears that he is not bound, nor ever was bound, to see the works of the contract through to completion. So however capricious the reason or however unfair to the contractor, the employer is apparently not in breach of contract by abandoning the works or by ordering the contractor off the site and completing with another contractor.

If that really was the case the employer could terminate in order to get the works completed at a lower price by another contractor; could terminate for 'any reason' to avoid the confrontation involved in terminating on the grounds of contractor's default; or, and most objectionable of all, could terminate for 'any reason' to deprive the contractor of his opportunity of lawfully terminating the contract.

However, the probability is that the employer does not have the freedom which clause 90.2 suggests. Firstly, the requirement of clause 10.1, that the parties shall act in a spirit of mutual trust and co-operation may act as a constraint on the employer such that termination 'for any reason' is open to challenge as a breach of contract. Secondly, the law may impose a test of reasonableness on the employer's action. See, for example, the Australian case of *Renard Constructions Ltd* v. *Minister of Public Works* (1992).

It may, perhaps, be argued that NEC 3 avoids unfairness to the contractor in that if the employer does terminate for 'any reason' then the amount due to the contractor is equivalent to the amount he would receive as damages for breach of contract. However, such an argument overlooks the potentially adverse impact that termination may have on a contractor's reputation or his organisational arrangements and it is, in any event, far from sound on financial grounds. The amount due on termination as calculated under NEC 3 may be considerably less than the contractor could claim as damages for breach of contract. The fee percentage, for example, is a figure obtained in competitive circumstances and it may not truly reflect the contractor's lost overheads and profit. Moreover the contractor may have liabilities to subcontractors and suppliers which are not fully recoverable under NEC 3's definition of 'defined cost'.

There is also the point that an innocent party may have two alternative claims in law for wrongful termination – one claim in contract as damages for breach; the other in *'quantum meruit'* for work done under the old rule established in the case of *Lodder* v. *Slowey* (1904). That rule, which operates only when the contractor is blameless, was expressed as follows by the New Zealand Court of Appeal prior to its affirmation by the Privy Council:

> *'The law is clear enough that an innocent party who accepts the defaulting party's repudiation of a Contract has the option of either suing for damages for breach of contract or suing on a Quantum Meruit for work done. An election pre-supposes a choice between remedies, which presumably may lead to different results. The nature of these different remedies renders it highly likely that the results will be different. If the former remedy is chosen the innocent party is entitled to damages amounting to the loss of profit which he would have made if the contract had been performed rather than repudiated; it has nothing to do with reasonableness. If the latter remedy is chosen, he is entitled to a verdict representing the reasonable cost of the work he has done and the money he has expended; the profit he might have made does not enter into that exercise. There is nothing anomalous in the notion that two different remedies, proceeding on entirely different principles, might yield different results. Nor is there anything anomalous in the fact that either remedy may yield a higher monetary figure than the other. Nor is there anything anomalous in the prospect that a figure arrived at on a Quantum Meruit might exceed, or even far exceed, the profit which would have been made if the Contract had been fully performed.'*

The advantage to the contractor of the application of the *Lodder* v. *Slowey* rule is that it enables him to escape from the prices in a poorly priced contract. It also acts as a restraint on the employer in preventing him from terminating when the contractor has performed underpriced early work but still has profitable later work in the contract.

Any employer contemplating terminating under NEC 3 for 'any reason' would be well advised, therefore, to take legal advice before proceeding on whether the amount due to the contractor as calculated under the contract really is the full extent of his financial liability.

18.4 *Termination under section 9*

Clause 90.1 – notification of termination

The first provision of clause 90.1 is that a party wishing to terminate should give notice to the project manager giving 'details' of his reasons for terminating. The second provision is that the project manager shall issue a termination certificate 'promptly' if the reason complies with the contract. It is not clear if the reference to 'details' in the first provision means simply that the notifying party must specify which of the twenty-one numbered reasons is relied on or whether, in the case of the employer terminating for 'any reason' the employer must also give details of that other reason. A requirement to give details in the latter case would suggest that to do so has some contractual effect – but this does not appear to be the case. 'Any reason' is a specified ground for termination by the employer so it is not open to the project manager to refuse a termination certificate once an application is made. And 'any reason' other than the numbered reasons attracts exactly the same procedures and assessment whatever its details (clause 90.2).

The requirement in the second provision for the project manager to issue a termination certificate 'if the reason complies' puts a heavy burden on the project manager to act with absolute fairness and impartiality between the parties. The project manager cannot be seen as the agent of the employer in this matter. He may have to decide on merit between contesting notifications and he may well find himself in conflict with the employer and obliged to act against the interests of the employer.

In the event of the project manager refusing to issue a termination certificate because, in his view, the reason does not comply with the contract, the parties are probably expected to continue performance until the matter is resolved by adjudication. If nevertheless, one or both of the parties proceeds with the termination in the absence of a termination certificate the probable effect is that all the termination procedures of NEC 3 are rendered ineffective and common law rules apply to any resulting dispute.

Clause 90.2 – the termination table

Clause 90.2 limits the contractor's rights to terminate under the contract to the reasons listed in the termination table which forms part of the clause. The employer, however, is permitted to terminate under the contract for 'any reason'. For comment see section 18.3. The application of the termination table is straightforward in that it schedules the procedures and the amounts due for each of the twenty-two permitted reasons (twenty-one numbered plus 'any' reason).

Clause 90.3 – implementation of termination procedures

This clause states only that the procedures for termination are implemented immediately after the issue of the termination certificate. Note that clause 90.1 refers only to a certificate being issued 'promptly' and that there is no timescale in terms of days.

Clause 90.4 – certification of amount due on termination

The project manager is required to certify within thirteen weeks of termination (which is presumably the date on the termination certificate) the final amount due to or from the contractor.

There appears to be an assumption here that in the event of the employer's insolvency there will be sufficient funds available from one source or another to pay the project manager for his efforts. Or alternatively it may be thought that the project manager has acquired duties to both parties by his appointment and is obliged to fulfil those duties irrespective of the prospect of remuneration.

It is probably not worth speculating on the contractual position where there is no final certification by the project manager following the employer's insolvency because in reality the contractor will lodge his claim with the receiver/liquidator regardless of whether or not he has a certificate.

One general aspect of clause 90.4 which is particularly worth noting is that certification of the final amount due after termination is not deferred until after the employer has completed the works and the costs of completion are known. Instead the final amount due is based on an assessment made by the project manager – see amount A3 (clause 93.2).

Clause 90.5 – cessation on termination

Clause 90.5 provides that after a termination certificate has been issued the contractor does no further work 'necessary to complete the works'. It may be arguable that work which is necessary for safety reasons is not work which is 'necessary to complete the works' but in any event the project manager, the employer and the contractor all have statutory obligations on safety and none can claim exemption by reference to contractual provisions.

18.5 Reasons for termination

Clause 91.1 – insolvency

Clause 91.1 details various financial failings in the nature of insolvency which are listed as reasons for termination, R1 to R10. Although separately numbered they attract identical treatment under the contract. Disappointingly, NEC 3 includes in its list of financial failings, as indeed do most other standard forms, administration and arrangements with creditors, both of which are patently attempts to stay in business.

Clause 91.2 – contractor's defaults

Clause 91.2 details three defaults which entitle the employer to terminate if the default is not rectified by the contractor within four weeks of notification:

- substantial failure to comply with obligations – reason R11
- non-provision of a required bond or guarantee – reason R12

- appointment of a subcontractor for substantial work before the project manager's acceptance – reason R13

It appears that the notification referred to in clause 91.2 is not the notice of termination referred to in clause 90.1 but is some earlier notice of dissatisfaction given to the contractor by the project manager. The intention is to put the contractor on notice of possible termination and to allow the contractor four weeks to rectify matters.

Reason R11, substantial failure to comply with obligations, is exceedingly general and clearly the project manager's notice would have to be specific to be effective. As to what is meant by 'substantially failed' in reason R11, that is a matter of judgment on the facts having regard to legal precedents. The evidence required to support this reason should it be challenged would have to be convincing.

The second reason, R12, failure to provide a bond or guarantee, is not uncommon. Project managers should be alert to the need to inform the employer of any default in the provision of a bond or guarantee if they are to avoid the possibility of being held responsible for losses arising from a contractor's insolvency.

The third reason, R13, appointment of a subcontractor for substantial work before acceptance by the project manager, is hard to reconcile with the first part of clause 91.2 which allows the contractor four weeks to put the default right. Either the contractor has appointed a subcontractor before acceptance or he has not. Perhaps the clause means that the contractor has four weeks in order to obtain acceptance from being notified of his default.

Clause 91.3 – contractor's continuing defaults

Clause 91.3 details two defaults by the contractor of a continuing nature – or, at least, that is what the words 'not stopped defaulting' appear to suggest. The defaults are worded:

- substantially hindered the employer or others – reason R14
- substantially broken a health or safety regulation – reason R15

It can be presumed that substantially hindered the employer or others has something to do with the performance of the contract and is not a general complaint about the business activities of the contractor. As to how such hindering might occur – clause 25.1 (co-operation) stipulates the contractor's obligation to co-operate with 'others' and to share the working areas with them. Hindering 'others' could clearly affect completion of the project if not completion of the works. Hindering the employer is a more difficult concept to grasp. Hindering the employer in what? Premature use and take-over of the works is one possible answer but is it conceivable that such a default attracts a harsher remedy than liquidated damages for late completion of the works?

Note that reasons R14 and R15 are grouped with reasons R11 to R13 in the termination table in clause 90.2. The distinction between the reasons in clause

91.2 and those in clause 91.3 appears to be therefore one of fact and not one of administrative significance.

Clause 91.4 – failure to pay

Failure by the employer to pay within thirteen weeks of the date of a certificate is one of the few reasons (R16), other than insolvency of the employer, entitling the contractor to terminate. The wording of clause 91.4 'if the Employer has not paid an amount certified' suggests an obligation to pay the certified amount in full but it is not clear how this would fit in with a validly served withholding notice.

Clause 91.5 – release under the law

Clause 91.5 of NEC 3 matches the second part of clause 95.3 of ECC 2. It states that either party may terminate if the parties have been released under the law from further performance of the whole of the contract (reason R17). NEC 3 omits the first part of the ECC 2 clause which allowed either party to terminate if war or radioactive contamination affected the contractor's works for 26 weeks.

The ECC 2 clause appeared in full to be a frustration clause – particularly as there was no separate frustration clause in ECC 2. At common law a contract is discharged and further performance excused if supervening events make the contract illegal or impossible or render its performance commercially sterile. Such discharge is known as frustration. A plea of frustration acts as a defence to a charge of breach of contract.

In order to be relied on, the events said to have caused frustration must be:

- unforeseen
- unprovided for in the contract
- outside the control of the parties
- beyond the fault of the party claiming frustration as a defence

In NEC 3, however, the prevention provisions introduced at clause 19.1 would seem to cover events in the nature of frustration and those find their way into the termination provisions of NEC 3 at clause 91.7 (reason R21). There are some important differences, however, between clauses 91.5 and 91.7 of NEC 3. The first is that clause 91.5 gives both the employer and the contractor rights to terminate – clause 91.7 gives rights only to the employer. The second difference is that clause 91.5 refers to release from further performance of the 'whole' of the contract whereas clause 91.7 can be seen as relating to problems of a partial nature. Thirdly, the events in clause 91.7 would not necessarily amount to events giving release under the law.

The intention of NEC 3 seems to be therefore that clause 91.5 remains the frustration clause of the contract and that clause 91.7 provides additional rights for the employer to terminate. Note that under the termination table the amounts due are the same for both clauses.

Clause 91.6 – prolonged suspension

Prolonged suspensions of work are grounds for termination under most standard forms of contract. NEC 3 avoids the term suspension but clause 91.6 deals with what is normally termed prolonged suspension by detailing the circumstances which entitle the parties to terminate when the project manager's instruction to stop or not to start work has not been lifted within thirteen weeks. The rules are straightforward:

- the suspension must relate to 'substantial work or all work'
- the employer may terminate if the instruction is due to default by the contractor – reason R18
- the contractor may terminate if the instruction is due to default by the employer – reason R19
- either party may terminate if the instruction is due to any other reason – reason R20

The clause puts considerable responsibility on the project manager since it is effectively his decision whether or not to lift any suspension. However, in the context of NEC 3 with its early warning and risk reduction procedures and its obligations on mutual trust and co-operation it is unlikely that the project manager would be unaware of the implications of allowing a suspension to remain in force for more than thirteen weeks.

Clause 91.7 – prevention

Clause 91.7, which is new to NEC 3, provides that the employer may terminate if an event occurs which:

- stops the contractor completing the works, *or*
- stops the contractor completing the works by the date shown on the accepted programme and is 'forecast to delay completion by more than thirteen weeks', *and which*
  — neither party could prevent, *and*
  — an experienced contractor would have judged at the contract date to have such a small chance of occurring that it would have been unreasonable to have allowed for it

This is, for the most part, the definition of a prevention event found in clause 19.1 of NEC 3. An important difference, however, is that clause 91.7 only comes into force in respect of delay to completion by the accepted programme date and when the forecast delay exceeds thirteen weeks.

But for the fact that clause 91.7 entitles only the employer to terminate it might be taken as a frustration clause – but see the comment on clause 91.5 (p. 310).

18.6 *Procedures on termination*

Clause 92.1 – completion of the works

This clause provides firstly, that the employer may complete the works himself and secondly, that the employer may use any plant and materials to which he has title – procedure P1. The provision in the corresponding ECC 2 clause that the employer could employ other people to complete the works is omitted presumably on the grounds that it was superfluous.

It is not wholly clear what purpose is served by clause 92.1 which purports to regulate the employer's conduct after termination. That would seem to be outside the scope of the contract. As to plant and materials the employer is arguably entitled to do whatever he wishes after termination with those to which he has title.

Clause 92.2 – withdrawal from the site

Clause 92.2 deals principally with withdrawal from the site by the contractor and the subsequent use of the contractor's equipment. The clause states three procedures which apply, either singularly or together, according to the reasons for the termination:

- Procedure P2 applies when the employer terminates for 'any reason' or the contractor is insolvent or in default. It entitles the employer to instruct the contractor to leave the site, remove equipment, plant and materials, and to assign the benefit of any subcontract or other contract related to the main contract to the employer.
- Procedure P3 applies when the contractor is insolvent or in default. It entitles the employer to use any equipment to which he has title and requires the contractor to remove such equipment when notified by the project manager that it is no longer required.
- Procedure P4 applies when the employer is insolvent or in default (or there is frustration or prevention). It entitles the contractor to leave the working areas and to remove his equipment.

The provision in clause 92.2(P2) for assigning the benefits of subcontracts is similar to provisions found in many contracts. In practice, however, such provisions amount to very little since novation is normally required to form the contractual relationships which the clause envisages and novations are concluded by agreement and not by compulsion.

For comment on the use by the employer of the contractor's equipment see Chapter 16, section 2.

18.7 *Amounts due on termination*

Clause 93.1 – payment on termination

Clause 93.1 deals with the valuation of the work completed prior to termination and the costs incurred in expectation of completion. It fixes amount (A1) due on termination by reference to five headings:

- An amount assessed as for normal payments. This will normally be the price for work done to date as clause 50.2 – but note clause 93.3 applying to Option A.
- The defined cost for plant and materials brought within the working areas or for which the employer has title and the contractor has accepted delivery.
- Other defined cost reasonably incurred in expectation of completing the whole of the works.
- Amounts retained by the employer.
- Unrepaid balances of advanced payments.

Amount A1 is the base for all amounts due whatever the reason for termination under the contract. It is much the same as the valuation at termination made under other standard forms of contract.

Clause 93.2 – other amounts due

Clause 93.2 details the adjustments to the amount A1 (the valuation on termination) which are made to determine the final amount due on termination having regard to the reason for termination. Three adjustment amounts are detailed:

- Amount A2 – the forecast defined cost of removing the contractor's equipment. This is included in the amount due to the contractor for all reasons except where the contractor is insolvent or in default.
- Amount A3 – the forecast additional cost to the employer of completing the whole of the works. This is deducted from the amount due to the contractor when the contractor is insolvent or in default.
- Amount A4 – the direct fee percentage applied to the difference between the tender total (or for Options E and F the first forecast of final actual cost) and the price for work done to date at termination. This is intended as a measure of the contractor's overheads and profit. It applies only when the employer has terminated for a reason not in the numbered list or when the employer is insolvent or in default.

Clause 93.3 – payment on termination – Option A

This clause makes the necessary point that the amount due on termination is assessed without taking grouping of activities into account. To that extent it modifies how clauses 11.2(28) and 50.2 are to apply to clause 93.1.

Clause 93.4 – payment on termination – Options C and D

> This clause applies to termination under the two target price contracts and
> it deals with how the contractor's share is to be calculated in the event of ter-
> mination. It effectively fixes the calculation of the contractor's share to the
> price for work done to date at termination. This amount is then to be paid in
> accordance with clause 53 (the contractor's share).

Chapter 19
Dispute resolution

19.1 Introduction

Dispute resolution in NEC 3 is dealt with in Options W1 and W2. Option W1 is to be used, according to its head note, unless the UK Housing Grants, Construction and Regeneration Act 1996 applies. Option W2, according to its head note, is to be used in the UK when the Act applies.

The employer is to state in the contract data, part one, which of these dispute resolution options is included in the contract. The key differences between the two options relate to the adjudication procedures. Option W1 specifies what disputes can be referred to adjudication; what notifications are to be given; and allows eight weeks for the adjudicator's decision to be given. Option W2, which is drafted to be compliant with the Act, is not restrictive of what disputes can be referred or when, and it allows four weeks for the adjudicator's decision to be given – subject to extension by consent.

Choice of Options W1 or W2

If the head notes to Options W1 and W2 are taken literally there is no choice to be made by the employer when entering W1 or W2 in the contract data. The proper option for any particular contract will apparently be governed by whether or not the contract is subject to the Act. However, that in itself might well be a matter in dispute and it is probably better that the employer should select which option is to be used rather than leave it for later debate.

That, of course, raises the question – what are the consequences if the employer selects the wrong option? The answer seems to be that if W1 is selected for a contract subject to the Act the referring party will have the choice of using that option (but only for disputes within its scope) or the relevant statutory Scheme for Construction Contract Regulations for any dispute. If W2 is selected for a contract not subject to the Act then W1 will have no application and all adjudications will have to be under W2 procedures.

It is quite possible, indeed probable, that for some contracts not subject to the Act, either within or outside the UK, the parties will prefer W2 procedures to those of W1 and will agree that W2 be adopted either formally in the contract or belatedly if W1 is already the stated option. It has certainly been common practice under ECC 2 for parties to opt out of the contractual adjudication provisions and to agree, sometimes as late as commencement of an adjudication, to use other procedures such as the ICE (Institution of Civil

Engineers), CIC (Construction Industry Council) or TeCSA (Technology and Construction Court Solicitors Association) rules. Amongst other things such rules deal with costs (something notably missing from W1 and W2) more directly than W1 or W2 where reference has to be made to the NEC Adjudicator's Contract to find costs mentioned.

Employer's right to commence adjudication

One factor which might influence an employer to prefer Option W2 to Option W1 is that it avoids incorporation into the contract of the W1 Adjudication Table. This table gives the employer only limited rights to refer disputes to adjudication. In particular it excludes rights to refer disputes on the project manager's or the supervisor's actions or lack of actions. The logic of this, which can be gathered from the Guidance Notes to NEC 3, is that the project manager and the supervisor act on behalf of the employer and the employer is not entitled to dispute that which is done on his behalf.

However, this is not something which fits comfortably with the long-standing acceptance in construction contracts of the need for impartial, if not wholly independent, contract administrators and certifiers. See, by way of comment, Chapter 5, section 6, and the views of the judge in the *Costain* v. *Bechtel* case. It will be interesting to see what approach courts will take if a case concerning adjudication under W1 or under the statutory scheme comes before them on the matter of whether the employer can dispute actions or lack of actions of the project manager or supervisor. The courts have had much to say in recent years on what constitutes a dispute but nothing on this particular point appears to be on record There is, however, in NEC 3, something not found in ECC 2 which may have a bearing on the point.

That is the new concept of 'a quotation for a compensation event which is treated as having been accepted'. Under W1 the employer is expressly given the right to dispute such a quotation and under both W1 and W2 the adjudicator is expressly given the power to revise and review any such quotation. On the face of it, if the employer has a right to dispute that which is treated as having been accepted he should have the right to dispute that which has been accepted and thereby dispute the actions or lack of actions of the project manager and the supervisor. But that may not have been what the draftsmen of NEC 3 intended.

19.2 Developments in dispute resolution

The Institution of Civil Engineers, promoters of the NEC contracts, has long been in the forefront of developments of dispute resolution. It was one of the first professional bodies to publish its own arbitration procedure (1983) and one of the first to introduce conciliation into a standard form of conditions of contract (1988). In 1991 when the first version of NEC was published it led the way in making adjudication the primary method of resolving disputes in a construction contract.

Adjudication, which at that time had very little to support its legal standing, has since made giant steps forward in becoming the predominant method of dispute resolution in all forms of construction contracts – a development greatly assisted by the recommendations in Sir Michael Latham's report *Constructing the Team* (1994) founded on his enthusiasm for the NEC, and the subsequent creation of the statutory right to adjudication brought in by the Housing Grants, Construction and Regeneration Act 1996.

Adjudication as it now exists is not quite what was intended in the early versions of NEC. That intention was to have a named adjudicator in each contract who would be on hand to deal with disputes as they arose so that as a matter of good project management all disputes were speedily resolved. To facilitate that aim the early NEC adjudication procedures imposed strict time limits for the referral of disputes to adjudication – some of which live on in Option W1 of NEC 3. But the 'get on with it quickly' approach of NEC suffered a blow when it was decreed in the Housing Grants, Construction and Regeneration Act 1996 that disputes could be referred to adjudication 'at any time'. To cope with this the adjudication procedures of ECC 2 had to be supported by the introduction of secondary option Y(UK)2.

However, this was not enough to make the adjudication provisions of ECC 2 fully compliant with the Act – see the case of *Mowlem & Co Ltd* v. *Hydra-Tight Ltd* (2000).

One result of this was that many, perhaps the majority, of adjudications under ECC 2 have been conducted in recent years under the statutory scheme rather than under the contractual scheme. That situation has now been addressed in NEC 3 by the introduction of Option W2 – which, on the face, is a fully compliant scheme.

However, although NEC has developed its adjudication proceedings NEC 3 has not kept pace with the growing trend for fully structured dispute resolution procedures. These include provisions for negotiations at various levels, expert determination, conciliation and/or mediation, dispute resolution boards, adjudication and, only finally, arbitration or litigation.

Indeed one of the most surprising omissions from NEC 3 is that it does not provide for mediation. The contract's prominently placed requirement for the parties to act in a spirit of mutual trust and co-operation seems to call out for mediation. And the unconventional wording of the contract, together with the complexity of some of its procedures, create genuine uncertainty as to the outcome of adversarially conducted processes. It may be said that NEC 3 does not preclude mediation although it does not provide for it, and that under ECC 2 many parties have found it appropriate and practical to mediate rather than to adjudicate. Both points have merit but not enough to excuse the omission.

19.3 *Meaning of dispute*

Although most construction and commercial contracts have dispute resolution clauses, few attempt to define the meaning of dispute. It is, however, a matter of some importance, particularly in contracts with conditions precedent to the commencement of dispute resolution proceedings or with conditions prescribing how and when disputes can be referred for resolution. Not surprisingly there is a string of reported cases going back for many years where the courts have been called upon to decide whether or not a particular referred matter was, or was not, a matter in dispute.

One judgment much relied on in recent years was the Court of Appeal decision in the case of *Halki Shipping Corporation* v. *Sopex Oils Ltd* (1998) which seemed to offer a simple solution to the problem by apparently suggesting that a claim made but not admitted constituted a dispute. However, the rapid growth of adjudication in the last decade has led to an influx of cases coming before the courts concerning disputes about disputes and an obvious need for a decisive statement of legal principles.

That statement has now been given by the Court of Appeal accepting, in two cases, *Collins (Contractors) Ltd* v. *Baltic Quay Management Ltd* (2004) and *AMEC Civil Engineering Ltd* v. *Secretary of State for Transport* (2005), a decision of first instance by Mr Justice Jackson in the latter case. This is what is said in the *AMEC* case Court of Appeal ruling:

> 29. From his review of the authorities, the judge derived the following propositions:
>
> '1. The word "dispute" which occurs in many arbitration clauses and also in section 108 of the Housing Grants Act should be given its normal meaning. It does not have some special or unusual meaning conferred upon it by lawyers.
> 2. Despite the simple meaning of the word "dispute", there has been much litigation over the years as to whether or not disputes existed in particular situations. This litigation has not generated any hard-edged legal rules as to what is or is not a dispute. However, the accumulating judicial decisions have produced helpful guidance.
> 3. The mere fact that one party (whom I shall call "the claimant") notifies the other party (whom I shall call "the respondent") of a claim does not automatically and immediately give rise to a dispute. It is clear, both as a matter of language and from judicial decisions, that a dispute does not arise unless and until it emerges that the claim is not admitted.
> 4. The circumstances from which it may emerge that a claim is not admitted are Protean. For example, there may be an express rejection of the claim. There may be discussions between the parties from which objectively it is to be inferred that the claim is not admitted. The respondent may prevaricate, thus giving rise to the inference that he does not admit the claim. The respondent may simply remain silent for a period of time, thus giving rise to the same inference.
> 5. The period of time for which a respondent may remain silent before a dispute is to be inferred depends heavily upon the facts of the case and the contractual structure. Where the gist of the claim is well known and it is obviously controversial, a very short period of silence may suffice to give rise to this inference. Where the claim is notified to some agent of the respondent who has a legal duty to consider the claim independently and then give a considered response, a longer period of time may be required before it can be inferred that mere silence gives rise to a dispute.
> 6. If the claimant imposes upon the respondent a deadline for responding to the claim, that deadline does not have the automatic effect of curtailing what would

otherwise be a reasonable time for responding. On the other hand, a stated deadline and the reasons for its imposition may be relevant factors when the court comes to consider what is a reasonable time for responding.

7. If the claim as presented by the claimant is so nebulous and ill-defined that the respondent cannot sensibly respond to it, neither silence by the respondent nor even an express non-admission is likely to give rise to a dispute for the purposes of arbitration or adjudication.'

30. In *Collins (Contractors) Limited* v. *Baltic Quay Management (1994) Limited* [2004] EWCA Civ 1757, Clarke LJ at paragraph 68 quoted Jackson J's seven propositions and said of them:

'63. For my part I would accept those propositions as broadly correct. I entirely accept that all depends on the circumstances of the particular case. I would, in particular, endorse the general approach that while the mere making of a claim does not amount to a dispute, a dispute will be held to exist once it can reasonably be inferred that a claim is not admitted. I note that Jackson J does not endorse the suggestion in some of the cases, either that a dispute may not arise until negotiation or discussion have been concluded, or that a dispute should not be likely inferred. In my opinion he was right not to do so.

64. It appears to me that negotiation and discussion are likely to be more consistent with the existence of a dispute, albeit an as yet unresolved dispute, than with an absence of a dispute. It also appears to me that the court is likely to be willing readily to infer that a claim is not admitted and that a dispute exists so that it can be referred to arbitration or adjudication. I make these observations in the hope that they may be of some assistance and not because I detect any disagreement between them and the propositions advanced by Jackson J.'

19.4 Adjudication under Option W1

As explained in section 19.1, Option W1 commences with the head note 'used unless the UK Housing Grants, Construction and Regeneration Act 1996 applies'.

Clause W1.1 – referral to adjudication

This clause requires that a dispute arising 'under or in connection with' the contract is referred to and is decided by the adjudicator. It is mandatory in its wording thereby giving rise to the presumption that unless the dispute is so referred there are consequences to follow. These seem to be twofold. Under clause W.1.3(9) the parties are to proceed as though the matter was not disputed and under clause W.1.4(1) the parties are not to refer the dispute to a tribunal (i.e. arbitration or litigation) prior to adjudication. In short, unless the dispute is referred to adjudication it is treated as though it does not exist. The clause is wide in its scope. It covers disputes arising 'under' and 'in connection' with the contract. Claims under the contract include not only contractual claims but also claims for breach of contract. Claims 'in connection with' the contract can include claims based on misrepresentation.

Clause W1.2(1) – appointment of adjudicator

This clause requires the parties to appoint the adjudicator under the NEC Adjudicator's Contract current at the starting date. Comment on this contract is given in section 19.7. It is not a contract of exceptional or unusual note. However, the overall impression given by the Adjudicator's Contract is that it is designed for use where the adjudicator is named in the construction contract and the adjudicator is appointed at or about the time the construction contract is let.

It is probable, therefore, that the obligation stated in clause W1.2(1) is intended to be unrelated to whether or not the parties are in immediate dispute. Its purpose can be seen as ensuring a state of readiness in case there is a dispute. Nevertheless, failure by one party to appoint the named adjudicator as required by the clause could have serious effects on the proper operation of Option W1 in the event of dispute – the remedy for which might have to be found in the courts.

Clause W1.2(2) – adjudicator to act impartially

The clause has two limbs. It states that the adjudicator:

- acts impartially, *and*
- decides the dispute as an independent adjudicator and not as an arbitrator

The statement that the adjudicator shall act impartially seems so obvious that it hardly needs stating. The courts are certainly reluctant to accept as valid and enforceable any decision which is not made impartially. But, in any event, it is questionable whether the construction contract is the right place to state the adjudicator's obligations. It may be, however, that all that is intended by stating that the adjudicator acts impartially is that any adjudicator named in the contract is to be taken as impartial, and obliged to act as impartial, whether or not he is independent of one of the parties. It is the case that some employers do name adjudicators from their own staff or with whom they have a connection.

The purpose of the statement that the adjudicator decides the dispute as an adjudicator and not as an arbitrator is not entirely clear. It may be intended to express the parties' agreement that the adjudicator should not be subject to the control of the courts and any applicable arbitration acts or it may be to express their recognition that the adjudicator's decision does not have the finality of an arbitrator's award. However, if the statement is intended to suggest that the process of adjudication is entirely distinct from the process of arbitration – following a view widely expressed in the early days of expansion of adjudication – that should be taken with care. The present approach of the courts seems to be that adjudication is a species of arbitration albeit subject to lesser court control.

Clause W1.2(3) – appointment by nominating bodies

This clause deals with the not uncommon situation when there is no adjudicator named in the contract data. It also deals with the appointment of any replacement adjudicator made necessary by resignation or the like. The parties may either choose the adjudicator by agreement or ask a nominating body to choose one.

The nominating body should be identified in the contract data as difficulties can arise when it is not. NEC 3, unlike some other contracts, does not have a named fall-back nominating body. Thus a situation can arise where there is no named adjudicator and no named nominating body. This does not greatly matter for adjudicators under a statutory scheme as the referring party can effectively choose his nominating body. But for adjudication under a contractual scheme such as Option W1 this is a complication which is best avoided.

Clause W1.2(4) – powers of replacement adjudicator

Clause W1.2(4) makes two points:

- a replacement adjudicator has power to decide a dispute referred, but not decided, at the time the original adjudicator left office
- time starts to run afresh from the date of appointment of the replacement adjudicator

Note that the clause does not deal with the situation contemplated in section 4 of the NEC Adjudicator's Contract that the parties may, by agreement, terminate the adjudicator's appointment for any reason. However, if there is to be a continuing adjudication and the parties have agreed to dispose of the original adjudicator it may be presumed that they have already agreed who is to be the replacement adjudicator.

Clause W1.2(5) – liability of adjudicator

This is another clause which seems to be more concerned with the relationship between the adjudicator and each of the parties than with the relationship between the parties. It states that the adjudicator, his agents and employees, are not liable to the parties for any action or failure to act in the adjudication unless done, or not done, in bad faith.

According to the Guidance Notes this clause appears in NEC 3 to protect the adjudicator from possible claims from the parties and, so it is said, it repeats a provision found in the NEC Adjudicator's Contract. If it was the case that such a provision was in the Adjudicator's Contract its repetition would seem to be pointless but oddly there is no such provision in the version of the Adjudicator's Contract published with NEC 3 – although there was in the previous version.

As it is, clause W1.2(5) seems to serve little purpose in the construction contract although it would have a purpose in the Adjudicator's Contract.

Clause W1.3(1) – the adjudication table

The adjudication table in clause W1.3(1) sets out which party may submit disputes to arbitration and the timescale for doing so. Note that in the table the discretionary phrase 'may refer' is used in contrast to the mandatory phrase 'are referred' in the introductory sentence of the clause.

For disputes about actions or inactions of the project manager or the supervisor the table states that only the contractor may submit disputes to adjudication. The employer it would seem is bound by their actions or inactions. The timing requirement is that the contractor may only submit a dispute to adjudication between two and four weeks after notification of the dispute has been given to the project manager. The lead time of two weeks is presumably to allow a brief period for negotiations. There is however a further qualification. The notification (which presumably means the notification of the dispute) must itself be made within four weeks of the contractor becoming aware of the disputed action or inaction. Thus the latest time for submission to adjudication is eight weeks after the contractor becomes aware of the disputed action or inaction.

There may be some scope for manoeuvre on the timing by arguing what is meant by when the contractor 'becomes aware' but otherwise the pace at which the contractor is propelled towards making his submission to adjudication is not something which fits easily in a contract designed to reduce conflict. However, in ECC 2 contracts common sense often prevailed and the parties, by agreement, abandoned the timescale requirements for adjudication to give themselves sensible time to consider the matters in dispute.

'treated as having been accepted'

The third section of the adjudication table which entitles the employer to refer to adjudication a dispute about a quotation for a compensation event which is treated as having been accepted is new to NEC 3. It follows the changes in compensation event procedures which deal with situations where the project manager does not reply to quotations within the contractually required timescale. The timescale for referral by the employer matches that given to the contractor for his referrals on actions or lack of actions and is between two and four weeks after the project manager's notification of the dispute to the parties with such notification being not more than four weeks after the quotation was treated as accepted.

The logic, and necessity, for putting into the compensation event procedures of NEC 3 fall-back provision for quotations to be treated as accepted in certain circumstances cannot be faulted. High on the list of problems with ECC 2 was that dilatory or recalcitrant project managers could intentionally, or otherwise, derail the compensation event assessment procedures – thereby leading to disputes for which the contract had no answers. However, it is neither obviously logical nor necessary that the employer should be able to dispute a quotation for a compensation event which has been treated as having been accepted. In the first place, unless it is the case that the employer can dispute a quotation which has been accepted (and that may be an unintended consequence of the changes in NEC 3) it is a contradiction in terms for a quotation which is treated as having been accepted to be treated differently from a quotation which has been accepted. Secondly, it casts doubt on whether under NEC 3 the employer stands behind the actions of the project manager as was obviously the intent in ECC 2. Thirdly, since the cause of a quotation becoming treated as accepted is in essence a default for which the employer should take responsibility it is not clear why the employer should be entitled to dispute the quotation.

There is, of course, the possibility of dispute between the parties as to whether a quotation has or has not become a quotation which is to be treated as having been accepted. And it might be thought that it is only that type of dispute which is referable under the third part of the adjudication table. However, two things go against that. Firstly, under clause W1.3(5) the adjudicator is expressly empowered to alter a quotation which is treated as having been accepted. Secondly, since it is more likely to be the contractor than the employer who asserts that a quotation should be so treated, it is the fourth part of the adjudication table dealing with 'any other matter' which would apply to a dispute on whether a quotation is to be treated as accepted.

'any other matter'

The fourth part of the adjudication table deals with disputes about 'any other matter'. Either party may refer such a dispute to adjudication and the referral is to be made between two and four weeks after notification of the dispute. There is no stated stipulation in the table as to the period between formation of the dispute and its notification and this, together with the provision that either party may refer, arguably gives greater flexibility than bestowed on the parties under the first three parts of the table. This is a matter of some importance not least because clause W1.4(1) of Option W1 makes referral to adjudication a condition precedent to referral to a tribunal. In other words if a party is out of time in commencing adjudication it has no remedy. Under ECC 2, which had a similar adjudication table (save for the part on quotations for compensation events), it was not unknown for disputes to be referred to adjudication on whether a dispute was about an action or inaction or was about 'any other matter'. Another point of argument under ECC 2, and one which may live on under NEC 3, was how the phrase 'notification of dispute' in the table was to be interpreted. On one view, notification of the dispute as mentioned in the table means the giving of formal notice of a pre-existing dispute; on another view it means the point of crystallisation of the dispute – as for example, a letter of rejection of a claim. Both views create problems.

The first leaves the time for commencing adjudication open-ended; the second opens up a new class of dispute on when a dispute crystallised. However, given the consequences of time-barring, the first view is probably the better view. It gives purpose to the phrase 'notification of the dispute' and it accords with the well established principle that legal rights are not lost except by clearly worded provisions. Thus to the extent that there is ambiguity in the phrase, the less draconian meaning is to be preferred.

Clause W1.3(2) – extensions of times

This clause states firstly that:

- the times in the adjudication table for notifying and referring disputes may be extended
- if the contractor and the project manager agree
- before the notice or referral is due

There is no mention of the employer in the clause, so presumably the project manager acts for the employer. But for disputes which arise from and relate to the project manager's performance this does not seem particularly satisfactory.

The second part of the clause requires the project manager to notify the contractor of agreed extensions. Again, there is no mention of the employer.

The third part of the clause states that if a disputed matter is not notified and referred within the stipulated times neither party may subsequently refer the dispute to an adjudicator or to a tribunal. It reinforces what can already be gathered from the adjudication table and clause W1.4(1). It may even go further because it seems to open the possibility of argument under clause W1.4(1) that an adjudication was held out of time and that the decision is invalid. The reference in the last sentence of the clause to 'the terms set out in this contract' is no doubt to be read as also applying to any agreed extensions of such times. But, given the purpose of the clause, it would be better if it said so.

Clause W1.3(3) – information to be considered

This clause lays down the basis of the adjudication procedure. It states that:

- the referring party includes in its referral information to be considered by the adjudicator
- any further information from 'a Party' to be considered by the adjudicator is to be provided within four weeks of the referral
- this period may be extended if the adjudicator and the parties agree

The clause appears to contemplate a documents-only procedure but it does not preclude information being provided at meetings. There may be some concern that the cut-off period for the submission of information could lead to ambush or denial of right to reply but adjudicators should be able to deal with this by fixing at the outset of proceedings a timetable for exchanges running through to the cut-off date. It is doubted if the clause can be interpreted as giving a party a right to lodge information immediately before the cut-off date thereby precluding a reply.

Clause W1.3(4) – joinder of subcontract disputes

It is not unusual for arbitration rules to provide for the joinder of main contract and subcontract disputes. However, joinder is fraught with difficulties – one being that the party in the middle is left facing both ways and in danger of perjuring himself in one or other of the actions. In adjudication there is a further inherent difficulty – that of timetabling and time limits. In practice, unless there is a good measure of co-operation between all the parties on the timetable and procedure to be adopted joinder rarely works.

Clause W1.3(4) of NEC 3 provides for joinder as follows:

- for a matter disputed by the contractor under, or in connection with, a subcontract
- which is also a matter disputed under, or in connection with, the main contract, *and*
- if the subcontract allows
- the contractor may refer the subcontract dispute to the adjudication at the same time as the main contract referral
- the adjudicator then decides the disputes together

The problem with the clause, apart from the general problems mentioned above, is that it starts in the middle of the contractual claim and it does not effectively deal with disputes which start, as many do, at the top or the bottom of the chain. Thus if the employer commences adjudication against the contractor in respect of design or workmanship, or if a subcontractor commences adjudication against the contractor in respect of adverse ground conditions, the simultaneous referrals contemplated in the clause do not occur.

Clause W1.3(5) – powers of the adjudicator

The powers of the adjudicator are not fully set out in the Adjudicator's Contract. Four specific powers are however detailed in clause W1.3(5) of NEC 3. These are:

- the power to review and revise an action or inaction of the project manager or supervisor or to alter any quotation which is treated as having been accepted
- the power to take the initiative in ascertaining the facts and the law
- the power to instruct a party to provide further information

- the power to instruct a party to take any other action considered necessary

Discussion on the first of these is given earlier in this chapter and in Chapter 8, section 2. The key questions are: does the power to review and revise actions extend to revising certificates and decisions; and how extensive is the power to alter a quotation treated as having been accepted.

The power for the adjudicator to take the initiative in ascertaining the facts and the law is common to most adjudication schemes. It may, however, be somewhat dated. It stems from a belief, borne when adjudication was in its infancy, that adjudicators should be pro-active rather than simply assessors of the material put before them. Perceptions of what an adjudicator can and should do have now changed. Essentially his role is to decide a dispute not to meddle in the affairs of the parties. The dangers of seeking out the facts and the law and, in the process, improving one party's case against the other are now well recognised, as are the dangers of deciding issues on the basis of things the parties have not had the opportunity to comment on. See, for example, the case of *Balfour Beatty Construction Ltd* v. *London Borough of Lambeth* (2002).

The power to instruct a party to provide further information has to be considered in the context of the timing requirements for the provision of information and for making the decision. It is a power which requires careful thought before being used. So also does the power to instruct a party to take other action.

Clause W1.3(6) – communications

This clause simply states the standard procedural rule that any communication between a party and the adjudicator is communicated to the other party at the same time.

Although the clause does not say so it is just as important that any communication between the adjudicator and a party is copied to the other party. To ensure that no problems arise in connection with this (i.e. one party claiming not to have received a copy) many adjudicators adopt the practice of addressing all communications to both parties.

Clause W1.3(7) – adjudicator's assessments

Clause W1.3(7) states that if the adjudicator's decision includes assessment of additional cost or delay he makes his assessment in the same way as a compensation event is assessed.

This seemingly innocuous clause conceals a complex and difficult problem which, by virtue of the new wording in clause 63.1 of NEC 3, will be worse in NEC 3 than it was in ECC 2. The problem arises firstly because compensation events are meant to be priced by quotations which include the contractor's risk forecasts; secondly, because the assessment process in clause 63.1 involves very detailed programming and costing tasks which, even if the adjudicator has the skills to undertake the task he is unlikely to have sufficient time. In ECC 2 adjudicators had some relief in that the assessment process allowed the retrospective examination of cost incurred. Under NEC 3 however, the new rule in clause 63.1 that the date when the project manager instructed or should have instructed the contractor to submit quotations divides the work done from the work not yet done means that assessments for disputed compensation events will, in many cases, have to be made on a forecast basis. This is not an appropriate task for an adjudicator.

There are some practical ways by which the difficulties can be avoided if the parties and the adjudicator agree to their adoption. One is to separate disputes about whether or not there are compensation events from disputes about their assessments. Indeed, there is a good argument to the effect that there cannot be a dispute about the assessment of a compensation event until there is recognition of the event and there are competing assessments. A prudent adjudicator may well therefore decline to deal with both entitlement and assessment issues in one adjudication on the basis that it is for the contractor and the project manager to deal with assessment in the first instance. Another method of easing assessment difficulties is for the adjudicator to let it be known to the parties that he proposes to decide simply between competing assessments subject, of course, to thorough examinations of those assessments. This approach is arguably the proper task of an adjudicator but, whether or not that be the case, it usually has the effect of producing sensible assessments from both sides.

One point worth noting is that the adjudicator is not given any power to utilise of his own accord the simplified assessment procedures allowed in the various main options which are stated to be subject to agreement between the contractor and the project manager. Agreement of the parties would be needed to the use of such procedures in adjudication.

Interesting questions arise as to the status of the adjudicator's decision if he does not make his assessment 'in the same way as a compensation event is assessed' as required by clause W1.3(7). Is it then an invalid decision which can be ignored at the will of either party or is it to be treated as a valid decision which one or both of the parties might find unacceptable? Would the decision be enforceable in the courts? One answer is probably that providing that the adjudicator purports to make a decision in compliance with clause W1.3(7) it will not be challengeable as invalid simply on assertions that it is not. However, blatant or intentionally expressed departure from clause W1.3(7) by the adjudicator might amount to exceeding jurisdiction such as to lead to invalidity.

Generally the courts recognise the difficulties of adjudication and uphold adjudicator's decisions notwithstanding patent errors or inconsistencies. The courts do draw the line, however, at jurisdictional excesses and certain departures from the rules of natural justice.

Clause W1.3(8) – notification of adjudicator's decision

Clause W1.3(8) requires the adjudicator to make his decision and to notify the parties of his decision within four weeks of the period for receiving information. It allows for extension of the period by agreement. Failure to make and notify the decision by the due date may well render it invalid.

Clause W1.3(9) – effect of notification of dispute

This clause states that:

- unless and until the adjudicator notifies his decision
- the parties, project manager and supervisor proceed as if the disputed matter was not disputed

It is questionable if the clause adds anything to the obligations of the parties as found in the main body of clauses and it is not entirely clear how it operates. Considering its context the clause presumably comes into effect only after a notice of dispute is served but if it is the case that the matter which is not to be disputed is to be determined from the notice of dispute some odd consequences could follow. Claims for compensation events, notified as disputes, would apparently stand unless and until defeated in adjudication. However, the true intention of the clause is probably the opposite – namely that claims and assertions which are disputed, remain disputed and are treated as such until decided in adjudication.

Clause W1.3(10) – status of adjudicator's decision

Clause W1.3(10) contains a number of provisions fixing the status of the adjudicator's decision:

- the decision is binding unless and until revised by a tribunal
- the decision is enforceable as a matter of contractual obligation and not as an arbitral award
- the decision remains final and binding if neither party notifies the other of dissatisfaction with the decision within the time allowed and states his intention to refer the matter to a tribunal

The first of these provisions confirms the temporary nature of the adjudicator's decision. The second appears to be to the same effect. The third transforms the decision from temporarily binding to permanently binding unless the disputed matter is referred to a tribunal within a stipulated time – four weeks under clause W1.4(2).

Clause W1.3(11) – correction of mistakes

This clause permits the adjudicator to correct clerical mistakes or ambiguity within two weeks of giving his decision.

The clause does not confine the adjudicator to doing so only on the application of one or both of the parties although correction normally follows such an application. In the event of there being opposition by one party to the application of the other the adjudicator needs to take great care in correcting alleged ambiguity. It is sometimes better if the decision is left as it stands.

19.5 *Adjudication under Option W2*

This option commences with the head-note 'used in the United Kingdom when the Housing Grants, Construction and Regeneration Act 1996 applies'. It replaces the adjudication provisions in secondary option, Y(UK)2, of ECC 2 and is intended to be and probably is compliant with the Act.

Clause W2.1(1) – referral to adjudication

This clause provides that a party may refer a dispute arising under or in connection with the contract to adjudication 'at any time'. This is significantly different than the position in Option W1 which regulates when disputes can be referred.

An important point to note in connection with clause W2.1(1) is that it is wider in its scope than the Act and the statutory adjudication schemes in that it includes for disputes arising 'in connection' with the contract as well as disputes 'under' the contract. In the case of *Strachan & Henshaw* v. *Stein Industrie* (1997) such disputes were held by the Court of Appeal to include disputes relating to misrepresentations.

Clause W2.1(2) – holiday periods

The clause states simply that time periods in Option W2.1(2) exclude Christmas Day, Good Friday and bank holidays.

There is no corresponding provision in Option W1 but the option states time periods in weeks whereas Option W2 states its periods in days.

Clause W2.2(1) – appointment of adjudicator

This clause is identical to clause W1.2(1) of Option W1. See the comment in the preceding section.

Clause W2.2(2) – adjudicator to act impartially

This clause is identical to clause W1.2(2) of Option W1. Again, see the comment in the preceding section.

Clause W2.2(3) – appointment by nominating bodies

This clause is essentially the same as clause W1.2(3) of Option W1 although set out differently. For comment see the preceding section.

Clause W2.2(4) – powers of replacement adjudicator

This clause is identical to clause W1.2(4) of Option W1. For comment again see the preceding section.

Clause W2.2(5) – liability of adjudicator

This clause is identical to clause W1.2(5) of Option W1. For comment again see the preceding section.

Clause W2.3(1) – notice of adjudication

Clause W2.3(1) has no direct counterpart in Option W1. It illustrates some of the major procedural differences between the two options. It requires:

- a notice of adjudication to be served before referral of a dispute to adjudication
- such notice to give a brief description of the dispute and the decision sought

It also requires the notice to be sent to the adjudicator named in the contract data and the adjudicator to notify the parties within three days of receipt whether he is able to decide the dispute or that he is unable to do so 'and has resigned'. If he does not so notify the parties either party may act as if he has resigned.

There is no express requirement for the notice of adjudication to be sent to an adjudicator chosen by a nominating body but as a matter of routine a copy will normally be provided by the nominating body or the parties to the adjudicator.

The provision in the clause that if the adjudicator named in the contract data states that he is unable to decide the dispute he is taken as having resigned probably means no more than resigned in respect of that particular dispute. It is doubted if this means that he is no longer the named adjudicator for subsequent disputes. However, this could lead to difficulties because under NEC contracts there are sometimes serial adjudications and these are best conducted by one adjudicator.

Clause W2.3(2) – referral to adjudication

The commencing part of Clause W2.3(2) requires the referral to adjudication to be made within seven days of service of the notice of adjudication. Compliance with this is best taken as a strict requirement for a valid decision. In the event that service of the referral is delayed it is best therefore, to re-serve the notice of adjudication.

Clause W2.3(2) also requires that the party referring the dispute to adjudication:

- provides the adjudicator with information on which he relies, including supporting documents
- provides to the other party copies of everything sent to the adjudicator

The clause also provides that further information from either party to be considered by the adjudicator is provided within fourteen days of the referral or such longer period as the adjudicator and the parties may agree. This is restrictive both in its timescale and in apparently disqualifying information provided outside the fourteen day period unless the parties agree to its inclusion. It begs the question of what is to be done with late information which is essential to a proper decision on the matter in dispute. It also appears to significantly limit the powers of the adjudicator to instruct further information under clause W2.3(4).

Clause W2.3(3) – joinder of subcontract disputes

This clause is identical to clause W1.3(4) of Option W1 save that it uses the phrase 'with the consent of the subcontractor' in place of 'if the subcontract allows' in connection with joining a subcontract dispute with a main contract dispute. Not much seems to turn on this and for comment on the clause see the preceding section.

Clause W2.3(4) – powers of the adjudicator

This clause is identical to clause W1.3(5) of Option W1. Again see preceding section for comment.

Clause W2.3(5) – non-compliance with adjudicator's instructions

This clause has no direct counterpart in Option W1. It deals with failure by a party to comply in timely manner with the adjudicator's instructions and empowers the adjudicator to make a decision based on the information and evidence he has received. It is ambiguous in its wording because on one interpretation, information received late is not to be considered but on another interpretation it may be considered.

Clause W2.3(6) – communications

This clause is identical to clause W1.3(6) of Option W1. See the preceding section for comment.

Clause W2.3(7) – adjudicator's assessments

This clause is identical to clause W1.3(7) of Option W1. Again, see the preceding section for comment.

Clause W2.3(8) – notification of adjudicator's decisions

This clause is similar to clause W1.3(8) of Option W1 except that it requires the adjudicator's decision to be given within 28 days of referral (instead of four weeks of receiving information) and it allows the period for giving the decision to be extended by fourteen days with the consent of the referring party (as well as allowing extension by agreement of the parties).

Clause W2.3(9) – effect of notification of dispute

This clause is identical to clause W1.3(9) of Option W1. Again, see the preceding section for comment.

Clause W2.3(10) – late decision

Clause W2.3(10) is another clause with no direct counterpart in Option W1. It provides that:

- if the adjudicator does not give his decision within the stipulated time
- the parties and adjudicator may agree to extending the time
- if they do not agree either party may act as though the adjudicator has resigned

The effect of the above is to deprive any decision given outside the stipulated or the agreed time of contractual standing. This matches the legal position that a decision given late is unenforceable.

Clause W2.3(11) – status of adjudicator's decision

This clause is identical to clause W1.3(10) of Option W1. For comment see the preceding section.

Clause W2.3(12) – correction of mistakes

This clause is identical to clause W1.3(11) of Option W1. Again, see preceding section for comment.

19.6 *Review by the tribunal*

NEC 3 does not contain a traditional arbitration clause in either Options W1 or W2. In both it contains provisions grouped under the marginal note of 'review by the tribunal'.

The tribunal is an identified term of NEC 3, not a defined term, so it is necessary that it be fixed in the contract data. It is likely to be either arbitration or litigation but if the contract data fails to state anything, litigation will apply by default rather than arbitration – there being no arbitration agreement for either party to rely on.

An important point to note is that the marginal note 'review by the tribunal' does not mean review of the adjudicator's decision. It means, as stated in both Options W1 and W2, settlement of the dispute by the tribunal. The word 'review' is used only in connection with review and revision of actions or inactions of the project manager and supervisor. It is possible that an inappropriate marginal note has been carried into NEC 3 from ECC 2 which did refer to review of the adjudicator's decision.

The point is important because in settling the dispute the tribunal will have regard to the arguments and evidence put before it not to arguments and evidence put before the adjudicator. In most cases the tribunal will have no interest in the adjudication proceedings or in the adjudicator's decision and may not even know of them. One difficulty which does occasionally arise, however, is that the claimant (referring party) in tribunal proceedings was the responding party in the adjudication and the question then is which party should have the burden of proof in the tribunal proceedings. Generally this is resolved by the parties agreeing to change places so that the original claiming party retains the burden of proof.

Review procedures in Options W1 and W2 compared

Clauses W1.4(1) to W1.4(6) deal with review procedures in Option W1. Clauses W2.4(1) to W2.4(5) deal with review procedures in Option W2. The five clauses in Option W2 are identical to five of the Option W1 clauses so there is only one difference between the two options on review procedures. This is that clause W1.4(3) of Option W1 is not found in Option W2.

Clauses W1.4(1) and W2.4(1) – referral to the tribunal

These clauses, which are identical in Options W1 and W2, state that a party does not refer any dispute under or in connection with the contract to the tribunal unless it has first been decided by the adjudicator in accordance with the contract.

The clauses clearly intend that adjudication shall be a condition precedent to tribunal proceedings and they are probably effective in this although it is doubtful if they have any effect unless they are cited as jurisdictional or condition precedent points in such proceedings. There is, however, one point of uncertainty and that is whether the requirement for adjudication in accordance with the contract is strictly binding. That seems to rule out other forms of adjudication including adjudication under statutory schemes. But, for reasons explained earlier in this chapter, the statutory schemes may be applicable in some circumstances. It is doubted if there was such an adjudication that a court would hold it to be of no effect in satisfying a condition precedent requirement.

More generally, note that the clauses presume that there has been an adjudicator's decision and that they do not deal with situations when there are late decisions or no decisions. Note also that it is the 'dispute' which is referable to the tribunal not the adjudicator's decision.

Clause W1.4(2) and W2.4(2) – notice of dissatisfaction

These clauses, which serve the same purpose and are almost identical provide:

- that if either party is dissatisfied with the adjudicator's decision
- he may notify the other party that he intends to make a referral to the tribunal
- providing that notification of referral is given within four weeks of notification of the adjudicator's decision

The difference between the two clauses is that W1.4(2) appears to refer the adjudicator's decision to the tribunal whereas W2.4(2) clearly refers the matter in dispute.

The general point of both clauses, however, is that they are intended to act as time-bars so that matters referred to adjudication are finally determined promptly rather than belatedly. However, the time-bar operates only on the notice of intention to refer. Its clauses do not go so far as requiring tribunal proceedings to be commenced within four weeks. But the parties need to take care if the contract stipulates particular arbitration rules and those rules link commencement of proceeding with the notice of intention to refer.

Clauses W1.4(4) and W2.4(3) – powers of the tribunal

These clauses, save for the occasional word and comma, are identical in options W1 and W2. They provide:

- the tribunal settles the disputes referred to it
- the tribunal has power to reconsider any decision of the adjudicator and to review and revise any action or inaction of the project manager or the supervisor related to the dispute
- a party is not limited in tribunal proceedings to the information, evidence (and in W1.4(4) arguments) put to the adjudicator

It is not clear why clause W2.4(3) should exclude 'arguments' as referred to in clause W1.4(4) but this may be no more than a printing error.

Clauses W1.4(5) and W2.4(4) – arbitration proceedings

These clauses are identical in Options W1 and W2. They simply make the point that if the tribunal is stated in the contract data to be arbitration then the arbitration procedure, the place of arbitration and the method of choosing the arbitrator are as stated in the contract data.

Straightforward as they may seem, complications can arise, as sometimes happened under ECC 2, if the contract data entries which are listed under 'Optional Statements' are left blank. There is then an agreement to arbitrate without any agreement as to procedure. That raises the question, is the arbitration agreement void, or is it that the arbitration is subject only to whatever statutory provisions apply – for example, in England, the Arbitration Act 1996? The answer, offered tentatively, is that the arbitration agreement, albeit bare, stands – subject to it being sufficient for procedural purposes when considered in conjunction with the applicable procedural law.

Clause W1.4(6) and W2.4(5) – adjudicator not to be called as a witness

These clauses are also identical under Options W1 and W2. They state only that the adjudicator shall not be called as a witness in tribunal proceedings.

Generally it would be unusual for an adjudicator to be called as a witness but it has been known for attendance orders to be served on arbitrators, adjudicators and mediators in court proceedings in various jurisdictions. It is doubtful if the clause is operable in all cases or if it affords much protection to an adjudicator served with a court attendance order.

Clause W1.4(3) – time-barring

This clause, which appears only in Option W1, states:

- if an adjudicator does not notify his decision within the stipulated time
- either party may notify the other that it intends to refer the dispute to the tribunal
- providing that notification of referral is given within four weeks of the date by which the adjudicator's decision should have been given

The clause supplements clause W1.4(2) which states a similar four week time-bar for decisions given but disputed. The probable explanation for why the clause is included in Option W1 but is omitted from Option W2 is that under Option W2, which incorporates the statutory right to adjudicate at any time, a dispute not decided by the adjudicator can be re-referred to adjudication at any time.

19.7 The Adjudicator's Contract

An updated version of the NEC Adjudicator's Contract was published in June
2005 as part of the NEC 3 family of contracts. It deals principally with the
terms and conditions of the adjudicator's appointment. It does not purport to
provide procedural rules for adjudication. Some of the clauses of the contract
are apparently drafted on the presumption that the adjudicator is a person
named in the contract data but both Options W1 and W2 require the contract
to be used for all appointments.

On the wording of the contract and from the inclusion in the contract data
of an entry as to when the adjudicator's appointment terminates, the intention
seems to be that the appointment runs for the period of the contract rather
than being dispute specific – although the fact that by clause 4.2 the adjudicator can terminate the appointment if he is unable to decide a dispute might
suggest otherwise. Under ECC 2 some parties appointed an adjudicator at the
outset of the project to deal with all disputes arising; others appointed adjudicators only when they were needed and only then on a dispute by dispute
basis. There are arguments in favour of both approaches involving familiarity
with the project on the one hand, and fields of expertise on the other, but
the big advantage of the project adjudicator approach is that it avoids the
often frantic late search for an adjudicator under the as-and-when-needed
approach.

Chapter 20
NEC 3 Engineering and Construction Subcontract

20.1 *Introduction*

Many standard forms of main contract have model forms of subcontract as part of a family of documents. Most step down provisions from the main contract to the subcontract so that as far as possible the obligations of the subcontractor are on a back-to-back basis with those of the contractor.

The NEC 3 Engineering and Construction Subcontract (NEC 3 subcontract) takes this to its limit in that it duplicates the main NEC 3 contract with little more than the names of the parties changed. It is, so far as contractual provisions go, a complete match of the main contract. It is, however, drafted in such detail that it is virtually independent of the main contract. It stands therefore as a subcontract which is fully back-to-back with the main contract but which, unusually, does not rely on examination of the terms of the main contract to give effect to its provisions.

That, at least, is the theory of the situation. In reality, however, with NEC 3 contracts much depends on the detail in the works information (subcontract works information for the subcontract) in fixing the obligations of the parties. So to obtain contracts which are back-to-back in both obligations and contractual provisions it is as important to match the works information as it is to match the standard provisions.

Use of the NEC 3 subcontract

Use of the NEC 3 subcontract is not mandatory with the NEC 3 main contract although its use is encouraged by clause 26.3 of the main contract. By that clause if the contractor does not use the NEC 3 subcontract he has to obtain the project manager's acceptance of any alternative conditions of subcontract.

Under ECC 2 which had a similar subcontract there was some reluctance on the part of main contractors to trade under its terms and conditions. The problem appeared to be threefold:

- concern at the administrative burden
- a perceived imbalance in remedies for breach
- loss of traditional caveats and control mechanisms

More is said on these points later in this chapter but if there is any generalisation to be made on why the NEC 3 subcontract should be treated with reservation it may well be that the commercial instincts of main contractors are to retain the use of simple standard forms which can be more readily adapted for particular projects.

There is another possibility, namely that main contractors may not be enthusiastic about affording the same opportunities for claims under compensation event procedures to subcontractors as enjoyed by themselves under the main contract.

Structure of the NEC 3 subcontract

The NEC 3 subcontract has the same structure as the NEC main contract with:

- core clauses
- main option clauses
- secondary option clauses
- schedules of cost components
- subcontract data – parts one and two

With just a few exceptions the wording of the standard NEC 3 subcontract documentation is identical to that in the main contract. And like the main contract, the subcontract places great reliance on documentation in works information, site information, contract data and programmes.

The basis of the transition of the standard documents from main contract documents to subcontract documents is that main contract references to the employer, the project manager and the supervisor, are replaced with references to the contractor; and references to the contractor are replaced with references to the subcontractor.

Main option clauses

The NEC 3 subcontract repeats the five main options A to E of the main contract but has no equivalent of Option F, the management contract. Clearly it is not appropriate that the management function of Option F should be subcontracted.

It is for the main contractor to choose which of the main options should apply and his choice will not necessarily be governed by the main option applicable to the main contract. For example, the probability is that main contractors working under Options C or D (the target contracts) will seek to let as many subcontracts as they can under the firm price Options A and B. Firstly, to maximise their gain share potential; and secondly to avoid the administrative burdens of the cost reimbursable arrangements of Options C and D. Even when the main contract is fully cost reimbursable under Option F the probability is that the majority of the subcontracts will be let under Options A or B.

Secondary option clauses

The NEC 3 subcontract has the same set of secondary options as the main contract but it is for the main contractor to select which of the secondary options should apply to the subcontract. There is no requirement that the secondary options in the main contract and the subcontract should match and the probability is that subcontracts will usually have a lesser number of secondary options than corresponding main contracts. This is because for most subcontracts some of the secondary options will not be commercially appropriate or necessary and for most subcontracts the full range of complexities in the main contract will not apply. See also the comment in section 20.4 on damages for late completion.

Core clauses

Except for the changes described above in nomenclature and a few other changes in detail the core clauses in the NEC 3 subcontract are the same as those in the main contract. Accordingly the comment on the core clauses which follows in this chapter is not on the detail of the wording but on differences of application between subcontracts and main contracts.

20.2 *Core clauses – general*

Actions

The requirement for the contractor and the subcontractor to act in a spirit of mutual trust and co-operation applies in NEC 3 subcontracts by application of clause 10.1 and in all subcontracts by application of clause 26.3 of the main contract whether or not NEC 3 subcontract is used.

Communications

Much of the criticism of ECC 2 contracts has been that they generate too much paperwork and are costly to administer. For subcontracts the burdens are multiplied according to the number of subcontractors – something which the main contractor has to allow and prepare for as a serious matter, taking particular note of the requirements in each NEC 3 subcontract for maintenance of a risk register.

Early warnings/risk reduction meetings

Main contractors, not unnaturally, like to be in control of what happens on site and have some difficulty coming to terms with provisions entitling the subcontractor to instruct them to attend risk reduction meetings.

20.3 Core clauses – the subcontractor's main responsibilities

Design

Note that by clause 22.1 the employer's rights in respect of the subcontractor's design are preserved as well as the contractor's rights.

Sub-subcontracting

The transfer of the full weight of NEC 3 main contract provisions on subcontracting to the subcontract seems heavy handed. Main contractors will not wish to find themselves burdened with considering, accepting or rejecting the terms of all sub-subcontracts but that appears to be what is envisaged since it is most unlikely that many sub-subcontracts will be let under the NEC 3 subcontract.

20.4 Core clauses – time

Completion

An important question main contractors have to decide in respect of time is whether or not to include secondary option X7 – liquidated damages for late completion. Most construction subcontracts leave damages for late completion unliquidated – not least because of the difficulties of making a genuine pre-estimate of loss when claims from other subcontractors may be a major element of any loss. Plant subcontracts, however, usually include liquidated damages as a means of limiting the liability of the subcontractor.

On a point of detail note that the main contractor has two weeks to certify completion against one week allowed to the project manager in the main contract.

Programmes

Another important question for main contractors, and a particularly difficult question, is what status to accord to programmes. Main contractors are frequently torn between conflicting objectives. One is to tie the subcontractor down to a programme so that any departure by way of late completion of an activity is a breach of the subcontract entitling the main contractor to damages. The other objective is to allow themselves maximum flexibility to direct the timing of the subcontractor's activities – so that they are not in breach of the subcontract by preventing the subcontractor starting and finishing each activity as shown on the programme. For a case on the complexities of the situation see *Pigott Foundations Ltd* v. *Shepherd Construction Ltd* (1993).

Main contractors will almost certainly be concerned that the NEC 3 subcontract gives them potentially the worst of both worlds in that the programme can form the basis of claims by the subcontractor under the compensation event rules but there is no express corresponding liability on the part of the subcontractor for failure to perform to the programme.

Take-over

Clause 35.2 is one of the five clauses of the NEC 3 subcontract where the employer is mentioned. The clause deals with the employer's use of the sub-contract works before completion and clearly it would not have been appropriate, in this clause, to replace the employer entirely by the contractor.

20.5 *Core clauses – testing and defects*

For testing and defects the main contractor under the NEC 3 subcontract assumes the roles of both the project manager and the supervisor although in some clauses the jurisdiction of the supervisor is still expressly recognised.

Uncorrected defects

Comment was made in Chapter 9 section 8 on the implications of the liability for uncorrected defects of the main contractor under clause 45.1 of the main contract. The same liability transfers to subcontractors under the subcontract – namely, liability for the assessed costs of uncorrected defects rather than for the actual costs incurred by the contractor.

With subcontracts this seems an even more repressive measure than with main contracts. Either the main contractor will correct the defect or he will not. In either case the financial implications can be properly ascertained. However, as clause 45.1 of the subcontract stands the subcontractor can be liable to the contractor for costs which he may never incur or which exceed those actually incurred.

20.6 *Core clauses – payment*

Under the NEC 3 subcontract the main contractor is required to assess and formally certify amounts due in like manner to the project manager under the main contract. However, there is some relaxation on the timing. Under the subcontract:

- the contractor has two weeks to certify (against one in the main contract)

- the contractor has four weeks from certification in which to pay (against three in the main contract)

The additional week allowed under the subcontract will obviously assist the contractor where the assessment dates in the subcontract and the main contract correspond. But by judicious timing of the subcontract starting date the contractor can gain more time.

Retention

Contractors need to be aware that retention only applies when secondary option X16 is included in the contract – and it is for the contractor to decide this irrespective of whether or not the corresponding option is in the main contract.

20.7 *Core clauses – compensation events*

In subcontracts financial claims flow in both directions whereas under main contracts financial claims from the employer are unusual – other than for liquidated damages or for the costs of remedying defects. This is in the nature of main contracts where the employer invariably has fewer stated entitlements to extra payments than the contractor.

Generally the intention of main contracts is that the employer should be able to liquidate his losses – defects apart. This is not the position in subcontracts and it is one of the objections to a straight transfer of main contract provisions into subcontracts as in the the NEC 3 subcontract. The effect is that the subcontractor has numerous stated entitlements under the compensation event procedure to claim against the contractor for his breaches but the contractor has little in return against the subcontractor except liquidated damages or common law claims for damages.

Under ECC 2, main contractors pruned the standard list of compensation events, sometimes quite severely, and it can be expected that under NEC 3 this will continue, with the new compensation event for prevention, clause 60.1(19), being a prime candidate for elimination.

Timing requirements

To ensure that the main contractor has time to pass on compensation event notifications to the employer where applicable the subcontract has timing requirements which are tighter than those in the main contract, thus:

- the subcontractor has seven weeks to give notice of a compensation event (against eight in the main contract) before it is time-barred, *and*
- the subcontractor has one week to submit a quotation (against three weeks in the main contract)

Note that the subcontract includes the new NEC 3 provisions for quotations to be treated as accepted if not replied to in time – another potential problem for the main contractor if there are many subcontracts to be administered.

20.8 *Core clauses – title*

These clauses should operate much the same under the subcontract as under the main contract.

20.9 *Core clauses – risks and insurance*

Risks

The subcontractor's risks are defined as those which are not the employer's risks or the contractor's risks.

The risks listed in the subcontract as the employer's risks and the contractor's risks match those listed as the employer's risks under the main contract. The arrangement looks clumsy and it may have the potential for confusion not least because it directly involves the employer in risks under the subcontract.

Insurance cover

To avoid the expense of duplication of insurance cover it is not unusual for main contractors to arrange insurances which provide some cover to subcontractors. The NEC 3 subcontract sets out a table of comprehensive insurance requirements but exceptions are allowed for any insurance which the contract data states are to be provided by the employer or the main contractor.

20.10 *Core clauses – termination*

Terminations are more common under subcontracts than main contracts so the NEC 3 provisions on termination require careful study – particularly the provision in clause 90.2 permitting the main contractor to terminate at will.

Another clause which deserves attention is clause 91.4 which states that the subcontractor may terminate if the contractor has not paid an amount he has certified within thirteen weeks of the date of the certificate. This appears to bind the contractor to each certificate such that any later downward correction or set-off is apparently an ineffective defence against termination.

Note, however, that failure to certify (as opposed to failure to pay on a certificate) attracts only interest under the subcontract (clause 51.2) and is not a stated ground for termination.

20.11 Dispute resolution

Dispute resolution options W1 and W2 of the main contract are incorporated into the NEC 3 subcontract largely unchanged, except for the names of the parties and the inclusion of additional provisions for joinder.

Option W1

Clause W1.3(4) of the main contract allows joinder of subcontract disputes with main contract disputes 'if the subcontract allows'. Clause W1.3(4b) of the NEC 3 subcontract addresses this by stating:

- within two weeks of notification of a dispute by the subcontractor to the contractor
- the contractor notifies the subcontractor if the matter is also disputed under the main contract
- the contractor may then submit the subcontract dispute to the main contract adjudicator at the same time as the main contract submission
- the main contract adjudicator then decides the disputes together

This scheme is not without potential complications since the subcontractor can, under the timing arrangements which apply to the subcontract and the main contract, refer a dispute to subcontract adjudication before the contractor can refer the same dispute to main contract adjudication, and there is nothing preventing different adjudicators being named in the main contract and in the subcontract.

Note that clause W1.3(4a) of the subcontract effectively steps down clause W1.3(4) of the main contract so that there are provisions for the joinder of sub-subcontract disputes with subcontract disputes.

Option W2

The same arrangements as for Option W1 apply except that the clause numbers are different.

Review by the tribunal

It is not obligatory that the subcontract adopts the same form of tribunal as the main contract but it is preferable.

Chapter 21
NEC 3 family of contracts

21.1 The contracts

From the launch in 1991 of consultative versions of the NEC main contract and subcontract the NEC family of contracts has steadily grown in size such that the set of contracts released in June 2005 under the generic title of NEC 3 comprised:

- the NEC 3 Engineering and Construction Contract
- the NEC 3 Engineering and Construction Subcontract
- the NEC 3 Engineering and Construction Short Contract
- the NEC 3 Engineering and Construction Short Subcontract
- the NEC 3 Term Service Contract
- the NEC 3 Framework Contract
- the NEC 3 Professional Services Contract
- the NEC 3 Adjudicator's Contract

The contracts are supported by NEC 3 guidance notes and flow charts and additionally there is a document entitled NEC 3 procurement and contract strategies.

All the contracts are written in the same style of language and all, with the exception of the Adjudicator's Contract, require the parties to act in a spirit of mutual trust and co-operation. The structure of core clauses and option clauses which is a notable feature of the NEC 3 Engineering and Construction Contract and its Subcontract is retained in the Professional Services Contract and the Term Service Contract, but the Short Contract and its Subcontract, the Adjudicator's Contract and the Framework Contract use the conventional approach of single sets of clauses. There is no separate partnering contract but the Engineering and Construction Contract and its Subcontract, the Professional Services Contract and the Term Service Contract all include partnering as a secondary option clause. Nor is there any separate construction management contract but by appointment of a construction manager under the Professional Services Contract and package contractors under other NEC 3 contracts, a workable construction management system can be achieved.

It is not intended that any detailed analysis of the various NEC 3 contracts should be undertaken in this short chapter. All that is attempted is a brief synopsis and identification of particular points of interest. Comment on the NEC 3 Engineering and Construction Subcontract is given in Chapter 20.

21.2 *NEC 3 Short Contract and Short Subcontract*

The Guidance Notes to the Short Contract suggest its use for contracts which:

- do not require sophisticated management techniques
- comprise straightforward work, *and*
- impose only low risks on the employer and the contractor

No suggestion is given as to the maximum contract value and, on the basis of the above criteria which could fit a contract of large financial value, that is understandable.

Structure

Both the Short Contract and the Short Subcontract comprise clauses grouped into nine sections:

- general
- contractor's (subcontractor's) main responsibilities
- time
- defects
- payment
- compensation events
- title
- indemnity, insurance and liability
- termination and dispute resolution

There is no choice of main options of the type A, B, C, D, E and F found in the main contract and main subcontract. Nor are there any secondary option clauses. The clauses themselves are, for the most part, clauses taken from the main contracts so the short contracts are genuinely short versions of the main contracts. In this the short contracts differ from conventional minor works contracts drafted independently of other contracts and of very simple style.

Management

No provision is made in the Short Contract for a project manager or any other contract administrator or certifier of professional standing. The employer fulfills the role. This is not entirely unusual in construction contracts but it can create difficult situations particularly if phrases such as 'the employer decides' are used – as they are in the NEC 3 Short Contract.

Price

For short contracts the pricing mechanism is usually very simple and straight-forward. In the NEC 3 short contracts prices are defined as 'the amounts stated in the Price column of the Price List'. But where a quantity is stated for an item in the price list, the price is calculated 'by multiplying the quantity by the rate'. This suggests that a contract may be on a lump sum basis, a remeasurement basis, or a combination of both. To the extent that this may leave unclear whether, in laymen's terms, this means that the contract is lump sum or a schedule of rates it is less than satisfactory.

Payment

The payment provisions of the short contracts illustrate one of the difficulties created by the absence of a project manager/certifier. In the main NEC 3 contract the project manager assesses 'the amount due' on interim certificates. In the Short Contract it is the contractor, and in the Short Subcontract, the subcontractor. The phrase 'the amount due' is one of significance, particularly so for contracts subject to the Housing Grants, Construction and Regeneration Act 1996 where the paying party is required to pay 'the amount due' unless a withholding notice is served. Thus where the party with the contractual power to determine 'the amount due' is the applying party, his application for payment has much greater status than when it is a certifier or the other party who has the power. Contractors may be pleased to be the party with power under the Short Contract but far less pleased that the subcontractor has the power under the Short Subcontract.

Compensation events

The core clause list of nineteen compensation events in the main contract is reduced to fourteen events in the short contracts and fifteen events in the Short Subcontract, omissions being:

- CE7 – instruction for dealing with objects of value
- CE9 – withholding an acceptance for a reason not stated
- CE11 – tests or inspections causing delay
- CE15 – take-over of part of the works
- CE16 – non-provision of materials etc.
- CE18 – breach of contract

The addition in the Short Contract is the compensation event, at clause 60.1(13) for 'a difference between the final total quantity of work done and the quantity stated for an item in the Price List'. The further addition in the Short Subcontract is the compensation event at clause 60.1(15) relating to changed completion dates.

It is difficult to detect any particular logic in the omissions but the absence from the short contracts of a compensation event for breach of contract seems to suggest that in these contracts common law rights are retained even if they are lost in the main contracts.

The compensation event at clause 60.1(13) of both short contracts is likely to attract considerable attention. It suggests that any quantities stated in the price list are effectively warranted and indicates that any change, increase or decrease, gives grounds for claim.

The short contracts retain some of the notification and quotation systems of NEC 3 main contracts but apply different assessment procedures. There are no schedules of cost components and defined cost approximates to actual cost. For most compensation events assessment is a costing exercise but for compensation events arising from actual quantities being different from these in the price list the assessment is by multiplying the changed quantities by the appropriate rates in the price list.

Late completion

As noted in section 21.2 the Short Contract does not contain secondary option clauses. At first sight the effect of this would seem to be to leave out of the short contracts provisions for liquidated damages for late completion. However, by virtue of a new clause found in both short contracts within the payment section, clause 50.5, the position is that instead of liquidation damages being an option in the short contracts they are mandatory. The clause reads, 'The Contractor (Subcontractor) pays delay damages for each day from the Completion Date until Completion.' For the situation which applies if no daily rate is stated see the comment on the *Temloc* v. *Errill* case in Chapter 3, section 8.

Dispute resolution

The dispute resolution procedures of the short contracts are considerably simpler than those in the main contracts. And instead of there being two options, W1 and W2, to cater for contracts without and within the scope of the statutory adjudication provisions of the Housing Grants, Construction and Regeneration Act 1996, there is, in both of the short contracts, a brief statement whereby, for contracts subject to the Act, instead of the parties being required to commence adjudication to a timetable specified in clause 93.3(1) that clause is replaced with a clause 94.1 allowing a dispute to be referred to adjudication at any time. This approach assumes that save for clause 93.3(1) the remainder of the provisions in clause 93.3 are compliant with the Act. This is probably the case, particularly as the time for giving the adjudicator's decision is stated as four weeks plus a further two, by agreement, or with the consent of the referring party.

21.3 NEC 3 Term Service Contract

The Term Service Contract carries the advice note: 'This contract should be used for the appointment of a supplier for a period of time to manage and provide a service.' The Guidance Notes expand on this with a number of explanations and suggestions:

- the contract is not restricted to construction works
- the contract is designed for managing and providing a service – not a project
- the service may be provided continuously over the period of the contract or on a task-by-task call-off basis
- the contract should not be used for very minor services, such as those involving a sole trader
- the service is usually provided on the employer's premises
- the service may include physical work such as cleaning and maintenance
- in the public sector the contract may be used for all contracted-out services, whether physical or not

Structure

The Term Service Contract uses an option structure similar to that in the main NEC 3 contracts but with only three main options, two dispute resolution options, and twelve secondary options.

Main options:

- Option A   – priced contract with price list
- Option C   – target contract with price list
- Option E   – cost reimbursable contract

Dispute resolution options

- Option W1   – non-compliant with HGCR Act 1996
- Option W2   – compliant with HGCR Act 1996

Secondary options

- Option X1   – price adjustment for inflation
- Option X2   – changes in the law
- Option X3   – multiple currencies
- Option X4   – parent company guarantee
- Option X12   – partnering
- Option X13   – performance bond
- Option X17   – low service damages
- Option X18   – limitation of liability
- Option X19   – task order
- Option X20   – key performance indicators
- Option Y(UK)2 – Housing Grants, Construction and Regeneration Act 1996
- Option Y(UK)3 – Contracts (Rights of Third Parties) Act 1999

Note, however, that there are no schedules of cost components for the Term Service Contract.

Text

For much of the text the Term Service Contract follows the style and, so far as is appropriate, the wording of the main NEC 3 contracts. There are some changes of terminology, for example:

- service manager instead of project manager
- plan instead of programme
- service information instead of works information
- affected property instead of the site

Such things apart, the Term Service Contract retains the same grouping of clauses as the main NEC 3 contracts and the same principles.

Management

The service manager fulfils the roles of project manager and supervisor and is either a member of the employer's staff or a firm appointed to provide management services. The contractor is permitted to subcontract under much the same rules as under the main NEC 3 contracts.

Scope of the contract

Questions often arise in respect of term contracts as to what type of contracts they are – or, put another way, what is their scope. One type of contract gives the appointed contractor the right to undertake all the work of the particular kind included in the contract required by the employer in a specified area for a specified period of time. Such a contract is an exclusive rights contract and it usually taken as a simple contract even though it may be operated with separate works orders for each job. Another type of contract is non-exclusive in that the employer can distribute his required work between two or more approved contractors utilising various criteria, one of which is usually price. The employer's works order is then effectively a freestanding contract for the job. A further type allows the contractor the option of whether or not to accept work offered to him. For the legal complexities of those matters see the cases of *Percival* v. *LCC Asylums Committee* (1918) and *Kelly Pipelines* v. *British Gas* (1989).

On the face of it, the NEC 3 Term Service Contract looks like the first type of contract but the suggestion in the Guidance Notes that the service may be provided on a task-by-task call-off basis suggests that it may be either the first type or the second type. This however, may be no more than a reference to secondary option clause X19 (task order). This option, when included, would seem to put the contract into the second type of term contracts since it sets out in some detail a range of provisions relating to individual task orders.

Pricing and payment

Subject to the above concerns as to whether there is one contract price or a series of works order prices under the Term Service Contract, the characteristics of the three alternative pricing mechanisms, A, C and E are as follows:

- Option A – this is described as a 'priced contract with price list'. The prices are the amounts in the price list and, if quantities are stated, the quantities multiplied by rates. The price for the services provided are defined as the price for each lump sum and quantities multiplied by rates. In some circumstances, depending on the composition of the price list and the manner of ordering work this might create a single lump sum contract but it looks more likely to create a schedule of rates contract.
- Option C – this is described as a 'target contract with price list'. The purpose of the price list is to create a target not to value the services. The price for the services provided are determined by reference to 'Defined Cost' – and in the Term Service Contract, defined cost is effectively actual cost. Option C is, therefore, a reimbursable cost contract with a target related gain/pain share mechanism.
- Option E – this is described as a 'cost reimbursable contract'. It includes provision for a price list but this has little or no contractual application.

Compensation events

The Term Service Contract includes a compensation event scheme very similar to that in the main NEC 3 contracts in respect to both its list of events and its procedures. However, it does not include compensation events for:

- finding of objects of interest
- adverse physical conditions
- adverse weather
- partial take-over
- prevention

The notification and quotation procedures for compensation events follow closely these in the main NEC 3 contracts but assessments are generally related to actual cost – there being no schedules of cost components.

Dispute resolution

The Term Service Contract incorporates options W1 and W2 without any substantial change from the main NEC 3 contracts.

21.4 NEC 3 Framework Contract

The Framework Contract carries the advice note: 'This contract should be used for the appointment of one or more suppliers to carry out construction work or to provide design or advisory services on an as instructed basis over a set term.' The parties are the employer and the supplier.

Framework agreements have become increasingly popular in recent years as a means of developing good working relationships between employers with on-going workload and selected firms. Frequently such agreements are informal or of limited contractual effect. The NEC 3 Framework Contract provides a formal basis for agreement whilst allowing either party the option of withdrawal.

The NEC 3 Framework Contract, which is extremely brief, is concerned only with the ordering of work or services. Other NEC 3 contracts are used for the management of the particular work packages. The basics of the Framework Contract are:

- when the employer requires work to be carried out within the scope of the framework contract he selects a supplier using the selection procedure – clause 20.1
- after selection, the employer instructs the supplier to submit a quotation for the proposed work package – clause 22.1
- the supplier submits a quotation in accordance with quotation information which the employer may then accept, request be revised, or reject (by notification that the package order will not be placed with that supplier) – clause 22.2
- either party may terminate their obligations under the contract at any time by notifying the other party – clause 90.1

21.5 NEC 3 Professional Services Contract

The Professional Services Contract is, as its name indicates, a contract for the appointment of a supplier to provide professional services. In the contract the parties are named as the employer and the consultant. The contract is designed primarily for use on projects where the construction contracts will also be from the NEC 3 family but its use is not so restricted and it can be used more generally.

Structure and text

The style, format and content of the Professional Services Contract is similar to that of other NEC 3 contracts. The notable differences from the main NEC 3 contracts are:

- there are only four main options
- consultant replaces contractor

- scope replaces works information
- a quality management system is required

Pricing and payment

The four main options are:

- Option A – priced contract with activity schedule
- Option C – target contract
- Option E – time based contract
- Option G – term contract

Option A is effectively a lump sum contract. Option C is a cost reimbursable contract based on time charges but with a target price mechanism included. Option E is a straightforward cost reimbursable time charge contract. Option G is a contract to provide professional services on a task basis and may be priced either as lump sum or time charges, or a combination of both.

Compensation events

The contract lists twelve events as compensation events:

- change of scope
- employer not providing access
- employer not providing something specified
- instructions to stop or not to start work or changes to key dates
- employer or others not working to accepted programme
- late replies to communications
- changes of decisions
- withholding of acceptances for reasons not stated
- correction of assumptions about compensation events
- breach of contract by the employer
- prevention
- consultant corrects defects for which he is not liable

Notification, quotation and assessment requirements are similar to those in other NEC 3 contracts with the exception that the assessments are made by references to effects on actual and forecast time charges rather than to defined cost.

Dispute resolution

Options W1 and W2 as the main NEC 3 contracts apply with only name changes.

21.6 *NEC 3 Adjudicator's Contract*

This is a tripartite agreement between the parties to a contract and the adjudicator. Its use is not confined to NEC 3 contracts but it is best suited to adjudicators appointed to serve for the duration of a contract rather than for particular disputes – see the comment in Chapter 17, section 17.

The contract is generally straightforward but it has some peculiarities such as providing for advance payment of fees, but not providing indemnity to the adjudicator against claims and costs arising out of his work.

21.7 *Concluding comment*

The New Engineering Contract has come a long way in a short time. Usage of the main contracts has probably exceeded the expectations of even the promoters. The contracts must be popular with employers to have achieved such usage even though there is still a body of lawyers, contractors and consultants with reservations, or what might be described as nervousness, about their use. There can be little doubt that even in the present period of ever-increasing proliferation of standard forms usage of NEC 3 contracts will continue to grow and the NEC family of forms will continue to develop. It will not represent failure if some of the interpretative problems considered in this book find their way to the courts for resolution. It will be a mark of the standing of the contracts. In the meantime open discussion of the contracts needs to be expanded and the involvement of lawyers in the process encouraged. If this book achieves that it will have been worth the effort.

Table of cases

Note: End references are to chapter sections.
The following abbreviations of law reports are used:

AC	Law Reports Appeal Cases Series
All ER	All England Law Reports
BLR	Building Law Reports
CA	Court of Appeal
CILL	Construction Industry Law Letter
CL	Construction Law
CLD	Construction Law Digest
CLY	Construction Law Yearbook
Const LJ	Construction Law Journal
EG	Estates Gazette
EWCA Civ	Court of Appeal, Civil Division (England and Wales)
EWHC	High Court (England and Wales)
EX	Exchequer Law Reports
KB	Kings Bench
LJQB	Law Journal Queens Bench
Lloyd's Rep	Lloyd's List Law Reports
NSWLR	New South Wales Law Reports
NZLR	New Zealand Law Reports
SACD	South African Court Decision
TCLR	Technology Court Law Reports
WLR	Weekly Law Reports

Table of clause references

The following pages provide an index of clause numbers and descriptions from NEC 3 engineering and construction contract references to chapter sections in this book. The chapter sections printed in bold are principal references.

The NEC 3 contract itself has a comprehensive index of subjects referenced to clause numbers so readers of this book who wish to have the benefit of a subject index will find it a straightforward matter to move from the subject index of NEC 3 to the chapter sections in the book.

Note: references are to chapter sections.

Core clauses

2   THE CONTRACTOR'S MAIN RESPONSIBILITIES

4 TESTING AND DEFECTS

Main option clauses

OPTION A: PRICED CONTRACT WITH ACTIVITY SCHEDULE

OPTION B: PRICED CONTRACT WITH BILL OF QUANTITIES

OPTION C: TARGET CONTRACT WITH ACTIVITY SCHEDULE